THE BEST OF THE
BEST
PLACES
IN THE WORLD

THE 100 MOST AWE-INSPIRING PLACES ON EARTH

Reader's
Digest

CONTENTS

6 **Introduction**

8 **Abu Simbel**, Egypt

14 **Acropolis**, Greece

18 **Afar Depression**, Ethiopia

20 **Alhambra**, Spain

24 **Altiplano**, Peru, Bolivia, Argentina, Chile

26 **Amazon Theatre**, Brazil

28 **Angkor Wat**, Cambodia

32 **Antarctic Peninsula**

36 **Aqua Tower**, USA

38 **Arena Chapel Frescoes**, Italy

40 **Astana**, Kazakhstan

42 **Lake Baikal**, Russia

46 **Banaue Rice Fields**, Philippines

48 **Banff National Park**, Canada

50 **Bell Rock Lighthouse**, Scotland

54 **Big Sur Coast**, USA

56 **Bird's Nest Stadium**, China or **Colosseum**, Italy

58 **Blue Mosque**, Turkey

62 **Boqueria Market**, Spain

64 **Bora Bora**, French Polynesia

66 **Carnac**, France or **Stonehenge**, England

68 **Chartres Cathedral**, France

72 **Chatsworth House**, England

74 **Chrysler Building**, USA

78 **Crac des Chevaliers**, Syria

80 **Cave of Crystals**, Mexico

82 **Culloden**, Scotland

84 **Delhi Old Town**, India

88 **Dubrovnik**, Croatia

92 **Easter Island**, Chile

94 **Eiffel Tower**, France

96 **Erg Chebbi**, Morocco or **White Desert**, Egypt

98 **Forbidden City**, China

102 **Mount Fuji**, Japan

104 **Galápagos Islands**, Ecuador

108 **Los Glaciares National Park**, Argentina

112 **Golden Gate**, USA or **Ponte Vecchio**, Italy

114 **Grand Canyon**, USA

118 **Great Wall of China**

120 **Gros Morne**, Canada

122 **Guggenheim Bilbao**, Spain

124 **Halong Bay**, Vietnam

128 **Haida Gwaii**, Canada

130 **Hawaii Volcanoes**, USA

134 **Heidelberg**, Germany

138 **Iguazú Falls**, Brazil, Argentina

142 **Kakadu Rock Paintings**, Australia

144 **Kanha National Park**, India

146 **Kerala's Backwaters**, India or **Britain's Canals**, UK

148 **Khao Sok National Park**, Thailand

152 **Kraków**, Poland

156 **Lalibela**, Ethiopia

158 **Leptis Magna**, Libya

162 **Louvre Museum**, France

BEYOND **COMPARE**

EASTER ISLAND

GALÁPAGOS ISLANDS

GREAT WALL OF CHINA

168 **Machu Picchu,** Peru

172 **Manú National Park,** Peru

174 **Matterhorn,** Switzerland, Italy

176 **Menin Gate,** Belgium

180 **Mesa Verde,** USA

184 **Milford Sound,** New Zealand

186 **Monasteries of Metéora,** Greece

190 **Monet's Garden,** France

194 **Nazca Lines,** Peru

196 **Neuschwanstein,** Germany

198 **Ngorongoro Crater,** Tanzania

204 **Olinda,** Brazil

206 **Pantanal,** Brazil, Bolivia, Paraguay

210 **Paro Taktsang,** Bhutan

212 **Petra,** Jordan

216 **Phong Nha Cave,** Vietnam

220 **Pokhara Valley,** Nepal

224 **Potala Palace,** China or **Versailles,** France

226 **Rhine Valley,** Germany

228 **Romania's Painted Churches**

232 **St Petersburg,** Russia

236 **San Gimignano,** Italy

240 **San Telmo,** Argentina

244 **Sana'a,** Yemen

246 **Santorini,** Greece

250 **Shwedagon Pagoda,** Myanmar (Burma)

252 **Staffa,** Scotland, and the **Giant's Causeway,** Northern Ireland

254 **Sugarloaf Mountain,** Brazil

258 **Svaneti,** Georgia

262 **Sydney Harbour,** Australia

266 **Taj Mahal,** India

270 **Teotihuacán,** Mexico

274 **Terracotta Army,** China

278 **Trevi Fountain,** Italy or **Dubai Fountain,** UAE

280 **Trunk Bay,** US Virgin Islands

282 **Tubbataha Reefs,** Philippines

286 **Uluru,** Australia

288 **Salar de Uyuni,** Bolivia

292 **Varanasi,** India

296 **Venice,** Italy

300 **Visby,** Sweden

302 **VW Transparent Factory,** Germany

304 **Wies Pilgrimage Church,** Germany

306 **Yellowstone National Park,** USA

310 **Zentralfriedhof Cemetery,** Austria

312 **Zollverein Coal Mine,** Germany

314 **Index**

319 **Credits**

TAJ MAHAL   **ULURU**   **VENICE**

INTRODUCTION

Our planet abounds in glorious locations, some natural, some man-made, some a mixture of both. From the breathtaking majesty of Arizona's Grand Canyon to the marbled magnificence of India's Taj Mahal, or from an other-worldly crystal cave in Mexico to the magical canals of Venice, it is easy to list such wonders – but, given such an astonishing variety of heart-stopping, jaw-dropping places, how can anyone pick the 100 'best of the best' places in the world – the hundred locations that outshine all the others?

Reader's Digest editors are famed for their editorial skills in selecting and distilling information, but this book set us perhaps our greatest – and most enjoyable – challenge as we struggled to define and then select the world's 100 'best' places. To meet it, we took advice from experienced travellers, world-heritage experts, international photographers, historians and naturalists, and then chose what we felt were the most beautiful, the most precious, the most treasured places on Earth. The range is dazzling, from gardens to rain forests, volcanoes to cathedrals, glaciers to palaces, remote islands to city skyscrapers.

But we didn't simply want to tell you the conclusions we reached – we wanted to demonstrate in words and pictures how we came to these conclusions; and also to tell you briefly about the other spectacular places that made up the competition for each entry – what we have called the 'best of the rest'.

Twice best Paris's Louvre Museum has the largest collections of any museum in the world, while the Eiffel Tower is the world's most recognised city icon.

What makes a place worthy of being called 'the best'? Which is the most spectacular palm-fringed tropical beach of them all? Which is the bleakest, whitest, ice-bound Arctic or Antarctic landscape? Where will you find medieval Gothic architecture in its most concentrated purity? Which is the world's greatest great museum? We asked and answered all of these questions – and, incidentally, chose the Louvre in Paris as the 'best' museum rather than the Metropolitan Museum in New York, London's British Museum or Madrid's Prado. Have we made the right choice? Do you agree? Here we give you all the information you need to form your own judgment. It is a book that (almost literally) opens your horizons.

We believe that the structure of the book adds variety and depth to the journey. In it, we take you around the world from A to Z, beginning with Abu Simbel in Egypt and ending with the striking Modernist buildings that incongruously grace the Zollverein Coal Mine Industrial Complex in Germany's Ruhr Valley. This alphabetical ordering makes it simple to find any place you may be looking for, but also gives the book a pleasing randomness – leading you on irresistibly from one fascinating entry to another. The ancient temples of Abu Simbel make way for the Parthenon (and other glories of the Athenian Acropolis), which yields to Ethiopia's forbidding Afar Depression, which yields in turn to the Moorish halls, courtyards and fountains of the Alhambra of Granada in southern Spain...and so on, in a constantly surprising parade.

Within each entry, special features include 'Best of the Rest' boxes describing some of the other places considered near-contenders when choosing the 'best of the best'. These boxes bring the total number of stunning entries in the book to more than 500. In a few entries, 'Small but Special' boxes take you to incredible places built on a human scale that are masterpieces in their own right; while six 'Beyond Compare' entries celebrate a category that is considered to be just that – beyond compare. To what, for example, could anyone compare Venice? Or the Taj Mahal? They are unique, one-offs. And the 'Ultimate' entries give you the choice. Which, for example, is the ultimate desert landscape, the classic sand dunes of Erg Chebbi in Morocco or the strange wind-carved rock shapes in Egypt's White Desert?

There are constant surprises. Which is the world's most iridescent coral reef? Australia's Great Barrier Reef is world famous and unquestionably magnificent, but many experienced divers give their vote to the Tubbataha Reefs in the Philippines – like so many places in this book a UNESCO World Heritage Site, but less well known in the wider world. Or more simply, how can we fully appreciate the beguiling beauty of the Taj Mahal – described as 'a solitary tear suspended on the cheek of time' – without also knowing the story of its builder, the Mughal Emperor Shah Jahan, mourning the death of his most beloved wife Mumtaz Mahal?

The book's subtitle says it all: 'The 100 most awe-inspiring places on Earth'. Each of the places in this book, from New York's Chrysler Building to Scotland's Culloden battlefield, is superlative whether for its beauty or its power to send a shiver down the spine. *The Best of the Best Places in the World* will entertain you, inform you, amuse you, perhaps even madden you as you beg to differ with its conclusions; but above all, we hope it will change for ever the way you look at our planet and its roll-call of wonders.

The Editors

ABU SIMBEL

Built by the great pharaoh Ramesses II and dramatically rescued from the rising Lake Nasser, the temples of Abu Simbel are the most extraordinary of ancient Egypt's many wonders.

Travelling south from Aswan, the journey to Abu Simbel can be made by light plane or by boat across Lake Nasser, but most visitors go by coach, setting off before dawn to cross the parched and rocky desert. The temples of Abu Simbel amply reward these modern pilgrims for their dedication. Waiting to greet them are vast statues of Ramesses II and his favourite wife, Nefertari, carved out of the golden sandstone more than 3,000 years ago.

WHERE ON EARTH?

Abu Simbel stands on the western bank of Lake Nasser in southern Egypt, almost 200 miles (300km) south of Aswan by road. The journey takes three hours by coach. Police-escorted convoys leave early in the morning and depart from Abu Simbel before 4pm. Flights are available from Aswan to the town of Abu Simbel.

The Great Temple

There are two temples on the Abu Simbel site standing about 100m (330ft) apart. The larger focusses primarily on Ramesses II, the smaller on Nefertari. At the larger temple, Ramesses appears seated on the facade in what was once a row of four massive identical statues. Towering 20m (65ft) high, they dwarf visitors with their unearthly scale, as befitting a ruler who was considered a god. Wearing the double crown of Upper and Lower Egypt, Ramesses sits alert and upright on his throne, smiling serenely. His hands rest on his knees with coiled energy, as if he might suddenly spring into action. At his feet are statues of family members – much smaller, but still larger than life-size. Beneath them, at the foot of the plinth, are statues of defeated enemies: Hittites, Libyans and Nubians.

In front of them is a line of statues of the hawk-headed sun god Re-Horakhty.

This cult temple has two themes: devotion to the gods and to war. It is dedicated to four gods: Re-Horakhty, Amun, Ptah (the three state deities, worshipped by the ruling elite) and to Ramesses II himself, the god-king. Ramesses is depicted twice in relief over the entrance to the temple, standing in worship on either side of Re-Horakhty, who is carved in deeper relief, crowned by a sun disc. High above, a long frieze of baboons, who were closely associated with the sun-god Re-Horakhty, raise their hands in seeming homage to the

Imposing facade The entrance to the Great Temple is guarded by monumental statues of Ramesses II that face into the rising sun with a poise that exudes timeless power.

RAMESSES 'THE GREAT'

Considered by many scholars to be the greatest of all the pharaohs of ancient Egypt, Ramesses II ruled for 66 years, 1279 to 1213 BC, dying at the age of about 90. He was an active warrior-king, scoring his proudest war-time triumph against the expansionist Hittites, who ruled from what is now Turkey. A threat to Egypt since about 1350 BC, the Hittites had not been effectively challenged by preceding pharaohs such as Akhenaten and Tutankhamen, but Ramesses

stemmed the Hittite tide. He also waged war against the Libyans on his western flank and the Nubians in the south.

Ramesses was an energetic builder, creating not only Abu Simbel, but also his own mortuary temple, the Ramesseum, at Thebes. This huge and splendid monument was built on the kind of ambitious scale that had not been seen in ancient Egypt since the construction of the pyramids 1,500 years before. He also built a new capital city, Pi-Ramesses, now in ruins, in the Nile delta.

rising sun, adding a light touch amid the grandiose solemnity of the other imagery.

Construction of the rock temples began in about 1264 BC, a decade after Ramesses claimed his greatest victory over the Hittites at the Battle of Kadesh in Syria. For their part, the Hittites also claimed victory, so the battle was probably more of a draw, but it resulted in an important peace treaty that was sealed by Ramesses taking a Hittite princess as one of his many wives. Abu Simbel was in the far south of Egyptian territory, in the land of their traditional rivals and enemies, the Nubians, so the sheer scale of the temple and its warlike theme was probably a deliberate act of intimidation.

An impressive interior

These themes of war and of Ramesses' prowess continue inside the temple, in the tapering progression of two primary chambers that lead to the sanctuary, hewn out of the rock. The first is the Great Hypostyle Hall, named for its massive 'hypostyle' supporting columns: eight statues of Ramesses in the form of the god Osiris, each 9m (30ft) high, serve as pillars lining the central passageway, four

THE BROKEN STATUE

One of the four statues of Ramesses II on the facade of the Great Temple is incomplete, the remains of its head and torso lying shattered at its feet. It was probably smashed in an earthquake in about 1248 BC, before the temple was complete. The left arm of the statue to the far right of the temple entrance also broke off at this time. Some restoration took place, but the head and torso remained where they had fallen.

During the 1960s rescue operation, there was much discussion about whether this broken statue should be restored to its intended form. In the end the team decided to position the head and torso as they had been found, face down in the sand in front of the temple – and that is where they remain to this day.

on each side. The walls are decorated with bas-relief images of Ramesses, either in worship or at war, personally pulverising his enemies. Ceiling paintings depict stars and vultures with outstretched wings representing Nekhbet, goddess of Upper

Egypt, associated with eternity and patron of the pharaohs. A passageway leads to the second chamber, similarly decorated, with Ramesses and Nefertari depicted with the sacred barque that they will use to cross the sky to reach the afterlife.

Finally, the visitor reaches the sanctuary, the holy of holies. Sculpture along the back wall, 60m (200ft) from the temple entrance, shows Ramesses seated alongside the three gods Re-Horakhty, Amun and Ptah. On two days of the year, February 21 and October 21 (possibly the birthday and coronation day of Ramesses), the rays of the rising sun would penetrate the chambers and light up three of the gods, but leave Ptah – god of the Underworld, regeneration and the night – in shadow. This still happens today, although no longer on precisely those dates.

Celebrating Nefertari

The second temple at Abu Simbel is smaller in scale and ambition than that of Ramesses, but in many respects it is similar. Six standing statues line the facade, in niches rimmed by hieroglyphs. Nefertari – the name means 'beautiful companion' – appears twice, on either side of the entrance, flanked by statues of Ramesses. All six statues are about 10m (33ft) high. Smaller statues of their

Great Hypostyle Hall The impressive tall statues of Ramesses II tower over visitors. Those on the left-hand side wear the white crown of Upper Egypt, while the double crown of Lower and Upper Egypt caps those on the right. When the rock temples were rediscovered in 1813, the statues were half-buried in sand.

children stand at their feet. The fact that Nefertari's statues are the same size as Ramesses is most unusual and significant. Queens were usually depicted on a much smaller scale beside their husbands so this indicates the reverence in which she was held.

Bas-reliefs and paintings on the walls of the inner chambers show Nefertari in acts of worship to Hathor, the goddess of joy, love, beauty, motherhood, music and dance. In several images Nefertari plays the sistrum, a kind of metal rattle sacred to Hathor. This may be Nefertari's temple, but Ramesses is very much present, again seen slaughtering his enemies while Nefertari looks on. In the innermost sanctuary, Hathor appears in the form of a heavily eroded statue of the divine cow, emerging from the back wall to offer protection to Ramesses.

Nefertari appears to have died somewhere between 1255 and 1250 BC, so she probably did not witness the completion of her temple.

Lost, found – and rescued

At some point after the final collapse of Egyptian power, Abu Simbel disappeared from view, buried beneath the drifting desert sands. Then, in 1813, the Swiss traveller and orientalist Johann Ludwig Burckhardt – famed also as the discoverer of Petra, in Jordan – came across the top of the head of one of the statues of Ramesses. It is said that Burckhardt named the site Abu Simbel after the local boy who was his guide. Unable to explore further, he mentioned the find to Italian explorer Giovanni Belzoni, who visited the scene and uncovered the temples four years later.

At this time, the temples stood beside the sacred River Nile, the annual flooding of which (from June to October) played a crucial role in the agriculture that sustained ancient Egypt. In the 20th century, as Egypt emerged into the modern world, the flooding had become a liability. In the 1960s, Egypt built the Aswan High Dam to control the river and supply hydroelectric power. This ambitious project created Lake Nasser, one of the world's largest artificial lakes,

best of the rest...

ANCIENT EGYPT

■ Made all the more impressive by its desert location, the **Step Pyramid of Djoser** at Saqqara consists of six superimposed tiers rising to 62m (203ft). Built in 2667-2648 BC, it was a prototype of the Pyramids of Giza, which followed only a century later.

■ The three **Pyramids of Giza** on the outskirts of Cairo are the classic pyramid group. Despite the encroaching suburbs, their stupendous scale still inspires awe today, as they have done for 4,500 years. The mysterious **Great Sphinx** forms part of this complex.

■ The greatest temple complexes of ancient Egypt are those of **Karnak** and **Luxor**, with forests of huge, hieroglyph-covered columns and bold connecting avenues lined with sphinxes. They were part of the ancient city of Thebes (on the site of the modern town of Luxor), capital of ancient Egypt in 1550-1290 BC .

■ The magnificent temple complex at **Dendera**, 40 miles (65km) north of Luxor, is one of the best-preserved of ancient Egypt. Started by the Ptolemies in the 1st century BC, it was dedicated primarily to the goddess Hathor.

■ The **Temple of Horus** at Edfu is one of the most intact ancient temples in Egypt. It was constructed by the Ptolemies, starting in about 237 BC and completed by Pharaoh Ptolemy XIII, father of Cleopatra.

Karnak's Great Hypostyle Hall

■ The unusual double-temple at **Kom Ombo** was built for the falcon god Haroeris and the crocodile god Sobek, at a place where sacred crocodiles used to bask beside the Nile. Started in the 2nd century BC, its walls, columns and ceilings are decorated with relief sculptures from the Ptolemaic era.

■ With a wide causeway leading up to its long colonnaded terraces, the huge **Mortuary Temple of Queen Hatshepsut** is astonishing in its design. It was built close to the Valley of the Kings by the queen who made herself pharaoh in about 1479 BC.

■ One of the most haunting sights of ancient Egypt is the **Colossi of Memnon**, a pair of heavily weathered, giant seated statues of Pharaoh Amenhotep III on the plain near Luxor. Created around 1350 BC, they were part of Amenhotep's large memorial temple.

Great Pyramid and Sphynx

Re-sited temples That Lake Nasser appears to have been Abu Simbel's natural home for thousands of years is testimony to the painstaking work of dismantling and reassembling the monument.

stretching for 300 miles (500km) along the Nile Valley behind the dam and including the site of Abu Simbel, as well as the homes of 122,000 people.

In 1964, with construction of the dam already underway, an international team sponsored by UNESCO set about rescuing the rock temples. They were sawn into carefully numbered pieces – 1,054 in total, some weighing up to 33 tonnes – and reassembled like a three-dimensional jigsaw on higher ground, 200m (660ft) to the west and 65m (220ft) above the original site.

Precision engineering
Relocation of the temples was a feat almost as extraordinary as the original construction. Whereas 3,275 years before, the temple facades had been carved out of a cliff face and the chambers gouged from the rock behind, the rescue engineers had to work in reverse. They had to remove 330,000 tonnes of surrounding rock to reduce the walls of the inner chambers to shells that could be lifted away in pieces. One by one, these sections were lowered onto

cushions of sand in large trailers and hauled up the hill to await reassembly.

The dam engineers, meanwhile, had their own schedule, and as the waters of Lake Nasser began to rise, a cofferdam was built around the temples to save them from the flooding. The Great Hypostyle Hall, its ceiling now resting on felt-topped steel girders, was one of the last parts to be removed, just three months before the whole site – now looking like a huge jaw with several teeth removed – was inundated.

Meanwhile, the restoration team was beginning the task of putting the temples back together on the levelled hilltop. The exterior sculptures were attached to steel bars to anchor them to poured concrete and knitted together with epoxy resin. Each piece was tirelessly and delicately edged into place using metal plates, wedges and wooden slats. Later, the fine saw slits and joints – totalling about 6 miles (10km) in length – were filled with mortar and painted to match the surrounding stone, so that they became virtually invisible.

A major setback occurred in 1966, when the dam engineers announced that the water level of Lake Nasser would be 1m (3ft) higher than formerly planned. Already one-eighth rebuilt, Nefertari's temple – which lay slightly below the

Great Temple in the original site – had to be dismantled again and raised to accommodate the new water level.

Completion in sight
In order to reproduce the original cliff-face setting, each temple had to be encased in an artificial mound. This presented another big challenge as the inner chamber walls now had to bear the weight of thousands of tons of rubble. To achieve this, engineers constructed a huge, reinforced-concrete dome behind each temple facade. At the forefront of building technology for their time, the domes bulged under the weight of the rubble and settled into their final shapes.

In 1968, after four years of precision work, the project was complete. Gradually the water rose up the cliff face, stopping just below the level of the re-sited temples. Ramesses II and Nefertari could look out once more across the waters of the Nile, now expanded into Lake Nasser. A marvel of the ancient world had become a marvel of the modern age.

Delicate move One of the heads of Ramesses II, cut into several blocks, is carefully removed from the original site. The temples were meticulously mapped so that each block would be repositioned in exactly the right place.

ACROPOLIS

Time stands still on the Acropolis, the ancient citadel of shrines and temples at the heart of Athens. The Parthenon has stood here for 2,500 years, the crowning glory of classical Greek architecture.

All around the Mediterranean world, the graceful ruins of temples and amphitheatres stand testimony to the glories of ancient Greece. But nowhere captures the spirit of that great civilisation with the intensity of the Athenian Acropolis. Most of the ruins here today – including the Parthenon, the greatest Greek temple of all – date from the age of Pericles, a golden era for Athens, but the history of the Acropolis goes back at least another millennium in time.

In around 1500 BC the Mycenaeans, a dominant force in Greece from about 1600 to 1100 BC, first built a palace on the massive bare plug of limestone that would later become the site of the Acropolis. The city of Athens gradually grew and spread around its base. The legend goes that Athena, goddess of wisdom and warfare, and the sea-god Poseidon vied for the honour of becoming the city's patron god. Zeus invited them to make gifts to the city. Poseidon thrust his trident into the rock and produced a salty spring. Athena touched the ground with her spear and an olive tree grew. The rest of the gods declared Athena the winner, and the Acropolis became her shrine. By the 6th century BC, it was packed with temples.

In 460 BC, following a war with the Persians during which Athens was sacked, the city emerged into a golden age under Pericles (lived

WHERE ON EARTH?

The Acropolis is in the centre of Athens. It is accessible from the surrounding streets such as Dionysiou Areopagitou. Tickets are sold at the Beulé Gate at the western end of the site. The 20-minute walk to the top of the hill is hard during the hot summer, so go there in the early morning or late afternoon.

GREECE

Athens
Acropolis
Piraeus

Mediterranean
Sea

around 495–429 BC). On his initiative, Athens underwent a grand rebuilding programme. All the most important surviving buildings on the Acropolis – the Temple of Athena Nike, the Propylaia,

Hill of power The Acropolis, with the Parthenon at its centre, inspired awe in Athenians and visitors alike, and quickly became famous all around the ancient world.

the Erechtheion, the Parthenon – were constructed and adorned by the leading architects and sculptors of the Periclean Age. Greatest among these were Iktinos, chief architect of the Parthenon, and the sculptor Phidias. The Acropolis that they and others created has influenced grand architecture ever since, from the schemes of the Romans for their own eternal city overlooking the Tiber, to the Lincoln Memorial in Washington, D.C. and the Madeleine Church in Paris.

Dedicated to Athena

Visitors enter the Acropolis by the western Beulé Gate (built in Roman times). The first building of significance is the diminutive Temple of Athena Nike (Athena of Victory), built between 432 and 421 BC. Designed by the architect Kallikrates, the temple perches on a delicate plinth and has four Ionic columns along the front and back. Relief sculptures illustrate battle scenes and the assembly of the all-powerful gods.

The Athenian architect Mnesicles started construction of the monumental entrance gates known as the Propylaia in 437 BC. The soaring colonnades through which people entered the Acropolis are formed from columns of Pentelic marble. Even in its present state, the entranceway has the power to impress. The Propylaia had two side wings, the northern one serving as a picture gallery that was decorated with either frescoes or hanging paintings.

On the northern edge of the Acropolis, the Erechtheion is famous for its marble maidens, or caryatids, that support the porch. The present statues are replicas of the originals; dressed in peplos gowns, they hold vessels in libation to the goddess Athena. Like many Greek temples, the Erechtheion was planned along symmetrical lines, but ended up asymmetrical. It was named after Erechtheus, an ancient

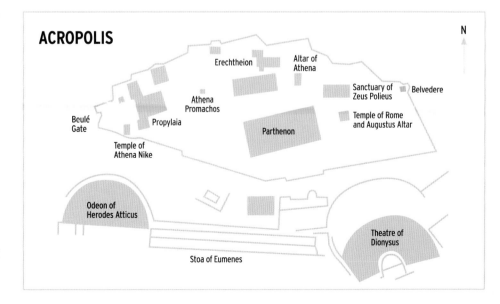

ACROPOLIS

N

Erechtheion
Altar of Athena
Athena Promachos
Sanctuary of Zeus Polieus — Belvedere
Beulé Gate
Propylaia
Temple of Rome and Augustus Altar
Parthenon
Temple of Athena Nike
Odeon of Herodes Atticus
Theatre of Dionysus
Stoa of Eumenes

king of Athens, and was the focus of the annual Panathenaic procession in honour of Athena, the highlight of the most important festival in the Athenian calendar. Within the temple are marks said to be those left by Poseidon's trident; the olive tree outside is a reminder of Athena's riposte.

Between the Erechtheion and the Parthenon stood the bronze statue of Athena Promachos ('Athena who fights

PHIDIAS'S DOWNFALL

In his day, Phidias (c. 480-430 BC) was revered as the greatest of all Greek sculptors though, as far as we know, none of his work has survived, except in copies. This is partly because his preferred medium was chryselephantine, pieces of gold and ivory supported on a wooden framework. He worked on a grand scale: in addition to his huge Athena Parthenos and his bronze Athena Promachos for the Acropolis, he was celebrated for his statue of Zeus at Olympia, one of the Seven Wonders of the Ancient World. When Pericles fell from power, Phidias was accused of embezzling gold intended for the Athena statue; he was arrested and died in prison.

on the front line'), created by the sculptor Phidias as a memorial to the Persian Wars. It stood 9m (30ft) tall, and when the tip of the gilded spear in Athena's hand glinted in the sun, it could be seen by sailors rounding Cape Sounion, 30 miles (50km) away, as they headed for the port of Piraeus.

A plaque at the Belvedere vantage point in the Acropolis's northeastern corner commemorates a more recent event. On the night of May 30, 1941, during the German occupation of Athens, two Athenians tore down the Nazi flag, inspiring the Greek resistance movement. The Greek national flag is raised on this spot each day by infantry soldiers in memory of the uprising.

Timeless temple

Dominating this hilltop site, the Parthenon temple is the focal point of the Acropolis and mercilessly upstages the other buildings. One of the largest Greek temples ever built, it was constructed of fine white marble quarried from Mount Pentelikon, 10 miles (16km) away. Although massive, it seems to soar, an effect brilliantly achieved by optical illusion.

The ground plan seems simple: 46 Doric columns line the outer edges; an inner set of columns originally lined

Influential ruin The Parthenon's pleasing proportions and clever symmetry achieve a perfection that not even war, explosions and looting have destroyed.

a large front chamber and a smaller back room. But this simplicity is deceptive. To counteract the optical effects caused by straight lines, the Parthenon's designers introduced various refinements. To the human eye, straight-sided columns appear narrower in the middle than at the top and bottom – the Parthenon's columns bulge slightly in the middle so that they appear straight. The corner columns are thicker than the rest to compensate for an apparent loss of mass when seen against the sky. The stylobate (floor plinth) is not flat but curves down at either side to give an illusion of flatness and perhaps to allow water to drain away. Every piece of stone was individually shaped, giving the building an organic vibrancy. The Greeks had used optical trickery elsewhere, but under the supervision of architects Iktinos and Kallikrates and the sculptor Phidias, it was brought to perfection.

The building was not designed for worship, but as the treasury, or *naos*, of the Delian League, the association of Greek city-states that had fought the Persian invaders. The League's wealth was stored in the smaller back room, while the front chamber was home to Phidias's oversized, gold-and-ivory statue of Athena Parthenos, 'The Virgin'. Although the statue vanished in the 5th century AD, copies and descriptions give an idea of what it looked like. Standing 10m (33 ft) tall, the crowned Athena held her spear and shield with her left arm and a winged figure of Victory in her right hand. Only priests, the ruling elite and important visitors were allowed inside the Parthenon. The public could only peer in through its large open doors, perhaps catching a glimpse of the vast gleaming statue inside.

Decline of fortune

The Parthenon was completed in 432 BC and remained in good condition for about 700 years. The Romans conquered Greece in 146 BC. Being admirers of Greek art, they studied what they could not plunder and added their own Monument to Agrippa near the Propylaia.

In the 6th century, the Parthenon was turned into a Christian church, then after the Ottoman conquest of 1458 it became a mosque. In 1687, the Parthenon suffered its greatest disaster. With Athens under siege by the Venetians, the Ottomans turned it into an arsenal. Bombarded by Venetian cannon, the stored gunpowder exploded. Columns toppled; sculptures were scattered.

More than a century later, the British ambassador to Ottoman Athens, Thomas Bruce, 7th Earl of Elgin, picked his way through the ancient ruins. The Ottomans had no interest in these broken marbles', so Bruce shipped half of them back to Britain. In 1816, he sold them to the British Museum, where they have remained ever since.

The New Acropolis Museum opened in 2009 and here the treasures that still remain in Greece are on display in pristine galleries. Other sights include

Substitutes The present caryatids on the Erechtheion are replicas, the originals having been moved to the New Acropolis Museum to protect them from pollution.

the Greek theatre of Dionysius and the Roman Odeon of Herodes Atticus. A walk through the woods brings the visitor to the Rock of Areopagus, a low hill to the northwest of the Acropolis where St Paul once preached. From here you can look out across the city and watch the sun set over the great crucible of Western civilisation.

best of the rest...

ANCIENT GREEK TEMPLES

■ The best preserved of ancient Greek temples lies near the Acropolis. The **Temple of Hephaestus**, fittingly the god of craftsmanship and metalworking, stands at the edge of the Agora in an area once

Temple of Apollo, Delphi

thronged with workshops. Designed by Iktinos, one of the architects of the Parthenon, it was built over a period of 30 years from 449 BC. It served as a church for 1,200 years until 1834.

■ Another temple designed by Iktinos is the **Temple of Apollo Epicurius** (Apollo the Helper) at Bassae, which stands in a remote mountain location in the western Peloponnese. It is unusual in that it has a north-south orientation, and contains columns in all three of the architectural orders: Doric, Ionic and the earliest Corinthian column. Some of the best friezes here were taken by British archeologists in the 18th century. Today, the remains of the temple are covered to protect the limestone from acid rain.

■ The sacred site of Delphi was home to the most celebrated oracle of ancient Greece. Most of the buildings are flat ruins, including much of the **Temple of Apollo**, but in this captivating mountain setting the force of history is palpable.

■ Colonists from the Greek city of Sybaris took their culture with them to southern Italy. A set of three Doric temples, all well preserved, has survived at **Paestum**, to the south of Naples. Two of the temples were dedicated to Hera, goddess of marriage and childbirth, and one to Athena. They date from about 550 BC to 450 BC.

■ In Sicily, too, Greek settlers left behind significant architectural treasures. The **Valley of the Temples** near Agrigento (actually a ridge rather than a valley) has the ruins of seven temples and various other remains. The Temple of Concordia (goddess of harmony), from the 5th century BC, is the best preserved.

AFAR DEPRESSION

Intense heat and volatile geology make this landscape the hottest in Africa in more ways than one. Though extreme and inhospitable today, millions of years ago this was the cradle of humankind.

The Afar, or Danakil, Depression in Ethiopia is the hottest place on Earth. Even in winter, the daytime temperature in this scrubland desert can soar above 42C (108F); in summer it exceeds 50C (122F). It is so dry and hot, and there is so little shade, that local people – mainly salt traders and nomadic herders – are often confined to their tents during the day. It is a political as well as climatic tinderbox. The Afar encompasses Ethiopia, Eritrea and Djibouti. War between Ethiopia and Eritrea combines with extreme physical hardships to make Afar almost uninhabitable.

Although the region is short on home comforts, it is a dynamic natural spectacle. The Depression is part of the Great Rift Valley that runs from Syria south to Mozambique, and three great splits in the Earth's thin outer crust meet at this point. As the African and Arabian continental plates drift apart, molten magma oozes up through the gap, a process more usually seen at the bottom of the ocean. All this geological activity produces a scorching cauldron of earthquakes, volcanoes and hydrothermal fields. In 2005 powerful earthquakes and volcanic eruptions shook the region for three days. Ash filled the air, rocks fell from the sky and the rift widened by a staggering 8m (26ft) in just ten days. Although the people were evacuated, large numbers of camels and goats were killed, swallowed up by fissures in the

WHERE ON EARTH?

The Afar Depression is to the northeast of Addis Ababa, capital of Ethiopia. It extends into Ethiopia's neighbours, Eritrea and Djibouti, and is part of the Great Rift Valley that stretches from the Middle East to southern Africa. It is the hottest place on Earth and one of the most inhospitable.

SAUDI ARABIA
Red Sea
ERITREA
YEMEN
Afar Depression
Gulf of Aden
DJIBOUTI
Addis Ababa
SOMALIA
ETHIOPIA

Unique landscape In the Dallol crater, multi-coloured mineral springs produce these unusual rock formations shaped like plates, mushrooms and cones, creating a landscape that resembles a vivid coral reef at low tide.

ground or hit by volcanic bombs. This geological unravelling, which began millions of years ago, will eventually lead to saltwater from the Red Sea flooding into the gash and forming a new sea.

Lava lakes and hot springs

The region's most memorable feature is Erta Ale ('smoking mountain' in the Afar language) in the remote northeast of Ethiopia. This active volcano's summit crater contains the world's oldest existing molten lava lake: known as the 'gateway to hell', it is thought to have been bubbling away like burned porridge for more than 100 years. The volcano, which attracts only the most intrepid tourists, explorers and archeologists, is most striking at night, when the summit glows an eerie red. The heat is so intense, and the sulphurous smell so overpowering, that visitors can stand no more than a few minutes at the edge of the crater looking down on the red-hot and searing-white molten lava, churning, hissing and spluttering.

At Dallol, a volcanic crater northeast of Erta Ale, the landscape changes daily. Constantly bubbling sulphur springs are coloured red, yellow, orange, green and white by the mineral deposits and bacteria that thrive in the extremely hot, acidic conditions.

EVOLUTIONARY ADVANCE

The Afar Depression is a cradle of humankind. In 1974, the fossilised bones of a female hominid were found at the village of Hadar. On the day of the discovery, scientists at the site were listening to The Beatles' 'Lucy in the Sky with Diamonds' so they named her 'Lucy'. She was 3.2 million-years-old. In 1992, at the Middle Awash site, archeologists found 'Ardi', another hominid fossil, estimated to be 4.4 million years old. And the oldest stone tools ever unearthed were found at Gona.

Salt and survival

Only drought-resistant trees and grasses grow here. The wildlife includes herbivores such as gazelle, oryx and the last population of African wild ass, along with hundreds of species of birds. Only hardy goats and camels can survive here; agriculture is out of the question. The economic mainstay of the Afar people is salt.

The region's lowest point is Lake Assal in Djibouti. At 157m (515ft) below sea level, it is the lowest point in Africa. Here, and at Lake Asele, are salt flats formed from circular tablets of salt, resembling a monochromatic patchwork quilt. People rise at 5am to chisel, lever and smash the salt into blocks – known as *amolé* – which are carried by camels to the trading settlements of Berahile or Mekclle.

Salt route Guided and guarded by nomadic traders, a salt caravan makes its way across the Danakil Desert. Political tensions have made these trips risky.

best of the rest...

EXTREME NATURE

■ Few places compare with Afar, but **Death Valley** in North America is one of them. It has a greater chance of rain, yet is still the hottest, driest and, at Badwater Basin, the lowest point in the USA - 86m (282ft) below sea level. Located in the Mojave Desert, California, the valley had the highest recorded temperature in the Western Hemisphere - a blistering 56.7C (134F) - on July 10, 1913, at Furnace Creek. Death Valley was named by pioneers trying to find a way across in 1849 - even though only one of the group died, they all assumed the valley would be their grave.

Death Valley

■ The lowest point on the Earth's surface is the shore of the **Dead Sea** on the Israel-Jordan border. At 423m (1,388ft) below sea level, it is part of the same Great Rift Valley that runs through the Afar Depression. With minimal water-replenishment from the Jordan River, high evaporation and extreme heat, the sea's level gets lower every year. Due to the high levels of calcium, potassium and magnesium in the salty, muddy water, and high air pressure, the Dead Sea has been a popular health resort for over 2,000 years, offering relief for both skin and respiratory conditions. The high level of salt increases the water's density, which in turn increases its buoyancy, so anyone can float in it, even non-swimmers.

ALHAMBRA

Behind the dazzling beauty of the Alhambra in Andalucia lies the complex and fascinating story of the Moorish empire in Spain and the finest surviving medieval Muslim palace in western Europe.

The last stronghold of the Moors in southern Spain towers above the modern city of Granada, with the red mountains of the Sierra Nevada rising behind. A Moorish citadel has stood on the site since the 9th century, but the surviving palace complex was begun in the mid-13th century by Muhammad ibn Nasr, first sultan of the Nasrid dynasty. The Alhambra's story is entwined with that of the Nasrid sultans, the last Muslim dynasty to rule in Spain.

In 1237, Muhammad ibn Nasr ibn al-Ahmar, the founder of the Nasrid dynasty, located his capital in Granada. Muhammad was seeking refuge from the Reconquista, the campaign of Spanish Catholics to take back power in Spain. The location offered good access to the coast further south and was protected by mountainous

Red fortress The royal city was named Qala't al-Hamra, after the Arabic word *hamra* for the dusty red colour of the clay from which the walls were built.

WHERE ON EARTH?

The Alhambra overlooks the city of Granada, in the Spanish region of Andalucia. The palace complex is accessible by foot (up the steep hill), local bus or by car. Entrance tickets, and tours of the palaces and gardens, are best booked in advance for either a morning, afternoon or evening session.

Madrid ●

SPAIN

Alhambra
Granada ●

Mediterranean
Sea

MOROCCO

terrain to the north. This defence was vital, since across the northern borders were the Christian kingdoms of Castile and Aragon. In 1246, Muhammad made a strategic truce with his Castilian neighbours that allowed the Nasrids to maintain their borders and religious freedom in return for submission to Castile as overlords. The peace and stability that resulted from this treaty lasted for 250 years, allowing Granadian culture to flourish.

Towering horizons

The palace sits on a 14ha (35-acre) plateau over a rocky outcrop of the Sierra Nevada Mountains. Even today, the forbidding walls with their 23 towers and four gates dominate the Granada skyline. The foundations were laid by Sultan Muhammad ibn Nasr in the 13th century, and the palace complex was completed in the 14th century by Yusuf I (reigned 1333–54) and Muhammad V (who reigned 1354–59 and 1362–91).

The self-contained city had palaces, prisons, homes for craftsmen, bathhouses, barracks, workshops and mosques. At one point it housed 40,000 people. The site also included the Royal Mint and necropolis. Only two of the original six main palaces survive – the Comares Palace and the Palace of the Lions. A separate summer palace sits in the Generalife gardens on a neighbouring hill. While traces of daily life here have vanished, the surviving palaces still give a glimpse into the life of the Nasrid sultans in all their splendour.

Palace contrasts

The two surviving palaces present very different visions of Nasrid royal architecture. The Comares Palace (Palacio de Comares) was built by Yusuf I and acted as the official palace for state visits and visiting dignitaries. The Palace of the Lions (Palacio de los Leones) was added by Muhammad V in

❝ In the old Moorish palace of the Alhambra I lived in the midst of an Arabian tale … everything spoke and breathed of the glorious days of Granada, when under the dominion of the crescent. **❞**

WASHINGTON IRVING
TALES OF THE ALHAMBRA (1832)

1370, and was used as a more private residence or place of learning.

The Court of the Myrtles (Patio de los Arrayanes) in the Comares Palace is dominated by a central pool of still water, making this a tranquil and contemplative space. The massive Comares Tower that

GENERALIFE GARDENS

These exquisite gardens, built during the reign of Muhammad III (reigned 1302–09), overlook the city of Granada and were used as a Nasrid summer retreat. The name comes from the Arabic *janna al-rafia*, meaning 'gardens of lofty paradise'. They offer terraces linked by arcades and water channels with abundant foliage, all set within a containing wall. Miradors frame extraordinary views across the Albaicin quarter of the city and the Alhambra. The gardens are a tribute to the *jannat al-firdaws*, the gardens of paradise described so eloquently in the Koran.

houses the Hall of the Ambassadors overshadows the pool and served as the throne room. Every part of this small, high space is covered with intricately carved plasterwork, brightly coloured wall tiles and exquisitely carved wood. The ceiling of inlaid marquetry is arranged in seven levels to represent the seven heavens of the cosmos – a heavenly canopy to protect the earthly sovereign who sat beneath. Carved in plasterwork below the wooden dome is a verse from the Koran known as *al-mulk* (kingship), which alludes to the majesty of the ruler.

In the Palace of the Lions, graceful columns cluster around a central courtyard, where the intimate atmosphere is enhanced by the sound of flowing water that is never silenced. The columns support galleries leading into two vaulted halls on the east and west, and two rooms with magnificent plaster-carved ceilings in the north and south. One of these is the reception room of the Hall of the Kings (Sala de los Reyes). Its domed ceiling is decorated with paintings of

Palace of the Lions Contained by 124 irregularly placed marble columns, the palace courtyard features an alabaster basin supported by twelve lions.

the Nasrid kings on stretched leather covered with gesso, a technique familiar in the contemporary Mamluk world. At the centre of the Palace courtyard is a pure alabaster basin supported by twelve marble lions, aquamaniles that spout into marble channels to bring cooling water into each of the rooms. Verses inscribed around the fountain's edge praise the beneficence of the ruler and the beauty of the water that flows over the brim.

Art of the master craftsmen

Every surface of the Alhambra is clothed with beautiful and intricate surface decoration; indeed, this is one of the distinguishing features of the Nasrid palaces at the Alhambra. While the structures of the building were made from strong and durable materials, such as marble for the floors and supporting columns, the decorations that covered the walls and ceilings were carved from wood, plaster and local clay.

Wood was used for ceiling decoration. In the Hall of the Ambassadors, for example, the ceiling is made up of more than 8,000 separate carved and painted pieces (perhaps to prevent distortion of the ceiling during the changing seasons). Extraordinary visual effects were achieved with plaster, as in the ceiling of the Hall of the Two Sisters in the Palace of the Lions, recognised as the finest *muqarnas* dome in the world. More than 5,000 individual plaster cells form the muqarnas – shapes resembling stalactites suspended in clusters to form stars, creating an effect like exploding fireworks, or the revolving heavens.

Plaster was carved for wall decoration, too, making good use of the raw materials available from gypsum quarries close to Granada. The plaster allowed craftsmen to achieve a flowing style of carving that suited the arabesque motifs and cursive script in the ornamental inscriptions that are woven throughout the fabric of the building. The most frequently used motif is the Nasrid emblem from the Koran. Other Koranic and moral inscriptions also appear, often set within cartouches, their purpose being to communicate the strong faith and power of the rulers. Finally, there are poetical inscriptions composed for specific parts of the palace, such as fountains, windows and niches.

Ceramic tiles were glazed and cut to create the tile mosaics that cover the lower parts of the walls and the floors. The technique involved glazing tiles before firing them, then cutting them

Mirador de Lindaraja A bay window in the Hall of the Two Sisters is decorated with elaborate *mocarabes* (honeycomb and stalactite decoration).

to shape and assembling them into complex patterns (such as 'exploding' star shapes). They were then placed upside down and back-filled with plaster to create panels that could be attached to the wall.

Wood, plaster and clay were the materials of choice because they were readily available and easily coloured. Traces of paint on the wood and plaster reveal that the surfaces were originally brightly coloured, while glazed and lustre-painted tile panels still shine with vivid hues. Woven silk textiles would have hung across windows, with rich carpets on the floors and silk cushions to recline on. Only the wealthiest rulers could afford such lavish and luxurious furnishings, and though the textiles are no longer in place, the overall effect is as impressive today as in the days of the Nasrid sultans.

Into a new era

In 1492, the Reconquista finally achieved its aim and the last Nasrid sultan, Muhammad XII, known as Boabdil, surrendered and was expelled from Spain. With the fall of Muslim Spain came the rise of the Catholic monarchs. The Alhambra passed to the new Catholic rulers, Ferdinand II of Aragon and Isabella, Queen of Castile. In the 16th century, Charles V ordered the demolition of part of the Alhambra to build the palace that bears his name. Its unique circular patio is the most important Renaissance building in Spain. In the 18th century the site was abandoned and it was not until the second half of the 19th century that the process of restoring this remarkable royal palace began.

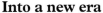

best of the rest...

MOORISH SPAIN

■ The **Great Mosque** of Córdoba, today known as the Cathedral of Córdoba, was commissioned in 785 by the Umayyad prince Abd al-Rahman I. Inside, the double horseshoe arches create a forest of

Great Mosque, Córdoba

coloured columns, while the exquisite mihrab niche is decorated with arabesque forms and mosaic calligraphy made by craftsmen from Byzantium. The courtyard of the mosque is planted with orange trees, as it was in the 8th century, making it one of the oldest continually planted gardens in the world.

■ The **Alcázar** in Seville is one of the most beautiful mudéjar palaces. The *mudéjares* were Muslims who remained in Spain under Christian rule; many were craftsmen who decorated palaces and churches for the Christian kings. The Castilian King Pedro 'The Cruel' (reigned 1350-69) employed mudéjares to rebuild an existing palace from the Almohad period. They used established techniques, such as polychrome tiling, carved wooden doors and muqarnas vaulting, that are reminiscent of the Alhambra in Granada. In fact, the decorative work at the Alcázar is often attributed to craftsmen sent from Granada.

■ Outside Córdoba lies a hidden city, **Madinat al Zahra**, where one of the world's most splendid palaces once stood. Parts have been excavated, but most of the palace remains hidden underground, still concealing its treasures. In 936, Abd al-Rahman III declared himself caliph and built this extravagant palace-city. Contemporary accounts describe the rich decoration: a pool of mercury dazzled visitors, the gold statues were encrusted with gems, and the walls were inlaid with ebony, jasper and ivory.

ALTIPLANO

Part desert, part grassland, the high Altiplano of South America has the air of the Wild West. Still home to its native people, it is a place where llamas graze and flamingos wade across isolated salt lakes.

Always chilly yet blessed with perpetual blue skies, arid yet home to massive lakes, the cradle of several ancient civilisations but relatively under-populated today, the Altiplano of South America is one of the globe's geographical conundrums. The high-altitude plateau extends for more than 600 miles (1,000km), spanning most of the terrain between Cusco in Peru and Jujuy in northern Argentina. Much of Bolivia sits on the Altiplano, as does a thin sliver of northeastern Chile. The name means 'high plains' in Spanish, a reference to the fact that the plateau lies at an average height of 3,650m (12,000ft)

above sea level. Higher still are the surrounding mountains – two branches of the Andes and solitary snow-capped volcanoes that are among the highest peaks in South America – that demarcate the Altiplano to the east and west.

Seismic variations

Scientists have long disagreed about what process formed these high plains. The plateau is undoubtedly associated with tectonic uplift of the Andes, caused by collision between the Pacific and South American plates, but is it the remains of a once-great inland sea or merely the result of millions of years of Andes erosion?

One of the Altiplano's defining features is the absence of an outlet to the ocean, despite its being a drainage basin

WHERE ON EARTH?

Running parallel to the Andes, the elongated, high-altitude Altiplano stretches from southern Peru to northern Argentina. The three aerial gateways to the region are Juliaca (Peru), La Paz (Bolivia) and Salta (Argentina). It can also be reached by coach or by train, more slowly and romantically.

Grazing lands Herds of domesticated alpacas graze the Altiplano grasslands. Members of the camel family, they are smaller than their close relatives, llamas. Their coats provide a fine yarn for rugs and clothes.

for water coming off the mountains. What rivers do exist here empty into Lake Titicaca on the Bolivia-Peru border and other lakes on the plateau. Titicaca is a geographical superlative in its own right, being the world's highest commercially navigable lake. It is also home to ancient people, some of whom still dwell on reed islands, attracting tourists by the boatload. The less well-known Lago Poopó in central Bolivia is also huge, as is the nearby Salar de Uyuni, a former lake that is now the world's largest salt flat.

Much of the Altiplano is high-altitude desert. In places that receive more moisture, grass, shrubs and cactus predominate. Wildlife is diverse, ranging from vicuña, a cousin of the domesticated llama and alpaca, to neon-pink flamingos, which breed along the shores of the salt lakes. There are also chinchilla, culpeo fox and the rabbit-like vizcacha.

Ancient peoples and new arrivals

Humans have occupied the Altiplano for at least 3,000 years. The Tiwanaku culture emerged around AD 100 on the shores of Lake Titicaca and developed into the area's most advanced civilisation. They built monumental temples and pyramids, made copper tools, cultivated a variety of crops and lived in mud-brick houses linked by paved streets. By the 12th century, the Tiwanaku had faded, perhaps the victims of a prolonged drought. The vacuum was filled by the

Lake Titicaca Local people still use reed canoes on the lake, which supports a variety of fish, including karachi and ispi, along with farmed trout.

Inca, who would dominate the Altiplano until the arrival of Spanish conquistadors in the early 16th century. Silver from a single mountain at Potosí bank-rolled the Spanish empire for centuries. Since the 20th century tin, zinc and lead have been mined by multinational companies.

The indigenous population remains in the rural parts of the Bolivian and Peruvian high plains, where the Quechua and Aymara languages – along with more than 30 other native tongues – are more often heard than Spanish. The Bolivian capital of La Paz is the Altiplano's largest city, followed by Cochabamba in Bolivia and Jujuy in Argentina. Yet it is Puno on the western shore of Titicaca that is the Altiplano's most evocative city. Birthplace of the Aymara civilisation, in modern times its crafts and culture have earned it the title of folklore capital of Peru.

best of the rest...

MOUNTAIN PLATEAUS

■ The world's largest and highest tableland is the **Tibetan Plateau** of central Asia. Often called the 'Roof of the World', the plateau is home to the unique Tibetan civilisation and the endangered snow leopard, takin and Tibetan blue bear. Despite rapacious logging and agricultural colonisation, what remains of Tibet's mountain plateau is a testimony to the beauty of these unending open spaces.

■ The **Colorado Plateau** of the American Southwest is best known as the highland through which the Colorado River cut

Tibetan yak

the Grand Canyon. It is, in fact, a huge basin ringed by highlands and filled with multiple plateaus. Sprawling across Utah, Arizona, New Mexico and Colorado, the Plateau covers 81,000 sq miles (210,000km²) of the USA: only Alaska, Texas, California and Montana are larger. Ancient lava flows, petrified forests and

rust-coloured mesas mark this vast desert expanse, which also includes the Navajo and Hopi Indian communities.

■ Most of central and southern India is part of the **Deccan Plateau**, formed more than 60 million years ago by a series of volcanic eruptions. The name 'Deccan' derives from a Sanskrit word for 'south'. The Western Ghats mountains block moisture from the southwest monsoons, so the northern part of the Deccan Plateau receives little rainfall. Key rivers feed in from the north and over stunning waterfalls, particularly at Hogenakkal and Shivasamudram. Many ancient civilisations took root in these highlands, the most powerful of which was the Vijayanagara Empire (1336-1646).

AMAZON THEATRE

The world's most extraordinary opera house is not in Sydney or Milan, but deep in the Amazon rain forest. Built against all the odds in the 1890s and recently restored, it still stands in all its opulent glory.

The second half of the 19th century was boom-time in Manaus, a steamy city that sprang up at the junction of the Amazon and Negro rivers, right in the heart of the Amazon basin. Brazil had a world monopoly on rubber, which grew naturally in the Amazon jungle, and Manaus was at the centre of this trade.

The immense wealth generated by rubber exports funded an extravagant lifestyle for the city's rubber barons, who lit their cigars with dollar bills and bought diamonds on a grand scale: more diamonds were sold in Manaus at this time than anywhere else in the world. The city became known as the 'Paris of the Tropics', but some residents wanted more than raw wealth. They yearned for culture and entertainment that could rank alongside the very best in Europe. The idea for an opera house, El Teatro Amazonas, was born.

Building the dream

Construction began in 1884 to a design by Italian architect Celestial Sacardim. No expense was spared as the finest materials were shipped across the Atlantic from Europe, then taken 900 miles (1,450km) inland up the Amazon. White Carrara marble was brought from Italy for the columns, statues and stairs. From Alsace came 36,000 yellow, green

WHERE ON EARTH?

The capital of the Brazilian state of Amazonas, Manaus is about 1,550 miles (2,500km) northwest of Rio de Janeiro on the Amazon River, where the Negro and Solimões tributaries merge. The city can be reached by air, road or boat: it takes five days from the port of Belém on the Atlantic coast.

Colonial culture An imposing neoclassical portico extends the full height of the front facade on a theatre that could have graced any European capital.

and blue tiles to crown the rooftop dome in the pattern of the Brazilian flag – a colourful nationalist statement visible for miles around. Louis XV-style furniture was imported from Paris. To top it all, the Amazon Theatre was fitted with electricity long before this was common in Europe or America: this building was state of the art. Murano glass from Venice was used in more than 30 of the almost 200 chandeliers that illuminate the interior.

Outside, Portuguese flagstones were used for the footpath and the nearby streets were paved with rubber-and-sand slabs to mute the sound of passing carriages, so the audience's listening pleasure would not be disturbed. When all was finally ready, the inaugural opera, *La Gioconda* by Italian composer Amilcare Ponchielli, was staged on January 7, 1897.

From decay to rebirth

The rubber boom was not to last. As production moved to plantations in Asia and Africa, the fortunes of Manaus waned. With the invention of synthetic rubber, they vanished. In 1907, a mere decade after that first operatic performance, the theatre saw its last. And the lights went out not just on the theatre, but on the whole city as it could not afford to run its generators.

Decay rapidly set in as the theatre fell prey to termites and the humid climate. Renovation was attempted in 1929 and again in 1974, but it was 1988 before a successful project got underway. Two years and $8 million later, opera finally returned to the stage there with a performance by Plácido Domingo.

The theatre's repertoire has been widened to include jazz, as well as classical favourites. The humidity plays

Restored to glory The ornate auditorium seats an audience of up to 640, beneath a ceiling painted with celebratory scenes of music, dance and theatre.

havoc with instruments and the grand piano has to be treated with special oils to keep it in concert condition. Yet the opera house and its orchestra attract some of Europe's best musicians, and its annual Amazon Opera Festival draws visitors from all over the world.

best of the rest...

OPERA HOUSES

■ Opera lovers attending the 20,000-seater **Arena di Verona** in Italy are part of a tradition dating back 2,000 years: audiences have been flocking here since Roman times. The arena has wonderful acoustics, with a summer opera festival taking place under open skies.

■ The **Berliner Philharmonie** in Germany is home to the Berlin Philharmonic Orchestra. The 2,440 seats in the pentagonal auditorium surround the central stage. No seat is more than 35m (115ft) from the orchestra, thereby eliminating the usual separation of artist and audience. Despite the unusual internal layout, the auditorium has excellent acoustics.

■ Situated on the Pearl River, the gleaming new **Guangzhou Opera House** in China has a double-auditorium in a shape suggestive of two boulders washed up on the shore. Folds and curves cut canyons through the public spaces, letting light into the building.

■ With its white marble facade, the **Oslo Opera House** in Norway appears to rise out of the water like an iceberg stranded on the shore of the Oslofjord. Here is a building you can walk on; the roof forms a plaza that gives access to the water at the base and views of Oslo from its highest point.

■ Both urban sculpture and performance space, **Sydney Opera House** in Australia is the jewel in Sydney Harbour. Danish architect Jørn Utzon worked with engineer Ove Arup for 16 years to make his innovative design of three groups of interlocking shells a reality.

Walt Disney Concert Hall

■ Formed from curved steel panels, the **Walt Disney Concert Hall** has been home to the Los Angeles Philharmonic since 2003, and forms a prominent landmark in the city. Designed by Frank Gehry, it is one of the world's most acoustically sophisticated concert venues, with a unique, hi-tech organ.

ANGKOR WAT

Monumental, perfectly symmetrical, Angkor Wat rises from the plain, an iconic 'temple mountain' built by mortals to please the gods.

The first sight of Angkor Wat is a heart-stopping moment, its appearance changing throughout the day – now bathed in a soft golden glow, now burning in the midday sun, or draped, stark and awesome, in deepening shadows. Sunsets are hauntingly beautiful, sending shivers down the spine as towers and turrets glow coppery gold in the shadow of Bakheng Hill where the first city of Angkor was built. A sandstone causeway leads across a wide moat sprinkled with lotus to an entrance in the outer wall, whose golden-coloured towers and colonnades are reflected in the still water. Orange-robed monks meditate in quiet corners. The past seems to cling to the old stones here.

Widely acclaimed by scholars as the pinnacle of classical Khmer architecture, this vast temple complex – generally acknowledged as the world's largest religious structure – ranks as one of South-east Asia's leading religious sites. It is just one of several hundred temples that was built in Angkor between the

WHERE ON EARTH?

Angkor Wat is part of Angkor Archaeological Park, a 150 sq mile (400km²) park north of the modern town of Siem Reap in northern Cambodia. It can be reached by bus, car or bicycle. The best time to visit is in the dry, relatively cool season from December to March. The nearest airport is Siem Reap International.

THAILAND

Angkor Wat
●Siem Reap
CAMBODIA
Gulf of
Thailand
●Phnom
Penh
VIETNAM

9th and 15th centuries, when the region served as the seat of the Khmer Empire.

With the decline of the empire from the 15th century onwards, the temples became abandoned, haunted only by holy men. The moat surrounding Angkor Wat probably protected the temple from being swallowed up by the fast-encroaching rain forest. Many smaller temples nearby were wholly or partially buried in dense undergrowth, while this, the grandest of them all, remained remarkably well preserved. Used first as a Hindu temple, then later as a Buddhist shrine, the complex survived both pilfering by locals and the ravages of time.

Although Portuguese travellers came upon the site in the 16th century, Angkor Wat did not attract world attention until French explorer Henri Mouhot published his travel tale *Voyage à Siam et dans le Cambodge* in the 1860s.

Today it is a World Heritage Site and a major tourist attraction – it is estimated that half of all foreign visitors to Cambodia come here. While no one doubts the extraordinary achievements of this temple – the sheer size of the complex, the technical problems encountered during its construction, the classical layout so pleasing to the eye – it is the bas-reliefs, above all else, that have brought it unrivalled fame.

The building of Angkor Wat

Angkor Wat was commissioned by the great Khmer king, Suryavarman II, in 1112 and dedicated to the Hindu god,

Focal point From each side of the main enclosure, porticoes and tiers of galleries lead the eye to the central tower of the temple.

Aerial vision This bird's-eye view of the temple complex reveals its huge scale and complexity, with the elevated central block representing sacred Mount Meru set within a series of enclosures.

Vishnu. Unlike other Angkorian temples, Angkor Wat faces west, the point of the compass that symbolised death, and bas-reliefs tell their story anticlockwise, the direction associated with ancient funeral rites. Scholars are divided on the significance of this, but the temple may have been intended as a royal mausoleum to house the king's ashes.

The temple is constructed partly of laterite, partly of sandstone blocks quarried some 30 miles (48km) away and brought down the Siem Reap River.

Evidence suggests that Suryavarman ordered work to begin simultaneously on all four sides of the temple. With limited means but plenty of labour, the project was completed in less than 40 years. In the late 13th century, the temple began to change to Buddhist use, and in the main sanctuary, Vishnu was replaced by Buddha images.

Architectural symbolism

At the heart of the temple complex, five mitre-shaped towers represent the peaks of Mount Meru, home of the Hindu gods and centre of the Hindu and Buddhist universes. The surrounding walls symbolise lower pinnacles, while courtyards represent the continents and

THE KHMER EMPIRE

Around 25 miles (40km) north of Angkor Wat lies Cambodia's sacred Koulen Mountain. Legend has it that Jayavarman II declared independence on this spot in AD 802, rejecting Javanese rule and proclaiming himself the 'universal monarch', or *devaraja* (god-king). Through conquest and diplomacy, he became the first ruler to unify the warring factions of what was then the Chenla Kingdom, setting down the foundations of what later became one of the greatest empires in South-east Asia.

Attracted by ample land and water for rice cultivation, the Khmer Court left its capital at Roluos in around 900 to settle in a new area to the northwest. It was here that the first city of Angkor was built. Massive temple building followed as new rulers, Hindu then Buddhist, wished to display power and wealth while keeping the gods on their side. The Khmer Empire survived for more than 600 years, controlling - to a greater or lesser extent and at different times - parts of modern Laos, Vietnam, Myanmar, Thailand and Malaysia.

Eventually, pressure on finances and labour weakened the kingdom. Quarries were exhausted, building halted, and in 1431 the Thai delivered the final blow, sacking Angkor city, and effectively bringing the Angkorian era to an end.

Stairway to heaven The steep stairways in the second enclosure that lead to the third, uppermost enclosure were designed to be difficult to climb, to symbolise the journey to heaven.

pools of water the oceans. The seven-headed snake, *naga*, is omnipresent, stretching like a rainbow bridge between humankind and the abode of the gods. Some scholars point to a correlation between Hindu philosophy and the temple layout, their theory being that the route to the centre represents a passage back to the creation.

A heavenly quest

A tour around Angkor Wat inevitably involves a step-by-step journey – inwards and upwards – towards the central tower. Starting at the moat, on the west side of the complex, the way leads through the west entrance, one of several *gopuras*, or gateways, in the wall (including one at each compass point). The entrance opens onto a second causeway, lined with nagas, that continues past libraries and reflecting pools and across a raised terrace. The space on either side of the terrace was occupied by the original palace and city of Angkor. Built of perishable materials, both have been destroyed by centuries of decay.

The temple itself consists of three rectangular walled enclosures, one inside another and each on a higher level than the previous one. On the west side of the temple, a cloister links the outermost enclosure to the second one. This cloister was once home to more than a thousand images of Buddha donated by pilgrims, and its walls bear inscriptions recording pious deeds.

In the second enclosure, flights of steps rise steeply to the four towers that mark

Dancing nymphs The walls of Angkor Wat are adorned with *apsaras*, mythological female figures said to be able to change form and seduce mortals. They were always shown dancing.

the corners of the third, and highest, level. These corner towers are smaller versions of the central lotus-bud-shaped tower. The palace's complex layout, with its many terraces, cloisters, courtyards, decorated pediments, pavilions and flights of steps from one level to the next, can be interpreted as representing the difficult journey up to heaven.

Swept by an intermittent breeze, the central tower marking the final stage of this skyward journey soars some 60m (200ft)

above the plain, where cicadas whir in the trees. It is a good place to linger for a while, enjoying the view over the plain and the jungle, which is sprinkled with other ancient buildings, and reflecting on the god-kings of a time long past and their anonymous temple builders.

The pride of Angkor Wat

Striking bas-reliefs embellish almost every surface within the main temple – walls, columns, lintels, roofs and, most stunning of all, the inner wall of the second enclosure, where a bas-relief frieze stretches for half a mile (0.8km) around the perimeter.

Most of the bas-reliefs date back to the 12th century, with some later additions. Intended to be instructional, they depict heroic scenes from the great Hindu epics of the *Ramayana* and *Mahabharata*. Here, mighty battles rage between demons and gods; Vishnu rides a great mythical bird, the *garuda*, and slays demon enemies as they approach him on all sides; and the legendary Battle of Lanka is told in a series of beautifully carved scenes, complete with monkeys, monsters and giants.

Elsewhere in this remarkable gallery, rewards and punishments are dealt out in the 37 heavens and 32 hells of Indian tradition. In the southwest section are historical scenes from the reign of Suryavarman II, including one of him on an elephant, leading his army in a triumphal battle march, fanned by his faithful servants and shaded by 15 umbrellas.

Most striking of all is a large frieze illustrating the legend of the Churning of the Ocean of Milk, in which gods and devils battle for possession of the elixir of eternal life. In the middle of the frieze, a snake is coiled around Mount Mandara. On one side of the mountain, a team of 88 devils tugs at the snake's head, and on the other side a team of 92 gods pulls at its tail, with Vishnu urging them on. According to the legend, the two teams took it in turns to pull on the snake. This action rotated the mountain back

> **" It has towers and decoration and all the refinements which the human genius can conceive of. "**
>
> ANTÓNIO DA MADALENA, PORTUGUESE MONK (1586)

and forth, churning up the ocean so that it eventually released the precious elixir, which the gods drank, securing their immortality.

The gods may have been charmed by the beautiful apsaras singing and dancing all around them. These graceful, heavenly nymphs are among the most endearing characters adorning the walls and pillars of Angkor Wat, alongside female temple guardians, or *devatas*, which are always shown motionless. Conservative estimates mention 2,000 such exquisite characters, displaying a range of hairstyles, garments, jewellery and flowers, all attractive, sensuous and often associated with fertility rites.

A spiritual legacy

It is impossible not to be impressed by Angkor Wat – by the scale and complexity of the site, the ambition of its builders, and the beauty of its exquisite decoration. But one also appreciates the level of pure devotion here, and its resonance throughout the temple, reflected in its intricate architecture and imagery. For many, this stirs thoughts of a spiritual nature that cannot be expressed in words.

best of the rest...

ASIA'S GREAT TEMPLES

■ In the late 12th century, the legendary Khmer king, Jayavarman VII, built a new capital, **Angkor Thom,** barely a mile (1.6km) from Angkor Wat, in Cambodia. A devout Buddhist, he commissioned a grand state temple, the Bayon, with 54 towers adorned by over 200 huge faces of Avalokiteshvara, a bodhisattva representing the compassion of all Buddhas. Some say these faces, which look down with just a hint of a smile, were modelled on that of the king himself.

■ Across the Siem Reap River from Angkor Thom, Jayavarman VII built the temple of **Ta Prohm** to honour his mother. Once a splendid complex in which more than 600 nymphlike apsara dancers entertained both king and gods, the site is regarded by some as the most atmospheric Angkorian temple. Left almost untouched, this is a haunting place, with dark corners and crumbling walls tangled up in creepers and roots. The jungle creaks all around and an eerie light filters through the large, leathery leaves of the surrounding banyan trees.

■ The **Ellora Caves**, in India's Maharashtra state, are widely acclaimed as the best example of rock-cut architecture in India. The 34 'caves' were carved out of the mountainside between the 5th and 10th centuries. Jain, Buddhist and Hindu temples are found close together, epitomising the religious tolerance of the time. Most stunning is the Kailasanatha temple dedicated to the Hindu deity, Shiva.

■ Located in Madhya Pradesh, India, the **Khajuraho** complex claims an imposing group of ancient Hindu temples. They are built of sandstone, on a spot where, according to legend, the god Shiva and the goddess Parvati were united. The temples owe much of their fame to the erotic carvings on the external walls, although scenes of daily life are also depicted. The smaller Eastern Group consists of Jain temples which are still used today.

■ Set in the Indian state of Tamil Nadu, **Mahabalipuram** showcases the early stages of Dravidian architecture and the transition from rock-cut to structural building. The monuments at this site consist of cave temples, carvings and *rathas* – shrines shaped like chariots, each cut from a single block of granite. The 8th-century Shore Temple is one of the oldest structural stone temples in southern India.

Ta Prohm

ANTARCTIC PENINSULA

Once described as a land that 'looks like a fairy tale', this lonely peninsula reveals the planet's most sublime icy landscape.

The first person known to set eyes on this stunning scenery was Fabian Gottlieb Thaddeus von Bellingshausen, a captain in the Russian Imperial Navy, but he did not recognise what he saw as land, believing it to be made up of ice. As a result it was William Smith and Edward Bransfield of the British Royal Navy, arriving just three days after Bellingshausen in 1820, who became the first to identify a new continent: Antarctica. They charted the extreme northern part of the peninsula, which later became known as Trinity Peninsula, reporting 'high mountains, covered with snow'.

In fact, the mountains here are an extension of the South American Andes, via a submarine ridge and the Scotia Arc of islands (such as South Georgia) that runs between the two. They emerge in the rugged, icy mountain chain that forms the backbone of the peninsula, rising to its highest peak at Mount Jackson 3,184m (10,446ft) above sea level.

Some of the most dramatic scenery is found in Lemaire Channel on the west side of the peninsula, between the mainland and Booth Island. Dark, snow-capped mountains with steep-sided cliffs line the waterway and at Cape Renard, at the channel's northern end, stand two striking basalt towers capped with ice. Just 500m (1,600ft) wide at its narrowest point, the channel enjoys millpond-like conditions, a rarity in the Southern Ocean.

The peninsula's climate is significantly different from the rest of the continent. Temperatures in the Antarctic interior average −49C (−56F) and in summer they rarely rise above freezing, even at the coast. The lowest air temperature ever recorded on Earth was −89C (−128F) at the Vostok research station in 1983. But on the peninsula, temperatures can average 2C (36F) in summer and have even been known to reach a heady 15C (59F). As a result, some of the snow and ice here melts, revealing moss-covered tundra and lichen-encrusted rocks, with rain and fog as likely as snow and, just occasionally, bright blue cloudless skies.

Ice and snow sculptures

Despite the summer thaw, large snow and ice fields persist throughout the year, both on the islands that fringe the peninsula and in the mountains on the mainland, and giant glaciers move inexorably to the sea. Wind, sea, rain and sun mould these natural features to create the enchanting ice sculptures that moved Norwegian polar explorer Roald Amundsen to describe this as a 'land [that] looks like a fairy tale'.

At Jougla Point, deep snowfields, precipitous snow cliffs and snow cornices with the fluffy smoothness of meringues dominate the natural harbour of Port Lockroy in the Palmer Archipelago. In Paradise Bay, glaciers end in towering ice cliffs that plummet into the sea, groaning and creaking as crevasses widen until another huge block of ice breaks off as a glacier calves a new iceberg.

WHERE ON EARTH?

The Antarctic Peninsula stretches northwest into the Southern Ocean towards South America. It can be reached by plane from Punta Arenas in Chile to King George Island in the South Shetlands, or by ship in a two-day journey across the Drake Passage from the port of Ushuaia in Argentina.

Weddell Sea

Antarctic Peninsula

South Pole

ANTARCTICA

Picture perfect The Lemaire Channel has been called the 'Kodak Gap' by cruise-ship tour guides on account of the number of photographs taken by visitors.

> **Below 40 degrees south there is no law, below 50 degrees there is no God.**

A 19TH-CENTURY MAXIM ON THE DRAKE PASSAGE SEPARATING SOUTH AMERICA FROM ANTARCTICA: THE ROUGHEST, MOST DANGEROUS STRETCH OF SEA ON EARTH

Glacier ice is packed so tightly that air bubbles are squeezed out and the ice absorbs most of the red and yellow light while reflecting the blue light. This is why icebergs glow a brilliant, almost transparent blue. Some icebergs are gigantic, the size of small towns. Others sport huge domes, towers, sharp pinnacles or crowns. Through some of them the sea has eroded great natural arches. All around, the sea surface is littered with icy flotsam. Some pieces are called 'growlers' because, when the ice melts, trapped air escapes with a sound like a growling animal. Others are known as 'bergy bits', a term that may sound insubstantial, but these small icebergs threaten shipping because they are harder to see than the larger icebergs.

Island wildlife

The many accessible islands on the western side of the Antarctic Peninsula are packed with wildlife. The islands have chinstrap, gentoo and Adélie penguin rookeries, as well as nest sites for kelp gulls, Antarctic skuas, fulmars, blue-eyed shags and petrels. Weddell

CHANGING HABITATS

Climate change is having an impact on the peninsula's penguins. A colony of emperor penguins has been newly discovered on the sea ice at Snow Hill Island on the eastern side of the peninsula, but a breeding colony on Emperor Island in Marguerite Bay, on the western side, has disappeared. The western side of the peninsula is one of the fastest-warming places on the planet, with winter temperatures a massive 6C (10F) higher than just 50 years ago. Penguin populations have decreased more than 50 per cent in the last 30 years. Scientists blame a reduction in their main food, krill. These shrimp-like crustaceans graze on algae on the underside of sea ice in early spring, but with less ice there is less krill, and less krill means fewer penguins.

Changing seascape Global warming is taking its toll. Each summer an increasing number of icebergs appear in the Weddell Sea, on the peninsula's east side, due to the break up of ice shelves and glaciers.

and crabeater seals haul out on beaches and ice floes, and leopard seals, armed with powerful jaws, hunt penguins close to shore. Offshore, pods of killer whales search for seals they can tip from ice floes, and humpback, minke and fin whales feed on enormous swarms of shrimp-like krill.

It is so cold for most of the year that only two plucky flowering plants grow here, mainly on the western side of the peninsula. One is a scruffy, hardy hair grass, and the other is a pearlwort, a cushion-shaped plant that hugs the ground and produces very small whitish flowers in summer. Primitive plant-like organisms that resist cold and desiccation, such as mosses, liverworts, lichens and algae, make up the rest of the flora.

Although there is a wealth of animal life in the waters around the peninsula, and penguins breed here in their thousands, none of these species live on the peninsula all year round. The biggest resident land animal is a flightless midge about 12mm (½in) long, and the top land predator is a tiny mite, no bigger than a pinhead, that

feeds on springtails. Many of the fauna species produce their own antifreeze to survive the Antarctic winter.

Last post

One of the peninsula's delightful little surprises is the southernmost branch of the British Post Office at Port Lockroy on Goudier Island. In summer, when it is manned on behalf of the United Kingdom Antarctic Heritage Trust, it attracts more than 6,000 visitors a year, which makes it the most popular stopping-off place

for cruise ships in the Antarctic. On the beach is the skeleton of a giant fin whale, a species second only to the blue whale in size. The skeleton is reconstructed every spring after the winter storms have demolished it, and it remains a sad reminder of a whaling industry that almost wiped out the world's whale populations during the 20th century.

Hope Bay rookery Adélie penguin rookeries like this one typically number more than 100,000 pairs of penguins. The males build nests from small stones.

best of the rest...

ICY WASTES

■ **Ilulissat Icefjord** on the west coast of Greenland, 185 miles (300km) north of the Arctic Circle, was declared a UNESCO World Heritage Site in 2004. The name Ilulissat translates from Greenlandic as 'the town of icebergs' because of the hundreds of icebergs, some 100m (330ft) high, that break away from the nearby Sermeq Kujalleq glacier, the largest glacier outside Antarctica.

■ The best icy wilderness in which to see polar bears is at **Churchill** in Manitoba, Canada. From mid-October to mid-November, the bears arrive here to wait for the sea ice to form so they can hunt seals once more in Hudson Bay. Huge 'tundra buggies' take visitors to the bears if the bears do not come to them. Nuisance bears are darted and carried out by helicopter; even so, they are known occasionally to end up in town, especially at night.

■ Fire and ice is the speciality of **Vatnajökull** glacier in Iceland, where active volcanoes perforate the thick ice cover. Grímsvötn, on the northwest side of the ice cap, is the most active and most scary because the glacier encases the slopes of the volcano. During an eruption, melting ice beneath the glacier can produce an explosive flood, known as a *jökulhlaup*. One such glacial outburst, in 1996, washed away part of Iceland's main ring road.

■ The best place to see ice on the ground and fire in the sky is at the **Aurora Sky Station** on Mount Nuolja in the Abisko National Park in northern Sweden. The aurora borealis, or 'northern lights', are visible on three out of four of the dry, dark winter nights between November and March. Visitors can stay overnight.

Ilulissat – town of icebergs

AQUA TOWER

Inspired by the waves that ripple across nearby Lake Michigan, the balconies of Chicago's Aqua Tower seem to spiral into the heavens.

Think of modern architecture and shiny surfaces, hard edges and sharp angles come to mind. But think again – modern design often uses natural forms, putting nature and eco-friendly elements at the heart of a building. Spanish architect Antoni Gaudí was the first to make use of irregular curves and motifs. Then, in Fallingwater, designed in 1935, Frank Lloyd Wright showed how nature can be an integral part of a home with a modern look and geometric shape.

Modern materials such as glass, concrete and steel freed architects from the tyranny of load-bearing walls. Le Corbusier, doyenne of modern architects, codified this in his five tenets: elevate the building to keep the ground open below; use the roof to reclaim space for nature; place walls where they look best; use horizontal windows; and design the facade freely.

Ripple effect

Chicago's Aqua Building is a sublime continuation of this tradition. Wave after wave of balconies curve around the 82-storey building as it rises into the sky, producing a rippling effect quite

WHERE ON EARTH?

Aqua is on North Columbus Drive in downtown Chicago, at the point where the Chicago River meets Lake Michigan. It is adjacent to Lakeshore Park and the Loop Busines District and within walking distance of the theatre district and most of the city's major museums.

unlike Chicago's usual square-cut style. Between the waves, planes of smooth glass mimic the surface of still water and glint in the sunlight. From inside there are unique and stunning views of Lake Michigan and the city. From street level, the facade resembles a multi-layered rock formation. From any angle, the 250m (820ft) high building is more sculpture than skyscraper, its appearance changing with the light at different times of the day.

The balconies, some of which stretch outwards as much as 3.7m (12ft), shade the facade from the sun and reduce the need for air-conditioning in summer. In autumn and winter, famously windy in Chicago, they break up wind streams

GLASS HOUSE

American architect Philip Johnson, who both designed and lived in the Glass House, famously said "I have very expensive wallpaper". The four exterior walls are glass, allowing views in all directions and integrating the house almost seamlessly with the surrounding landscape. A place to live in or a stage? Or both?

The view of the Connecticut countryside changes constantly during the day and through the year. In spring, the sun filters through young, pale green leaves; in autumn, the leaves change colour to shades of yellow and red. All this can be experienced from inside the house.

Completed in 1949, the house is an early example of the use of industrial materials such as glass and steel for a private, residential structure. But what makes the building so special is that the idea of transparency and reflection in architecture could not be better realised.

Sun sensitive Balconies ripple upwards, shading the interiors. Six different types of high performance glazing further moderate the sun's heat.

so that the tower needs less resistance against them. Architect Jeanne Gang, a bird lover, even took into account how birds perceive their environment in order to help them avoid collisions with the building. The irregular pattern created by the balconies and windows is more visible to birds than a regular repeating pattern of glass panes.

New technology

The striking design is combined with the latest in sustainable technology. Visitors arriving by electric car find a public charging station in the building, and the apartments are equipped with energy-efficient lighting.

The tower also displays its green credentials on the roof of the three-storey podium around the base of the tower. This is the largest green roof in Chicago and features a pool, hot tubs and a running track. Its beds are planted with succulents, grass and shrubs that absorb water. When the sun shines, the water evaporates, cooling the air and reducing the urban heat-island effect. Perhaps here more than anywhere else in this remarkably modern building, one sees how technology can make life better for people while lessening impact on the planet, and how relevant Le Corbusier's principles of design still are today.

best of the rest...

MODERN HOMES

◼ Elegantly integrated into the surrounding Pennsylvania landscape, **Fallingwater's** cantilevered terraces seem to levitate above the waterfall. Frank Lloyd Wright built the house above, rather than next to, the waterfall so that the sound of falling water became part of life in the house. Large windows connect the natural environment around the house with its interior.

◼ Behind the elegantly curved facade of the **Copan Building** in São Paulo, designed by Oscar Niemeyer and completed in 1966, is a vertical town with its own quarters and zones. The 32-storey residential block, the largest structure ever built in Brazil, is home to 5,000 people.

◼ The glass-and-steel **Stahl House** designed by Pierre Koenig and completed in 1959, has a breathtaking site in the Hollywood Hills, USA, and a light and elegant design. The living room with floor-to-ceiling glass walls appears to hover above the city.

◼ Le Corbusier's **Villa Savoye** in Poissy, on the outskirts of Paris, France, is an elegant modernist manifesto that floats above the ground on pilotis. The flat roof functions as a terrace and non-loadbearing walls are placed only where aesthetically desired. Clean geometrical forms contrast with curving reinforced concrete walls inspired by maritime architecture.

ARENA CHAPEL
FRESCOES

A fresco cycle of unmatched beauty and humanity adorns a small chapel in Padua. Painted more than a century before the start of the Renaissance, it set a standard for others to follow.

In the early 1300s, wealthy Paduan banker Enrico Scrovegni asked the Florentine painter Giotto di Bondone (who lived around 1267–1337) to decorate the newly completed Scrovegni family chapel. Giotto chose for his subject a series of scenes from the New Testament, then set about his task using the fresco technique, which involves painting directly onto wet plaster. In a decisive break with the art of the immediate past, which favoured subdued colours and stylised figures, Giotto injected an unprecedented degree of realism and emotion into his retelling of the Christian story. In doing this, he blazed a trail for the great Renaissance artists who followed.

Jewel-like interior

Giotto covered every inch of wall space around the chapel's nave with scenes from the lives of the Virgin Mary and of Jesus, all executed in glorious, glowing colours. Adjacent scenes were separated with bands painted to imitate inlaid marble and precious stones. On the west wall is a vast Last Judgement where,

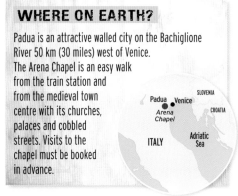

WHERE ON EARTH?

Padua is an attractive walled city on the Bachiglione River 50 km (30 miles) west of Venice. The Arena Chapel is an easy walk from the train station and from the medieval town centre with its churches, palaces and cobbled streets. Visits to the chapel must be booked in advance.

The art of storytelling Giotto's innovative style was an instant hit with visitors to the chapel, striking an emotional chord as well as an aesthetic one. He laid out the story in almost cinematic style.

among the throngs of the saved, Giotto included his patron, Enrico, presenting a model of his chapel to the Virgin Mary. The barrel-vaulted ceiling above is a brilliant blue studded with glittering golden stars, and Giotto repeated the blue in the background of several scenes.

Master storyteller

The powerful effect of the chapel lies more than anything in Giotto's narrative skill. He laid out the chosen scenes in chronological sequence, beginning at the top of the walls with the lives of Mary's mother and father, Anna and Joachim, and the Virgin's early life. The earthly life of Jesus is depicted along the central tier, finishing with the Passion cycle and Resurrection. Giotto also placed thematically related scenes above and below each other: the miracle of Jesus raising Lazarus from the dead, for example, is above the resurrection of Christ, the first scene foreshadowing the second.

Selecting the key moment in each story – the reaction to a miracle, Judas's betrayal of Jesus with a kiss – Giotto imagined how the characters must have acted and felt, and represented the emotion of the story through their facial expressions, physical gestures and postures. In the Lamentation, Jesus's followers wring their hands, their faces tense with grief, as Mary holds the body of her dead son. Elements such as folds in clothing, horizon lines, looks and gestures direct the viewer's attention to the central event. Giotto's innovative use of light and shade to model solid figures, and diagonal lines to create depth, added realism, as did the contemporary styles of dress and architecture, all helping to draw viewers into the drama unfolding on the walls around them.

Lasting influence

Consecrated in 1305, the chapel was an instant success with visitors, to the consternation of the Augustinian monks living nearby. The monks appealed to Pope Benedict XI to close the chapel on the grounds that it was too big, its decorations too opulent and – to cap it all – its bells too loud. But the Pope disagreed: he had already granted indulgences to all visitors, reducing

The Lamentation Giotto's ability to convey drama and depth was groundbreaking. Universal sorrow reaches out from every element of the scene: the limp body of Christ, the thrown-back arms of John (in the centre), and Mary's gaze at her beloved son.

their time in Purgatory by a year and 40 days. Visitors in later centuries included Masaccio, Leonardo da Vinci, Michelangelo and Raphael, all of whom built on Giotto's artistic innovations.

best of the rest...

ITALIAN FRESCO CYCLES

■ In 1348–50, under the patronage of Cosimo de' Medici, the Dominican monk Fra Angelico painted the monks' cells in the friary of **St Marco**, Florence, with serene, contemplative frescoes of scenes from the life of Christ.

■ In the 1420s, in the tiny **Brancacci Chapel** in Florence, Masaccio created frescoes of the life of St Peter. The first painter to fully master the use of perspective, Masaccio deployed sculptural modelling and bold colours to produce convincing human figures and settings.

■ Piero della Francesca's *Legend of the True Cross* fresco cycle in the basilica of San Francisco, in **Arezzo**, completed in 1466, is considered among the masterworks of the Renaissance. Piero combined a mastery of perspective with a strong feel for light in scenes that have grandeur and colour.

■ Michelangelo laboured almost singlehandedly for nearly four years, from 1508 to 1512, to decorate the vast ceiling of the Vatican's **Sistine Chapel** with events from the book of Genesis. The finished ceiling featured more than 300 figures. Seen from below, the ceiling appears to recede upwards, culminating in the creation of Adam. The frescoes represent a high point of Renaissance art.

ASTANA

This cutting-edge showpiece of contemporary architecture on the wild steppes of Kazakhstan is the realisation of one man's dream, outshining other modern cities such as Shanghai and Hong Kong.

Kazakhstan is a colossal country. The ninth largest in the world by area, four times the size of France, it stretches from the Caspian Sea virtually to Mongolia. Its northern border with Russia is 4,650 miles (7,500km) long. The country's original capital, Almaty, nestles in the far southeast, in the foothills of the Tien Shan Mountains – closer to Kyrgyzstan and China than to most of its own nation. In 1995, Kazakhstan's king-like president, Nursultan Nazarbayev, announced that he wanted a new capital in the heart of the country. The site chosen was Akmola, a small industrial city on the Ishim River and major railway junction nearly 600 miles (1,000km) northwest of Almaty – not exactly in the centre, but at least in the middle of the vast steppes that shaped the character of the nation. The new name was to be Astana, meaning simply 'capital'.

This vast area was formerly notorious for its Soviet prison camps or gulags. Winter here lasts for six months and temperatures can drop to −40C (−40F). In contrast, summer can be baking, with temperatures topping 40C (104F). Undeterred by the hostile climate, President Nazarbayev envisaged an ultra-modern city, with air-conditioning and open green spaces. He had the resources to achieve this. Drawing on

WHERE ON EARTH?

Astana is in north-central Kazakhstan. It is served by a new airport and is on a rail junction connecting with the main cities of the country and the wider region, including Urumqi in western China. As expected of a national capital, Astana has a range of high-class hotels.

RUSSIA

● Astana
KAZAKHSTAN

Bayterek Tower The tower rises to 105m (345ft). The observation deck is at 97m (318ft), symbolic of the year 1997, when Astana became Kazakhstan's capital.

Kazakhstan's vast oil, gas and mineral wealth, he could hire the services of the world's top architects to create his prestige capital. Japan's Kisho Kurokawa (1934–2007) was entrusted with the masterplan, which came to fruition in 1997, when the capital city was officially opened for business.

The Bayterek Tower

President Nazarbayev himself made the first sketches for Astana's most famous monument: the Bayterek Tower. The name means 'tall poplar' and the design embodies a popular legend. The golden ball that tops the tower represents the egg of the Samruk (or Simurgh), the mythical bird of happiness which, according to folklore, lays its magic egg each year in a poplar tree. The observation deck provides views of the entire city. Like all of Astana's key monuments, the tower is spectacularly illuminated at night.

The President's workplace is the handsome palace known as Ak Orda (White Horde), overlooking the broad Ishim River. This relatively conservative building finished in white Italian marble was loosely modelled on the White House in Washington, but extended upwards, as if pulled skywards by its neat blue dome and golden spire. Close by, Kazakhstan

Petal-like design The vision of Manfredi Nicoletti, architect of Astana's Central Concert Hall, was to build the 'Flower of the Steppe'.

Central Concert Hall provides a striking contrast. Designed by the Italian architect Manfredi Nicoletti, the dramatic, leaning exterior curls around three concert halls like shavings of steel. Inaugurated in 2009, the hall contains one of the world's largest classical-music venues, with 3,500 seats.

President Nazarbayev brought in British architect Norman Foster to build the extraordinary Palace of Peace and Reconciliation. This 62m (203ft) high granite and glass pyramid contains a museum, library and opera house, as well as a congress hall with a huge circular conference table, designed for the delegates of the triennial Congress of World and Traditional Religions.

At the other end of the city's main east–west avenue is the Khan Shatyr (Royal Marquee), an entertainment centre resembling a massive leaning tent – another brainchild of President Nazarbayev realised by Norman Foster. With a polymer roof suspended from cables rising to 150m (490ft), this is the world's highest tensile structure. Opened in 2010, it contains shops, theme-park rides and even a beach. At night it glows with changing colours from inside.

Still growing

Government buildings and apartment blocks have been similarly designed in inventive shapes and colours – such as a set of three wavy, blue-green skyscrapers entitled the Northern Lights. Boulevards and green spaces are adorned with formal gardens, clipped hedges, and artificial trees that light up at night.

Most of this new city is to the south of the Ishim River. The old Soviet-style town to the north is gradually being replaced as the population swells towards 800,000. Capital cities 'built from zero', such as Canberra in Australia and Abuja in Nigeria, can take a while to gain the patina that lends character. A capital only since 1997, Astana is too young for that, but its citizens appear to like it. It is new, spacious and visually stunning. But you might have to wrap up well to enjoy it.

best of the rest...

MODERN PLANNED CITIES

■ **Brasília**, the modern capital of Brazil, was erected on the savannah of south-central Brazil in just four years, beginning in 1956. Urban planner Lúcio Costa fashioned the city with a street design shaped like an aeroplane or a bird in flight. In the 'wings' are the residential *superquadras*, or apartment blocks. A huge lake, the Lago do Paranoá, sweeps around the nose, where government buildings are located, and is now spanned by the zigzag arches of the Juscelino Kubitschek Bridge.

Costa brought in the modernist architect Oscar Niemeyer to design the landmark buildings. The most imaginative include the National Congress, with its huge cup and bowl; the waterfall-like arches of the Itamaraty Palace; the Palácio da Alvorada, the President's official residence; and the stark crown of thorns of the Metropolitan Cathedral of Our Lady of Aparecida.

■ At **Masdar** in the Gulf emirate of Abu Dhabi a new city is being built in an attempt to create an energy-sustainable, zero-carbon conurbation. Streets are narrow and shady. Terracotta meshes on the outsides of buildings protect them from the sun's glare while allowing breezes to circulate. The only vehicles are solar-powered podcars.

Brasília's Cathedral of Our Lady of Aparecida

LAKE BAIKAL

The oldest and deepest lake on Earth is a place of outstanding natural beauty, often cloaked in fogs and violent storms. It holds a fifth of the planet's unfrozen fresh water and is home to some unique wildlife.

Set in the remote mountains and dense forests of southern Siberia in the Russian Federation, this vast, crescent-shaped stretch of water extends for nearly 400 miles (640km), its slate-blue surface regularly churned up by the wind.

What it lacks in surface area – it is smaller than North America's Lake Superior and Africa's Lake Victoria – Lake Baikal more than makes up in depth, plunging to 1,642m (5,387ft) at its deepest point. The creatures living in its lower regions, such as sponges and shrimp-like amphipods, are more reminiscent of those found in the deeper parts of the open ocean than in a freshwater lake.

Above the water line, the scenery is dramatic and stunningly beautiful. Rugged mountains surround the lake: the high Baikal Mountains lie to the west and the lower Zabaikalsky Mountains to the

Shaman Rock Looking east across the lake from Olkhon Island, the craggy outcrop of the sacred Shaman Rock dominates the view.

Lake Baikal is in southeastern Siberia, sandwiched between the Russian federal subjects of Irkutsk Oblast and Buryatia. It is on the route of the Trans-Siberian Railway between Moscow and Vladivostok, which skirts the southern part of the lake. Irkutsk, at the lake's southern end, has an international airport.

east. Their lower slopes and the northern lakeshore form part of the great northern forest, the taiga, which stretches across the high northern latitudes of North America, northern Europe and Asia and is home to a third of all the trees in the world. Ancient larches and 500-year-old cedars, as well as younger birch and pine,

grow down to the water's edge. The pines growing on sandy ground appear to stand on stilts, their roots exposed by the wind. In autumn, the larches colour the whole region orange.

Sacred beauty

Local people have always recognised the special beauty of Lake Baikal – modern Russians call it the 'pearl of Siberia'. The Buryats, who arrived in the region with the Mongolian warrior Genghis Khan in the 13th century, practised Shamanism and chose the craggy rock outcrop now known as Shaman Rock, at the tip of Cape Burkhan on Olkhon Island, as a site for their rituals. Practising shamans lived in a cave at the foot of the rock. The Buryats also used Shaman Rock as a place of judgment, forcing those accused of crimes to stay here overnight in winter. If a criminal survived exposure to the cold, he was set free; if he succumbed, he was clearly guilty.

In the 17th century, Tibetan Buddhism arrived in the area from Mongolia, partly absorbing and partly displacing Shamanism as the local religion. Converts took over the cave as a sacred site and inscribed the walls with Buddhist prayers that can still be read by visitors.

Some artefacts discovered in the area go back much further in time. Rock paintings of people, bulls, dogs and swans, estimated to be more than 4,000 years old, adorn the rose-white limestone rocks at Sagan-Zaba Cliffs on the lake's western shore, and Bronze- and Iron-Age tools and weapons have been found at sites dotted all around the lake.

Unique wildlife

Lake Baikal is rich in wildlife. Nearly 300 species of birds nest around the lake, and many more stop off on their seasonal migration, especially in the marshy delta of the Selenga River. White-tailed eagles patrol the shores for carrion, and brown bears are forest residents. More than a third of plant and animal species living here, such as the Baikal sturgeon, are found nowhere else in the world.

Baikal's most famous residents are the steel-grey nerpas, a species of freshwater seal. How seals came to be here is a mystery, although scientists speculate that they swam up rivers from the Arctic Ocean and were cut off from the sea during the last Ice Age. When the ice melted they never went back, but became isolated in the lake. Nowadays, seals can be seen basking on rocks on the Ushkany Islands and other central and northern parts of the

Freshwater seal The nerpa seal is unique to Lake Baikal, the only mammal found in its waters. It is a small, solitary seal that can often be seen in summer in the lake's central and northern sections.

lake. Nerpas feed mainly on golomyanka, or Baikal oilfish, the most common fish in the lake. These bottom-dwellers come close to the surface to feed at night. Oilfish lack a swim bladder but have a high oil content and porous bones, which allows them to move up and down in Baikal's water unaffected by changes in pressure.

Another notable resident of the lake is the omul, a small, silver-sided, salmon-like fish occasionally caught by nerpas and the primary catch of local fishermen. Smoked omul is a delicacy sold in markets around the lake and popular with travellers; locals prefer their omul salted. A traditional dish, known as *stroganina*, consists of a salad of finely cut strips of freshly frozen, raw omul served with onion, salt and black pepper.

Nerpas and lake fish can be seen in the aquariums of the small museum of the Limnological Institute of the Russian

ANCIENT RIFT

Lake Baikal is in the world's deepest continental rift valley. The tear in the Earth's crust here is pulling apart at a rate of 2cm (³/₄in) a year, causing frequent earthquakes and creating numerous hot springs. The lake itself is 25-30 million years old, making it not only the world's oldest, but also one of the longest-lived lakes in geological history. It is fed constantly by no fewer than 336 rivers, including the mighty Selenga, and it drains through the Angara River, a tributary of the Yenisei, the largest river system to flow north into the Arctic Ocean.

Academy of Sciences, in the village of Listvyanka on the lake's southwestern shore, but there is also a good chance of spotting them in the wild, for Baikal's waters are unusually clear. The clarity of the water is maintained by the poppy-seed-sized copepod *Epischura baikalensis* that dominates the plankton, gobbling up miniscule particles of food and specks of pollution to make Baikal one of the clearest lakes in the world. On a good day, visibility is at least 40m (130ft). When Vladimir Putin descended to the bottom of the lake in the submersible *Mir* in 2009, he declared: 'We can see the bottom of Lake Baikal, which is very clean and beautiful. The water is pure from an ecological point of view, but in fact it is a kind of plankton soup.'

Wild weather

Summers at the lake are relatively short. The warmest month is August, when the air temperature reaches 18C (64F) on the lake and 25C (77F) on the surrounding land. It stays warm in September. In early summer and late autumn, fogs are frequent.

High winds lash the lakeshore during autumn – at this time of year there are, on average, an incredible 18 storms a month. The winds blow from different directions, each with a distinct character and local name. The shelonnik blows from the southeast, the verkhovik from the northeast. As the verkhovik wind strengthens, the water turns almost black, with white-capped waves that push towards the southern shore. The kultuk blows from the southwest, accompanied by grey, leaden skies and low cloud. The barguzin howls down the valley of the Barguzin River on the east side of the lake; the sarma, from the Sarma River flowing in from the west, can reach hurricane strength. The equally ferocious gornaya appears suddenly, causing 6m (20ft) high waves to break on the cliffs along the eastern shore. Clearly, Lake Baikal can be a stormy place. Even so, on average there are 2,277 hours of sunshine each year – similar to Melbourne, Australia, and parts of the Bordeaux region in France. The driest and sunniest place is Zagli Bay at the southern end of Olkhon Island, the largest of Lake Baikal's 27 islands.

In winter the lake is transformed into a white wonderland. Mists rise from the surface in December and the surrounding vegetation is covered with hoar frost. By late January the surface water is frozen solid to a depth of about a metre (3ft), and the air temperature can drop to –27C (–17F), even plunging to –39C (–38F) in the surrounding

Ice formations In winter the lake's surface freezes solid, but daily fluctuations in temperature cause the ice to contract and expand, alternately creating fissures then pushing up great triangular slabs of ice.

countryside. The ice is unusually clear, so in the shallows you can still see right through to the bottom of the lake. As dusk approaches, the sinking sun's rays colour the ice golden, then pink, then finally red.

In April the ice turns cloudy and breaks up. This is often accelerated by deep-water currents and sometimes by bubbles of methane rising from the bottom of the lake. The bubbles push up from the depths to cause patches of clear water, or 'springs' as they are known locally. Small icebergs might still be floating in the northern part of the lake in June, when the water is colder than in December. Despite this, in relatively shallow bays, such as the 15-mile (24km) wide, sandy-shored Barguzine Bay, the water reaches a comfortable 22–23C (72–73F) – warm enough for a swim.

Preserving Baikal

Lake Baikal's outstanding beauty has impressed visitors for centuries, so it should come as no surprise that the region has a long history of conservation. As early as the 13th century, Genghis Khan forbade any building around the lake so the area would remain pristine. In 1912 Tsar Nicholas II proclaimed the eastern shore as Russia's first nature reserve, known as the Barguzinsky Reserve. Today, half of the lake's shoreline is protected. Tough laws ensure that sustainable tourism, such as kayaking and hiking, prevails over mass development, so maintaining this unique tradition of preserving the natural habitat for the forseeable future.

Small but SPECIAL

CHINA'S FIVE FLOWER LAKE

Set in the striking karst landscape of the Jiuzhaigou Valley in Sichuan province, Five Flower Lake is extraordinarily clear, with visibility to a depth of 40m (130ft) revealing a lattice of ancient fallen tree trunks on the lakebed. Five Flower is one of a series of blue, green and turquoise-coloured lakes dammed by rock falls, but it differs from the others as its waters change colour, looking sometimes yellow, sometimes green, but usually diamond-blue. In winter Five Flower never freezes, though the others do, and in summer it never dries up. Local wildlife living in the adjacent mountain forests include the rare giant panda and the golden snub-nose monkey.

best of the rest...

LAKES

■ The deep-blue waters of **Crater Lake** in the northwestern US state of Oregon fill the caldera of an ancient volcano that collapsed 7,700 years ago. Its strangest occupant is the 'Old Man of the Lake', a 9m (30ft) tall tree stump bleached pure white by the elements, which has bobbed upright in the water for more than a century. No rivers enter the lake. Evaporation in summer is compensated by winter snow and rain, the entire body of water being replaced every 250 years.

■ Surrounded on three sides by the Lipontine Alps, and touching the plain of Lombardy to the south, **Lake Maggiore** is Italy's longest lake. Considered part of the country's lake district – which also includes lakes Como, Garda and Lugano – it is shared with Switzerland. Temperatures here are mild all year and a

Crater Lake

Lake Maggiore

Mediterranean-style climate prevails. This has given rise to some of northern Italy's most magnificent gardens, including the English-style Giardini Botanici dell'Isola Madre, the Italianate gardens of Palazzo Borromeo on Isola Bella, and gardens with subtropical plants on the larger Isola di Brissago, which appear to float like flower-decked boats on the water.

■ Ancient **Lake Ohrid** has been around for about 5 million years and straddles the mountainous border between Macedonia and Albania. It has unique plants and wildlife, including the Ohrid brown trout and the 'plashica', a fish endemic to the lake. The scales of the plashica are used to make Ohrid pearls.

■ **Phewa Lake** in Nepal is famed for its still, crystal-clear waters, which offer a picture-perfect reflection of sacred Mount

Machapuchare. Belonging to the Annapurna range of peaks in the Himalayas, Machapuchare is revered by locals and climbing it is forbidden. Visitors can take a boat to an island in the middle of the lake that is home to the 18th-century Hindu Tal Barahi temple.

■ The **Plitvice Lakes** in the mountains of central Croatia are a series of 16 blue-green lakes connected by spectacular waterfalls and natural dams of travertine rock. The shifting landscape of this limestone region was formed by several small rivers that eat away at the underlying rocks, picking up sediment in one place and depositing it in another as they flow from lake to lake.

■ Mid-November at **Lake Tekapo** on New Zealand's South Island is Russell lupine time. From now until January, the roadside verges and untended ground around the lake are carpeted with the dense, bright-coloured flower spikes of lupins. The lake lies at the base of New Zealand's Southern Alps, its milk-blue colour the result of powdered rock, ground up by glaciers, that remains suspended in the water reflecting the light.

Lake Tekapo

46

BANAUE RICE FIELDS

Thousands of neatly manicured rice terraces, created more than 2,000 years ago, hug the hillsides of central Luzon, giving a serene, sculptural beauty to an otherwise densely wooded region.

From hilltop vantage points above the towns and villages, it is clear that whole hillsides have been carved into flights of terraces as far as the eye can see. The low stone or mud walls that contain the terraces follow the natural contours of the landscape: this is a contour map made physical reality, each level crisply delineated. The terraces are filled with water, so their surfaces are uniformly, spirit-level flat. In places, summits of ridges are ringed by walls to create a top as flat as a wedding cake.

Nowhere else on Earth has a landscape been so intricately sculpted on such a scale – 4,000 sq miles (10,000km²) carved out of the forested hills by countless generations of Ifugao farmers. The region has been recognised by UNESCO and enshrined as a World Heritage Site embracing five traditional rice-growing communities and towns, the most famous of which is Banaue.

The Ifugao people are the original inhabitants of this rugged region at the heart of the Cordillera Central mountain range. Remote, independent

WHERE ON EARTH?

Luzon is the main northern island of the Philippines and Banaue is 220 miles (350km) north of the capital city, Manila. The best time to see the terraces is in the two months leading up to the rice harvest in late June or July when the crops are fully grown. Visitors usually arrive by road.

and with a fearsome reputation for headhunting in the distant past, they were largely bypassed by the Philippines' colonial rulers. Such was the region's inaccessibility at the end of World War Two, the Japanese forces made their last stand here, at Mount Napulawan.

Agricultural traditions

All the while, in their partial isolation, the Ifugao observed a precisely honed pattern of rice growing. Building, flooding, irrigating and cultivating rice terraces on steep terrain requires an unusual degree of social cohesion, and water – sourced from the rain forests above the terraces – has to be shared equitably between farmers.

Until recently, Ifugao shamans called *mumbaki* were at the heart of rice-growing communities. They led the rites to ensure the blessing and protection of the gods and spirits. The rituals, where still conducted, may involve incantation and chanting, rice wine, the sacrifice of chickens and dancing. Wooden carvings, called *bulol*, represent the spirits of the rice fields and are the focus of devotions. Kept in the granaries, the bulol depict men and women seated with a bowl on their knees. For rituals, dances and celebrations, villagers dress in traditional striped kilts and feather headdresses.

Precarious future

Traditional Ifugao rice is highly prized for its quality and flavour, but the work is back-breakingly hard and profits are slim.

Wet work Once the terraces have been cleaned by the men and then flooded, the work of planting the rice seedlings (above) and harvesting the crop is traditionally carried out by women.

Cycle of colour At the start of the season, the water-filled terraces reflect the sky and wooded hills. Gradually, the terraces turn green as the rice grows, then gold at harvest time – an ever-changing setting for the village of Bangaan.

The terraces need constant maintenance, all of which has to be carried out by hand: the structures are too delicate for machines. As young men and women have been lured away by the promise of easier lives in the cities, many terraces on the margins have fallen into disuse.

One incentive to maintain the Ifugao rice terraces is that they have become a major tourist attraction – although, there again, many local people prefer to work as guides or in the hospitality industry rather than toil in the fields. This landscape is in a critical phase with an uncertain future. As Ifugao elders point out, the deterioration of the terraces has coincided with a time when the mumbaki have converted to Christianity, perhaps thereby forfeiting the protection of their traditional local gods.

best of the rest...

CULTIVATED LANDSCAPES

■ Rows of neatly trimmed tea bushes cloak the hills beneath the Indian town of **Darjeeling**. Since a British doctor planted the first tea bush here in 1841, tea has been grown on its celebrated tea estates, thriving at a high altitude against the backdrop of the snowy Himalayas.

■ In the western Netherlands, before the landscape could be cultivated, it had to be created from scratch. Reclaimed from the sea and protected by dykes, the **Dutch polders** are land threaded by canals. Windmills have pumped water to maintain the polders since the 16th century.

■ The art of fine wine is closely tied to soil, climate and landscape. In the **Rhine Valley** between Koblenz and Mainz in Germany, the vine terraces cling to steep hillsides under the watchful eye of medieval castles.

■ Around **Coruche**, northeast of Lisbon, is the heart of Portugal's *montado* - the magnificent oak forests where cattle graze and pine trees grow alongside the self-renewing cork oak trees. The bark is harvested for cork.

BANFF NATIONAL PARK

Ice fields and exquisite blue lakes are set amid breathtaking Rocky Mountain scenery. This is true wilderness country, with wildlife to match.

Among towering snow-capped mountains, a crown of permanent ice fields – the Waputik, Wapta and Columbia – feed glaciers that push down like huge white tongues against the dark rock. The meltwater forms torrents that plunge through precipitous gorges and over thundering waterfalls. Some of that meltwater feeds into glacial lakes, bringing with it a fine dust known as 'rock flour'. As sunlight hits the water, the dust absorbs all the colours of the spectrum except blue, which is reflected back from the surface. This accounts for the many shades of turquoise seen in the lakes here: Moraine Lake, backed by the Valley of Ten Peaks, is a pale teal-blue; Peyto Lake, ringed by forests, is baby-blue; Lake Louise is a milky turquoise.

Twenty-dollar view This view looking north across Moraine Lake once featured on the Canadian $20 bill.

WHERE ON EARTH?

Created in 1885, Banff National Park is Canada's premier national park. It occupies 2,500 sq miles (6,475km²) of the Canadian Rockies. The town of Banff, in the park's southeast corner, is 75 miles (120km) west of Calgary on Trans-Canada Highway 1.

BRITISH COLUMBIA — ALBERTA — CANADA — Banff National Park — Calgary — Vancouver — MONTANA — WASHINGTON — IDAHO — USA — OREGON

Large animals are commonplace in the park. Black bears and moose feed on dandelions in spring and berries in autumn; wolves lope along the banks of the Mistaya River; bighorn sheep clamber over jagged cliffs; hoary marmots sunbathe near Peyto Lake. All of this combines to explain why Banff is the epitome of raw Rocky Mountain beauty.

best of the rest...

ROCKY MOUNTAIN SCENERY

■ The Canadian Rockies are blessed with many stunning national parks, of which **Jasper National Park** in Alberta is the largest, second only to Banff in natural spectacle. It is the wilderness home to an enormous diversity of animals, including herds of woodland caribou.

■ To the southeast, **Grand Teton National Park** in Wyoming, USA, has the youngest mountains in the Rockies, rising up steeply from the floor of Jackson Hole.

■ **Yoho National Park** on the western slopes of the Canadian Rockies has pristine wilderness around Lake O'Hara. It is also home to the Burgess Shale, whose rocks contain the fossils of primitive creatures from 500 million years ago, the ancestors of all the major animal groups living today.

Grand Teton National Park

BELL ROCK LIGHTHOUSE

Against daunting odds, this elegant lighthouse was built miles offshore on a treacherous reef that is uncovered only at low tide. It is the oldest sea-washed lighthouse operating in the world.

Since 1811, the lamps of the Bell Rock Lighthouse have warned North Sea sailors off the east coast of Scotland to beware the infamous sunken reef known as the Bell Rock. Building on top of that rock was fraught with difficulties and danger. The rock is 12 miles (19km) off the coast in the fierce North Sea, and completely submerged except for a few hours each day.

That the Bell Rock Lighthouse has endured the constant assault of the waves for 200 years without any significant deterioration to its masonry is testimony to the genius of Scottish engineer Robert Stevenson and a tribute to the masons, joiners, smiths, mould-makers, stonecutters and carpenters who, with unsurpassed skill and courage, and at great personal risk, undertook its construction over four years.

Dangerous shores

The Scottish coastline, with its submerged rocky moraines, is known for its hazards to navigation. The Bell Rock (also known as Inchcape Rock) extends 427m (1,400ft) across the shipping routes between the firths of the Forth and Tay, and is particularly insidious because, except at low tide, it lies completely hidden by the waves. From the earliest days of sail, shipwrecks here were common. A local legend tells of a 14th-century abbot of Aberbrothock (modern Arbroath) who ordered a bell to be hung on a timber buoy attached to the rock, where its clanging in the restless waves would serve as a warning. The structure gave the rock its name, but did not last long. By the 18th century, ship losses on the coasts around Britain were so frequent that merchants lobbied Parliament in Westminster to build lighthouses. This led to the establishment, in 1786, of the Northern Lighthouse Trust.

Life-saving light At high tide, the tower appears to rise magically straight from the sea: there is no hint of the razor-like rocks that lie a few feet below. The sloping base was designed to deflect the force of the waves.

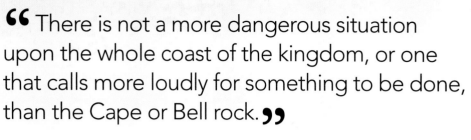

❝ There is not a more dangerous situation upon the whole coast of the kingdom, or one that calls more loudly for something to be done, than the Cape or Bell rock. **❞**

ROBERT STEPHENSON, REPORT TO THE COMMISSIONERS OF THE NORTHERN LIGHTHOUSE BOARD (1800)

Stevenson takes the lead

In 1799 Robert Stevenson, then a young civil engineer eager to make his name, first proposed a lighthouse on the Bell Rock, but it was not until 1804, when the Royal Navy ship HMS *York* foundered there, taking 491 lives, that the sceptical Lighthouse Board agreed to the expensive (and, many believed, foolhardy) project. Stevenson already had some experience – when he was just 19, he had supervised construction of a lighthouse at Little Cumbrae on the Firth of Clyde – but he was still relatively unknown and so the cautious Lighthouse Board appointed John Rennie, an eminent engineer of the day renowned for canals and aqueducts, to supervise the project.

The upstart Stevenson treated Rennie with a cannily aggressive respect: the barrage of letters (more than 82 exist) that he sent to Rennie during the construction, dutifully requesting counsel and reporting on progress, served to keep Rennie usefully employed back in London, writing careful replies full of sage advice that Stevenson did not hesitate to ignore when it suited him. Stevenson was also fortunate that Rennie suffered from seasickness; he visited the rock only twice during construction.

Strength and precision

In planning the lighthouse, Stevenson and Rennie took note of the work of their engineering forebear, John Smeaton (1724–92). Stevenson based the initial design on Smeaton's Eddystone Lighthouse (completed in 1759), which had a broad base tapering to a slender tower. Smeaton had been inspired by the shape of an old oak tree that could withstand the storms that toppled less stable trees. Rennie's experience now came into play, as he adapted Stevenson's design for the rigorous conditions of the Bell Rock by insisting on a broader base and more gradual slope to deflect the battering forces of the waves.

Because of the violence of the sea and the surge of the tides, construction could proceed only in summer, when storms were less severe, and only during the few hours of low tide when the rock was exposed. If low tide was at night, the crew was expected to work by torchlight. Stevenson referred to the craftsmen working on the reef as 'artificers', a word that evokes the skills and adaptability needed to overcome the destructive forces of nature.

During the earliest days of construction, the artificers lived on a boat anchored off the reef. Later, they built barracks, perched on stilts next to the lighthouse and connected to it by a rope catwalk, where they lived in the middle of the stormy sea. One young man who worked as a smith fell from the catwalk and was swept into the sea and drowned. He was the only fatality on the rock itself, although four men died in other incidents related to the lighthouse construction.

While enduring gruelling weather and primitive living conditions, the men were engaged in hard labour and pushing the boundaries of engineering achievement. The foundations (which, due to the pitiless force of the sea, had to be extra deep) were hacked out of the rock with pickaxes. These required constant sharpening, so a forge was set up on the rock, where the smith was often working knee-deep in water.

Each of the 2,835 blocks of Aberdeen granite or sandstone had to be cut to precise dimensions. The work included the crucial dovetailing that would allow them to fit together (as Stephenson said 'with great nicety') in a minutely calculated, interlocking pattern of

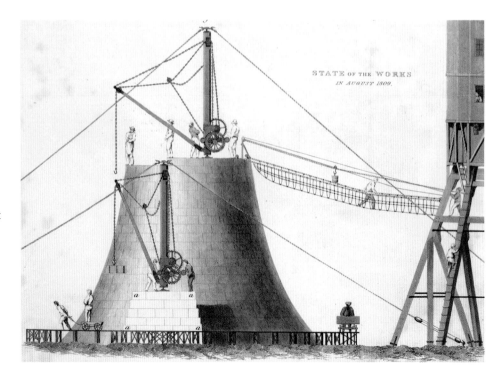

'courses', or layers. The finished stones were then loaded onto boats. Out at the rock, they were unloaded onto rails that encircled the tower, winched up into position by pulleys and secured with wooden wedges. Ninety courses of masonry took the tower to a height of just over 31m (102ft); with the addition of the glass light-room, the finished lighthouse topped out at 35.3m (115ft 10in).

Lighting the way

The Bell Rock's source of illumination was revolutionary for its era. Smeaton's Eddystone Light had attempted to penetrate the infamous Scottish fogs with nothing more than a chandelier mounted

Under construction An old illustration shows the system of winches and pulleys for lifting the stone blocks and the precarious rope-bridge that linked the half-built tower and the artificers' living quarters.

with candles. For Bell Rock, Stevenson and his stepfather, Thomas Smith, a former lamplighter in Edinburgh, designed an apparatus of 24 silver-plated reflectors on a revolving frame, with panes of red glass fronting the reflectors on the two short sides. Power to turn the frame was supplied by a drum wound with a weighted, descending rope. As the rope unwound, the drum turned. The resulting intermittently flashing red light became Bell Rock's signature.

In February 1811, the first revolving light shone forth, visible for 35 miles (56 km). That original system operated for 30 years before the first upgrade, and the light has changed with technology several times since, being lit over the years by spermaceti (whale) oil, paraffin, diesel and acetylene gas. Today, the light is powered by batteries charged by solar panels, with generator backup, and is fully automated. The lighthouse was manned until 1988.

Still saving lives

The Bell Rock Lighthouse has been called one of the 'seven wonders of the industrial world'. Beautiful and lonely, it has inspired artists and poets including J.M.W. Turner and Sir Walter Scott. But it is ordinary fishermen and sailors, whose lives it continues to save, who most appreciate the efforts of the brave men who built it.

Small but SPECIAL

ENOSHIMA LIGHTHOUSE

The lighthouse as modern sculpture? Japan's Enoshima Lighthouse, also known as the 'sea candle', glows on the highest point of Enoshima island in the city of Fujisawa, overlooking Mount Fuji and Sagami Bay. Renovated in 2003, this modern lighthouse consists of a spiral staircase surrounded by an open steel superstructure. At night it is bathed in light that changes between violet, pink, green and amber. Visitors can either climb the stairs to the observatory at the top or take an escalator - either way, the ascent is through a corona of coloured light. The lighthouse is nearly 60m (200ft) high and rises 36m (120ft) above sea level, so the view is panoramic.

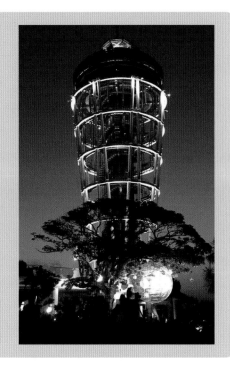

best of the rest...

LIGHTHOUSES

◾ In profile it resembles a slim white arrow topped by a powerful beacon shaped like a candle flame. The **Coastwatcher's Memorial Lighthouse**, built in 1959, at Madang in Papua New Guinea, memorialises the Australians and New Guineans who monitored enemy activity in the Southwest Pacific during World War Two and transmitted coded intelligence on enemy movements to the Allies via radio stations dotted across the islands.

◾ Buddhism and beautiful sunsets are features of the **Kanchanaphisek** lighthouse set on a headland at the extreme southern end of Phuket, Thailand. The lighthouse, built in 1996, to mark King Rama IX's accession to the throne, is topped by golden sculptures of elephants, Buddhist symbols of mental wisdom and physical strength. It overlooks Promthep Cape, Kho Man Island and the Andaman Sea.

◾ Erected in 1752 at the most southerly point of mainland Britain, **Lizard Lighthouse** warns shipping of the hazardous waters around Lizard Point, Cornwall. Its twin towers are connected by a cottage with views of both lights. Comfort-minded superintendents were said to snooze on a couch in the cottage at night, waking occasionally to peer at the lights. If the lights dimmed, the keeper, still reclining, blew a cow horn, startling the poor bellows-keepers into stepping up their efforts to fan the lighthouse fires. The lighthouse provides a welcome light to vessels approaching from the Atlantic Ocean.

Leander's Tower

◾ The **Cape Elizabeth Lighthouse** is one of the most handsome cast-iron lighthouses in New England, USA. The rocky Maine settlement of Cape Elizabeth, named after the sister of the British monarch, Charles I), has had a lighthouse since 1828; the current structure dates from 1874. The lighthouse and its surrounding buildings were immortalised in paintings by American artist Edward Hopper, including *Lighthouse at Two Lights*, in which the isolated tower is bathed in glorious sunshine.

The lighthouse emits four white flashes every 15 seconds and its fog signal presents two distinct blasts every 60 seconds. It remains an active aid to coastal navigation, and its optical equipment is still maintained to modern standards by the US Coast Guard.

◾ An ancient, now modernised, Byzantine lighthouse clings to a tiny island in the Bosphorus strait in Istanbul, Turkey. Known as **Leander's Tower**, or Maiden's Lighthouse, it has been used through the ages as a fort, a prison and a quarantine hospital, and boasts competing legends to explain its presence. Today's tower was built by the Ottoman Turks in 1725, and has become a symbol of the city. The interior space is now a restaurant, and there are daily excursions running from the shore.

Pointe Sainte-Mathieu

◾ **Pointe Sainte-Mathieu** Lighthouse stands on the rugged westerly point of Finistère ('end of the Earth'), in Brittany, France, where fjord-like inlets create a treacherous coast and the sea is prone to violent storms. The current structure was built in 1835 in the imposing ruins of a 13th-century Benedictine abbey, replacing a system of warning lights that had been provided by the monks.

The building is 37m (121ft) high, and its white light, which has a range of 29 miles (46 km), flashes across the Atlantic Ocean every 15 seconds to guide boats towards Brest harbour. The lighthouse equipment was fully automated by 1996. The structure was designated a national historical monument in November 2010.

Lizard Lighthouse

BIG SUR COAST

A magnet for writers and artists, home to rare plants and animals, California's Big Sur is intimidating, yet inspiring. Since 1937 it has been served by a road that no one thought could be built.

Stretching for 90 miles (145km) between Carmel and Cambria is the slice of California coast known as Big Sur. Even the name sounds magical, a polyglot of Spanish and English meaning 'big south'. Gazing south from Carmel, it is easy to see how settlers arrived at that name: colossal mountains rise straight up from the Pacific Ocean, some of them weathered into 400m high (1,300ft) cliffs, often besieged by monstrous waves. This coast is a ship-killer, too, a place that skippers avoided lest they fall into its rocky claws. No wonder pioneers took so long to trickle down this stretch of coast. Even today it is largely uninhabited.

Formed at the same time as the Sierra Nevada to the east, the Santa Lucia Mountains give the coast its geological backbone and scenic backdrop. A mild Mediterranean climate is complemented by coastal fog, endowing Big Sur with a variety of microhabitats from lush redwood forest to arid chaparral. The wildlife is also diverse: migrating grey whales and monarch butterflies, endangered California condors and sea otters, coyotes and cougars.

WHERE ON EARTH?

Big Sur lies about 150 miles (240km) south of San Francisco and 300 miles (480km) north of Los Angeles. It is not served by public transport: visitors must drive themselves or join a private group tour. Accommodation is limited, but several of the state parks have camp sites.

The Spanish arrived in 1770 and created a mission in Carmel and in the provincial capital, Monterey, but they shunned the rugged coast further south. A century later, enterprising Yankees thought Big Sur would yield the same gold and timber bounty as the rest of California. But the region proved too inaccessible and by the early 20th century the miners and lumberjacks had left.

A new dawn

Locals had long called for a road along the coast to aid shipwreck victims and improve access to isolated communities. Construction started in 1919, and

18 years, 32 tonnes of dynamite and 33 bridges later, the Big Sur stretch of California Highway One was complete.

The implausible route, with its myriad twists and turns and dramatic drop-offs, became an instant classic. The author and painter Henry Miller fled to Big Sur in 1944 and stayed for nearly two decades. Photographer Edward Weston and Beat Generation bard Jack Kerouac fell under its spell. By the late 1960s, San Francisco's counterculture revolution had swept down to Big Sur, and the likes of Joan Baez and Joni Mitchell performed on the cliff tops.

Much of Big Sur is now protected within the confines of the Ventana Wilderness, Los Padres National Forest, Monterey Bay National Marine Sanctuary and half a dozen state parks. Cruising down Highway One is a quintessential California experience. And Big Sur itself remains much as it always was: awesome, astonishing and surprisingly pristine.

Wild beauty Big Sur's dramatic coastline weaves in and out of rocky inlets that are constantly pounded by the Pacific Ocean.

best of the rest...

DRAMATIC COASTLINES

Italy's iconic **Amalfi Coast** stretches along the south side of the Sorrento Peninsula south of Naples. Long a picturesque retreat of the rich and famous, the coast is speckled with whitewashed villages on precipitous limestone cliffs. The island of Capri is a ferry ride away.

The **Lycian Coast** of southwest Turkey blends ancient ruins and pine-forested mountains with dreamy turquoise bays like Olu Deniz. The region's white-sand strands and offshore isles are surprisingly empty.

Amalfi Coast

The **Gulf of Porto**, on the west side of the French island of Corsica, is a largely undeveloped coast featuring some beautiful medieval villages. Rugged red rocks emerge from the sea to tower above secluded bays and the occasional sandy beach.

With the Indian Ocean to the west and the Timor Sea to the north, Australia's northwest **Kimberley Coast** is accessible only by boat and virtually uninhabited. Dramatic headlands alternate with deep, sandy bays, and more than 2,500 islands lie close to the shore. Classical features of the region include its towering red-rock cliffs, tremendous sweeping tides and its crocodile-infested estuaries.

Kimberley Coast

" This is the California that men dreamed of years ago… this is the face of the earth as the Creator intended it to look. **"**

HENRY MILLER,
BIG SUR AND THE ORANGES OF HIERONYMUS BOSCH
(1957)

BIRD'S NEST STADIUM

Built as the principal stadium for the 2008 Summer Olympic Games, the Beijing National Stadium seems as much sculpture as architecture. Its angled, undulating form, created by seemingly random straps of steel, quickly earned it the nickname 'Bird's Nest'. Swiss firm Herzog & de Meuron designed the stadium, and Chinese artist Ai Weiwei was the artistic consultant. Despite its size, every aspect is tailored for the individual. It holds more than 80,000 people, yet every seat has a direct sightline to the arena. There is no single, grand entrance; instead, a multitude of entrances allow visitors to seep in. Inside, the criss-crossing beams and stairways break up the vastness of the space. It is a wonderful example of a public space with a huge capacity that yet retains a sense of intimacy.

Beijing
● Beijing National Stadium

East China Sea

CHINA

THE ULTIMATE STADIUM?

Stadiums are the last word in entertainment venues: the largest – the Great Strahov Stadium in Prague, completed in 1934 – holds 220,000 people. They are the theatres of the people, too big to be exclusive to the elite. And they become symbols of local or national pride. The best live up to this high status, their outer shells drawing the eye with sweeping

shapes and decorative flourishes. But they are also driven by functionality. Tens of thousands of people must be able to arrive and leave safely within minutes, which requires pinpoint planning of entrances and stairs. Even the highest, most distant seats must have a clear view. Good acoustics are essential: the crowd will roar, but players must be able to hear the referee's whistle. The wonder of it is that the Romans cracked the formula: the Colosseum provided the template from which virtually all stadiums have borrowed ever since.

COLOSSEUM

The Colosseum in Rome, at the heart of the Roman Empire, was designed to be the greatest and best: a showpiece entertainment centre worthy of the imperial Roman capital. An audience of 60,000 could gather in this amphitheatre to watch gladiator fights, combats with exotic animals and even mock sea battles with the arena artificially flooded. With its marble columns, statues, silk cushions, fountains and vast awning for shade, this was a prestige building. Commissioned by Emperor Vespasian in a bid to curry public favour, it was inaugurated in AD 80 by his son and successor, Titus, with a 100-day festival of combat and slaughter. The Colosseum remained in use for almost 500 years. Its skeletal ruins today lay bare its ingenious engineering without diminishing its muscular physical presence – impressive even after 2,000 years.

ITALY

Rome
● *Colosseum*

58

BLUE MOSQUE

The noble exterior of this great mosque can only hint at the diverse legacy of the Ottoman Empire that lies within – blue Iznik tiles, delicate Venetian glass, swirling arabesques and exquisite calligraphic texts.

Turkey's great metropolis, Istanbul, straddles the Bosphorus – a stretch of water that separates Asia in the east from Europe in the west. This ancient city claims, among other things, more than 3,000 mosques, some nestling in quiet corners, others rising majestically, all cascading domes and minarets, above the city skyline. They rival each other to the glory of Allah, but none is more imposing than the Blue Mosque, built by Sultan Ahmet I, and hence known locally at the Sultanahmet Mosque.

Youthful ambition

When Ahmet came to the throne in 1603 he was just 13, but already a pious young man well versed in matters of faith. He disapproved of the traditional art of miniature painting (figurative art being disrespectful to divine creation), brought back a ban on alcohol, and aimed to make Friday prayers and alms-giving compulsory. Before long, he had set his heart on building a new mosque – an act of benevolence and devotion funded by his lavish fortune. A hospice, public baths and kitchens, a bazaar and a school would be included in the mosque complex for the benefit of all.

The Chief Imperial Architect, Sedefkar Mehmet Aga, was put to the task – a daunting prospect since one of his predecessors, judged to lack ability, had been executed a few years earlier. Having learned his trade from the celebrated

WHERE ON EARTH?

The Blue Mosque is in the Sultanahmet district of Istanbul, at the southern end of the Hippodrome. Hagia Sophia and the Topkapi Palace are nearby. Istanbul has two airports: Ataturk 14 miles (22km) west of the city and Sabiha Gökçen 22 miles (35km) to the east of the city centre.

BULGARIA · Black Sea · Istanbul · GREECE · Blue Mosque · TURKEY

Built to impress The Blue Mosque's central dome, supported by a mass of lesser domes, and six sky-piercing minarets look across the junction of the Sea of Marmara and the Bosphorus.

> **"** ... the long approach reveals one dome after another, peeping through an archway, topping another, rising as you walk up the steps, until the central dome appears above all others ... **"**

Mimar Sinan, who had completed more than 300 buildings, Mehmet Aga set to work in close cooperation with his sultan.

The first step was to find a suitable site. After much debate they chose the old Roman Hippodrome, which had been a venue for chariot racing. This ample space at the heart of the city was near the Topkapi Palace, while the former Byzantine church of Hagia Sophia stood at its northern end. Dating from AD 537, Hagia Sophia was the largest cathedral in Christendom for 1,000 years until the Ottomans overran Constantinople, as Istanbul was then called, in 1453 and converted it into a mosque. For Sultan Ahmet I, the ultimate challenge was to create a building better, bigger and, because it would be untainted by the past, 'purer' than Hagia Sophia.

On November 9, 1609, Sultan Ahmet attended the foundation ceremony, digging with a velvet-handled tool – now

HAGIA SOPHIA

When Byzantine Emperor Justinian I entered his new Church of Hagia Sophia (Divine Wisdom) in AD 537, he is reported to have exclaimed: 'Solomon, I have surpassed thee'. Huge piers, arches and semi-domes lead the eye up to a massive dome, 31m (102ft) in diameter, around whose base 40 windows allow light to flood in. Precious objects and materials were brought from the furthest corners of the empire. Marble and porphyry line the walls and pillars. Most dazzling of all are the gold-leaf mosaics that embellish the upper walls and ceilings, their tiny pieces angled to reflect maximum light. The church is now a museum.

on display in the Topkapi Palace – until he was tired. The foundation work continued for three months, and on January 4, 1610, nobles from the sultan's court were invited to lay their own stones. The devout sultan often visited the site, supervising workers and handing out advice and orders. When it was half completed, he wrote a 'foundation charter' in his usual poetical style, setting out the function of each building and donating substantial sums of money for this purpose. The mosque was officially completed in 1617. Sultan Ahmet I died of typhus shortly afterwards, at the age of 27. His architect died later that year.

During his short life, the young sultan had achieved a great deal. He was an accomplished poet, encouraged scholars

Inner courtyard The mosque is approached through a large arcaded courtyard with carved marble columns and a marble-paved floor.

and calligraphers, married twice and, according to some records, had five sons. Today his legendary mosque, officially called the Sultanahmet Mosque but internationally known as the Blue Mosque for its interior decorations, is both an iconic landmark and a living place of worship.

First impressions

Situated above the shores of the Sea of Marmara, the mosque is an elegant structure with stepped domes. It has six minarets, where other mosques have four, and some scholars have suggested

that confusion may have arisen because the Turkish words for 'gold' and 'six' are similar and Sultan Ahmet had in fact requested the former. Whether a misunderstanding or an innovation, the six that were built competed with the Masjid al-Haram in Mecca, the world's holiest mosque, causing much controversy. This was only quelled, the story goes, when Ahmet offered to fund a seventh minaret in the Holy City.

An iron chain hangs across the main entrance in the outer wall so that even the sultan, who entered on horseback, had to bow his head as a sign of respect. Gate, forecourt, steps, another gate – narrow but monumental – and finally the inner courtyard: the long approach reveals one dome after another, peeping through an archway, topping another, rising as you walk up the steps, until the central dome appears above all others, standing some 43m (141ft) high. It is an

ingenious design inviting pilgrims to look higher and higher towards heaven. As you stand by the ablutions fountain, the minarets, archways, domes and cupolas cannot fail to take your breath away.

The dome-based structure was borrowed from Byzantine churches, as seen in the nearby Hagia Sophia, but with true inspiration and innovative techniques, including the use of smaller domes to support the main dome, Ottoman architects made it their own. They also devoted attention to the building's external spaces, with outer and inner courtyards providing quiet oases where devotees could reflect and prepare before entering the main sanctuary.

A sense of light and space

Step inside the mosque and the first impression is of light and space – a space that can accommodate 10,000 worshippers. The lofty central dome

Uninterrupted space A complex arrangement of arches and domes encircles a vast interior where natural light floods in through tiers of windows.

draws the eye upwards, supported by massive, yet elegant, fluted piers. The prayer hall is a vast open room with just two essential elements: the elegantly carved marble mihrab, the niche indicating the direction of Mecca, and an elaborate minbar, or pulpit, where the imam addresses the congregation during Friday prayers. The hall has been designed in such a way that, however large the crowds, the imam can be seen by every worshipper.

Natural light filters into the hall through more than 200 windows. Little of the original stained glass, donated by the Signoria of Venice, now remains, but the new windows let in a dappled light, creating shafts of golden rays that sweep through the shadows as the sun moves round. Blue, white, red or gold, the patterns on the walls are forever changing, enhanced by large circular chandeliers that hang low over the prayer floor. It is said that ostrich eggs were placed on the chandeliers to prevent spiders making their cobwebs there.

Exquisite decoration

The generous light illuminates the Iznik tiles that decorate the walls and piers. Iznik, in the Bursa province of Turkey, was a renowned centre of pottery, specialising in the blue and white, Chinese-style ceramics favoured by the Ottoman sultans. Ahmet was no exception and more than 20,000 tiles were ordered for the mosque from Iznik and other centres, the best from master potters Kasap Haci and Baris Efendi. With such a large number of tiles came a wide range of designs, the most ornate representing trees, flowers and fruit.

The most highly regarded of all Islamic art forms is calligraphy, which is used to transmit the spoken word. Great calligraphers regard their work as a spiritual act, a holistic experience engaging mind, body and soul. Much of the Blue Mosque calligraphy was entrusted to Seyyid Kasim Gubari, one of the finest calligraphers of his time. He inscribed verses from the Koran in delicate friezes, on square or circular panels and in banner-like strips on gates, pillars and domes. Gold script

on a blue background, gold on black or on green above the gates, the fine, flowing display of scrolls and strokes appears all around the interior. Beautifully restored by contemporary artist Hasan Celebi, it remains one of the most inspiring features of the mosque.

The red carpets covering much of the floor have floral motifs with a marked preference for blue volutes and arabesques, including tulips and leaves. The originals, of hand-woven silk, have been replaced by gifts from devotees. The lavish use of arabesque decoration is seen at its best on the dome, semi-domes and archways. A fundamental element in Islamic art, the arabesque's continuous interlacing of foliage, tendrils, flowers, scrolls and plain lines of arabesque patterns is believed to symbolise the infinity of creation and the unity of all believers.

A unifying legacy

Inevitably, time has worn away some of the lustre of this incredible interior, and to call the mosque 'blue' is, today, rather an overstatement. Yet few people doubt that Sultan Ahmet's grand design marked the pinnacle of classical Ottoman architecture, a masterpiece of engineering, with a lofty prayer hall matching a stunning exterior.

Delicate patterns Though blue was the main colour of the tiles, it was not used exclusively; red and gold also feature. Motifs were often taken from nature.

The sultan rests near his noble creation in the royal mausoleum. Worshippers and visitors flock to its gates, including, in 2006, Pope Benedict XVI who stood with the imam of the Blue Mosque, praying for 'all believers to identify with the one God and bear witness to true brotherhood'.

best of the rest...

MOSQUES

■ The **Badshahi Mosque** in Lahore was commissioned in 1671 by Emperor Aurangzeb. Completed in just two years, it remains the second-largest mosque in Pakistan, accommodating up to 100,000 people in its prayer hall and courtyards.

Badshahi Mosque

Built on a platform facing the Lahore fort, it is a symbol of Mogul splendour, rich in carvings, marble inlay on red sandstone, fresco work and stucco tracery.

■ Set on the flood plain of Mali's Bani River, the **Great Mosque of Djenné** is the largest adobe (mud-brick) building on Earth. Regarded as the world's best example of Sudano-Sahelian architecture, the mosque sits on a platform above the marketplace and its exterior is decorated with bundles of rodier palm sticks. Every year, the local community repairs the walls during a lively festival, the palm sticks acting as a ready-made scaffold. Dating in its present form to 1907, the mosque is among Africa's best-known landmarks.

■ Jutting into the Atlantic Ocean on reclaimed land, Morocco's largest mosque, the **Hassan II Mosque** in Casablanca, has the world's tallest

Great Mosque of Djenné

minaret. Standing 210m (689ft) tall, it displays fine elements of Moorish architecture. The marble and plaster interior decorations, mosaics and painted ceilings are the work of 6,000 artisans and took over five years to complete. According to the Koran, 'God built his throne on water', and a glass section in the floor allows devotees to look down to the sea. It was inaugurated in 1993 and has space for 105,000 worshippers.

BOQUERIA MARKET

Both Barcelona's gastronomic heart and one of the world's most vibrant places to shop and eat, La Boqueria is a riot of colours, smells and flavours in the heart of Catalonia's capital city.

What makes a great food market? Is it the glorious displays of just-picked fruit and vegetables, the savoury aromas of home-cooked local dishes to eat on the spot, the chance to taste artisan cheeses and other delicacies, the sight of fresh fish and crustaceans glistening on shaved ice, the cries of the market vendors hawking their wares? Beneath its high, hangar-like roof, Boqueria has all these in abundance. The vast, open-air structure is crammed with 250 stalls and nearly a dozen bars and restaurants, offering a taste of everything from local fruits and vegetables to speciality meats and cheeses and home-cooked Catalan dishes.

La Boqueria (official name Mercat de Sant Josep) is one of the oldest food markets in Europe. Its roots go back to the mid-18th century, when travelling markets and vendors scattered along the street called La Rambla had become a public nuisance. The city's efforts to relocate and centralise the sellers, a process that began in 1837, was intended to clean up the area; few could have predicted that it would eventually result in a veritable food lovers' Mecca.

Construction of the building that houses the legendary market began in 1840; a few years later, a portico of large stone columns was erected and still frames the market today. The following decades brought iconic additions, like

Temple to gastronomy Barcelona's shield hangs over the entrance to the market, where more than 30,000 different types of food are sold, from local specialities such as peppers, salt cod and salami, to exotic fruits.

WHERE ON EARTH?

Mercat de Sant Josep (La Boqueria) is off La Rambla, Barcelona's main pedestrian thoroughfare, a five-minute walk from the Plaça de Catalunya. The closest Metro station to La Boqueria is Liceu. The market is open every day, except Sunday, from 8am and begins to wind down at about 3pm.

FRANCE

ANDORRA

SPAIN   Barcelona ●   Boqueria Market

Mediterranean Sea

IBÉRICO HAM

The charcuterie stalls of Boqueria Market are hung with hams. The best are designated Jamón Ibérico, which are produced according to strict rules. The rich, red flesh is marbled with translucent fat - the ham comes from pigs grown plump on acorns foraged beneath holm and cork oak trees. Ham from pigs fed only on acorns is the most expensive: for the very best look for the label *jamón ibérico de bellota*. Hams from pigs fed on grain are *jamón ibérico de cebo*; *jamón ibérico de recebo* indicates a mixed diet of grain and acorns. Served in wafer-thin slices, the ham is sliced just before serving so that it remains moist.

the dramatic Modernist arch at the main entrance, rendered even more dazzling by the Gaudí-esque stained-glass mosaic.

Early each morning the market's vendors, many of whom are third and fourth-generation sellers, begin arranging their offerings: piles of Valencian oranges, luscious strawberries, purple-tipped artichokes and strands of dried chillies at produce stands; pristine whole fish and molluscs, fat Palamós shrimp and langoustines in the fishmonger's section at the market's centre; the country's famed Ibérico hams, chorizo and other cured meats at charcuterie stands; and a vast range of fresh meat and poultry, mushrooms, dried fruits, spices, sweets, and everything in between (sheep's and cows' heads, offal, even dried insects).

Tapas on the trot

A thorough exploration of the market's crowded aisles can take hours, but a bite to eat at one of the cramped, no-frills restaurant counters shows that there's nothing wrong with fast food when it's this fresh. Two outstanding counters are Bar Pinotxo, near the market's entrance, and El Quim de la Boqueria, towards the rear. At these popular spots, nab a prized bar stool at the jam-packed counter to watch the cook griddle razor clams, sauté squid in garlic and olive oil, or serve up savoury stews.

Veteran proprietors scour the market stalls each morning for the best ingredients, featuring them in soulful dishes like slow-cooked chickpeas with pork-blood sausage (at Pinotxo) or a sauté of baby squid and eggs sprinkled with sea salt (at El Quim). Regardless of the hour, it is customary to wash down the food with a glass of crisp cava and cap it off with a *cortado* (Spanish espresso).

Quality is king

Though La Boqueria is one of Barcelona's main tourist attractions, the majority of its patrons are Barcelonans – mothers shopping for dinner, students meeting between classes, chefs seeking inspiration, elderly couples sharing lunch. (Visitors should resist the urge to touch food displays or face a sharp rebuke from vendors.) The variety of patrons, and

Charcuterie choice Shoppers pause to consider a range of cured meats, including Ibérico hams hanging from hooks above the display cabinet.

the market's sweeping scope of edibles, reflects the city's passion for good food.

Maybe that's why this market remains superior to all others. Everyone, from the mushroom vendor who has written a book on the subject, to the talented yet humble chefs turning out tasty dishes in tiny kitchens, to the home cook who makes a beeline for the same seafood vendor every time, is serious about eating well, and that means an almost obsessive focus on excellent ingredients. Plus, where else could you find wild hare, olives and goose barnacles under the same roof?

best of the rest...

FOOD MARKETS

One of Vietnam's largest floating markets, **Cai Rang** consists of hundreds of boats that meet early in the morning in the Mekong Delta to trade bananas, papayas, pineapples and leafy greens, as well as noodles, rice, coffee, beer and wine.

Cai Rang

At Mexico City's sprawling **Mercado de la Merced** more than 5,000 stalls are packed into several gigantic buildings. Patrons take their pick from limes, *nopales* (cactus paddles), guavas and more in the vegetable produce market; the butchers' section offers local specialities like *chicarrón prensado*

(pressed, spiced blocks of pork skin); and there is no shortage of stews and *quesadillas* (tortillas filled with a savoury mixture).

London's bustling 257-year-old **Borough Market** is bursting with stalls, shops and restaurants. Shoppers munch chorizo and

arugula (rocket) sandwiches from Brindisa, potted shrimp in butter from Furness Fish & Game, or artisan cheese from Neal's Yard.

Named for the red jackets once worn by children at a nearby orphanage, **Marché des Enfants Rouges**, a covered market in Paris's Marais district, offers all the makings of an excellent meal: fresh produce, crusty bread, charcuterie and wine. Prepared dishes, such as North African-style couscous or rotisserie Bresse chicken, are also sold.

In a tangle of narrow streets in Palermo, Sicily, **Vucciria** market is the place to go for just-caught fish, seasonal produce and delicious, salty, fried snacks: calamari, artichokes, and chickpea-flour patties.

BORA **BORA**

Dramatic events on the ocean floor millions of years ago gave rise to what many judge to be the most perfect tropical island in the world.

With mountain slopes cloaked in verdant forests, plantations sprinkled with yellow, orange and red hibiscus, and surrounded by a wide and protective coral reef, Bora Bora is many people's idea of paradise. But this heaven on earth had a fiery birth, being the tip of an extinct volcano, whose two main peaks, Mount Pahia and Mount Otemanu, cut a dramatic profile against the ocean. Between the island and its encircling reef lie the blue waters of a crystal-clear lagoon.

Life below water

The reef's coral gardens and vast lagoon teem with darting sea creatures: clownfish hide among the deadly tentacles of brightly coloured sea anemones; parrotfish graze on algae and triggerfish grind the coral; and needle-toothed moray eels lurk in crevices ready to grab a passing victim. Larger predators, such as blacktip and whitetip reef sharks, scour the reefs, while aggressive grey reef sharks patrol the steep drop off into the cobalt blue of the deep sea. Deeper down in the ocean, squadrons of manta rays, along with swordfish, bonitos, mahi mahi and tuna, feed along the reef wall. On the reef's scattering of islets, each fringed with white sand beaches, huge robber crabs, the largest land-living crustaceans, climb the palm trees to harvest coconuts.

Bora Bora has inspired a host of visiting writers and artists, including the novelist James Michener, who described it as the most beautiful island on Earth, comparing it to an emerald surrounded by turquoise and encircled by a necklace of sparkling pearls.

Iridescent beauty For snorkellers and divers Bora Bora's sparkling lagoons offer an underwater kaleidoscope of colourful fish and coral gardens.

WHERE ON EARTH?

Bora Bora lies within French Polynesia in the Pacific Ocean. Its airport is on Motu Mete, an islet in the north – Air Tahiti runs daily flights to and from Tahiti. Vaitape, the largest town, is on the western side of the island opposite the main channel into the lagoon. French is the official language.

● Motu Mete

FRENCH POLYNESIA ● Bora Bora
● Vaitape

Pacific Ocean

---

best of the rest...

TROPICAL PARADISE ISLANDS

■ **Socotra**, at the tip of the Horn of Africa in the Indian Ocean, is a genuine desert island so its scrubby plants are designed to conserve or store water. The desert rose resembles a bottle with prominent projections, while the dragon's blood tree looks like an inside-out umbrella that channels dew to its red-sapped roots.

Socotra – dragon's blood trees

■ The tropical volcanic islands of **São Tomé and Príncipe**, in the Gulf of Guinea off Africa's west coast, lie close to the Equator. The palm-fringed beaches, crystal-clear waters and unexplored forests are shared with few visitors and the pace of life is agreeably slow.

■ **Pitcairn** in the South Pacific is as remote and unspoiled as it was in 1790, when the mutineers from HMS *Bounty* settled there. Plants include the yellow fatu – one of the rarest flowers in the world.

CARNAC

There are some 4,000 standing stones – or menhirs – at Carnac, France's most celebrated set of megalithic monuments. Roughly hewn and of varying sizes, they form parallel avenues (alignments) and circles stretching more than 2.5 miles (4km) – a scale not matched anywhere else in the world. Laid out in pre-Celtic times between about 4500 and 2000 BC, they are part of a huge concentration of standing stones, dolmens and burial mounds in southern Brittany. The purpose of this enterprise is disputed: perhaps the alignments were processional routes associated with burial sites in the area, or were connected to astronomical readings. Although in summer visitors can access the area only with guided tours, they have the chance to walk among great fields of stones in one of the world's oldest grand-scale endeavours.

FRANCE
Carnac • Vannes
BRITTANY
Bay of Biscay

THE ULTIMATE MEGALITHIC SITE?

Thousands of years after they were erected, the giant stone megaliths (from Greek, meaning 'large stone') of prehistoric Europe still prompt wonder - and questions. How and why were they built? And by whom? For some reason, prehistoric people set themselves tasks at the extreme limits of their technology and physical ability. We can only assume that these monuments had religious or spiritual

significance. Many are associated with burials; or aligned to observations of the cosmos, perhaps reflecting the importance of the seasons to early farmers. The circles and lines of standing stones, in particular, seem to exude a palpable spirit of place, perhaps by virtue of their immense age or the beauty of their settings. Megalithic monuments have been found across Europe, from the stone circles of the Cromeleque dos Almendres in Portugal, to the dolmens (rock shelters) in southern Russia and the Caucasus, to the rings of Brodgar and Callanish on islands off Scotland.

STONEHENGE

The sheer concentration of massive standing stones gives Stonehenge an intensity that sets it apart from other megalithic structures. Set on windswept Salisbury Plain, these stones are the surviving legacy of around 1,500 years of building on the site, from about 3000 to 1500 BC. They include 4-tonne megaliths that were dragged – no one is sure quite how – all the way from Wales, 140 miles (220km) away. How Stonehenge looked in ancient times is not known; some of what is seen today was reconstructed in Victorian times. As to its use, alignments suggest it was perhaps a kind of cosmic calendar centred on the summer solstice. The site is now hemmed in by two roads, and the volume of visitors prevents close access to the stones, but Stonehenge retains the aura of timeless mystery that underpins its status as the icon of Britain's ancient past.

● Stonehenge
● Salisbury
ENGLAND ● Southampton

CHARTRES CATHEDRAL

Shards of coloured light from the incomparable medieval stained glass illuminate this supreme example of the Gothic cathedral.

WHERE ON EARTH?

Chartres is the capital of Eure-et-Loir, a department of northern France, 60 miles (100km) southwest of Paris. Easily accessible by road or rail, the journey from Paris takes about an hour. The town centre is small and walkable, with the train station in the west. The cathedral rises on a hill to the east.

English Channel

Le Havre

FRANCE   Paris

Chartres

River Loire

North transept rose window The intense colour and luminosity of Chartres's stained glass has intrigued experts and visitors for more than eight centuries.

Seen from a distance, the spires of Chartres cathedral rise from the flat expanse of the Beauce plain, dominating a landscape dotted with grain stores and water towers. From closer in, the sheer size and audacity of the building, the profusion of sculptures on its exterior and the soaring windows of brilliantly coloured stained glass impress modern travellers and pilgrims, just as they have done for the past eight centuries. The cathedral's exceptional state of preservation is another of its most important features. The vast majority of the stained-glass windows are original, and the overall architecture has undergone only minor changes since the early 13th century.

Erected between 1194 and 1250, the current cathedral is the last of six churches to have been built on the site. The *portail royale* (Royal Portal) on the western facade is the oldest surviving element of the cathedral's Romanesque predecessor, which was largely destroyed by fire in 1194. The cathedral's most famous relic also survived the fire: the Sancta Camisa is believed by Roman Catholics to be the tunic worn by the Virgin Mary at Christ's birth. An outpouring of religious fervour followed the much celebrated miracle of the tunic's survival, prompting local towns and villages to donate substantial funds and labour for the new building. They were suitably rewarded by the grandeur of the cathedral that rose 25 years later.

Gothic splendour

The main nave is 34m (112ft) high, 130m (427ft) long and 16m (53ft) in width, the widest nave in France. The massive external walls are supported by equally sizeable flying buttresses around the outside of the building. Strikingly elegant in their own right, these supporting structures counterbalance the lateral forces created by the cathedral's lofty vaulting. With the flying buttresses taking the weight of the vaulting, the architects could increase the size of the windows and allow light to flood the interior.

In its design, the cathedral generally resembles contemporary Gothic cathedrals, such as those at Laon, Amiens and Reims, though distinctive features at Chartres include the lofty arcades, the slender triforium (arched gallery) and the immense clerestory (upper-level windows) above the nave, all supported by the flying buttresses. Among the few alterations that have been made, the most important is the northwest tower's distinctive Flamboyant Gothic spire added in the early 1500s.

Narratives in stone

Before stepping inside the cathedral, it is well worth pausing to admire the prolific sculptural decorations around the doorways, which recount numerous stories from the Old and New Testaments. Christ and the Virgin Mary are the main subjects of the Royal Portal. Christ is depicted in the central bay seated in glory, with statues of the 12 apostles along the lintel below. The bay to the right shows scenes from the nativity, while more unusually the bay to the left includes, among other things, beautifully crafted sculptures representing the 12 signs of the zodiac.

MEDIEVAL GLASS

The light-enhancing qualities of the glass at Chartres are considered to be unique. They are thought to have been achieved using techniques that appeared in the early 12th century and were lost a century later. Chartres Blue, a hue enhanced with traces of red, was first used on the three Romanesque windows on the western facade. Contrasting colours - red, yellow, green - were added to make the biblical stories more vivid. Recent research has determined that the use of sodium compounds in the glass made it more resistant to dirt and deterioration. The earliest window, Our Lady of the Beautiful Window - located in the south choir - is widely considered the loveliest of all. The blue of the Virgin's dress has allegedly never been reproduced exactly, despite countless attempts by monks and alchemists.

The sculptures on the north portal recall Old Testament stories such as Adam and Eve in the Garden of Eden. Carved figures include the prophets Isaiah and Jeremiah, an emaciated John the Baptist and St Peter dressed as pope. The New Testament is the focus of sculptures on the south portal, complete with scenes from the Last Judgement.

Chartres's crowning glory

As visitors enter the cathedral through the Royal Portal, they are greeted by an uninterrupted view of the semicircular apse at the east end of the church. The gaze is drawn upwards, rising from the elaborately carved choir screen, past three tiers of arched windows and on up to the rib-vaulted ceiling high above. All is imbued with the deep richness of colour that emanates from the stained glass, surely Chartres's greatest treasure.

Almost incredibly, of 176 original stained-glass windows – a greater number than was created in any other church in France – 152 remain intact today. The glass covers 2,600m² (28,000sq ft). Like the sculptures in the portals, the windows were created to offer an illustrated version of the bible in an era when literacy was far from widespread. The five windows arranged in a semicircle around the choir depict facets of the life and legend of the Virgin Mary. The north transept's rose window portrays figures from the Old Testament, while the south transept represents the New Testament, its rose window showing the Apocalypse.

Floodlit glory The shorter of Chartres's two towers, from an earlier church, was constructed in the 1140s. The taller, more ornate tower was added in the 1500s.

Pilgrimage in miniature

Labyrinths became a regular feature in Gothic cathedrals, though many were later removed or destroyed. The labyrinth at Chartres is an 11-circuit design divided into quadrants. It was laid into the floor as a pavement maze in the year 1200 by a master mason known only as Scarlet, and measures some 12m (40ft) in diameter. A walk through the Chartres labyrinth weaves through each of the four quadrants

Elegant forms The flying buttresses have sculptural as well as structural beauty, their appearance lightened with piercings and niches.

several times before finally reaching the centre. At the heart of the labyrinth is a rosette design symbolising enlightenment, with the four arms of the cross providing Christian symbolism. The labyrinth was intended as a pilgrimage to be walked, or crawled, for repentance, or as a quest that visitors to Chartres undertook in the hope of coming closer to God.

SACRED GEOMETRY

Keith Critchlow (born 1933), an expert on religious architecture, has written widely on the subject of sacred geometry. He points out that Chartres's architects - the Masters of the Compasses - calculated the building's proportions using compasses that were set at a fixed distance. For example, the diameter of the western rose window matches that of the labyrinth exactly, and other structural measurements in the church relate directly to the same diameter. Similarly, the height of the western facade is as tall as the apse is long; if laid flat on the floor of the church, its rose window would lie directly over the labyrinth. Such harmony in the proportions of the building gives rise to a deep spiritual experience.

The road to Jerusalem
Often used as a substitute for an actual pilgrimage to Jerusalem, the Chartres maze came to be known as the 'Chemin de Jerusalem'.

Today, the labyrinth is usually obscured by the chairs that line the nave, but these are traditionally removed each year on midsummer's day and, more recently, on Fridays during the summer months. This allows modern pilgrims and visitors to walk the ancient labyrinth.

An enduring monument

Chartres remains almost unchanged today, 800 years after being built. It survived the political and religious upheavals of the 16th century with only minor damage. Both its structure and its glass remained unharmed during the French Revolution, when so many churches were destroyed during a process of de-Christianisation. A wooden sculpture of the Virgin Mary was, however, burned outside the church during the Revolution. Restorations were carried out during the 19th century after fire damaged the roof in 1836.

More recently, all of the stained glass was removed for protection during World War Two. Preserved during the hostilities, it was later cleaned, releaded and returned, restoring the church to its 13th-century glory once more. More than any other cathedral of its time, Chartres remains as it was in medieval times.

Survivors in stone The sculptures on the cathedral's exterior, like the stained glass, have weathered the centuries relatively unscathed.

best of the rest...

EUROPE'S GOTHIC CHURCHES

■ **Saint-Denis**, Paris, was completed in 1140 and is widely recognised as the first and most daring experiment in Gothic architecture, characterised by the inclusion of immense expanses of glass and a new organisation of space. Based on Norman models such as Saint-Étienne de Caen, Saint-Denis made use of the pointed (ogival) vaulting that better distributes the weight of the columns, allowing larger upper-level windows (clerestory).

■ Found on the Île de la Cité at the heart of medieval Paris, **Notre Dame Cathedral** is one of the city's most visited buildings. Work began in 1163 and continued for 150 years. The cathedral's impressive western facade is a masterpiece of geometric design, combining the vertical pull of its two towers with horizontal elements formed by balustrades and galleries. At the centre of the facade is a 9.5m (31ft) diameter rose.

■ The cathedral at Chartres was followed by the lofty **Our Lady of Reims**, where work started in the early 13th century. Like Chartres, Reims is dedicated to the Virgin Mary and famous for its flying buttresses, rose windows and unity of style. The 138m (453ft) long nave is a mere 30m (98ft) wide, which adds to the perceived illusion of height.

Reims Cathedral

■ The **Church of the Jacobins** in Toulouse, begun in 1230, is a fine example of the simplicity and functional economy of line in early Gothic architecture, in contrast with the ornamental complexity of later Gothic art. Surprisingly lofty amid the narrow streets of Toulouse, one of the church's most striking features is the row of seven 22m (72ft) high octagonal columns with palm-tree vaulting that support the roof. Light streams in through the stained-glass windows, while a mirror on the floor reflects the superstructure, allowing marvellous views of the 22-spined palm-tree vaulting over the choir.

■ The Rayonnant Gothic style that developed in France around the mid-13th century is characterised by the further elimination of solid wall surfaces in favour of graceful grids or frameworks of stone tracery and glass. **Sainte-Chapelle** in Paris has walls composed almost entirely of glass, with only a skeletal web of masonry binding the elegant structure together.

■ French cathedrals inspired the German churches of the 13th century, with **Cologne Cathedral**, northern Europe's largest and most eloquent example of Gothic architecture, based on the cathedral of Amiens. Begun in 1248 and not completed until the late 19th century, Cologne cathedral, officially dedicated to Sts Peter and Mary, is notable for its huge spires and the dizzying height of its choir, which also has the largest height-to-width ratio of any medieval church.

■ The far-reaching influence of the French Gothic style is clearly evident at **Burgos Cathedral** in Spain. Begun in 1221, the early construction was overseen by Frenchmen. Dedicated to the Virgin Mary, this large-scale building shares many structural elements with cathedrals like Notre Dame and Chartres, not least an imposing western facade with central rose window and lateral banding, flanked on

Cologne Cathedral

either side by a square tower. At Burgos, each tower is finished with an octagonal spire with elegant tracery.

■ Early Mediterranean Gothic architecture attained its paradigm at Barcelona's **Santa María del Mar** (1329–83). In the interior, stonemason and master builder Berenguer

Sainte-Chapelle

de Montagut made light the main protagonist of a breathtakingly soaring and relentlessly symmetrical basilica. Sixteen slender octagonal columns rise up 16m (52ft), supporting cross vaulting that reaches a height of 32m (105ft) above the floor.

■ In Britain, the chapel of **King's College**, Cambridge, (built 1446–1515) is one of the finest examples of late Gothic architecture. Its elegant ceiling spanning 25m (82ft) is the world's largest fan vault. The strikingly tall stained-glass windows were largely the work of Flemish craftsmen. Dating from the early 16th century, most remain intact today.

CHATSWORTH HOUSE

For all its grandeur, its world-class art collection, its rare furnishings, its rolling parkland designed by Capability Brown, and centuries of history, Chatsworth House remains, at heart, a family home.

The magnificent yellow stone building nestling in the lush green valley of the River Derwent, against a backdrop of wooded hills, seems like a survivor from a bygone age – as indeed it is. But it is also a living and working community. This stately home, the grandest in England, is the ancestral seat of the 12th Duke of Devonshire and arguably the most impressive of all the homes of the English aristocracy.

The story of Chatsworth began in the 16th century, when Sir William Cavendish married the Countess of Shrewsbury ('Bess of Hardwick'). They bought the manor of Chatsworth in Derbyshire in 1549 and began rebuilding it in 1552. On their deaths, the house and estate passed down the Cavendish

Golden facade A perfect example of English Baroque style, the west front has nine bays with a central pediment supported by four columns and pilasters.

WHERE ON EARTH?

Chatsworth House is 3.5 miles (5.6km) northeast of Bakewell in the Peak District National Park, Derbyshire. The closest railway station is Chesterfield, which has bus connections to the estate. Main attractions are the house, gardens, farm and playground (closed in winter) and the park, which is open all year.

Leeds

Chatsworth House ● ● Chesterfield

ENGLAND

line. In 1684 another William Cavendish became the 1st Duke of Devonshire. Little of the original building remains as the house has been extended and updated several times, with most of the work carried out in the 17th and 18th centuries.

Rich interiors

Chatsworth House has been created on a grand scale, with 300 rooms, 17 staircases, 1,044m (3,425ft) of passages, 359 doors and 30 baths. The Grand Staircase has swirling paintings by Antonio Verrio; the State Rooms are hung with paintings by Old Masters, including Tintoretto, Rembrandt and Salvator Rosa among many others. Silks, velvet and marble abound. The State Music Room has gilded leather wall coverings and an intriguing *trompe l'oeil* violin on the door. The Queen of Scots Apartments are a reminder that Mary, Queen of Scots, was imprisoned here at various times between 1570 and 1581. The Queen of Scots Dressing Room, along with the Wellington Dressing Room, are decorated with hand-painted Chinese wallpaper.

A family of collectors

From the Elizabethan needlework to the contemporary art, the collections on display reflect the varied tastes and interests of successive generations of the family. The

Fine dining The Great Dining Room is laid for a banquet, with 18th-century silver and furniture designed by William Kent. Seven family portraits by Sir Antony van Dyck grace the walls.

tapestries in the State Drawing Room, based on cartoons by Raphael, were bought by the 1st Duke. The large collections of Old Master drawings and paintings were started by the 2nd and 3rd Dukes. The 18th-century scientific instruments originally belonged to the scientist Henry Cavendish, grandson of the 2nd Duke. The collection of William Kent furniture was inherited by the 5th Duke from his grandfather, the 3rd Earl of Burlington,

together with the earl's art collection. The 5th Duke's wife, Georgiana, was painted by Thomas Gainsborough and Sir Joshua Reynolds. Both portraits are on display, together with her jewellery and collection of minerals. The 6th Duke added the large sculpture collection. Modern additions include a group of family portraits by Lucian Freud and a digital portrait created by Michael Craig-Martin.

External artistry

Surrounding the house and blending into the landscape of the Peak District National Park are 42ha (105 acres) of superb gardens and grounds, including an Elizabethan garden that dates back to the estate's foundation under William Cavendish and Bess of Hardwick; the 300-year-old Cascade water feature; and a maze made up of 1,209 yew trees.

The gardens provide the perfect accessories for a perfect stately home – except that Chatsworth is no ordinary stately home. Unlike others of its kind, this is not just a museum or historical monument, but a genuine residence where favourite family objects, such as an American football, sit alongside historic gems, such as Henry VIII's rosary beads. You are even likely to see the current Duke or Duchess milling around among the estate's annual 650,000 visitors.

best of the rest...

GREAT HOUSES

■ In France's Loire valley, the romantic manor house of **Chenonceau** was built in the 16th century beside and across the Cher River. It was lived in first by Henri II's mistress, Diane de Poitiers, and then by his widow Catherine de Medici. It has exceptional collections of Old Master paintings and Flemish tapestries. The gardens include many rare plants, particularly roses.

■ **Bran Castle**, Romania, is often referred to as 'Dracula's Castle', although there is no connection with Bram Stoker's novel. Built as a fortress in the 13th century to protect the lands of the king of Hungary from Ottoman incursion, it passed through the

hands of the Hungarian aristocracy. It was the home of Queen Marie of Romania in the first part of the 20th century and is now a museum of medieval art, paintings and furniture.

■ Set within an estate of 3,238ha (8,000 acres), **Biltmore House** is America's largest private residence. Conceived by millionaire George Washington Vanderbilt, it was styled after a French chateau and completed in 1895. The house has 250 rooms, including a banquet hall with a 21m (70ft) high ceiling. Among its many treasures are 40 bronze sculptures and Napoleon's chess set. The estate also has an award-winning winery.

■ The **Wurzburg Residence** in Bavaria, southern Germany, is one of the most important baroque palaces in Europe. Completed in 1780, its interiors include a grand staircase, chapel and grand salon, and ceilings painted by Gian Battista Tiepolo. Much of the building was destroyed during World War Two and has been restored.

Wurzburg Residence

CHRYSLER BUILDING

Wildly eccentric and supremely stylish, the shimmering, seven-tiered Art Deco dome crowning New York's Chrysler Building makes it one of the most spectacular skyscrapers in the world.

Although it is an iconic landmark today, the Chrysler Building did not always seem destined for fame and adoration. Its tremendous height and glorious design were secured during New York's skyscraper mania of 1928–9, when automobile magnate Walter P. Chrysler became personally involved with architect William Van Alen's plans to design the world's tallest skyscraper. The building was to be built on the corner of Lexington Avenue and 42nd Street.

Size is everything

Van Alen was told to spare no expense in creating a building that would capture the optimism of the modern era. He was also instructed to beat the height of all other skyscraper projects.

This was a tough challenge since there were several other projects running in the city. Van Alen's former business partner, H. Craig Severance, was designing the Manhattan Company Building (known today as the Trump Building) and was planning to break the world record for tallest tower. Another competitor was the Lincoln Building, designed by J. E. R. Carpenter, whose claims galvanised Van Alen into upping his own ambitious designs. Technological developments made it possible for skyscrapers to reach new heights and these towering symbols of modernity presented the fastest route to architectural and commercial stardom.

THE FLATIRON BUILDING

A predecessor to the Chrysler Building is New York's striking, wedge-shaped Flatiron Building at the intersection of 5th Avenue and Broadway at 23rd Street. Designed by Chicago architect Daniel H. Burnham and constructed in 1902, it is a classic example of the Beaux-Arts style that preceded Art Deco. Measuring only 1.8m (6ft) across at its rounded, prowlike front, the 22-storey skyscraper provoked immediate criticism from sceptics who insisted it would never withstand the city's strong winds. In the end, the 3,680-tonne steel structure clad with terracotta and Italian limestone successfully jump-started the area as a commercial district. Today it is one of the most photographed buildings in New York. Although the Flatiron's restaurant and observation deck closed long ago, visitors still stream into the lobby or stand at street level, gaping up at the triangular wedge.

Shocking revelations

Construction of the Chrysler and Manhattan buildings entered 1929 with opposing building crews hawkishly monitoring each other's progress from across the city skyline. Soon, all of New York City was caught up in the feverish skyscraper race. At the Chrysler Building, a team of men worked around the clock to turn nearly 30,000 tonnes of steel into an indestructible frame for the building. Despite the frantic pace, no one died during construction – an incredible achievement for the time, when working on buildings higher than 15 storeys routinely resulted in fatalities.

When newspapers reported that the Chrysler Building, near completion, would top off at 282m (925ft), Severance seized his chance and ratcheted his building slightly higher before calling it finished. It was then that Van Alen unveiled his secret weapon – a gleaming 57m (187ft) metal spire, which had been secretly assembled in pieces in the building's fire shaft. On September 28, 1929, the spire sections were raised to the tower's peak, fitted together and bolted into place – all in just 90 minutes. It was as if, Van Alen said, 'a cloud-piercing needle' had unexpectedly appeared. At that moment the Chrysler Building, at 319m (1,046ft), became the world's tallest building – and the ultimate symbol of American ambition. The claim to the title would be short-lived: the height of the Empire State Building surpassed the Chrysler Building's in 1931.

Attention to detail

After clinching this historic victory, Van Alen turned his attention to the exterior and interior details. Nearly 4 million bricks were used to clad the frame in a handsome white with grey trim. Expounding the favourite motifs of Art Deco style, the architect used curves and zigzags freely, as well as forms that

Lighting up the sky The stainless steel crown of the Chrysler Building glows in the rising and setting sun.

glorified the automobile and his patron. Jutting out from the corners of the 31st floor are ornamental replicas of 1929 Chrysler radiator caps. Thirty floors up, eight eagle-headed gargoyles guard points of the compass. All of these adornments, combined with the building's distinctive steel cupola punctuated with triangular windows, add up to a building that resembles a fantastical flying machine.

The city had never seen anything like it before. Yet when it officially opened to the public, on May 27, 1930, critics were quick to slam it. They were especially scornful of the spire, which many dismissed as a gimmick. Douglas Haskell wrote in *The Nation* that the building 'embodies no compelling, organic idea'. But considering the devastating effects of the stock market crash at the end of October 1929 and the ensuing economic depression, it is

Going up? The Art Deco elevator doors in the Chrysler Building are one of its most eye-catching features. Each door design is slightly different.

notable that the Chrysler Building was completed in the same spirit of opulence in which it was first conceived.

Particularly lavish, even by today's standards, is the Y-shaped lobby, the only portion of the building still open to the public. Three separate entrances lead into a sweeping space that once served as a Chrysler car showroom. Giant slabs of red Moroccan marble line the walls of the grand foyer; the floor is tiled in Sienna travertine imported from Germany. Even the lighting is beautiful as well as functional: vertical clusters of metal-fronted light bars are backed by Belgian blue marble and Mexican amber onyx, resulting in a warm, ambient glow.

Also surprisingly lovely are the lobby's 32 elevators. Split into five banks, these tiny spaces are composed of exotic woods whose names alone are appealing: Japanese ash, English grey harewood, Oriental walnut, Cuban plum pudding and Philippine mahogany. Spanning a lush range of colours, these hardwood veneers form stylised flower patterns,

best of the rest...

SKYSCRAPERS

Empire State Building

■ At 443m (1,454ft) the grand Art Deco **Empire State Building** is topped by an imposing lightning rod, and rivals the Chrysler Building as New York's best-loved skyscraper. Tourists flock to the observatory on the 86th floor, but New Yorkers are partial to the view from afar: its rotating tower lights change frequently to celebrate holidays and special events, and span more than 400 colour combinations.

■ Officially named as 30 St Mary Axe, London's futurist **Gherkin** is known for its plump, unusual shape. Since opening in 2004, the Gherkin has breathed new life into the city's skyline with its lattice of glass triangles and striking spiralling pattern; the attractive plaza at the base is open to the public.

■ Known as Europe's first 'green' skyscraper, Frankfurt's innovative **Commerzbank Tower** uses a central atrium to capitalise on natural light and ventilation. On nine different floors, expansive 'sky gardens', resplendent with vegetation from different parts of the world, act as sanctuaries for office workers.

The Gherkin

and although all of the cabs fall into four basic designs, no two are exactly alike. The rich wood is another nod to the automobiles of the era, which sported beautiful wooden dashboards and trim.

Tribute to the modern era

Another record-breaking feature of the lobby is the ceiling mural, entitled *Transport and Human Endeavor* and measuring 30x23m (100x76ft). Painted by artist Edward Trumbull on canvas, then cemented to the three-storey-high ceiling, the piece echoes the building's tribute to mechanical progress. To match the epic scale of the building, the mural was the largest in the world at the time of completion.

Trumbull and Chrysler agreed that the mural should convey the manpower that made the Chrysler Building possible. It is fitting, then, that the central image is the bare torso of a man with rippling back muscles. The mural, which was restored in 1999, also depicts the Chrysler Building itself, shooting towards the Lexington Avenue entrance, in shades of orange, brown, yellow, red and blue.

Other once-celebrated features of the building have not stood the test of time. A 71st-floor observation deck closed in 1945. The regal duplex apartment that housed Walter Chrysler for years has been stripped down to an anonymous office suite. The exclusive Cloud Club was shut down in 1979. Its members were the city's most prominent advertising, steel, oil and automobile executives, and it boasted everything from a Tudor-style lounge to lockers for stashing alcohol during Prohibition. Today, all 77 usable floors of the building are office space.

Lasting legacy

Van Alen could hardly have predicted that his once-controversial skyscraper would become such an integral component of New York's skyline and one of the world's most beloved buildings. The criticism he faced for the design was only the beginning of his misfortune: a dispute with Walter Chrysler over payment led to a lawsuit that eventually guaranteed his fee, but resulted in negative public perception, ruining his chances for future work. His death in 1954 went largely unnoticed.

Yet it is important to recognise that together Chrysler and Van Alen created a true architectural marvel that pays homage to a unique moment in time. Chrysler, with his outsized ego and ambition to expand his brand, harnessed with Van Alen's bold vision, brought into being a skyscraper unlike any that has shot up since.

The giddy hope that characterised the late 1920s and informed much of its architecture was permanently altered by the Depression. Never again would a building reflect such individual tastes. No skyscraper since the Chrysler Building is as elegant or timeless, as compelling upclose as it is far away, or as stunning at any time of day, whether gleaming in the morning sun or illuminated by spotlight beams at night.

Turning Torso

■ Spanish architect Santiago Calatrava based the design for his gravity-defying **Turning Torso** residential tower in Malmö, Sweden, on his steel and marble sculpture of the same name. Consisting of a stack of nine twisted cubes, reinforced by a structural 'spine', the building is compelling when viewed from afar: it seems to constantly change shape as the observer moves around it, appearing in turn bowed, then skewed, then terrifyingly top-heavy.

■ Dubai's ultra-modern **Burj Khalifa** stands at 829m (2,720ft) and has held the title of the world's tallest building since it opened in 2010. It houses private residences, offices, a luxury hotel and restaurant. The extensive park at ground level has gardens and fountains. The skyscraper's design borrows from traditional Islamic architecture.

■ **Taipei 101** is a 101-storey office block standing 508m (1,667ft) tall. Its record-breaking lifts travel at 0.6 miles/min (1km/min), and there are observation points on the 89th and 91st floors. Its spire is inspired by Taiwan's native bamboo, while the interiors draw on classic Chinese motifs. The 800-tonne steel shock-absorber is a key provision against earthquakes and typhoons.

Taipei 101

CRAC DES CHEVALIERS

Like many of the most evocative castles, Crac des Chevaliers has a violent past that contrasts with its present-day serenity.

The passing of the centuries haunts the sunlit courts and jutting turrets of the mighty Crac des Chevaliers. Nowhere in the world is it easier to get close to the medieval crusader spirit than in the castle's vaulted Hall of the Knights or the dark passageways that thread their way round its walls. The site itself, 650m (2,130ft) up on a hilltop, provides the archetypal setting for a castellated fortress to dominate the plain below. T.E. Lawrence (Lawrence of Arabia) called it 'perhaps the best preserved and most wholly admirable castle in the world'. Viewing the stronghold from outside the ramparts, it is easy to see why. Built to guard the main route south through Syria, Crac des Chevaliers, the Knights' Castle, is the world's most spectacular example of medieval military architecture and an enduring monument to the Crusades.

The knights in question were crusaders, part of the armies of Roman Catholic Europe that were fighting to wrest the Holy Land from Muslim control. History knows them as the Knights Hospitallers, a closed order of warrior monks initially dedicated to caring for Christian pilgrims travelling to Jerusalem. Although devoted to good works, they soon found that the military demands of life in a threatened outpost in hostile territory forced them to take up the sword. Their austerity and discipline quickly turned them into some of Christendom's most fearsome champions.

A model castle

When the Knights Hospitallers took possession of the hilltop site, it was occupied by a Muslim fortress that had fallen to the crusaders in 1110. Employing every defensive trick known to medieval military architects, the new owners set about turning the existing structure into a state-of-the-art stronghold with curtain walls and square towers surrounding an inner courtyard. In the 13th century, following a series of earthquakes, the knights remodelled the castle and added a second wall, producing a showpiece concentric castle with two massive rings of defensive walls. Although 9m (30ft) high, the outer wall is on a lower level than the inner one, giving troops on the inner wall a clear view of the slopes below the castle and

Mighty stronghold Crac de Chevalier's massive sloping inner wall rises from the bedrock and was designed to be impossible for attacking forces to scale.

the surrounding terrain and leaving attackers who managed to scale the outer wall nowhere to hide. At the eastern end, where the defences were at their weakest, a reservoir cum moat fed via an aqueduct from a nearby spring separated the two walls.

Each line of fortifications was studded with protruding bastions from which defenders could pour a steady fire of arrows, stones and boiling oil on attackers outside the perimeter. A single, heavily fortified gateway gave onto a vaulted passageway studded with 'murder-holes' through which the defenders could fire missiles at intruders. Inside the castle, there was room for up to 2,000 people, their horses and

EVOCATIVE CASTLES

■ **Qal'at Salah El-Din**, about 50 miles (80km) north of Crac des Chevaliers, also retains its former grandeur. Built by Byzantines in the 10th century, it features a 28m (92ft) deep moat.

■ Scotland's **Eilean Donan**, near the village of Dornie in the western Highlands, sits on an island in Loch Duich. The mountainous backdrop adds to the sense of remoteness.

■ **Harlech Castle**, overlooking Tremadoc Bay in west Wales, was built in the 13th century by England's King Edward I. Its most notable feature is a gatehouse with two pairs of cylindrical towers.

Alcázar de Segovia

■ Southern Spain boasts the picturesque 12th-century **Alcázar de Segovia**, perched on a rocky crag like the bows of a ship extending out from the city walls.

■ Spanish settlers built the triangular fortress of **San Felipe de Barajas** in Cartagena, Colombia, which played an important role in colonial conflicts with France and England.

equipment. Cisterns and underground storerooms could hold enough stores of water and food to last several months.

Never overrun

The builders did their job well, and in the 150 years that it spent in Crusader hands the castle withstood 12 separate sieges, one of them conducted by the great Islamic leader Saladin himself. It also survived a major earthquake that ravaged the region in 1170, although much rebuilding was required.

The castle eventually fell a century later to the Mamluk sultan Baybars, who broke its resistance by using siege engines, catapults and battering rams to smash into the gate-tower of the outer ring of walls. The defenders managed to hold out in the inner precinct for a further two weeks. When that fell, the

surviving knights conducted a last-ditch defence in the massive south tower, eventually negotiating safe conduct for themselves to the Christian port of Tripoli (in modern-day Lebanon). Within two decades Baybars had mopped up the last Christian resistance, and the lands of the Levant were back in Muslim hands.

Standing in one of Crac des Chevaliers' sunlit courts, the ancient stones speak to the imagination, for this castle is the chief surviving monument of a unique time of religious idealism and violence. To go there is to travel back in time, to an era that still echoes in the present.

Built to impress Perched on a hilltop, the castle dominates the fertile plain below. Its position made it difficult to approach or to use siege equipment against. Even so, it was eventually taken by force.

CAVE OF CRYSTALS

The most spectacular geological discovery of modern times is this beautiful but dangerous chamber, deep below ground in North Mexico.

It was the year 2000, and two brothers were working in the Naica lead and silver mines when they came across a chamber quite by chance. They found it packed with some of the biggest natural crystals on Earth: huge translucent beams and obelisks of selenite or moonstone, a form of gypsum. The largest were 11m (36ft) long and more than half a million years old. It was a spectacular discovery.

Intense heat

This extraordinarily beautiful place is also perilous. Molten magma deep below the cave keeps the temperature constantly high at around 50C (122F). This, together with 90 to 100 per cent relative humidity, is potentially lethal. To avoid heat stroke, visitors to the cave must wear suits packed with ice cubes and face masks blowing ice-cooled air.

Yet it is this heat that is key to the crystal formation. For millennia, the chamber was flooded with mineral-rich water, and the hot, stable conditions were ideal for crystals to form. When, in 1985, water was pumped from the mines, the crystal formation ceased. There is now a danger that, having been exposed to the air, the giant crystals will slowly collapse, and there are calls to preserve the site.

Crystal wonder Visitors to the cave are dwarfed by the giant crystals in what looks like a movie set for *Superman*. Most stay for only 20 to 30 minutes; any longer and they risk dying from the heat.

WHERE ON EARTH?

The Cave of Crystals lies 300m (1,000ft) below ground level in the Naica mines near the town of Delicias in Chihuahua State, northern Mexico. They are working mines, so access to the Cave of Crystals is restricted. Visits are possible to the Cave of Swords, containing sword-sized crystals.

best of the rest...

TREASURES IN THE EARTH

■ The walls of the **Lascaux Caves** in southwestern France are decorated with Palaeolithic rock art more than 17,000 years old. The images are of large animals, including a 5.2m (17ft) long aurochs (the ancestor of domestic cattle), as well as horses (below left) and deer. Today, access to the caves is restricted to scientific experts, but a replica of the two main halls of the cave, known as Lascaux II, is open to visitors.

Lascaux Cave Art

■ Deep under the Gabon rain forest in west central Africa, the **Abanda Caves** are host to an enormous roost of up to 100,000 bats of different species. But while looking up, visitors must also watch their steps below. Living on the floor of the caves is a small population of crocodiles, including a curiously orange-coloured male. The first proper exploration of these caves was made as recently as 2010.

CULLODEN

The spirits of Scotland's troubled past haunt Culloden Moor, where Bonnie Prince Charlie's dream of kingship came to a violent end.

A fresh wind blows away the last grey cloud: the sky is blue and open, arched across by a sudden rainbow to the east. One final flurry of sleet and the summer afternoon seems set fair. The sunshine makes the wet grass sparkle and lights up the purple heather, tingeing with warmth what might have been a chill and barren scene. Rough and rugged, the field stretches away to where it is bounded by a distant line of trees. Yet it doesn't matter how radiant the sun, how beautiful the

landscape here: the atmosphere always feels unsettled, the mood overcast. For history hangs over this Highland landscape like menacing clouds. It was on an April afternoon, nearly three centuries ago, that Bonnie Prince Charlie's army was cut down, his dream of a Jacobite succession to the English throne destroyed.

Frail hopes

There have been more important battles than Culloden – battles in which more participants were killed or on which more momentous changes hung. This was no Waterloo or Stalingrad. France's Louis XV had seen a chance to make difficulties for England's Hanoverian rulers by backing Charles Stuart, the grandson of James II, in the Jacobite cause, which sought to reclaim the

WHERE ON EARTH?

Culloden Moor lies just outside the village of Culloden, on the northeast side of Inverness, Scotland. Inverness is accessible by road (via the A9, A82 and A96), train and air. You can drive to Culloden or take one of the direct buses that run hourly from Inverness city centre.

SCOTLAND
North Sea
Inverness ● ●Culloden

Graves of the clans Lying along the path through the battlefield, memorial headstones bear the names of the clans who perished in the battle.

British Crown for a Stuart king. Bonnie Prince Charlie landed from France in July 1745, and soon found support among the Scottish clans.

That September, Charles and his army of clansmen secured a victory over British forces under the Duke of Cumberland at Prestonpans, near Edinburgh. For a brief while, it looked as though the ensuing invasion of England might succeed, but it ran out of steam at Derby, and the Jacobites retreated back to Scotland. By spring 1746, with supplies dwindling and money running out, the cause was all but lost.

As the Duke of Cumberland and his troops pursued the Jacobites north, Bonnie Prince Charlie took the fateful decision to face them at Culloden, to the east of Inverness. His forces were tired, hungry, outnumbered and far better suited to guerrilla tactics than a pitched battle. As dawn broke, the French envoy pleaded with Charles to withdraw, but

> **"** The Battle of Culloden was fought on this moor 16th April 1746. The graves of the gallant Highlanders who fought for Scotland and Prince Charlie are marked by the names of their clans. **"**
>
> INSCRIPTION ON THE MEMORIAL CAIRN AT CULLODEN
> ERECTED BY DUNCAN FORBES IN 1881

with Cumberland's army in sight, the Prince's pipers began to play and the army struggled into position.

Bogged down

Even then it did not have to be such a disaster. Having rejected all advice with his decision to make a stand on Culloden Moor, Charles then failed to use his greatest strength: the charge of his Highland infantry with their broadswords raised. This fearsome weapon was effectively cancelled when he kept them standing ready for an hour within enemy range. By the time he gave the order to charge, hundreds had already been slaughtered. Those who survived to hear the signal had to cross the rough, marshy ground, with British cannon and musket fire continuing all around. The ragged group that reached the Redcoat lines found their enemy prepared with bayonets fixed, ready to answer their whirling broadswords stroke for stroke.

Within an hour – about the same time it takes to tour the battlefield on foot today – the Jacobites had been driven from the field. Between 1,500 and 2,000 Jacobites were killed or wounded, compared to English losses of 50 dead and 259 wounded. Cumberland's troops

killed a similar number as they lay injured or tried to flee. The dead clansmen were identified for burial by their clan badges (plant sprigs worn in their bonnets).

In the months that followed, Cumberland and his troops drove a swathe of destruction through the Highlands, burning villages, driving off livestock and laying waste to crops, earning him the title of 'Butcher'. Communities were broken up, the clan system dismantled and Highland culture banned. In the ensuing years, thousands went into exile.

Highland ghosts

The ghosts of the Culloden Highlanders are said to return on April 16 each year to refight the battle; some say they hear their war cries and clash of broadswords. There are claims of sightings of a Jacobite soldier lying dead on one of the grave mounds.

No tactician ever argued that the Jacobites should have won the Battle of Culloden. Few historians believe that Britain would have been the better for a further spell of Stuart rule. Why, then, does Culloden cast such a long shadow? What makes this empty stretch of moorland so poignant a place? Ultimately, perhaps, because all of us have a soft spot for a lost cause, once it is truly lost.

best of the rest...

LAST-STAND BATTLEFIELDS

■ **Roncesvalles Pass**, in the Pyrenees, was the place where in AD 778 a Basque force defeated the Emperor Charlemagne's Frankish army as it returned to France, and killed Roland, one of the Frankish commanders. The battle inspired 'The Song of Roland' – the oldest surviving work of French poetry.

■ **Little Bighorn Battlefield National Monument** and **Indian Memorial**, Montana, commemorate the Battle of the Little

Bighorn of 1876, where General Custer's troops were overwhelmed by the Native American attack. The victors' success was short-lived as they were overrun by white settlers, losing their lands and way of life.

■ South Africa's **Rorke's Drift** is the historic site of the struggle mounted by 150 British soldiers against 3,000 Zulus in 1879.

■ In 1244, at the height of the Albigensian Crusade, 200 members of the Catholic Cathar sect were killed by the French army after a nine-month siege of their citadel at **Montségur** in Aquitaine, France.

DELHI OLD TOWN

Built 400 years ago by the Mughal emperor Shah Jahan, Old Delhi still pulses with life: chaotic, colourful, bustling and vibrant.

Now a labyrinthine jumble of exquisite Mughal architecture, faded mansions and narrow lanes buzzing with activity, Old Delhi was commissioned by Shah Jahan in 1638. It was said that during his reign, revenues from the Mughal Empire were at their greatest, and travellers spoke of a most magnificent court, flourishing trade and dazzling arts and architecture. With such wealth and talent at his disposal, Shah Jahan could well afford a new capital. On the banks of the Yamuna River, surrounded by cool woodlands and fertile fields, a city of avenues, gardens, canals, mosques, markets, mansions and a fortified palace – the Red Fort – were completed in just ten years.

The Old Delhi that survives today is the most recent of seven cities built on this site by a succession of rulers. At first called Shahjahanabad, 'the City of Shah Jahan', the area is now known as Old Delhi to distinguish it from New Delhi, the city built in the 1920s under the British Raj.

WHERE ON EARTH?

Delhi is northern India's largest city. Old Delhi is on the west bank of the Yamuna River, just north of New Delhi, the current capital of India. Most visitors arrive at Indira Gandhi International Airport and take a train, bus or taxi to the city centre. Rickshaws offer an ideal way to explore the old city.

THE MUGHALS

In 1526 a warlord by the name of Babur, a descendant of the Mongol warrior Ghengis Khan, defeated the ruler of the Delhi Sultanate and proclaimed himself emperor. Thus began the powerful Mughal dynasty of conquerors, patrons of the arts and prolific builders that came to control much of modern India and Pakistan. The Mughals ruled until 1857, when, following the failed Indian Mutiny against the British Raj, the last emperor was exiled to Burma. The Mughal Empire reached its golden age under the fifth emperor, Shah Jahan, who came to the throne in 1627 and is now best known as the builder of the Taj Mahal.

A slice of life

At the heart of Old Delhi is Chandni Chowk, or Moonlight Square, the main street that runs across the old town to the Red Fort. It was laid out around a network of canals designed to reflect the moonlight. By day, the broad thoroughfare was a bustling market. It also provided the perfect venue for the grand Mughal processions that made their way across town on special occasions. The tradition was revived in 1903, when the Delhi Durbar celebrated the coronation of King Edward VII and Queen Alexandra.

Today the canals have gone, but Chandni Chowk and the streets to either side remain as vibrant, colourful and crowded as ever. Rickshaws garlanded with tinsel weave perilously through the traffic, and the honking of three-wheeler taxis, buses and cars drown out the constant chorus of bicycle bells. Bakers and cooks, snake-charmers and bead-sellers ply their trades on the crowded pavements; cows, protected by their sacred status, wander calmly through the dust and commotion. Shops are piled high with embroidered fabric, silver bangles, antiques, books, sandals, scarves and shawls, herbal remedies and spices that release myriad fragrances in the heat. Children munch on deep-fried

vadas soaked in yoghurt, noodles and cheese balls, while women in fluttering saris sip ice-cream drinks flavoured with saffron or rose syrup. Sweet shops do a brisk trade, offering more than a thousand different delicacies

In the alleyways, craftsmen shape clay figurines and pots, beat silver, mend shoes, fix punctures, weave rugs, polish lacquerware or put the finishing touches to inlaid marble and wood.

Old Delhi is a slice of modern India, but amidst all the frenzy, the past lingers on in traditional neighbourhoods, known

as *kuchas*, where the men still all share the same trade, and in the residential areas, where the old haveli mansions, their once ornately carved and decorated exteriors set with frail balconies, sport a satellite dish here and there.

City of mansions

The havelis were often built around an inner courtyard with a central fountain and had lavish interiors. Now deteriorating, most are mere shadows of their former selves but they remain popular haunts on the heritage trail. Well-known ones include Ghalib Ki Haveli, home of the 19th-century Mughal poet, Mirza Ghalib, and the well-preserved Chunnamal Haveli, built by a family of textile merchants. The Khazanchi Haveli was where Shah Jahan's accountants lived. It was linked to the Red Fort by a tunnel so that money could be moved safely between the two.

The renowned Bhagirath Palace has been swallowed up by a commercial complex, but its story never fails to please. It was built in the early 1800s for Begum Samru, a poor dancing girl

Chandni Chowk Old Delhi's central street is one of the liveliest street markets in the world. Temples, mosques and churches are spread along its route.

who married a European mercenary who later led his army to save Emperor Shah Alam. She became extremely rich and powerful, and lived to the age of 89.

Mihrabs and marigolds

No Mughal capital would be complete without a central mosque. Shah Jahan chose a hillock to the southwest of the Red Fort, where 5,000 men set to work

Centre of power Named for the colour of its encircling walls, the Red Fort is one of the finest examples of Mughal architecture in the world.

on the Jama Masjid at a cost of 1 million rupees. Every Friday, the emperor left his palace on elephant back, perched in a gold *howdah*, to attend at the mosque's central *mihrab* and kneel in the niche facing Mecca. He left the palace by the Delhi Gate and returned by another route as this was considered more auspicious. At the top of a steep flight of steps, across a paved courtyard, a cool ablution pool reflects the slender minarets, cloisters and domes. The sandstone and marble, pillars and arches, calligraphy and inlaid panels create an atmosphere of spacious, undisturbed calm.

Old Delhi is dotted with places of worship, all with their own distinctive cultural traditions. The Sikh Gurudwara Sis Ganj is a modest but captivating temple marking the spot where Guru Tegh Bahadur, the ninth Sikh guru, was beheaded on the orders of Emperor Aurangzeb (Shah Jahan's son). Before entering the temple, worshippers remove their shoes and wash their hands and feet; food is sometimes offered to departing visitors.

The Anglican St James' Church, built in 1836, is Delhi's oldest church. It was commissioned by Colonel James Skinner, son of a Scotsman and his Rajput wife.

The Jain Digambar temple is an impressive red sandstone building complex and reflects the power and

Small but SPECIAL

CARCASSONNE
The historic heart of picture-perfect Carcassonne dates back to Gallo-Roman times and was restored in the 19th century. Rising like a fairytale castle above a medieval bridge on the Aude River in southwest France, it is enclosed by a double line of ramparts with 52 towers and fortified gateways. Within the walls are cobbled lanes, busy in summer, a castle with dungeon and drawbridge, and a basilica. Views from the ramparts stretch from the new town across the Languedoc plain to the snowy tops of the Pyrenees.

influence that the Jain community have exercised on the city's history and the social status that they still retain.

The Hindu Gauri Shankar temple was reputedly built by a wounded soldier and dedicated to the god, Shiva. Within lies an 800-year-old bejewelled lingam statue and the marble chair of a Hindu saint who lived in the temple for more than 50 years. It is a colourful shrine, with votive cotton threads and offerings of red powder mingling with sandalwood and the marigold garlands that are sold to visitors.

The Red Fort
'If there is paradise on earth, it is here, it is here', reads an inscription in the Red Fort, or Lal Qila. The fort represents the pinnacle of Mughal artistic and architectural achievements and is the greatest symbol of its empire. Rising above a dry moat, it bristles with turrets, crenellations and bastions, a formidable structure with a once-palatial interior.

OLD CITIES

■ Japan's World Heritage sites around **Ancient Kyoto** cover 17 separate locations, and are listed for their historical buildings and scenic beauty. Rebuilt over time, the 300 Shinto shrines, 1,700 Buddhist temples - many set in gardens designed to prompt meditation - pavilions and castle represent the hub of Japanese culture.

Kyoto

■ **Old Damascus**, Syria, claims to be the world's oldest continuously inhabited city. The old town is partly surrounded by a wall and dotted with churches, shrines, madrassas and mosques, including the vast Umayyad. There are also traditional Damascene houses, such as Azm Palace, and caravanserai.

■ At the heart of a modern city, **Old Jerusalem** in Israel is a centre of pilgrimage for Jews, Christians and Muslims. Significant locations include the Dome of the Rock and the al-Aqsa Mosque on Temple Mount, the Western Wall and the Church of the Holy Sepulchre. The old walled city has more than 200 historical monuments and a bustling market.

■ Dating back to the 13th-16th centuries, **Tallinn Old Town**, Estonia, has brightly painted and gabled houses, towers, spires and cobbled lanes. There are grand churches and medieval markets, secluded courtyards, old passageways and traditional craft shops.

The two main gates (the Delhi Gate and the Lahore Gate) lead to a covered bazaar where merchants traded with the Mughal court.

The complex consisted of two sections, one for administration, the other residential. The pavilions and palaces of the living quarters were close to the river to catch the breeze, and were set within elaborate gardens in the Mughal style. These included the Moonlight Garden, filled with flowers that bloom at night, the Life Bestowing Garden and the Streams of Paradise. Every building was a treasure house of Mughal art, which is characterised by the fusion of Islamic, Persian and Indian elements.

After the departure of Shah Jahan, the Red Fort's golden age soon ended. Emperor Aurangzeb added the Pearl Mosque, but later alterations were less sensitive. Looting, vandalism and the destruction that occurred under British rule also took their toll. Yet in this vast complex, sheltered from the city's 21st-century roar, the remaining buildings bear witness to a glorious past, from the Imperial Apartments to the Palace of Colours, reserved for the ladies of the court, to the Royal Baths and the Audience Halls and in the cool white marble, the *pietra dura* inlays of flowers and birds, scalloped arches, fountains, latticed screens and decorated ceilings and walls. Best preserved is the Hall of Private Audience, an open marble pavilion glittering with semi-precious stones and once home to the legendary Peacock Throne, carried off by Persian invaders in 1739.

Each year on August 15, the anniversary of India's independence, the Indian Prime Minister addresses the nation from the quiet of the Red Fort. But in the old town beyond the fortress walls, life never stops amid the cacophony of vehicles, the swirling colours and the scent of spices.

DUBROVNIK

The red-tiled roofs, Renaissance palaces and breezy coastal location give little clue to the long struggles for freedom of this old city, its port protected by fortified walls that no enemy ever breached.

To marauding pirates or would-be invaders, this fortified port, with rugged mountains on one side, sheer cliffs on the other and Lokrum island protecting the bay, must have appeared impregnable. Even today, all that visitors can see as they arrive by boat is the formidable stone wall encircling the old town and harbour, hugging every contour of the land and flanked by towers, bastions and forts. They are considered among the largest and best-preserved defensive walls in Europe, a remarkable testimony to the skill of the builders who created a structure strong

enough to resist earthquakes, to the cooperation of the citizens, and, above all, to the astute diplomacy of a free city that managed to keep peace with the rival powers of the Ottoman Empire to the east and the Venetian Republic to the west. For the people of Dubrovnik, the walled port remains a symbol of independence and prosperity.

The protective wall

The wall that shelters this jewel of the Adriatic stretches 1.2 miles (2km) in its entirety, climbing to the town's highest point in the northwest corner, snaking

Beauty in strength A view of Dubrovnik from the hills above shows the extent of the city's medieval walls. In the past, chains slung across the harbour entrance at night completed the circle.

along the cliff top, then dipping back down to the harbour. Rebuilt and altered many times, it reaches a height of 25m (82ft) in places and is up to 6m (20ft) thick, though less on the seaboard side, where limestone cliffs provided the first line of defence.

A walk along these ancient ramparts is breathtaking in every sense. Swept by a cool breeze or blazing in the summer heat, the outlook extends from rocky ridges on the hill above the city down to the Adriatic, from the meandering coast and glistening harbour to the old town with its jumble of red roofs sprinkled with spires and domes. Bells chime in the clear air and flagstones, polished by centuries of footsteps, shine like silver.

Construction of the current walls began in the 12th century and continued for the next 500 years. But why did this relatively small, southern European port need such hefty fortifications? As early as the 12th century, the autonomous city-state of Ragusa, as Dubrovnik was then known, found itself caught between a series of rival powers – the Byzantines and Venetians to the north and west and, later, the Ottomans to the east – as they vied to control the lucrative trading routes that crossed the Adriatic Sea. With astute diplomacy, Ragusa managed to maintain its autonomy while gaining protection from the Byzantines and, later, from the Venetians.

In 1440, Ragusa became a vassal state of the Ottomans but continued to operate as a free state, acting as a trading post between the Venetians and Ottomans. It was a time of great prosperity. The city's fleet transported salt, wine, olive oil, dried fruit, leather and wool across the Mediterranean Sea and beyond. Aristocrats, ship-owners, merchants, bankers and an educated elite made the port their home.

Forts and gates

When Constantinople fell to the Ottomans in 1453, followed by Bosnia in the 1460s, Dubrovnik decided the time had come to strengthen its defences. At the highest point of the ramparts, the circular Minceta Tower went up around an earlier fort, itself surrounded by thick walls and battlements. Fort Bokar was designed to defend the Pila Gate, the main entrance on the land side of the town. Believed to be the oldest casemented fortress preserved in Europe, its massive cylindrical structure protrudes from the wall.

Formidable fortifications A walk round the walls is one of steep, narrow steps and precipitous drops. In places, the main wall is protected by an outer one.

Guarding the port entrance in the southeast of the city, the mid-14th century St John Fortress was remodelled. At night, chains were stretched across the harbour entrance from the fortress to the Kase jetty, another protective barrier, to prevent access. To the east, the Revelin Fortress – erected in the 15th century and rebuilt in the 16th – could fend off any land approach.

Most forbidding of all is the St Lawrence Fortress, a triangular fort perched on a precipitous rock just outside the western wall and rising 37m (121ft) above the water. According to ancient documents, the Venetians had long planned to take over this strategic spot, but Dubrovnik claimed it first and built the fort in just three months. A haunting place with terraces and arches, thick walls on the seaboard and two drawbridges, it is a popular setting for productions of *Hamlet*. Above the fortress gate is inscribed the motto so dear to the people of the city: 'Freedom is not to be sold for all the gold in the world.'

Four gates give access to the old town: two from the harbour – Ponte to the west of the Great Arsenal and the Fishmarket

Gate to the east – and Ploca and Pila on the land side. Pila is an imposing structure with multiple doors, a moat, a stone bridge and a wooden drawbridge. Above the gateway is a carving of St Blaise, patron saint of Dubrovnik.

The old town

The medieval thoroughfare known as Stradun leads from the harbour straight across the city, flanked on both sides by a grid of equally straight lanes that allowed messengers to move swiftly in all directions – from fort to fort, across

> **“** For the people of Dubrovnik, the walled port remains a lasting symbol of independence and prosperity. **”**

town or down to the port. Rebuilt after an earthquake in 1667, Stradun is an elegant, traffic-free esplanade paved with limestone. Both ends are marked by a lofty bell tower and a 15th-century fountain. The larger fountain, at the western end, has a massive dome surrounded by at least a dozen carved heads spouting fresh water piped from a spring more than 7 miles (11km) away. Several historic buildings grace Stradun and the adjacent Luza Square, including two palaces in Gothic-Renaissance style.

The Sponza Palace, where merchants, bankers and poets once met, houses the 17,000 volumes and manuscripts of the Dubrovnik Historical Archives. Baroque churches and monasteries stand proudly within the walls, while here an old granary, there a noble mansion with balcony and coat of arms, a stepped passageway, a tiny garden ablaze with sunflowers and pomegranates are tucked into side streets. Dark archways provide shade and in bustling squares the scent of lavender rises from market stalls.

The price of freedom

During the 19th century, Ragusa lost the freedom it cherished so highly – first to Napoleonic and then Austrian rule. A turbulent 20th century culminated in the Croatian War of Independence in the early 1990s, when forces of the Yugoslav People's Army encircled and bombarded the city and its historic buildings for three months until a Croatian counterattack lifted the siege. Peace eventually returned and the damage was repaired.

Every hour on the hour, two bronze figures known as the 'green men' strike the old bell in the clock tower on Luza Square, while in the glittering Renaissance palaces and along the fortifications looking out to sea, the free spirit of Dubrovnik lives on.

best of the rest...

WALLED PORTS

▨ Known by the Phoenicians as Gadir, 'walled fortress', **Cadiz** sits on a narrow peninsula in southwest Spain, guarding a strategic bay. It was a formidable stronghold and is Spain's oldest settlement. Remnants of the ancient walls still cling to the Old Town, punctuated by gates, forts and 18th-century watchtowers.

▨ The medieval town, or 'Ville Close', of **Concarneau** in Brittany, France, is on an island in the harbour with a bridge connecting it to the mainland. It became a major fortified stronghold in the 14th century. The walls were rebuilt from 1451 onwards by Pierre II, Duke of Brittany, and his successors.

Essaouira

▨ In the 18th century, Sultan Mohammed III of Morocco commissioned a new fortified town and port, **Essaouira**, to open up trade on the Atlantic coast, close to Marrakech. The work was entrusted to foreign engineers, namely the French Cornut, pupil of Vauban. Two sets of fortifications were built to protect the new kasbah - now the old town - and the port. Walls, bastions and gates are well preserved and old bronze cannon still look out to sea.

▨ **Kotor**, Montenegro, claims a spectacular setting, deep in a fjord-like bay backed by mountains. The defensive wall was built under Venetian rule, which began in 1420. More than 2.5 miles (4km) long and up to 15m (50ft) wide, it stretches around the old town, then climbs up the steep slopes to the fort of St John, before coming back down to the harbour.

▨ **Valletta**, Malta, owes its defenses to the Knights of St John, a crusading order granted the island by the King of Spain in 1530. After the Great Ottoman Siege of 1565, the knights decided to build a fortified city on the Sceberras peninsula to deter any future Islamic invasions. The city was protected by a double line of land fortifications, while at the tip of the peninsula Fort St Elmo commanded unrivalled views over two natural harbours.

EASTER ISLAND

Symbols of both Polynesian culture and the artistic heights that ancient civilisations were able to reach, the giant stone sculptures of the Rapa Nui have a mystical allure.

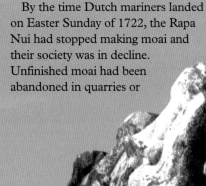

WHERE ON EARTH?

Easter Island is one of the world's most isolated landfalls, a tiny speck in the Pacific Ocean. Its nearest neighbours are Pitcairn Island, 1,243 miles (2,000km) to the west and Chile, 2,175 miles (3,500km) to the east. There are flights from Santiago in Chile and Papeete in French Polynesia. The town of Hanga Roa has visitor facilities.

● Easter Island
● Hanga Roa
South Pacific Ocean

Few human achievements have aroused as much curiosity and controversy as the giant stone statues, the *moai*, of Easter Island. To this day, archeologists cannot say for certain how or why the monolithic sculptures were erected, what their exact purpose was, or why the society that created them went into decline.

Rapa Nui (the indigenous name for both the island and its inhabitants) was settled around AD 300 by peoples from the west, and it is remarkable that Polynesian mariners even discovered such a remote speck of land, let alone established a 1,000-year colony there.

Monuments of stone

By the 10th century, the colonists were sculpting effigies from volcanic stone. The statues probably had religious significance and may have been images of deified ancestors. Local legends say that the moai walked from the quarries themselves to the sacred sites (*ahu*). Modern researchers believe that each one was pulled and pushed by hundreds of islanders along a bed of toromiro palm trunks, then erected on the rectangular ahu to serve as a place of worship and, at some periods, tombs.

Over time, the moai evolved in style and size. The earliest statues are small and roughly hewn, with round heads and eyes. By the 16th century, they were enormous – up to 21m (70ft) high and weighing 270 tonnes – and amazingly sophisticated, with long faces and meticulously carved hands. Archeologists speculate that the increasing size reflects an environmental and social crisis that afflicted the island. Dwindling food and resources, sparked by climate change, natural disasters and overpopulation, may have caused the islanders to believe that they had offended their gods. To win back the gods' favour, the chiefs ordered the construction of ever larger statues. But as the situation deteriorated, civil war and cannibalism followed.

By the time Dutch mariners landed on Easter Sunday of 1722, the Rapa Nui had stopped making moai and their society was in decline. Unfinished moai had been abandoned in quarries or

Mysteries of stone The moai heads, which face away from the ocean, could represent clan chiefs acting as channels of communication with the Rapa Nui gods.

left lying on ceremonial roads. Conflict continued over the next century: the statues were vandalised and the population dwindled. In 1888, Chile claimed the island and the remaining 100 islanders were moved to Hanga Roa village, where they worked as virtual slaves for British sheep farmers who leased the island.

The heads might have passed into obscurity if not for Father Englert, a German missionary living on the island between 1935 and 1969. He had an avid interest in Rapa Nui culture and catalogued numerous archeological sites. The treasures he recorded were eventually put under the protection of the island's National Park, which now covers 90 per cent of Rapa Nui.

Today, the moai, many restored to upright positions, stand guard over a starkly beautiful landscape of rugged low-slung volcanoes, open beaches, windswept moors and precipitous cliffs, mute monuments to a lost civilisation.

the best because...

■ It is home to the world's greatest collection of ancient sculpture – almost 900 stone statues have been counted.

■ The statues are an enduring mystery. Despite extensive research, no one knows how or why the Rapa Nui erected them, or why the culture declined.

■ Today's tiny population of 5,000 means the island remains almost as it was when the last giant moai were erected.

■ Rapa Nui National Park also features dramatic volcanic landscapes.

■ Now part of Chile, the island's modern culture is a unique blend of Polynesian and Latin American influences.

EIFFEL TOWER

Think of Paris: picture the Eiffel Tower. A cliché, you might think? Only until you visit it and witness its size and monumental beauty.

All great cities want an icon – a bold and exceptional building or monument that embodies the spirit of the city and captures the imagination of the world. The Eiffel Tower is just such a building, an instantly recognisable emblem of Paris – even for people who have never visited the city.

The concept was bold from the start. The city authorities wanted to create the world's tallest structure to mark the 1889 Universal Exposition held to celebrate the centenary of the French Revolution. They set the mark at 300m (984ft), almost twice the height of the Washington Monument in Washington DC, which held the record at the time, and put the design out to competition. The winning entry among 107 submissions came from Gustave Eiffel (1832–1923), the French engineer already famous for his bridges, domes and viaducts.

Massive triumph

No one had built anything quite like this before, or on such a scale. In little more than two years, around 100 workmen fixed together the tower's 18,038 pieces of iron, weighing 7,300 tonnes, using 2.5 million rivets – a breathtaking engineering feat with no other purpose than to create pleasure and astonishment. The effect has not diminished with time. With its gently tapering curves and ornamental filigree lattice, from a distance the Eiffel Tower has a remarkable elegance and lightness of touch. It is a shock, therefore, to stand at its base, between the four legs, and see just what an outlandishly colossal structure it is.

Lifts or stairs (there are 704 steps to the second floor) take visitors to three separate viewing platforms, each with multiple visitor attractions. Even the second floor, at 115m (377ft) above the ground, can seem dauntingly high; and the fretwork structure, open to the elements, can be unnerving. But the views over Paris are magnificent – especially from the comfort of the Jules Verne

Pinnacle of civic pride Around 75 per cent of visitors to the Eiffel Tower come from outside France, making it the showcase of Paris. It is the world's most visited paid-for monument.

restaurant or the informal buffet. The top floor is nearly two-and-a-half times higher still. On a clear day you can see for 80km (50 miles), right across Paris and into the surrounding countryside beyond the city.

Saved for the nation

The Eiffel Tower was not always universally loved by Parisians. It caused a storm of controversy when it was built, with astonishing speed, in 1887–9. Protestors dismissed it as a 'black factory chimney', a 'barbarous mass overwhelming and humiliating all our monuments', but criticism diminished when visitors began to experience the Eiffel Tower first hand and recognised it as a wonder of the industrial age.

Originally planned as a temporary structure, the Eiffel Tower was scheduled to be dismantled after 20 years, but it was reprieved in the 1890s when it acquired a new purpose. It became a transmission tower in the early days of radio, and also functioned as a weather station. It held the title of the world's tallest structure until 1930, when it was overtaken by the Chrysler Building in New York.

Since Gustave Eiffel was an authority on the aerodynamics of tall, iron-framed

Iron giant The massive base of the Eiffel Tower dwarfs the streets and traffic below. Looking southeast, as here, its grand arch frames the lawns of the Champ de Mars and the buildings of the École Militaire.

best of the rest...

CITY ICONS

■ The **Statue of Liberty** was a gift from France to mark the centenary of the American Declaration of Independence. With an internal structure by Gustave Eiffel, the statue was erected on an island in New York Harbor and inaugurated in 1886. It was the first American landmark encountered by arriving immigrants and became a symbol not just of New York but of the entire USA.

■ Not only the look, but also the sound of **Big Ben** in London is familiar the world over. Completed in 1859, the Clock Tower was part of Charles Barry's rebuilding of the Houses of Parliament following a devastating fire in 1834. The name 'Big Ben' actually belongs to the great bell that strikes the hour.

■ The **Leaning Tower of Pisa** was designed as a campanile, or freestanding bell tower, for the cathedral of Pisa in Italy. It is an unusual and attractive round tower, built over two centuries to 1372 along the classical lines of ancient Rome. As a result of subsidence, it leans at an angle of about 4°. The tower has now been stabilised, retaining the idiosyncratic lean.

buildings, he calculated the curve of the legs at the base of the tower that would most efficiently resist wind load. In addition, the iron latticework is so minimal that the wind cannot get a grip on the tower. Such was Eiffel's engineering wizardry that even in strong winds the tower never sways more than 11cm (4½in).

Today, the Eiffel Tower is one of the world's top tourist attractions, with nearly 7 million visitors every year.

During the winter season, a temporary ice rink is installed on the first floor, while down at ground level the original 1899 lift machinery is open to the public for pre-arranged guided tours.

The Tower's pulsating evening lightshow – which lasts for five minutes on the hour, every hour until 1am – gives it continuous visibility, while innovative illuminations to mark special events ensure that its status as an unparalleled city icon is constantly refreshed.

ERG CHEBBI

A vast, swelling sea of sand, Erg Chebbi is the classic image of a desert. Covering 42 sq miles (110 km²) of eastern Morocco, on the border with Algeria and the Sahara desert, the dunes rise to 150m (500ft), looming like a sand tsunami over outlying towns and villages, such as Merzouga. They form long, curvaceous ripples running north to south for 14 miles (23km), perpendicular to the prevailing winds, which constantly brush against the soft mounds of sand, pushing loose grains over the scimitar-shaped ridges. The dunes are permanently on the move, as they have been for at least a million years. Little can survive in this hot, dry, mobile environment: the footfalls of passing camels and humans sink deep into the sand. Yet the place has a magnetic beauty that beckons exploration.

Atlantic Ocean

MOROCCO

Marrakech ●

Erg Chebbi ●

ALGERIA

THE ULTIMATE DESERT?

Much of our Solar System is waterless and lifeless. The Earth, by contrast, flows with water and life, deserts being an exception. Receiving less than 250mm (10in) of rain a year (the official definition of a desert), and in many cases baked by relentless sun, deserts test the very limits of survival. Yet they can also be places of awesome beauty, where the bare, raw geology of the Earth is exposed in unfettered

palettes of colour and shading, especially at the start and end of the day. At night, clear cloudless skies yield to a star-spangled heaven. By challenging life, deserts also produce marvels of adaptation among plants and animals that cling to the gifts of night-dew and occasional rain showers. After rain, a desert may suddenly bloom into a carpet of flowers. Dormant shrimps awake to complete an entire life cycle in days, before a puddle dries. Cacti roots suck moisture into their trunks. The greatest deserts are paragons of such extremes, poised on the knife-edge of life.

WHITE DESERT

S and is a great sculptor. Whisked up by the wind, it forms a carpet of sharp-edged corrosive particles capable of stripping a car of paint or etching away at rock. This is what has happened in one of the world's most remarkable natural landscapes in the super-dry Western Desert of Egypt. The White Desert, now a national park, is filled with outlandish natural sculptures that rise from the flat desert floor and take on all manner of shapes in the imagination of the human observer: portrait heads on narrow necks, birds in flight, sails, mushrooms, nipples, yurts and spires. Chiselled out of a deep layer of chalk laid down by a long-lost sea millions of years ago, the rock formations are dazzlingly white in full daylight. At dawn and dusk they are cast in soft pink and orange hues that turn an eerie silver in the deep silence of a moonlit night.

FORBIDDEN CITY

In China's labyrinthine Imperial Palace, every detail is symbolic of the absolute power of the emperor enthroned at its centre.

There is a line that cuts the ancient walled city of Beijing exactly in two. This meridian passes through the Yongding Men, a recently rebuilt central gate in Beijing's southernmost wall, and runs north up a broad avenue to the twin towers of the Zhengyang Men, a gate in the wall that once separated the older, northern city from its southern extension. Continuing north, the line passes through the middle of the Forbidden City's three largest halls, before continuing north through the Bell and Drum Towers – once Beijing's timekeepers – and out through a long-vanished gate in the north wall.

When the emperor sat on his throne in the Hall of Supreme Harmony, the Forbidden City's grandest hall, the meridian line passed right through him. He sat at the centre of all power as symbolised by the labyrinth of ceremonial buildings, residences, offices, gardens and other amusements symmetrically laid out around him, as was Beijing itself. Seen from the main entrance, gates to sections of the palace on the left side have 'right' in

WHERE ON EARTH?

The Forbidden City is in Beijing, northern China, in Dongcheng - one of the four districts that make up the city centre. Entry is through the Meridian Gate (south gate), to the north of Tiananmen Square, which can be reached by subway. Visitor numbers are restricted at peak times.

Beijing
●Forbidden City

East China Sea

CHINA

their name, and vice versa. Everything is arranged around the enthroned emperor's south-facing viewpoint.

Imperial grandeur

Beijing's walls have now been replaced by ring roads and all but a handful of their gate towers have been pulled down, but the palace's imposing pavilion-topped Meridian Gate still stands beyond the palace moat, providing access through the 10m (33ft) high palace walls. Most of the buildings face south to make the best of the sun and to turn their backs

on baleful northern influences. They sit on marble plinths with elaborately carved balustrades and projecting water spouts in the shape of dragons. The main pillars are single tree trunks, heavily lacquered in red, the colour of prosperity.

The grandest building in the Forbidden City, the Hall of Supreme Harmony, is eleven bays wide and reputedly the largest wooden building in China. Here, on ceremonial occasions, the enthroned emperor reviewed a vast multitude of gaudily costumed courtiers prostrated on the wilderness of flagstones that line the palace's largest courtyard.

Now officially called the Palace Museum, the Imperial Palace is still better known as the Forbidden City. One

Dragon throne At the centre of the Hall of Supreme Harmony, the emperor's seat of power is richly ornamented with the imperial dragon motif.

Chinese name for it was Zijin Cheng, often translated as 'Purple Forbidden City'. But the Chinese character for purple in this case referred to the Pole Star towards which the complex was aligned.

The palace was originally constructed over a period of 14 years to a layout prescribed in the *Rites of Zhou*, a text probably from around the 3rd century BC. Construction is said to have involved 100,000 artisans, but this is the kind of round figure the Chinese love to use when they mean 'many'. The palace was completed in 1420 and the Yongle emperor of the Ming dynasty moved in shortly afterwards, the first of 24 Ming and Qing emperors to live here up to 1924.

Figures of up to 9,000 or more are given for the number of rooms in what is the largest and best-preserved group of historic buildings in China. That count really applies to bays – the spaces

between pillars in the courtyards and hall facades – but nevertheless the site occupies a vast area, approximately 1,000m (3,300ft) by 750m (2,500ft).

Rich symbolism

The palace's grandeur lies not just in its scale, but also in the small details, none of which occur by chance – all have practical, political or occult significance. Yellow roof tiles, for example, could only be used with imperial consent. Lesser buildings, and those assigned to princes, had green tiles. One palace library had a black-tiled roof, a colour associated with water and seen as an aid to fire-fighting. Buildings reserved for functionaries had grey tiles.

The huge wooden doors are studded with large golden knobs. These have been likened to golden fish eyes, bowls and *mantou* – Chinese steamed bread rolls. One story has it that they

City of gold Viewed from the north, wave after wave of steeply curved roofs proceed southwards, the grandest and highest centred on the meridian.

were inspired by conches, symbols of tightness and security. The number of knobs, usually arranged nine by nine, seven by seven or five by five, indicates the rank of the door.

The two beasts facing inwards along the spine of each roof are water dragons, supposed to resist the attacks of lightning and fire. Rows of ceramic figures run down the eaves – at the tip is a man, followed by a succession of animals. Traditionally, this figure is a tyrannical prince of a pre-Chinese state who was overthrown by his neighbours and hanged from the roof of his palace. The people erected images of the prince on their roofs, mounted on a chicken that was unable to fly and with a Chinese

Chamber (or *The Story of the Stone*), about the life and fortunes of a feudal family in Beijing.

The nearby three-storey Rain and Flowers Pavilion has huge golden scampering dragons on its roof, beautiful blue tiles and subsidiary dragons emerging from its eaves.

The last emperor

The palace's rearmost courtyard is known as the Imperial Flower Garden, and features small temples, ancient bamboo and an enormous rock garden topped by a small pavilion. A building on the west side was used as a schoolroom by Sir Reginald Johnston, the British tutor of the last emperor. The room was furnished with heavy Victorian furniture, Nottingham lace curtains and Axminster carpets to make him comfortable. Johnston, Isabel Ingram (the American tutor of the empress) and the imperial couple are said to have had al fresco lunches here in the garden.

The northeast section of the palace includes Beijing's finest opera theatre, the Pavilion of Pleasant Sounds, built in 1776, with a ceiling of painted clouds, trapdoor mechanisms and other performance machinery.

Nearby, drama of a different kind was played out in 1900 when, as the imperial family prepared to flee the arrival of foreign troops, the Dowager Empress Cixi ordered the murder of the Guangxu emperor's favourite consort, who was promptly drowned in what is now known as the Well of the Pearl Concubine.

dragon at his back to prevent him escaping. Other figures may include a lesser dragon, a phoenix, lion, unicorn and a celestial horse. Halls used by the emperor have nine of these figures, with the exception of the Hall of Supreme Harmony, which has ten.

The heavily restored towering palaces and broad open spaces on the main axis remain intimidatingly impressive, but it is in the smaller, more human spaces of the residential quarters that

the ghosts of drowned concubines and Machiavellian eunuchs must reside. The Palace of Eternal Spring, in a knot of small courtyards on the west side of the complex, was formerly the residence of several well-known concubines. Passages to the right and left end in ingenious *trompe-l'oeil* paintings that make them appear infinitely extended. In other parts of the courtyard are paintings of scenes from the classic 18th-century Chinese novel, *The Dream of the Red*

best of the rest...

SEATS OF ROYAL POWER

■ A formidable fortress, barely altered for almost seven centuries, what Britain's **Tower of London** lacks in scale it makes up for in atmosphere - especially in its dungeons - and in the magnificence of its treasures, including the British Crown Jewels, encompassing an amazing 23,578 gems. Enduring traditions at the Tower include the colourful Yeoman Warders - all ex-soldiers - and six large ravens fed daily on raw meat and blood-soaked biscuits.

■ The elegant **Winter Palace** at St Petersburg was home to the Russian Tsars for nearly 200 years until the revolution of 1917. Behind its broad green-and-white frontage lie 1,500

Tower of London

rooms, now better known for their contents. Founded by Catherine the Great in the 18th century, it houses one of the world's greatest collections of fine art and antiquities.

■ Istanbul's fortified **Topkapi Palace** sits on the European side of the Bosphorus, but is unlike anything else in the West – a vast, asymmetric agglomeration of minarets, domes and courtyards for ceremonial, residential and administrative purposes. Frequently adapted over five centuries, it contains hints of the Byzantine as well as the Islamic, and so is also quite unlike anything else in the East.

The same quarter holds the Flower Garden of the Palace of Peaceful Old Age, with paths winding between small, secluded pavilions, rockeries and tall, ancient trees.

Exhibition pieces

The best of the treasures from the Forbidden City are now held in the National Palace Museum in Taiwan, but various halls on the east side of the palace hold striking exhibitions of toys, jewellery, costume and artworks. The Clock and Watch Exhibition contains many timepieces and automata given to the emperors to curry favour. Perhaps the most impressive is a British clock of 1780 that incorporates a figure holding a calligraphy brush and writing the eight Chinese characters meaning: 'People come from everywhere to pay their respects to the emperor.'

The Palace of Great Benevolence houses donated bronzes and stoneware. Neighbouring halls display ceramics, including 110 pieces of tea ware from the palace collection. Imperial patronage made the now ubiquitous unglazed Yixing earthenware popular, and sets were commissioned specifically for imperial use.

The Western-style Water Hall of 1909, also known as the Crystal Palace, was commissioned from a German construction company. Never completed, it was bombed in an attack that ended the brief restoration of the last emperor in 1917. Its frame of iron,

partly clad with marble, was designed to be surrounded by water. The Nine Dragon Screen of 1773 features colourful dragons that writhe in relief along an assemblage of large tiles, one of which is said to be a wooden copy hurriedly created to replace a tile broken during assembly, but which could not be replaced before inspection.

Fight for survival

In 1999 the Forbidden City received a partial, long-overdue touch-up, with some courtyards re-paved and roofs mown, but substantial vegetation still tops many buildings. It might be argued

that the distressed state of the site is in any case more historically correct, since maintenance was always minimal and repairs undertaken only when they almost amounted to complete reconstruction. Photographs from 1900 show rotting wood, sagging beams, fallen plaster and peeling paint, while journalists wrote of dingy interiors. Today, just under half the site is open to the public, but its sprawl of peeling grandeur is more than enough to get lost in for days.

Ornate interior This lavish bell room is one of 24 structures in the Flower Garden of Peaceful Old Age, the emperor's intended retirement quarters.

MOUNT FUJI

The perfect snow-capped volcanic cone, Mount Fuji beckons pilgrims to test themselves on the arduous six-hour climb to the summit.

Mount Fuji's lone conical peak silhouetted against a crisp blue sky has been revered since ancient times. Standing at 3,776m (12,388ft), 'Fuji-san' is Japan's tallest and most holy mountain. Believed by Buddhists and Shintoists to be the home of deities, the mountain acquired its shape from volcanic eruptions that occurred several hundred thousand years ago (the most recent major eruption was in 1709). The resulting symmetrical proportions have inspired poets and artists, among them Katsushika Hokusai, who created the series of prints, *36 Views of Mount Fuji*.

The entire Japanese nation tracks the seasonal changes around Mount Fuji. A snow-covered mountain marks the start of winter; in spring, cherry blossoms decorate the foothills, followed by brightly coloured azaleas in summer. The mountain opens to climbers on July 1, after the snow melts, although ice remains in places all year round. Above the treeline alpine roses greet the first climbers, and during the short summer season 300,000 people make the trek.

In late August, the Yoshida Fire Festival marks the end of the climbing season. This is held in Fujiyoshida City to appease the goddess of Mount Fuji and petition her to prevent the volcano from erupting. Following a five-centuries-old tradition, people carry shrines believed to contain the goddess's soul through the streets in a torchlight parade. The correct procedures must be followed to avoid arousing her anger.

A sacred pilgrimage

Some pilgrims climb all night, their way lit by torches, to see the sun rise over the sea of clouds that usually cloaks

WHERE ON EARTH?

Situated 62 miles (100km) southwest of Tokyo on Japan's main island, Honshu, Mount Fuji is in the Fuji-Hakone-Izu National Park. Regular train and bus services run from Tokyo's Shinjuku station to the Kawaguchiko-Yoshidaguchi trail, which is one of four paths to the summit. The mountain is open in July and August.

HONSHU
JAPAN
●Tokyo
● *Mount Fuji*
Pacific Ocean

Picture perfect Fuji's nickname, Konohana-Sakuahime, means 'causing the blossom to bloom brightly', referring to the pink cherry blossoms that frame the mountain in springtime.

best of the rest...

SACRED MOUNTAINS

■ **Mount Shasta**, California, is the tallest peak in the Cascade Mountains. It is sacred to Native Americans and is now also a New Age spiritual destination.

■ **Mount Sinai**, Egypt, is the biblical site where Moses received the Ten Commandments from God. There are two trails up to the summit, both starting at the Greek Orthodox St Catherine's Monastery. The easiest way up is by Bedouin camel.

■ A million pilgrims a year trek up **Croagh Patrick** in County Mayo, Ireland, to pray, do penance or just enjoy the views. It was a site of pagan pilgrimage before the arrival of Celtic Christianity. St Patrick reputedly fasted on the summit for 40 days, then threw down a silver bell, knocking the she-demon, Corra, from the sky.

the lower slopes. This sunrise, known as *goraiko*, or holy light, is worshipped as a deity. Accounts of climbing this sacred mountain go back centuries. In a celebrated haiku, the 18th-century poet, Issa, exhorts a lowly snail to keep climbing, with majestic Fuji-san its unlikely and seemingly impossible destination. Today, crowds of the devout are joined by the merely curious as they wind snail-like up the four main trails, anticipating the revival of their spirits and souls as they emerge on the peak to the age-old beauty that surrounds them.

BEYOND COMPARE

GALÁPAGOS ISLANDS

The only place in the world where lizards feed in the sea, penguins live at the Equator and creatures have no fear of humans.

Strange and unique, the species of the Galápagos Archipelago sparked naturalist Charles Darwin's theories about natural selection. Geographic isolation turned these remote volcanic islands into a natural genetic laboratory as, separated from each other and from the rest of the world by the vast Pacific Ocean, species that live here evolved in isolation: 6 per cent of the birds, 32 per cent of the plants, 90 per cent of the reptiles and 46 per cent of the insects exist only here.

The islands straddle the Equator but are bathed by the cold, food-rich Humboldt Current that flows north from the Antarctic. The current creates an environment that nourishes the islands' unique and surprising array of wildlife. Penguins, fur seals and sea lions – animals more common to polar and temperate seas – live alongside creatures that are at home in the tropics, such as iguanas, frigate birds and giant tortoises. And the greatest delight of all is that these animals are unafraid of people: they do not run, swim or fly away, and so can easily be observed.

Marine iguanas nod at each other in defiance, sneeze salt or slither from the dark volcanic rocks into the water to graze on seaweed below the surface – the only lizards on Earth to live and feed in the ocean. The world's largest cormorant – flightless and unique to the islands – holds out its stubby wings to dry. Blue-footed boobies parade their bright blue feet, and great frigate birds puff out their red throat sacs like red balloons to impress a mate. Flamingos and white-cheeked pintail ducks busy themselves about a lagoon close to the beach. Inland, a Galápagos hawk perches on a giant tortoise, a handy lookout point to watch for lava lizards and iguanas.

WHERE ON EARTH?

The Galápagos Islands rise from the Pacific Ocean floor to reach a high point of 1,707m (5,600ft) at Wolf Volcano on Isabela. Part of Ecuador, they lie about 600 miles (1,000km) west of the mainland, a 30-minute flight from the city of Guayaquil. The growing human population now exceeds 30,000.

Galápagos Islands: Darwin, Wolf, Pinta, Marchena, Genovesa, Santiago, Fernandina, Isabela, Santa Cruz, San Christóbal, Pacific Ocean, Floreana, Española

In a shallow bay, squadrons of golden rays flap effortlessly over the sandy seabed. Offshore, schools of scalloped hammerhead sharks swim back and forth, resting during the day before hunting in

Evolutionary flexibility The marine iguana, a land reptile, has adapted to graze on seaweed. Sally Lightfoot crabs provide it with grooming services.

Blue-footed boobies The Galápagos is home to about half of the world's breeding pairs of blue-footed boobies.

a sight that still greets visitors today on Santa Cruz (Indefatigable) island, which has the largest surviving tortoise population.

From the late 16th century, pirates used Galápagos as a base while sacking Spanish treasure ships. They found that the tortoises lived for a year without food, so they stacked them in their holds, alive and upside-down, as a ready supply of fresh meat. Crews of passing ships helped themselves until the 20th century, decimating the population.

In 1684, a crude navigational chart was prepared by the English buccaneer Ambrose Cowley, who gave each island an English name. The Ecuadorian government has now given the islands Spanish names – except for one, still known as Nameless Island – but scientists call them by the English names that were in use when Charles Darwin visited in 1835.

Darwin's laboratory

Once ashore, one of the first things Darwin noticed was that the giant tortoises on one island had different carapaces (shells) to those on another. Some were saddle-like, enabling the tortoise to stretch its neck up to browse on bushes and cacti, while the ground-

Ocean-feeder The scalloped hammerhead shark has a relatively small mouth and feeds mainly on fish, squid, octopus and crustaceans.

smaller groups at night. On the beach at dusk, green sea turtles haul themselves out of the water to lay their eggs in the sand, while with ear-splitting screams a colony of swallow-tailed gulls, the world's only nocturnal gull, takes off to collect squid and small fish that rise to the surface of the ocean at night.

Explorers and pirates

At first sight, the richness and diversity of life on the islands is not apparent. Barren, black, jagged volcanic rocks and desert plants greeted the earliest European visitors and they were not impressed. Spaniard Fray Tomás de Berlanga, Bishop of Panama, discovered the islands by accident in 1535 when his ship drifted from the Ecuadorian mainland. He described them as 'worthless'.

They appeared on a world map of 1570 by Flemish cartographer Ortelius. He labelled them 'Insulae de los Galopegos', a reference to the giant tortoises that de Berlanga had seen –

ISLAND UPSTARTS

At 3 million years old, the Galápagos Islands are relatively young. They sit on a geological hot spot, where the Earth's crust is melted by magma, causing volcanoes and new islands to form. Each year, they move 5cm (2in) southeastwards. The older islands, such as Española (Hood), have moved away from the hot spot and are being slowly eroded by the sea. The younger central and westerly islands, such as Isabela (Albemarle) and Fernandina (Narborough), are over the hot spot and still being formed. Isabela is the largest island, with six volcanoes fused together. The most recent eruption was on Fernandina in 2009, when La Cumbre volcano spewed lava from a fissure measuring 200m (650ft).

BEYOND COMPARE

grazers had rounded shells. He also saw that mockingbirds were similar to those on the mainland, but slightly different on each island. He shipped many specimens back to England – mainly in the form of preserved skins, but also some nests – for further study.

Studying finches

Darwin was not an expert on birds, so on his return to London he gave his collection to English ornithologist James Gould. Gould recognised that all the Galápagos 'finches' were related, the descendants of a single mainland species (identified through DNA analysis more than 150 years later as a grassquit). About 2.3 million years ago, it seems grassquits were blown to the Galápagos, where they came to land on different islands. Separated from others of their kind, the birds were faced with local conditions and

> 66 [The tortoises] ... appeared most old-fashioned antediluvian animals or rather inhabitants of some other planet. 99
>
> **CHARLES DARWIN**

foods, which are different on each island, the older, easterly islands being more lush than the younger, westerly ones.

Darwin speculated that birds with the traits needed for survival in a new environment adapted and bred, a process he called 'natural selection'. He believed that the birds had evolved into distinct species on each island, with differently shaped bills for different foods. Some evolved robust bills for eating seeds, others slender bills to catch insects. One species learnt to use a 'tool' – a cactus thorn – to winkle out grubs from wood, and there

is a bird on Wolf (Wenman) and Darwin (Culpepper) islands that pecks the skin of boobies to drink their blood – the so-called vampire finch. It was this diversity, as well as the mockingbirds and giant tortoises, that Darwin drew on to form his theory of evolution.

Favourable weather

The Galápagos Islands would be a barren desert if it were not for the fogs and regular rainfall coming off the ocean. Even though the islands are on the Equator, the temperature stays at

a pleasant 21–29C (70–84F) all year, moderated by the cold Humboldt Current that brings frequent drizzle. There are two distinct seasons: the dry season, or *garúa*, between July and December, when mist obscures the highlands; and the warm, wet season between January and June, the wettest months being March and April with a daily, cleansing downpour. The weather changes with altitude, being colder and wetter on the higher ground at the centre of each island. The vegetation here is more lush, with pale grey-green palo alto trees and tree-sized *Scalesia*, the plant world's equivalent of Darwin's finches due to its variety.

Today, the Galápagos Islands are a living laboratory where scientists study evolution in action. It is a delicate ecosystem and 'Lonesome George', a giant tortoise who died in 2012 aged about 90 years old, was a symbol of that fragility. He was the last Pinta tortoise from Isla Pinta (Abingdon), where introduced goats, pigs and rats badly affected tortoise numbers. Active conservation work now protects the remaining wildlife. The islands that Darwin first believed to 'show little sign of life' have turned out to be so rich in such a wide variety of life that they are key to understanding the origin of species.

Remote bathing spot The population of giant Alcedo tortoises – seen here on Isabela Island – was cut by an invasion of feral goats from a neighbouring island who ate their source of food. The tortoises are now protected.

the best because...

■ Visitors see plants and animals that are not found anywhere else on Earth.
■ Temperate, polar and tropical species of animal live together.
■ The wildlife is easy to see and tolerates visitors.
■ These young volcanic islands are still active and in the process of formation.
■ Variations between plant and animal species across the islands formed the basis of Darwin's theory of evolution.

LOS GLACIARES
NATIONAL PARK

High on Argentina's Patagonian plateau, more than 200 spectacular glaciers large and small carve away at the southern Andes.

Los Glaciares National Park encompasses part of the largest ice mantle outside Antarctica and Greenland. With a third of the park buried beneath the Southern Patagonian Ice Field, it includes the third-largest store of fresh water on the planet. This is one of the few places on Earth where rugged mountains with sheer rock faces shaped by ice are found alongside glaciers that are expanding rather than retreating.

The ice field feeds 47 large glaciers – 13 of which flow towards the Atlantic Ocean, the rest towards the Pacific – and more than 200 smaller glaciers. Many of the glaciers are accessible at unusually low altitudes. In other non-polar locations, glaciers are generally found above 2,500m (8,200ft), but here they start at 1,500m (5,000ft) and gouge their way down through the mountains to just 200m (650ft) above sea level, where icebergs are calved effortlessly into the milky waters of long glacial lakes.

Mountain high, valley low

The Viedma Glacier in the north of the park is criss-crossed by canyon-sized crevasses and striped lengthwise by glacial debris. It calves into Lago Viedma, which stretches for 50 miles (80km). Ice has scoured the valleys all around, creating a uniformly brown landscape of smoothly polished rocks. In the south, 100-mile (160km) long Lago Argentino is fed by three major glaciers. The Perito Moreno Glacier can be accessed from land and is overlooked by a conveniently

WHERE ON EARTH?

Los Glaciares National Park is in the Austral Andes of southwest Argentina, on the border with Chile, 1,694 miles (2,727km) from Buenos Aires. The village of El Chaltén is the gateway to the mountains and glaciers, and the nearest airport is at El Calafate on the southern shores of Lago Argentino.

CHILE
ARGENTINA
Los Glaciares National Park • El Chaltén
Atlantic Ocean
Pacific Ocean

Icy embrace The advancing Perito Moreno Glacier is viewed from a platform: the immense wall of ice marches over everything in its path.

positioned viewing platform. The fast-flowing Upsala Glacier – the third-largest in South America – and Spegazzini Glacier, with its 135m (443ft) ice wall, can only be approached by boat.

Sailing too close to a glacier's 'spout' is fraught with danger because great slabs of ice the size of large buildings crash down from the terminal ice walls. The only warning is a small icefall and, maybe, a gush of meltwater, accompanied by what sounds like a barrage of artillery fire. Moments later, massive blocks of ice crash into the water with a thunderous roar and a mountain of spray, producing a huge wave that can swamp smaller boats. The ice blocks disappear briefly, and then bob back up to the surface to float as new, electric-blue icebergs.

Glacial advance

Perito Moreno is one of the few glaciers in the world that is still actively growing despite global warming, although not steadily. Rather, it advances and retreats in a cyclical pattern. Sometimes the 3-mile (5km) wide ice front advances so far that it forms a natural dam across the

lake. Water builds up on one side, rising some 30m (100ft) higher than in the rest of the lake. The enormous pressure eventually ruptures the ice dam, and the water smashes through in a spectacular and frightening torrent, sometimes washing away entire forests as it goes. Then the process starts again.

World's toughest mountains

In the extreme north of the park, not far from the Viedma Glacier, are the world's most challenging mountains. Highest is the saw-toothed granite peak of Cerro Fitz Roy, measuring 3,405m (11,171ft), and named after the captain of HMS *Beagle*, the ship that took Charles Darwin around the world. Seeing the mountain's reflection in the cobalt waters of Laguna de los Tres, it is hard to appreciate its notorious reputation, but mountaineers did not scale its peak until 1952.

To the west is windswept Cerro Torre. At 3,102m (10,177ft), it is the highest of a series of four peaks. This vertical spike of granite is topped by a mushroom-shaped cap of rime ice, making it virtually impossible for mountaineers to reach the summit. The first undisputed ascent of Cerro Torre was by an Italian expedition in 1974. Because of the sheer rock faces, ascents of both mountains are rare. While 100 people a year might reach the top of

Everest, which is more than twice the height of Fitz Roy or Torres, there is barely one successful ascent a year here.

One great creature that is at home in this rugged terrain is the Andean condor. It nests or roosts on inaccessible rock ledges high in the mountains, from where

Jagged peaks The Cerro Torre mountain is known for fearsome rain and wind, its almost impossibly pointed peak and a crown of hanging white ice.

it launches itself effortlessly into the air. Using its long, narrow wings – at 3.2m (10.5ft) it has the longest wingspan of any land bird – with upturned primary feathers at the tips, the condor soars on updraughts and thermals, like a glider, over mountains, glaciers and forests. It can travel 120 miles (200km) in a day in its search for carrion, preferring the carcasses of larger mammals such as guanaco, deer and foxes.

Cold-climate forests

The flora in Los Glaciares grows in three well-defined areas: the highland semi-desert, the forested woods and the steppe. Below the semi-desert and dark mountains of the ice field are sub-polar forests populated with three types of hardy beech tree: the lenga, guindo and ñire (Antarctic beech). The deciduous lenga grows 30m (100ft) tall and tolerates temperatures of −30C (−22F). In the most exposed places, the trees are bent and twisted by the fierce, freezing winds. Some have no branches on the windward side, forming what are known as 'flag trees'.

The stunted, shrub-like ñire beech, with its waxy, sweet-scented leaves, survives in even harsher conditions; it even grows on Hoste Island, to the south on the southern shore of the Beagle

Channel, making it the world's most southerly tree. With their arid, cold and windy conditions, the steppes support creased, rigid grasses that form low, thick mattocks and circular tussocks.

Animal life

Life here must be tough to survive, but more than 100 types of native bird make their home in Los Glaciares. Torrent ducks swim and dive in fast-flowing, white-water rivers, plucking aquatic invertebrates from submerged rocks, while aggressive caracaras are always on the lookout for something edible to filch and squabble over. The region's only native bird of prey is the powerful black-chested buzzard, which has a wingspan of 149–200cm (59–79in). It hunts rabbits and skunks, and sometimes competes with condors for carrion.

Rabbit-like viscachas with long, bushy tails leap between rocks with surprising agility, but the most significant mammal in the park is the critically endangered huemul deer. They live at high altitudes in summer, then move down the mountains in autumn to spend winter in sheltered forest valleys. With their stocky build and short legs, they clamber over the rocky terrain on bluffs and grasslands close to the glaciers,

Looking for lunch The endangered grey fox inhabits the arid Patagonian steppes to the east of the ice field, where it survives on small mammals such as hares and rodents, birds, fruit and carrion from puma kills.

always alert to the presence of mountain lions, their only predator. Although this creature is fast and agile, and able to migrate vast distances in search of food, its population has been reduced by a loss of habitat to agriculture.

Changeable weather

Weather in the park is fickle. The mountains hold most of the moisture blown in from the Pacific Ocean, with fresh snow falling even in summer at high altitude. Winds blow up to 75mph (120km/h). Despite these conditions, there are sunny summer days with an average daytime temperature of 20C (68F) at the town of El Calafate and, at this relatively high latitude, the days are long: stretching out to 17 hours in midsummer.

Further east, the land is in semi-permanent rain shadow and buffeted by the constant drying wind, so the forests give way to the arid steppe of Patagonia, the realm of the grey fox, mara (a relative of the guinea pig) and flightless feathery rhea – a relative of the ostrich and emu – South America's largest bird.

best of the rest...

GLACIERS

■ Pakistan's **Biafo Glacier**, in the Karakoram Mountains, joins with the **Hispar Glacier** to form an ice highway stretching 60 miles (100km). It is the longest glacial system outside the polar regions. Today, hardy trekkers clamber along the Biafo Glacier to reach the Snow Lake, one of the largest basins of ice in the world. It is the realm of the wild snow leopard, but sightings are rare.

Biafo Glacier

■ Both New Zealand's **Fox Glacier** and **Franz Josef Glacier** are advancing rather than retreating. They descend from the Southern Alps in the Westland Tai Poutini National Park on the west coast, their terminal ice walls standing less than 300m (980ft) above sea level in lush temperate rain forest. Located 12 miles (20km) apart, they are easily accessible.

■ Alaska has more than 100,000 glaciers, the best of which are in **Glacier Bay National Park and Preserve**. Seven tidewater glaciers calve into the sea. While the Grand Pacific Glacier (credited with carving the bay) is receding, the Margerie Glacier is stable, and its entire length from Mount Root is visible from cruise ships travelling along the deep water close to the terminal wall. The mighty Johns Hopkins Glacier is advancing - it calves such huge masses of ice from its 76m (250ft) high face that even large ships keep 2 miles (3km) clear. The melting icebergs in the bay sometimes fizz and pop as they release trapped air, an effect known locally as 'bergie seltzer'.

■ The **Furtwängler Glacier**, close to the summit of Tanzania's Mount Kilimanjaro, the highest mountain in Africa, is a remnant of an ice cap that was once the dormant volcano's white crown, but which is disappearing fast. Furtwängler and Kilimanjaro's other lingering equatorial glaciers inspired Ernest Hemmingway to write *The Snows of Kilimanjaro*.

■ On the Chilean side of the southern Andes is the **Torres del Paine National Park** with the spectacular Torres del Paine (Tower of Paine). Torres means 'tower' in Spanish, while Paine is the local Indian word for 'blue'. These three granite monoliths are shaped by ice and rise up 2,500m (8,200ft). The area also offers Los Cuernos del Paine (Horns of Paine), the white tongues of the Grey Glacier; the awesome Valle del Francés with its views of Paine Grande; and the turquoise-coloured glacial waters of Lake Nordenskjöld and Lake Pehoé.

■ China's glaciers of the sacred **Jade Dragon Snow Mountain** in Yunnan province stand on one side of Tiger Leaping Gorge, one of the

Jotunheimen National Park

deepest river canyons in the world. The receding glaciers are the most southerly in the Northern Hemisphere and the most accessible in China. They are approached via a cable car and wooden stairs and, because of the effect of the high altitude - 4,680m (15,354ft) - some visitors hire oxygen bottles to combat the thin air. A local name for the mountain is Wuluyoucuige, meaning the 'place for lovers that die for their love'.

■ With Norway's two highest peaks - Galdhøpiggen and Glitterind - and many accessible glaciers within its boundaries, **Jotunheimen National Park** is the 'home of the giants'. In the nearby **Jostedalbreen National Park** is the Jostedal Glacier, a plateau glacier and the largest in mainland Europe. At both sites, visitors go glacier-trekking, including 'blue-ice walks' on the Nygard Glacier (a tongue of the Jostedal Ice Field), but always with an experienced guide.

Torres del Paine

GOLDEN GATE

The extraordinary span across the entrance to San Francisco Bay more than lives up to its reputation. A superlative example of Art Deco architecture, the Golden Gate is both a feat of engineering and an enduring symbol of San Francisco and the 'golden state' of California. From its completion in 1937 until 1964, it was the world's longest suspension bridge at 1,280m (4,200ft). The twin towers kept the world record for tallest suspension towers until 1998. The bridge derives its name from the burnished cliffs on either side of the blustery strait, christened 'Chrysopylae' in 1846 by Captain John C. Fremont, who became one of California's first senators. A century later no one bothered with ancient Greek anymore and the bridge became known by the English translation: the Golden Gate.

THE ULTIMATE BRIDGE?

What makes a bridge transcend mere stone and steel? Any span that has become a household name – the Brooklyn Bridge, Sydney Harbour Bridge or Tower Bridge in London – is equally icon and engineering wonder. The Romans took the first great leap forward with massive arched aqueduct bridges like the Pont du Gard in France. By the Middle Ages, bridges had become works

of art - as seen in the Rialto in Venice and the Bridge of the 33 Arches in Isfahan, Iran. The Industrial Revolution brought a golden age of aerial engineering, starting with the Niagara Falls Suspension Bridge in the 1850s. For the next hundred years, many in the West could name the world's longest bridge. Not so in recent times, as aesthetics have once again overtaken size as the criterion by which bridges are judged. Spans like the Millau Viaduct in France and England's Gateshead Millennium Bridge are both architectural and cultural icons.

PONTE VECCHIO

Henry Wadsworth Longfellow penned the finest words about Florence's fabled Ponte Vecchio: 'Florence adorns me with her jewelry. And when I think that Michael Angelo hath leaned on me, I glory in myself.' Built in 1345 across the River Arno, the Ponte Vecchio is a survivor of almost six centuries of natural disasters, warfare and general wear and tear. Giotto disciple Taddeo Gaddi designed the bridge as a combined transport corridor and marketplace where butchers, tanners and blacksmiths could hawk their goods. In the 16th century the bridge caught the eye of the Medici, the rulers of Florence, who added a second deck – the Vasari Corridor – above the merchant shops to link their palaces, and cast out the artisans in favour of goldsmiths and jewellers. The Ponte Vecchio is the only one of Florence's bridges to survive World War Two.

ITALY
Florence
Ponte Vecchio

Tyrrhenian
Sea

GRAND CANYON

Descending from the Colorado plateau into Arizona's mile-deep, river-hewn chasm is like stepping into a geological time machine. Forty different rock layers are exposed – some almost two billion years old.

No matter how many photographs or paintings of the Grand Canyon you've seen, nothing prepares the first-time visitor for its sheer jaw-dropping magnificence. Writers have searched for words to describe the experience. British author E.M. Forster called it 'the most astounding natural object I have ever seen'. Hard-boiled novelist Henry Miller literally cried on the brink of the enormous gorge. 'It's mad, completely mad,' wrote Miller,

WHERE ON EARTH?

The Grand Canyon stretches across half of northern Arizona between Lake Mead and Lake Powell. The nearest international airports are Phoenix, Arizona, and Las Vegas, Nevada. Most visitor facilities are in Grand Canyon Village on the south rim, accessible by highway and the daily Grand Canyon Railway.

NEVADA
UTAH
Grand Canyon
Las Vegas ●
CALIFORNIA
USA
● Los Angeles
ARIZONA
Phoenix ●
MEXICO

'and at the same time so grandiose, so sublime, so illusory that when you come upon it for the first time, you break down and weep with joy.'

Arizona's 'big ditch' is grand indeed, measuring 277 river miles (446km) long, 18 miles (29km) wide at its broadest point and a mile (1.6km) deep. A chasm

Sheer drop Toroweap Overlook is one of the narrowest and deepest points in the canyon. The rock layers here include lava flows and long-gone lake beds.

of similar size in Europe would stretch all the way from Paris to Amsterdam. And even if you doubled the height of the world's tallest building, Dubai's Burj Khalifa, and placed it at the bottom of the canyon, it would still not reach the rim.

Nature's forces

More than anything else, the Grand Canyon is testament to how water, wind and gravity – working in concert over millions of years – can bring extreme change to the Earth's surface, and even create an entirely new landscape. Nearly two billion years ago, the region that now supports the Grand Canyon was a shallow inland sea that gradually filled with silt, sand, mud and volcanic ash. Movements in the Earth's crust later compressed and uplifted these layers of sediment into a broad plateau that was subjected to further volcanic activity and other geological forces. Three hundred million years of steady erosion did the

rest, most of it carried out by the snow-fed Colorado River tumbling down from the Rockies' western flank on its turbulent journey to the Gulf of California.

The geological cross-section exposed by this erosion is one of the world's most complete. Almost 40 different rock layers span most of the best-known geologic timeframes, from the Late Precambrian to the Mesozoic 'Age of Dinosaurs' and the Cenozoic 'Age of Mammals'. The oldest rock is the dark grey Vishnu Schist along the banks of the Colorado, which was formed 1.75 billion to 1.73 billion years ago. But it's the orange, ochre and red rocks at higher elevations that leave the greatest impression, especially at sunrise and sunset, when the canyon walls glow like fire.

The chiselled buttes, pyramids and towers that speckle the gorge, even more than its sheer walls, give the Grand Canyon a charisma few other geological wonders can match. During his landmark

canyon survey of the 1880s, Clarence Dutton of the US Geological Survey gave them names such as Shiva Temple, Vulcan's Throne and Tower of Ra, drawn from ancient mythology and exotic faiths, linking the canyon with great civilisations of the past and endowing it with a whole new layer of mystique.

A range of habitats

Owing to its huge size and depth, the Grand Canyon harbours several major ecosystems, including five of the seven life zones found in North America. A descent from rim to river is the ecological equivalent of travelling from Canada to Mexico, a journey from boreal forest and subalpine grasslands to the stark, almost barren Lower Sonoran Desert. Altitude is the primary force in shaping these diverse ecosystems, but they are also affected by moisture levels: parts of the North Rim routinely receive 3–3.5m (10–12ft) of

Ancient store rooms Side canyons contain remnants of human habitation, as here in these cliff-face granaries in Nankoweap Canyon, which were used by the Pueblo people around AD 1050–1100.

snow each winter, while desert areas in the canyon bottom are lucky to receive 18cm (7in) of rain in a year.

Yet life survives, and even thrives, in the canyon. More than 1,700 types of plant are found in the Grand Canyon National Park, ranging from towering ponderosa pines and twisted junipers that pose along the rim, to the cacti, mesquite and sagebrush of the desert areas. With a constant water supply, the canyon's river habitats form rich, oasis-like pockets and 'hanging gardens' where willows, aquatic plants and even orchids grow around small ponds, springs and streams.

Animal life is highly diverse and specialised to deal with the variations in altitude, terrain and climate. At the top of the food chain are predators like the mountain lion and bobcat, which move in and out of the canyon in pursuit of prey. The largest creatures roaming the park are elk, mule deer and black bear. The canyon is also home to javelinas (wild pigs), skunks, porcupines, coyotes and many other mammals. Reptilian life ranges from six species of rattlesnake to delicate tree frogs and poisonous Gila

monsters. More than 370 bird species have been counted in the skies above and around the canyon, while the Colorado River hosts 17 different types of fish.

Human activity

Although their impact has been insignificant compared to that of mother nature, humans have long been part of the Grand Canyon, too. People have lived in the chasm for more than 11,000 years, going back to the last Ice Age. These ancient people were nomadic hunters and gatherers who left their mark in the form of temporary camps, caves and rock-art galleries below the rim. By around 3,500 years ago, people here were experimenting with agriculture, growing maize, beans and squash in places with permanent or seasonal water. In the so-called Formative Period (AD 500–1540), small villages were established in and around the canyon. The canyon's cliff dwellings were created at this time.

Captain Garcia Lopez de Cardenas and a small group of Spanish soldiers were the first Europeans to happen upon the Grand Canyon. Part of Francisco Vásquez de Coronado's expedition to find the fabled Seven Cities of Gold, they reached the South Rim in September 1540. It was another 200 years before Europeans saw the

canyon again. By the mid-19th century, Americans were exploring the canyon region, culminating in Major John Wesley Powell's epic three-month boat trip down the Colorado in the summer of 1869. As word of the massive, multi-coloured chasm spread across the globe, visitors flocked to the canyon, among them US President Theodore Roosevelt.

JOHN WESLEY POWELL
After losing an arm in the Battle of Shiloh during the American Civil War, Major John Wesley Powell headed west in pursuit of adventure and a career in natural history. He explored the Rocky Mountains, then set his mind on becoming the first person to navigate the Colorado River through the bottom of the Grand Canyon. Gathering upriver in the spring of 1869, Powell and his ten-man team had no idea what lay ahead in terms of terrain, water conditions or wildlife. Yet they plunged ahead, running the river in four small wooden boats that somehow withstood the violence of numerous waterfalls and rapids. Three months later the expedition emerged from the western end of the canyon, completing one of the most remarkable journeys in the exploration of the American West.

An ardent conservationist, he awarded the canyon federal protection after his 1903 visit. By 1919 it was listed as a national park.

Expanded over the years, Grand Canyon National Park is now one of America's largest, spreading across 1,904 sq miles (4,932km²) of northern Arizona. Over the last century more than 180 million people have visited the park, making it one of the world's most popular natural attractions.

Preserving the park

In recent years, park authorities have taken bold steps to return the canyon to a more pristine state. New flight rules limit helicopter and aeroplane traffic in the canyon and restore natural quiet. Private vehicles are banned on some popular rim roads, which are now accessible only on foot or by shuttle bus, many running on relatively clean natural gas. To reduce the park's reliance on outside energy sources, photovoltaic solar panels have been installed at the new South Rim Visitor Center and elsewhere in the park.

The authorities have also introduced measures to protect the park's historic structures, especially those in the South Rim's Grand Canyon Village Historic District. Many of these buildings are icons of American national park architecture. Opened in 1905, the El Tovar Hotel is a national historic landmark. The design is an eclectic clash of styles, including elements of Southwest Indian, California Mission,

Western pioneer and even Swiss Alpine. Pioneering architect Mary Colter designed several of the park's outstanding structures, including the pueblo-inspired Hopi House (1905), Desert View Watchtower (1932) and Phantom Ranch (1922) in the bottom of the canyon.

Native caretakers

Two Native American tribes – the Hualapai and Havasupai – are also caretakers of the Grand Canyon. Their reservations are along the West Rim and include many spectacular overlooks and side canyons. Most notable of the

Walking on air The cantilevered Skywalk bridge, whose design was inspired by views from a helicopter trip, suspends visitors in midair.

latter is Havasu Canyon, home to the small village of Supai and a number of spectacular waterfalls that plunge into turquoise pools. Farther west, the Hualapai have constructed the spectacular but controversial Skywalk – a U-shaped viewing platform with a glass floor some 1,200m (4,000ft) above the Colorado River. Visitors can walk out over the canyon for a bird's-eye view of this vast chasm, two billion years of history etched into its sheer sides.

best of the rest...

CANYONS AND GORGES

■ The massive **Barranca del Cobre** (Copper Canyon) in northern Mexico consists of a network of six canyons that merge into one another. Reached by a precipitous highland railway, the Ferrocarril Chihuahua al Pacífico, the canyon is home to a native people called the Rarámuri.

■ South America's most significant canyon is **Colca Canyon** in southern Peru, about twice as deep as the Grand Canyon but not nearly as steep. Famed for its resident condors, the gorge is still populated by indigenous people who farm the canyon's pre-Inca stone terraces.

Colca Canyon

■ Stretching more than 100 miles (160km) from end to end, **Fish River Canyon** in southern Namibia is the largest canyon in Africa and the world's third largest overall. The canyon's stark desert scenery is deeply reminiscent of the Grand Canyon, making it a popular hiking destination.

■ The River Danube's **Iron Gates Gorge**, a rock-and-water boundary separating Romania and Serbia in the central Balkans, is Europe's most spectacular gorge. From the time of prehistoric man to that of Roman legions and medieval knights, the chasm has a long and colourful human history. Several dams built since the 1970s have partially flooded the gorge, easing navigation.

■ **Yarlung Tsangpo Canyon** in Tibet, China, is considered by some to be the world's largest canyon, although this is disputed. Largely unexplored and inaccessible, the chasm plunges 6,009m (19,714ft) at its deepest point and stretches around 300 miles (500km) across the Tibetan plateau in southern China. The gorge was carved by the snow-fed Yarlung Tsangpo River.

GREAT **WALL** OF **CHINA**

Draped like a ribbon of stone across China's mountainous terrain, the wall created long ago to keep barbarians out now draws travellers in.

China's Great Wall is the most extensive, impressive and, in parts, remote defensive wall ever built by any people in history. Stretching right across northern China, it is actually a series of walls that have been built, linked, rebuilt and extended over a period of more than 2,000 years.

The wall's length is almost impossible to calculate. Estimates range from 1,500 miles (2,400km) to 3,100 miles (5,000km) for the wall built during the Ming dynasty (1368–1644), which runs from Shanhaiguan on the shores of the East China Sea to Jiayuguan near the edge of the Taklamakan Desert. In some areas two or three walls overlap each other; in others there are gaps. Long defensive spurs spread out from the main route, and many sections lie separate and disconnected.

The Ming wall

Before the mid-to-late Ming period, the majority of the walls were made of rammed earth and most remained so. China's Ming rulers took on the task of turning these defences into formidable fortifications.

What many people today think of as the Great Wall was built for the most part between 1522 and 1620. Averaging 8m (26ft) high and 6m (20ft) thick, it is made of rubble and earth clad with stone and topped with brick. Watchtowers rise above the main structure at strategic intervals. The style varies according to the terrain, the general in charge of construction, the available materials and the perceived level of threat. Most of the wall is wide enough for three or four horses to ride abreast, but at some particularly high points it narrows to a single strand of brick.

Though intimidating, the structure did not always succeed in deterring intrepid nomads, who worked their way around the ends of separate sections, found holes where the wall had not been properly maintained, outflanked the garrisons at key points or simply bribed their way in.

In 1549 the Mongols gave advance warning of an attack on Beijing. Despite the wall and the warning, Altan Khan was able to lead 700 mounted tribesmen up to one of the city's gates the following year. The wall-building intensified, costing up to three quarters of the Ming annual budget and contributing to the already tottering dynasty's collapse in 1644. Today most of the wall is dilapidated, and yet it still stands – a sprawling ruin of leaning battlements and crumbling watchtowers overlooking overgrown slopes.

the best because...

■ It is ancient: the earliest constructions date from the 5th-3rd centuries BC.

■ The Great Wall is the longest defensive structure ever built in the world.

■ In an unparalleled feat of engineering, the wall stretches between the highest and most inaccessible points in the mountainous terrain.

■ In places it is possible to turn through 180 degrees while keeping the wall in view at all times.

Stone border The restored Jinshanling section of the wall, just an hour's drive from Beijing, includes 60 watchtowers and many other original features.

GROS MORNE

Rugged, uninhabited mountain tablelands combine with glacier-carved lakes and fjords in this dramatic area of eastern Canada.

More than 600 million years ago, two of the tectonic plates that make up the Earth's crust collided far beneath modern-day Newfoundland and Labrador. The force of the impact thrust 1.3 billion-year-old chunks of the Earth's mantle and oceanic crust skywards, creating the massive rock outcropping known today as the Tablelands – now part of Gros Morne National Park. This stretch of Newfoundland's coast was further shaped by glaciers into a landscape of fjords and sheer cliffs, lakes and waterfalls, plateaus and coastal lowlands that make up one of Canada's most striking wilderness areas.

WHERE ON EARTH?

Gros Morne National Park is tucked into the coast round the Gulf of St Lawrence on the western edge of the Great Northern Peninsula of Newfoundland and Labrador, Canada. The main route through the park is Highway 430, which follows the coast heading north from the town of Deer Lake.

CANADA
NEWFOUNDLAND & LABRADOR

Gulf of St Lawrence

Gros Morne

Glacier-carved waters Western Brook Pond in the northern sector of the park is a freshwater fjord that has become cut off from the sea.

The park takes its name from Gros Morne Mountain. At 806m (2,644ft) this is the tallest peak in the park's four mountain ranges and second highest in the province of Newfoundland. The earliest known human habitation in the region dates back 5,000 years to the Maritime Archaic Indians who crossed the Strait of Belle Isle from Labrador. But it is the British explorer Captain James Cook who first mapped and named many of the area's natural features, including the Tablelands.

Earth's mantle exposed

The stretch of high, flat-topped mountains of orange-brown rock that make up the Tablelands are the most accessible place on the planet to observe exposed sections of the Earth's upper mantle, the rock layer normally found deep below the outer crust. Lacking the nutrients to support plant life and containing a high level of heavy metals, the sheets and slabs of exposed rock are bare and barren.

A hiking trail provides the best access to this rocky landscape, which can also be viewed from a boat trip on the 9-mile

(15km) long fjord known as Trout River Pond. Boat trips also allow visitors to explore Western Brook Pond, the national park's most spectacular fjord. Pissing Mare Falls, the highest waterfall in eastern North America, plunge 350m (1,148 ft) down precipitous cliffs into its serene, inky-black waters.

The park's wild inhabitants

A number of endemic animal species, including the Canadian lynx, live here. Sightings of moose, woodland caribou, red foxes and snowshoe hare are common along roadsides and hiking trails. Harlequin ducks, blackpoll warblers and two species of terns also breed here. Rock ptarmigan, members of the grouse family, are often spotted on the upper slopes of Gros Morne Mountain, along with arctic hares.

The park's exceptional scenery, coupled with its immeasurable geological and biological diversity, rank it not just among Canada's top national parks but also as one of the world's greatest natural treasures.

best of the rest...

LAND AND SEA

■ Located on the west coast of Scotland, **Applecross Peninsula** is defined by raw oceanic splendour and windswept vistas at every bend in the road. Quaint hamlets stretch around sheltered bays in what is considered one of the remotest places in the UK. It is only accessible via a single-track coastal road or a challenging mountain route over Bealach na Bà, at 626m (2,054ft) above sea level the highest pass in Scotland.

■ Formerly a private estate, the **Glenveagh National Park** is an unspoiled wilderness area in Ireland's County Donegal, noted for its pristine sylvan lakes, rugged mountains, deep peat bogs and glacier-scraped cliffs. Birch and oak forests host a thriving population of red deer. Golden eagles, a reintroduced species, soar above Lough Veagh, the park's main lake. A tour of the late-19th century Glenveagh Castle provides an insight into the property's history.

■ Several coastal inlets, or *rías*, interrupt the craggy coastline of Galicia in northwestern Spain. Known as **Rías Baixas**, these fjord-like fingers jut far inland from the Atlantic Ocean. The wild seascapes are offset by centuries-old villages and lush vineyards plump with grapes where *albariño* wines are produced. The frequent fog and rain give the area a mist-shrouded, ethereal quality, adding to its mysterious beauty.

GUGGENHEIM BILBAO

More famous than the art within, this radical museum set new standards of design and put its home city on the international map.

With its twisting curves and interlocking structures, all covered with a gleaming metallic skin, Bilbao's Guggenheim Museum seems to flex and stretch towards the sky. The shape of this titanium-clad building has been described as 'frozen motion'. Or is it like a huge metallic flower? Or a ship? From each viewpoint, the architecture suggests a different interpretation. And in this riverside setting Californian architect Frank O. Gehry has made the most of titanium's reflective properties and its ability to take on the colour of the changing light. Go on a misty day and the museum seems to hover over the adjacent Nervión River. At other times, the building glows golden in the sun or appears covered in silvery scales.

New approach to architecture

In designing this contemporary icon, Gehry made no reference to previous architectural styles. Instead, curving and sharp-edged forms appear precariously balanced on top of one other. But the building's innovation goes beyond its radical form. Gehry and his team used three-dimensional digital modelling and software designed for the aviation industry to create the free-form curves and calculate the exact specifications for the titanium, limestone and glass parts used in the building's construction.

Star of the show

The museum epitomises and celebrates the revitalisation of a decaying industrial city. In the 1980s, Bilbao's industries were in decline. Rebounding in the mid-1990s, Bilbao made the transition from a post-industrial to a service economy. It was supported in this by what has become known as the 'Guggenheim effect', where one unique building puts the whole city on the map.

The Guggenheim opened in 1997 with a collection that focused on artists working after World War Two. Sunlight floods in through the glass roof of the atrium, which leads to galleries displaying works by artists such as Mark Rothko, Andy Warhol, Gerhard Richter and Richard Serra. Since opening, the museum has had more than 10 million visitors. Yet it is the building itself – as much a work of art as anything found inside – that is the main attraction.

Is it a ship? Seen from the Nervión River, the museum's flowing shapes resemble an ocean liner. Guarded by Jeff Koons' flower *Puppy* (right) it makes a surprising sight set against Bilbao's narrow streets.

best of the rest...

INNOVATIVE ARCHITECTURE

■ A building's facade usually conceals its interior workings, but the **Centre Georges Pompidou** in Paris does the opposite: giant pipes for air and water, electrical conduits and escalators inside large glass tubes are on display on the building's exterior. They give the building, designed by Richard Rogers and Renzo Piano in the 1970s, a futuristic look, though some of the apparently structural components are purely decorative.

■ The roof of the pilgrimage chapel of **Notre Dame du Haut** in Ronchamp, France, designed by Swiss architect Le Corbusier, looks like a sail billowing in the wind, supported by gently curving walls. Inside, the roof appears to float above the walls, an effect achieved by raising it on low columns widely spaced around the top of the walls. Windows between the columns allow light to stream into the building.

■ The **German Chancellery** was built in 1999, following German re-unification. The main facade allows views into and through the building, emphasising the government's idea of transparent politics. The Chancellery demonstrates that official buildings can be playful, representative and monumental simultaneously.

HALONG **BAY**

Generations of artists and photographers have attempted to capture the dreamlike quality of these exquisite limestone seascapes.

O f all the extraordinary limestone landscapes in the world, many of which are to be found in the Far East, the most beguiling is the watery world of Vietnam's Halong Bay. Restored junks drift in and out of the bay's waterways, their distinctive sails, shaped like the wings of a moth, silhouetted against a surreal backdrop of jagged peaks. At dawn, clusters of conical hills emerge from wreaths of mist over the water, their tops appearing to float in

midair. Kayaks bearing passengers set off from the junks to explore secret lagoons, secluded beaches, caves bristling with stalagmites and stalactites, and floating fishing villages. The television aerials that poke from the tin roofs of village houses bring a touch of the present to these timeless waters.

Formed by rain and sea

Halong Bay means the 'Bay of the Descending Dragon'. At the dawn of Vietnam's history, so the legend goes, the gods sent a family of dragons down to Earth. Out of their fiery mouths spewed forth a stream of jade and jewels that solidified into the almost 2,000 precipitous pillars and spectacularly sculpted islands in the bay, forming a

WHERE ON EARTH?

Halong City in Vietnam, 105 miles (170km) east of the capital, Hanoi, is the gateway to Halong Bay in the Gulf of Tonkin. Spread over an area of more than 600 sq miles (1500km²), Halong Bay is best visited between November and March, although there is a chance of rain at any time of year.

VIETNAM
• Hanoi   Halong City
Halong Bay
Gulf of Tonkin

Aquatic maze The waters of Halong Bay wend their way around seemingly endless strings of limestone cliffs and islands. Overleaf: A passing junk is dwarfed by one of Halong's many sea stacks.

barrier more than 100 miles (160km) long against invaders from China.

In fact, the rock that forms these gemlike islands was once part of the sea bed, a layer of sedimentary rock made up of the compacted fossilised shells and skeletons of countless tiny sea organisms. Over the course of hundreds of millions of years, forces deep within the Earth raised this layer of rock high above sea level and exposed it to the elements. Torrential rains, which are such a feature of the region in summer, seeped into fissures in the limestone; and the acid in the rainwater etched channels in the easily eroded rock. These were then exploited by the incoming sea, eventually leaving towers, or islands, several hundred feet tall: all that remains of what was once a vast limestone plateau. The tropical climate and monsoon rains nurtured the vegetation on these islands, swathing them in a deep emerald green and endowing them with rich biodiversity.

best of the rest...

LIMESTONE LANDSCAPES

Huanglong Valley

■ Like Halong Bay, the limestone landscape of **Huanglong Valley** in Sichuan province, China, is a UNESCO World Heritage site. And also like Halong Bay, it is named after a dragon: *Huanglong* means 'Yellow Dragon' in Chinese and the valley is said to resemble a golden dragon as it winds through dense forest on either side. For a stretch of 2.2 miles (3.6km), the Huanglong River cascades over a series of waterfalls between ponds formed by limestone deposits. The opal waters of the ponds, framed by the golden tracery of limestone, evoke the scaly skin of a dragon.

■ Limestone landscapes are popular locations in James Bond films. Halong Bay featured in *Tomorrow Never Dies*, while **Phang Nga Bay** was the setting for *The Man with the Golden Gun*, filmed on Khao Phing Kan off the south coast of Thailand. The sheer limestone outcrops soar 300m (1,000ft) into the sky from the turquoise waters of the Andaman Sea, and the brilliant white beaches are among the most beautiful in the world.

HAIDA GWAII

Primeval rain forests, ancient monuments, unique wildlife and a traditional way of life survive in harmony at the very edge of the world.

Untouched for centuries, fairytale temperate rain forests of giant western red cedar and Sitka spruce grow right down to Canada's Pacific shoreline. Bald eagles soar overhead and black bears forage on the beach. Pods of killer whales stalk seals off the rocky coast, and tightly packed carpets of brightly coloured starfish litter the shallows. This is Haida Gwaii, the 'islands of the people', the only place in the world where a national park protects everything, from the top of the highest mountain to the depths of the surrounding ocean. In 2005, the region was selected as the top national park in the whole of North America.

The islands in question – the more northerly Graham Island and Moresby Island to the south of it, surrounded by clusters of smaller islands (as many as 150 in total) – lie a short distance out

WHERE ON EARTH?

Haida Gwaii is 60 miles (100km) west of the British Columbia coast. The islands were formerly called the Queen Charlotte Islands, but on June 3, 2010, they became officially known as Haida Gwaii. Scheduled daily flights and a regular ferry service operate between the mainland and the islands.

CANADA

BRITISH COLUMBIA

Haida Gwaii

Queen Charlotte City

Pacific Ocean

Towering tradition Carved totem poles several metres high dot the forest. Trees are felled for carving, then the finished poles are re-erected.

from Canada's northwest coast. The park is the Gwaii Haanas (Islands of Wonder) National Park and Haida Protected Area, which occupies the southern third of Moresby Island. The people, thought to number fewer than 4,000 today, are members of the Haida Nation.

Ravens and eagles

For more than 13,000 years, Haida folk have lived in harmony with the land and the sea. They are skilled seafarers and traders, taking to the water in ocean-going canoes with 60 paddlers. They revere the plants and animals among which they live, and this is reflected in their highly stylised memorial and mortuary poles, many of which are more than 100 years old.

These 'totem' poles of elaborately carved cedarwood are unique to the people of the Pacific Northwest. The vertically stacked crests, usually depicting local animals, show the lineage of the owner and whether he or she is a child of the Raven or of the Eagle clan, the two principle clans recognised here. Many poles have three human figures carved into their upper sections, representing lookouts – known as Guardian Watchmen – whose job was to guard the land and sea and who raised the alarm when enemies approached.

During summer, modern-day Haida watchmen guard the surviving poles and ancestral longhouses in the earliest settlements, known as First Nation

villages, the best preserved of which is on the island of SGaang Gwaii, off the southernmost tip of Moresby Island. The watchmen are now hosts rather than warriors, ready to beguile visitors with intriguing tales of their cultural and natural heritage.

Galápagos of the north

The islands are exposed to the full wrath of the Pacific Ocean and winds are often strong. Waves reaching 35m (115ft) high crash onto their western shores; more rain falls in the west than in the gentler, sheltered east. The abundance of moisture sustains ancient, moss-covered

Mortuary pole Totem carving is done by skilled craftsmen, who then paint the wood in bright colours using natural pigments. Each carved figure represents a different story in the owner's life.

temperate rain forests harbouring animals whose predecessors sought refuge here during the last Ice Age, for the islands remained ice-free.

When the ice on the mainland melted, these creatures became isolated on the islands and subsequently evolved into new subspecies. This is a feature the islands share with the Galápagos Islands much further south – hence their nickname, 'Galápagos of the north'. Haida Gwaii's subspecies of black bear, for instance, is the world's largest, with a massive skull and large crushing cheek teeth. When the salmon are running, the bears catch what they can, but they are careless and discard much of the fish. Then Haida Gwaii's subspecies of stoat moves in, along with the real eagles and ravens, to pick at what's left on the bones.

Coastal wildlife

A million-and-a-half seabirds fill nesting colonies around Haida Gwaii's coastline. At Delkatla Wildlife Sanctuary in the north, migrating birds such as endangered sandhill cranes travelling the Pacific Flyway put down to refuel.

Inshore are kelp forests and eelgrass meadows, and a rich intertidal zone hides the rare northern abalone. Offshore, humpback whales feed on shoals of herring and krill, grey whales stop by on their migration north and, recently, blue whales, the largest known animals to have lived on Earth, have made a welcome return for the first time in decades.

HAWAII VOLCANOES

Created by a hot spot in the middle of the Pacific Ocean, Hawaii's volcanoes show the Earth's dynamic forces in action, illustrating in dramatic fashion how it changes every day.

Situated on the southeast side of Big Island, the U-shaped Hawaii Volcanoes National Park has two of the world's most active volcanoes – towering Mauna Loa and slow-slung Kilauea. As these and many other volcanoes are readily accessible in the park, visitors can witness the continuing birth of the Hawaiian Islands in real time.

The park itself sprawls across one of the largest wildernesses in the Pacific Ocean: 505 sq miles (1,308km²) of lava fields, volcanic desert, cinder cones and glowing lava rivers framed by lush rain forest, rugged coastline and high-altitude ecosystems that seem more like arctic tundra than a tropical island.

Long mountain

Mauna Loa looms over the park, and indeed the whole island, a beast of a mountain that is often impossible to

WHERE ON EARTH?

Hawaii Volcanoes National Park is on Hawaii's Big Island, the most southerly of the island group. The Visitor Center is 30 miles (48km) south of Hilo on State Route 11 and 90 miles (145 km) from the Kona Coast (via Naalehu). Camping is permitted at several spots, with indoor accommodation at the hamlet of Volcano.

USA
HAWAII
● Kohala
BIG ISLAND ● Mauna Kea
● Hualalai ● Hilo
Mauna Loa ● ● Kilauea
Hawaii Volcanoes
National Park
Pacific
Ocean

MAUNA KEA

Big Island's third great volcano, Mauna Kea (meaning 'White Mountain') is older and less active than its neighbours. At 4,205m (13,796ft), the top is higher than Mauna Loa, making it the world's highest mountain when measured from its base on the ocean floor to its summit - about a tenth taller than Everest. Perched at the top is the world's largest collection of observatories for optical, infrared and submillimeter astronomy: only skilled drivers make it to the summit in 4WDs. Further down the mountain is the Onizuka Center for International Astronomy. 'White Mountain' alludes to the snow that sprinkles Mauna Kea in winter, prompting locals to bring out skis and snowboards.

see from the coast because its massive bulk is regularly shrouded in mist. The name means 'long mountain' in the Hawaiian language, an apt description of its elongated, loaf shape. Rising 4,169m (13,678ft) above sea level, it is one of the highest peaks in Polynesia. Snow is not uncommon during winter months, and temperatures at the summit often plunge below freezing. But that only tells part of the story, because Mauna Loa extends a further 5,486m (18,000ft) below the surface of the sea, part of a massive seamount that is actually the largest mountain on the planet in terms of mass.

Constant flow of lava

Being a classic shield volcano, Mauna Loa's eruptions are slow and quiet compared to fire-breathing conical stratovolcanoes. But they happen often: 33 times in the past 150 years, about half on the summit and the remainder in the rift zones and radial vents on the mountain's flanks. One radial event, in 1877, occurred below sea level. Although they may not be spectacular, Mauna

Sunrise glow Sparks fly and the eastern sky is obliterated during a dawn eruption of Kilauea. A long trail of lava moves slowly down towards the coast.

Loa's eruptions often produce copious amounts of molten lava that slowly but surely flow into the ocean. Mauna Loa's dynamic plate tectonics also produce severe and frequent earthquakes; past quakes have measured as high as magnitude 8 on the Richter scale.

Kilauea is a marked contrast. Although it is also a shield volcano, it is so low it can hardly be called a mountain. The squat volcano is more like a giant hole punched into the Earth's surface. But size and shape can be deceptive because Kilauea is rated the world's most active volcano. Over the last 150 years, it has erupted 61 times. The current episode has been going on since 1983 – the planet's longest and most consistent volcanic event. Although these eruptions are usually mild mannered, Kilauea can erupt with explosive fury, producing violent events that take human life. Given this hyperactivity, it comes as no surprise that the name means 'spewing' or 'much spreading' in the native language.

The volcanoes trace their roots to underwater volcanic activity that probably started around a million years ago. Researchers believe that Mauna Loa broke the surface around 400,000 years ago, forming the 'seed' that sprouted into Big Island. The summit collapsed 660,000–700,000 years ago, leaving a deep caldera. Kilauea is younger, its first underwater eruption pegged at 300,000–600,000 years ago. Both volcanoes squat on the Pacific tectonic plate atop a huge plume of upwelling magma. Although the hot spot remains fixed, the plate itself is gradually shifting westwards at a rate of 13cm (5in) per year. Eventually – perhaps half a million years from now – the volcanoes will no longer be over the hot spot and will become extinct, while new volcanoes start to grow from the seabed.

Human activity

The island's first human inhabitants were Polynesian settlers, who arrived from the South Pacific around 1,600 years ago. Once established, about 800 years ago, they evolved a completely independent Hawaiian culture, with a healthy respect for the volcanoes and their geothermic power. Those who lived in the shadow of the volcanoes left a rich assemblage of archaeological evidence: temples, tombs, trails, canoe landing sites, rock art and

PELE'S CURSE
The Hawaiian goddess of fire and lightning, Pele is said to dwell in the Halema'uma'u Crater at the bottom of Kilauea. According to legend, all of Big Island's volcanic activity is an outward expression of Pele's heartbroken pining for a long-lost lover. It is also said that anyone who carries away volcanic stones from the area is cursed - until those stones are returned to their rightful place. Even in modern times, the US Post Office at the volcano site and local hotels occasionally receive packages containing volcanic rocks from visitors who claim they were afflicted with bad luck after taking them home.

carvings etched in the cooled lava. There are even footprints preserved in hardened ash, remnants of house platforms, caves and livestock pens.

The arrival on the Big Island of English explorer Captain James Cook, in 1778, set the stage for European exploration. British naturalist Archibald Menzies made the first recorded ascent of Mauna Loa in 1794, his climbing party surviving on coconuts harvested at the coast.

Changing coastline Constantly seeping lava from Kilauea spills into the ocean. The ebb and flow of the sea water moulds the lava as it cools, creating new layers of rock along the coast.

In 1823, the missionaries William Ellis and Asa Thurston made written records of the eruptions on Kilauea. It was Thurston's grandson, a Honolulu newspaper publisher, who led the early 20th-century drive to establish a national park based around volcanoes on Big Island and Maui, a dream that came to fruition in 1916. Hawaii Volcanoes became a separate reserve in 1960.

Rare plants and animals

While the park's volcanic activity and landscapes are its main attractions, rare flora and fauna inhabit ecosystems that have evolved here in almost complete isolation for 70 million years. Among the park's distinct biological zones are the coast and ocean areas, woodland, rain forest, subalpine and alpine (aeolian) regions.

Endemic plants and animals range from koa trees and the threatened high-altitude silversword plant, to the equally vulnerable nene geese, Hawaiian petrel and pueo short-eared owls to critically endangered hawksbill turtles. There are carnivorous caterpillars, the largest dragonfly in the United States, crickets

that cluster around new lava, and Hawaii's only native mammal – a bat.

Hot magma hikes

Visitors have been travelling to the park since the 1840s, when the Volcano House hotels were established on the

Rare beauty To save the native silversword, volunteers have planted more than 10,000 seedlings on Mauna Loa since 2000. Nearly all survive.

rim of Kilauea caldera. The oldest of these (dating from 1877) now houses the Volcano Arts Center. Most of the park's 1.6 million annual visitors stick to the Crater Rim Drive that circles Kilauea, the Chain of Craters Road down the coast and Holei Sea Arch, leaving most of the park virtually deserted for those who choose to venture off the main roads. A network of trails runs through the remote wilderness areas of Ka'u Desert, Napau Crater and secluded shorelines such as Apua Point. Two trails climb to the summit of Mauna Loa, where a cabin provides overnight shelter and fresh water.

Because of the region's dynamic and dangerous character, the park authorities are vigilant when it comes to volcanic activity. Roads, trails, camping grounds and other facilities are closed at a moment's notice, especially when the northeast trade winds weaken and poisonous fumes, such as sulphur dioxide, infiltrate the visitor areas. Hikers are advised to move uphill and upwind of any eruptive activity they may come across.

At their own risk – and against the advice of the Park Service – hikers also venture into the active lava-flow zone between Pu'u O'o Crater and the coast in the park's eastern section. This hike is most often done in the late afternoon or early evening to view the molten lava glowing neon orange in the dark as it creates the newest land on Earth.

best of the rest...

VOLCANOES

■ The Canary Islands off the northwest coast of Africa are in an active volcanic zone. The archipelago's **Pico del Teide** on Tenerife is the world's third-highest volcano, at 3,718m (12,198ft) and, because the islands are governed by Spain, is technically Spain's highest mountain. **Timanfaya** volcano on Lanzarote rises from a multicoloured landscape that is said to resemble Mars.

■ Perched at the eastern end of Siberia, the Kamchatka Peninsula is one of the globe's most active volcanic regions. Of the

Karymsky Volcano

160 volcanoes in the area, 29 are still active, including the massive **Klyuchevskaya Sopka**, the largest active volcano on the Eurasian landmass. **Karymsky** is the most active volcano in the eastern section. Kamchatka's most renowned volcano is the perfectly conical and perpetually snowcapped **Kronotsky**.

■ Italy's smouldering giants are **Mount Etna** in eastern Sicily, **Mount Vesuvius** near Naples and **Stromboli**. Etna is in an almost constant state of eruption and produces vast amounts of lava. It has erupted more than 60 times in the past 400 years, including four events since the turn of the 21st century. Vesuvius is notorious as the volcano that destroyed the Roman cities of Pompeii and Herculaneum in AD 79.

■ **Piton de la Fournaise** (meaning 'Peak of the Furnace') lies on the French island of Réunion in the Indian Ocean. Its cauldron-like caldera is 5 miles (8km) wide and is surrounded by high cliffs on the rim. The caldera is breached to the southeast and drops to the ocean. Research suggests that further collapse could cause a megatsunami.

HEIDELBERG

Cupped by the wooded valley of the River Neckar, Heidelberg has been a centre of academic learning for 600 years. University life is threaded into its soul, but it wears the weight of its history lightly.

The very best university cities are more than the sum of their parts: the university is an integral and indivisible part of the city's personality. Heidelberg is just such a place. Amid modern shops, offices, cinemas and hotels are the old university buildings: colleges and faculty departments, libraries and lecture theatres, student halls of residence and grand assembly

rooms where degrees are bestowed on each year's crop of graduates, dressed for the occasion in gowns and mortarboards.

Old university towns are quite unlike other towns and the students are a big part of that difference. The universities

Heidelberg panorama The wooded hinterland, historic castle, compact street layout and delightful river combine to make the city a perfect place to study.

WHERE ON EARTH?

Heidelberg is set on the River Neckar, in the state of Baden-Württemberg in southwestern Germany. It is 11 miles (18km) southeast of Mannheim. International travellers fly into Frankfurt airport, 50 minutes away by train. Choose term-time to visit, to witness the vibrancy of the university life.

pride themselves on their hard-earned academic reputations, shored up by time-honoured traditions and historic buildings, and every year they receive a new injection of the very brightest young people, who spill out into the streets and reinvigorate the city.

Germany's oldest university

Founded in 1836, Heidelberg has all the gravitas and poise that centuries of excellence imbue, but what strikes the visitor first is its beauty. Mark Twain was a fan, and spent almost three months here in 1878, describing his experiences in his travelogue *A Tramp Abroad* (1880). Staying at a hotel above the castle, he wrote, 'I have never enjoyed a view which had such a serene and satisfying charm about it as this one gives…The town lay, stretched along the river, its intricate cobweb of streets jewelled with twinkling lights… One thinks Heidelberg by day – with its surroundings – is the last possibility of the beautiful, but when one

sees Heidelberg by night, a fallen Milky Way, … he requires time to consider upon the verdict.'

The view Mark Twain admired is still there today. Occupying the southern bank of the River Neckar, the Altstadt (Old Town) is clustered around two central squares. The Universitätsplatz (University Square) is the original home of the university and still its focal point. The Marktplatz (Market Square) is the site of the Gothic Heiliggeistkirche (Church of the Holy Ghost), completed in about 1400, and the city's most prominent landmark. For more than 200 years, up until 1936, the church was divided in two in a most unusual way: one half (the choir) was for Catholics, the other (the nave) for Protestants. It is now a fully Protestant church with an austere but elegant interior. The old university buildings, including the faculties and the library, are scattered around the town and along the main street, the Hauptstrasse.

The dominant style of Heidelberg's historic buildings is Baroque: very little of the medieval city remains. The old city gate, at the southern end of the Carl-Theodor Bridge, is a rare survivor, albeit adorned with Baroque pepperpot crowns; so too is the Marstall, the stable block and arsenal built by the river in 1510, now used as a dining hall. But these are exceptions because serious damage was caused to the old city by Louis XIV of France. In a bid to wrest control of the region during the War of the Palatinate Succession, Louis' troops laid siege to Heidelberg in 1689, occupied it, then razed it to the ground in 1693. The city

White towers Visitors who enter the Old Town over the stone bridge are greeted by the Haspeltor gateway of 1788, with its bell-top Baroque towers.

was swiftly rebuilt in the Baroque style of the era, but on the same medieval street plan. The result is architectural grandeur on an intimate footprint.

The Schloss

One part of the city that was not rebuilt was the Schloss, a red sandstone castle set in woods above the city centre and an inseparable part of Heidelberg's landscape. This was the castle of the prince-electors of the Palatinate of the

HORTUS PALATINUS

When Frederick V and Elizabeth Stuart, daughter of James I, married in London in 1613 they were just 16 years old. In contrast to most dynastic marriages, this proved to be a love match. Back in Heidelberg, Elizabeth created a beautiful garden in the Italian Renaissance style next to the castle. Designed by the French hydraulic engineer Salomon de Caus, it contained a series of flower and topiary terraces, statues, grottoes, mazes, trick fountains, a water organ and even mechanical singing birds. Named the Hortus Palatinus, it was held to be a marvel of its day and dubbed 'The Eighth Wonder of the World'. Its glory was short-lived: work stopped when Frederick and Elizabeth were exiled, and the garden was used as an artillery base during the ensuing Thirty Years' War. But today it is still possible to trace the rudiments of this magnificent monument to pleasure.

Rhine, one of seven Electors who ruled on behalf of the Holy Roman Emperor and selected future emperors. So Heidelberg was not just home to one of Europe's most respected universities; it was also a centre of power.

During the 18th century, Charles Theodore, Count Palatine and Elector of Bavaria, started to rebuild the castle, but in 1764 it was struck by lightning and work ceased. It remains a curious hotchpotch of medieval and Renaissance ruins attached to restored interiors from the 18th, 19th and 20th centuries. This blend of grand ambition and decay appealed to Romantic poets, who flocked to Heidelberg in the 19th century.

Early days

The valley of the River Neckar has been inhabited since pre-history: the jawbone now on display at the Kurpfälzisches Museum is a copy of an original bone that belonged to 'Heidelberg Man', a 600,000-year-old precursor of Neanderthal Man and *Homo sapiens*. Wind the clock forward and you also find a Roman fort and a 9th-century Christian abbey set on the Heiligenberg, or Holy Mountain, a possible origin of the city's name.

Conrad of Hohenstaufen, half-brother of Holy Roman Emperor Frederick Barbarossa, took over Heidelberg's castle in 1155, and made it his base as Count Palatine of the Rhine. Elector Rupert (or Ruprecht I) founded the university in 1386. It soon became a magnet for

> **"** I have never enjoyed a view which had such a serene and satisfying charm about it as this one gives. **"**
>
> MARK TWAIN
> *A TRAMP ABROAD* (1880)

academics across Europe and heralded the university's first heyday. The rise of Protestantism and the religious disputes and wars of the 16th and 17th centuries sent Heidelberg and its university into the political and economic doldrums.

Fraternity culture

The city was injected with a new lease of life under Charles Frederick, Grand Duke of Baden, in the 19th century.

As a result of his patronage, the official name of the university is now Ruprecht-Karls-Universität (or Ruperto Carola), in honour of its two founders, who lived four centuries apart. By the time Mark Twain came to Heidelberg in the 1870s, the university's reputation was restored and it attracted students from around the world, especially America. It had its own local traditions, not all of which enhanced its reputation.

The all-male student body split into drinking clubs, each with their own rules and uniforms – notably, natty peaked caps – and consumed unbounded quantities of alcohol. If students misbehaved, they were arrested by the university constables and thrown into their own prison, the Studentenkarzer – a spell in which was considered essential for any self-respecting student. Their graffiti and initials can still be seen gouged into the woodwork of the Karzer, and the echoes of these traditions still

Heidelberg castle The ruins host annual cultural festivals and provide a dramatic backdrop for open-air music performances.

reverberate in the student pubs, such as the 17th-century Zum Seppl and the 18th-century Zum Roten Ochsen. The militaristic aspect of the student drinking clubs also manifested itself in character-building 'academic fencing', or Mensur, a tradition founded in Heidelberg. Participants wore padded protection and goggles, but left their faces exposed so that cheeks would be vulnerable to razor-sharp swords and were often left with a scar – evidence of bravery and a source of pride.

Perhaps the greatest monument to Heidelberg's reputation for copious drinking is the 'Heidelberg tun' (Grosses Fass), one of the world's biggest wooden barrels and a key side-attraction – along with the Apothecary Museum – of the castle. Constructed in 1751 and estimated to have a capacity of 195,000 litres (43,000 gallons), it is the youngest survivor of a series of four huge barrels that supplied wine to the castle refectory. Legend recalls tales of the gargantuan drinking feats of an 18th-century court jester who was put in charge of the tun. He was nicknamed Perkeo, supposedly from the Italian *perchè no?* (why not?), which was always his response when offered a drink. The story goes that when Perkeo was in his eighties and fell ill, his doctor mistakenly gave him water to drink, which proved such a shock to his system that he promptly died.

Spared from bombing

During the 1930s, Heidelberg proved fertile ground for Nazism; the leading Nazi architect Albert Speer was brought

University lecture hall For more than 300 years students have defended their doctoral theses and received their degrees in this hallowed chamber.

up in the city. Another legacy of this era is an outdoor amphitheatre called the Thingstätte, set on the Heiligenberg above the city, and one of many built for Nazi rallies. The site is still used for concerts and festivals.

The US fascination with Heidelberg grew during the Nazi era, enhanced by the successful Broadway musical *The Student Prince* (1924), which was set in the city. American money helped to fund the Neue Universität, built in the heart of Heidelberg, just when the university was collapsing as a third of its staff, many Jewish, were forced out by the Nazis.

Heidelberg was spared Allied bombing during World War Two, mainly because it had no strategic industries, but also because of its reputation as a venerable

university city. After the war, it became the headquarters of the US Army in Europe, and later of NATO's Allied Land Forces in Central Europe. The military base to the south of the city has a housing area named Mark Twain Village.

The University of Heidelberg remains a leading research university and home to the Max Planck Society for the Advancement of Science. Just as Goethe, the Romantic poets and Mark Twain wandered along the 'Philosopher's Walk' and enjoyed the city's views, modern students can absorb what makes Heidelberg the ideal university city.

best of the rest...

UNIVERSITY CITIES

■ Founded in 1134 and given a royal charter in 1218, the University of **Salamanca** rose to be Spain's most celebrated medieval university. With a skyline dominated by two magnificent cathedrals, the city has numerous historic university buildings, as well as a thriving modern university.

■ The hilltop city of **Perugia**, in Umbria, Italy, has preserved the face of its medieval and Renaissance past in its churches, public buildings and art collections. Its original university, founded in 1308, is now based at a former monastery.

■ The University of **Oxford** – 'city of dreaming spires' – is the oldest in the English-speaking world, dating back to the 11th century. The students live in colleges around the city; many of these retain their original courtyards and wood-panelled dining halls. The university also boasts the Radcliffe Science Library, housed in the Palladian Radcliffe Camera building.

Radcliffe Camera, Oxford

■ A group of academics broke away from Oxford in 1209 to form another university at **Cambridge**. With the River Cam meandering through it, the city is startlingly picturesque. Old Court in Corpus Christi College is the oldest enclosed courtyard in the university and one of many highlights.

■ The University of **Michigan** was founded in Detroit in 1817, but moved to Ann Arbor in 1837, and since then the city – still priding itself on its 'small-town' charm – has grown up around its four main campus areas. Among the university's landmarks are the neoclassical Angell Hall, the 1930s Burton Memorial Tower, with its keyboard-operated carillon, and the Earl V. Moore Building designed by Eero Saarinen in the 1960s.

IGUAZÚ FALLS

Thundering water and colossal power are the hallmarks of the world's greatest waterfall, where water pours over the edge of the Paraná plateau like an ocean pouring into an abyss.

WHERE ON EARTH?

The Iguazú (Iguaçu) Falls straddle the border between Brazil and Argentina, where the Iguazú River runs off the Paraná plateau. The falls lie about 1,850 miles (3,000km) from both Buenos Aires and Rio de Janeiro, and are accessible from Argentina's Cataratas del Iguazú airport and Brazil's Foz do Iguaçu airport.

PARAGUAY • Foz do Iguacú **BRAZIL**

ARGENTINA • Iguazú Falls

Cataratas del Iguazú •

Stretching for more than 1.5 miles (2.4km), the Iguazú Falls – where the Iguazú River pours over the rim of the Paraná plateau – are the world's widest true waterfall, wider than Victoria Falls, and second only to Niagara in average annual flow (Iguazú exceeds Niagara at the peak of its annual flood).

In the local Guaraní language, *iguazú* simply means 'big water'. It's a fitting name, for these falls are immense, made up of nearly 300 individual waterfalls and cataracts, each with its own name, with rocky, palm-crested islands separating the silver cascades.

When the river is in full spate, and tinted red with iron-rich silt, 12,800m³ (452,000cu ft) of water plunges down the 80m (260ft) drop every second. Half of it ends up in the long, narrow, U-shaped chasm known as the Devil's Throat, where the river pours in from 14 waterfalls around its three sides. On a clear day the spray creates sparkling, dancing rainbows in the gorge. The river marks the border between Brazil and Argentina, and the Devil's Throat is divided between the two.

The first Europeans to set eyes on the Iguazú Falls arrived in 1541. They were an advance party travelling with the Spanish explorer Álvar Núñez Cabeza de

Cascading colour Blue sky, green forest and red silt in the water complement the rainbows that form within the Devil's Throat.

Vaca, one of only four survivors of the ill-fated Narváez Expedition to North America. The Spanish were drawn by the roar of crashing water, which can be heard several miles away. The Alvar Nuñez Falls on the Argentinian side are named after the explorer.

Open to the world

After this discovery, the region was left undisturbed by outsiders for more than 300 years. Only the native Tupi-Guaraní tribes lived here and, sporadically, a Jesuit mission. But in 1902, Carlos Bosetti (whose name was given to the picturesque Bosetti Falls) and Jordan Hummel

BIG BANG
Iguazú Falls formed when hard basalt rock resisted natural erosion to create the lip of the falls. Softer rocks were washed away to form the narrow chasm. The hard rock, known as 'flood basalt', formed from solidified lava that spewed out during a volcanic eruption about 132 million years ago. This eruption is thought to have been the single largest explosion to have taken place on Earth. The same basalt rocks are found in Namibia, in southern Africa, because at that time Africa and South America were joined as one continent. Despite the hardness of the basalt, it is eroding very slowly, so that the falls are moving upstream at a rate of about 1m (3ft) every thousand years.

organised the first tourist trip to the falls, and floodgates of a very different nature were unleashed as visitors came from far and wide to see this natural spectacle.

The right bank of the Devil's Throat cascade – about 20 per cent of the total falls – is in Brazilian territory. The rest is in Argentina. Walkways and trails on the Argentinian side enable

spray-soaked waterfall-watchers to get right into the action, the upper circuits overlooking the drop and the lower circuits positioned next to the thundering water. Buses, helicopter tours, a train and boats venture right into the Devil's Throat.

The falls are home to a wealth of wildlife, especially birds. Swifts and

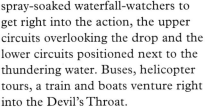

Under the falls Boat tours into the Devil's Throat allow visitors to feel the full power of the spray and view birds that nest on the rocks.

swallows swoop around the cascading water. Large numbers of aerobatic great dusky swifts nest and roost on the basalt rock walls behind the falling curtains of water, which keep them safe from predators. They are one of the few species of swift to perch on exposed rock, clinging with their sharp, curved claws and supported by their stiff tails. They construct cup-shaped nests made from moss and stones, held together and securely 'glued' to the wall with a mixture of mud and saliva.

The swifts fly directly through the deluge rather than around it. This carries a risk of being swept away and drowned, so they have developed special techniques

Dramatic catwalk Viewing platforms take visitors to the very edge of the plateau at the top of the falls on the Argentinian side.

for flying in and out. On their way in, they turn on their side to reduce resistance through the water. When leaving, they first drop vertically behind the waterfall to gain enough speed to punch their way out. They fly low over the river or high over the forest to catch the flying insects on which they feed, returning to the falls to feed their chicks and rest.

An altogether bigger bird, the striking but endangered black-fronted piping guan, occupies rocks close to the falls. It has jet-black feathers flecked with white, a bright red throat wattle with an electric blue base, white rings around the eyes and a distinguished white crown of slicked-back feathers on its head – unmistakable and unforgettable.

Rain-forest jewels

The waterfalls are surrounded by lush, emerald-green, sub-tropical forests that are protected as national parks. Orchids, bromeliads and begonias, palms and ferns thrive, and the forest is radiant with the bright red flowers of the ceibo, or Cockspur coral tree – Argentina's national flower – and the vivid pink or stark yellow blossoms of trumpet trees,

Water-loving bird The chestnut-eared araçarí mainly frequents wet habitats near lakes, rivers and flooded ground.

or Ipês. The rare 40m (130ft) tall Palo Rosa tree is a favourite with bees and beekeepers for the fine nectar produced by its flowers. Several species of toucan are common, including the chestnut-eared araçarí with its yellow belly and red breast. The vinaceous-breasted Amazon parrot – which has green plumage with a hint of red on the breast – is rarer. Even more extravagant is the metallic green of the sparkling violet-ear, a hummingbird that beats its wings so fast it hovers in front of the flowers on which it feeds.

Upstream, the river supports Yacaré caimans. Bat hawks hunt for dragonflies by day and small bats at night. Snail kites search for apple snails and butterflies, including the Turquoise Emperor, are everywhere. Huge harpy eagles soar above.

Hidden deep in the forests are South America's most charismatic mammals – tapirs, anteaters, ocelots, capybara, hogs and deer, although they are hardly ever seen. The elusive jaguar also lives here and the footprints of these excellent swimmers and climbers can often be seen along the riverbanks. They prey on other mammals, as well as turtles, lizards, birds and fish. Coatis, on the other hand, are common around the falls, and will approach visitors and even eat out of their hands.

best of the rest...

WATERFALLS

◼ The waters of **Angel Falls** pour down from a remote flat-topped mountain, or tepui, that towers over the Venezuelan rain forest. At 979m (3,212ft) high, they are the highest in the world. The water drops 807m (2,648ft) in one cascade, splattering in rapids and cascades across a slope at the base of the falls. Angel Falls are named after Jimmie Angel, who saw the falls from his plane in 1933 and crash-landed at the top in 1937. Locally it is named Kerepakupai Merú, meaning 'waterfall of the deepest place'.

◼ The three cascades of **Niagara Falls**, Horsehoe, American and Bridal Veil, on the Canada-USA border have the greatest average water flow of any waterfall. The falls lie on the Niagara River that drains from Lake Erie into Lake Ontario. They are significant because of the combination of height and volume of falling water. The falls are moving back by up to 60cm (2ft) each year, and will eventually disappear into a series of rapids.

◼ Yosemite's **Bridalveil Fall** in California is a mere 190m (620ft) high but charms viewers with its swaying flow as the waters move in

Angel Falls on Auyantepui

the wind. The waters thunder down just after the snow melts in May and June; at other times the flow is weaker.

◼ While Iceland's Dettifoss is Europe's most powerful waterfall, it is **Gullfoss** to which visitors flock. The waterfall plunges into the canyon of the Hvítá River in two drops at right angles to each other, the first with a drop of 11m (36ft) and the other at 21m (69ft). The canyon runs on again at right angles to the bottom waterfall. The river seems to disappear into the ground because the waterfall flows into the recess.

◼ On Africa's Zambezi River, on the Zambia-Zimbabwe border, are the **Victoria Falls**, or Mosi-oa-Tunya, 'the smoke that thunders'. Named by David Livingstone after Queen Victoria, the falls have, during the flood season, the largest single sheet of falling water in the world, more than 1,600m (5,250ft) wide and 108m (354ft) high. The water plunges into a transverse canyon and drains through to deep, steep-sided gorges.

KAKADU ROCK PAINTINGS

An extraordinary legacy of rock paintings has survived in the stone-sheltered galleries of Kakadu National Park, revealing 20,000 years of culture and day-to-day living.

WHERE ON EARTH?

Kakadu National Park is 155 miles (250km) east of Darwin in Australia's Northern Territory. In the dry season the road to the park's northern entry (Arnhem Highway via Stuart Highway) is accessible by conventional vehicles; in the wet season only 4WDs can make it. Airstrips at Jabiru and Cooinda in the park offer scenic flights.

Darwin · Jabiru · Kakadu National Park
AUSTRALIA

Aboriginal people have lived on the vast lands bounded by Australia's Kakadu National Park for at least 50,000 years. Evidence of their occupation is scattered throughout, and includes campsites, stone tools and grindstones. Concealed in the rugged stone country of the drier south is their greatest legacy of all: more than 5,000 art sites that make up the world's greatest concentration of rock art.

Ranging in age from more than 20,000 years old to the present day, the art represents one of the longest records of any group of people on Earth. Covering the walls and ceilings of rock shelters are paintings illustrating the activities of ancestral beings said to have roamed the country forming its features. They show the relationship of the people to the land, the plants they gathered and the animals they hunted. The earliest paintings, dating from the time of the last Ice Age, when the sea level was lower and the climate drier, show animals now extinct. The most recent depict the first contact with Europeans.

Revealing layers

For the Kakadu artists, the primary purpose was to tell a story rather than leave an image for posterity, so paintings were often superimposed one over another. Distinctive artistic styles are associated with three environmental phases: the pre-estuarine, estuarine and freshwater periods. The oldest (pre-estuarine) images are direct imprints of hands and objects onto the rock, paintings of land animals and stylised human figures carrying boomerangs.

About 8,000 years ago, the rising sea levels that followed the end of the Ice Age transformed river valleys into estuaries. New foods, such as barramundi fish and crocodiles, appear in the art of this estuarine era, as well as new tools such as spear-throwers. A new art style also emerged, known as X-ray painting for its detailed representations of the skeleton and internal organs.

About 1,500 years ago, a build-up of silt blocked the inflow of salt water, and freshwater wetlands replaced the tidal flats. Once again new game, such as magpie geese and water turtles, and plants such as the waterlily with its edible tuber, were reflected in the art. The style was still X-ray, but became more decorative than anatomically accurate.

The best-known sites are at Nourlangie Rock and Ubirr, a rocky outcrop close to the food-rich waters and floodplains of the East Alligator River. Rock art at Ubirr includes depictions of possums and wallabies, barramundi and turtles, and a thylacine (Tasmanian tiger). Standing 230m (755ft) above the surrounding plain, Nourlangie Rock is the site of the large Anbangbang rock shelter. In regular use for at least 20,000 years, its walls are a gallery layered with paintings.

Estuarine art Paintings at Ubirr depict a barramundi fish and two figures, male and female. They are typical of the style known today as X-ray painting.

best of the rest...

ROCK PAINTINGS

■ The **Tassili N'Ajjer National Park** in southeast Algeria comprises a vast and barren plateau fissured into rugged 'forests' of rock. These eerie wind-and-sand-sculpted formations date back 70 million years. Surrounded by the Sahara Desert, the area is home to some of the most important prehistoric art in the world, an astonishing collection of more than 15,000 rock paintings and engravings depicting aspects of the evolution of human life, animal migrations and climate change. The images include many animal species, such as giraffe, rhinoceros and horses, long gone from this once-fertile region.

■ Sometimes referred to as the Sahara Desert's 'secret garden', the spare grandeur of the **Ennedi Plateau** in northeastern Chad, with deep gorges cut by long-vanished watercourses, forms a sandstone bulwark against the stretching desert. Over the millennia erosion and increasing aridity have produced stark, rocky landscapes and sheer-sided sandstone canyons that are home to a collection of rock art. The sweep of history depicted here includes animals such as early horned cattle and giraffe, as well as village life, musicians and hunting scenes.

Tassili N'Ajjer National Park

KANHA NATIONAL PARK

India's largest national park is billed as the 'land of the tiger' and offers the best chance of seeing the majestic Asian tiger in the wild.

'It was seven o'clock of a very warm evening in the Seeonee Hills …', wrote Rudyard Kipling at the beginning of his classic tale, *The Jungle Book*. Those hills, glowing first pink then gold in the setting sun and now deep in Kanha National Park, were his inspiration. Shere Khan is here, the tiger being one of Kanha's top predators, along with Bagheera the leopard (although Kanha's are spotted rather than black), Baloo the sloth bear and Tabaqui the jackal. Sadly, Akela the wolf is becoming increasingly rare, but is replaced by the dhole, or Indian wild dog.

They all live in India's Kanha National Park (which includes the Kanha Tiger Reserve) in the Central Indian Highlands of Madhya Pradesh, recognised as the most beautiful reserve in the whole of India. At its core are two main river valleys,

WHERE ON EARTH?

Kanha National Park is in the Mandla and Balaghat districts of Madhya Pradesh, 110 miles (175km) southeast of Jabalpur. There are three airports in the region: Jabalpur, Raipur and Nagpur, all with roads to Kanha. Tour operators and (infrequent) buses serve the towns near the park.

Jabalpur • 　Kanha National Park
Nagpur • 　• Raipur
INDIA
Bay of Bengal

the Banjar and Halon, surrounded by forested mountains, ravines, meandering streams, meadows and plateaux known as *dadar*. From Bamni Dadar, the highest point in the reserve, the sunset over the jungle is stunning, earning Bamni the nickname Sunset Point. When the reserve was designated, the area's villages, such as Ourai and Sondar, were cleared of people and are now home to the wildlife that gathers to drink from the communal pools and ponds once used by the villagers.

Green valley gems

The sheer variety and quantity of birds and animals in the reserve ensure satisfaction for nature lovers. The

Reaching up Kanha is the only home of the endangered hard-ground barasingha, which inhabits the large tracts of grassland mixed in with the forest.

highland forests of haldu and bija trees are filled with the song of painted partridges and golden orioles, carefully observed by speedy Shaheen falcons flying overhead. The lowland forests of sal trees and bamboo are interspersed with meadows ('maidans') and populated by tigers, whose arrival is greeted by a cacophony of alarm calls from other animals, especially the cry of the peacock. The grasses are vital food for herbivores such as barasingha swamp deer – brought back from the brink of extinction in a conservation success story. The Kanha barasingha differ from their northern relatives by living on hard ground, rather than in swamps. They share the territory with blackbuck, chital and langurs.

Warning signs

Langurs and monkeys spot an approaching tiger or leopard from lookout posts in the trees, while the chital deer can smell the big cat's presence from afar, so the

Tree house Despite their size, tigers are good climbers and quite at home in trees, whether in pursuit of prey or in search of shady places to take a nap.

two species stick together and warn each other of danger. Safari jeeps wind their way carefully through the forest so that visitors can observe the unfolding animal drama in real time.

The forest around Bamni Dadar is also home to sambar, barking deer, Indian gaur (wild ox), wild boar and the chousingha (four-horned antelope). This small, primitive species is no higher than 60cm (2ft) to the shoulder. Male chousingha have four horns, rather than the usual two – an unusual arrangement among mammals.

Nocturnal mouse deer, or chevrotains, have recently been discovered here, too, so with the food chain working from the ground up, this is a huge natural larder for hungry carnivores … paradise for Shere Khan.

best of the rest...

ASIAN NATURE RESERVES

■ When western Sichuan's Wolong National Nature Reserve, China's most famous Giant Panda sanctuary, was hit by the 2008 earthquake, the door was opened on other important conservation areas - most importantly at **Foping National Nature Reserve** in Shaanxi's Qinling Mountains, which has the greatest density of pandas in China.

■ The southern part of Mount Everest sits in eastern Nepal's **Sagarmatha National Park**. The higher slopes of this region of mountains and valleys is the terrain of snow leopards and Himalayan black bears, along with tahrs, serows and gorals (goatlike mammals), yak, blood pheasants and choughs.

■ Japan's **Jigokudani Monkey Park** is the only place in the world where Japanese macaques bathe in hot springs. Jigokudani means 'Hell's Valley', for steam and boiling water flow from the ground, and the monkeys take full advantage. In summer they forage in the forest, but in winter they take a daily warming bath here, before returning to the forest and surrounding cliffs to sleep.

Jigokudani Monkey Park

KERALA'S BACKWATERS

THE ULTIMATE WATERWAY?

The quiet waterways around Alleppey, south of Kochi, are typical of the Kerala backwaters in southwest India, where lakes and lagoons are linked together via a complex system of rivers and canals. Creating an extensive 560-mile (900km) network, the waterways serve a number of thriving communities, while providing the only access to remote corners of this tranquil coastal state. Kerala's backwaters have natural beauty and character in abundance. Waterborne travellers dodge flocks of ducks on narrow channels bordered by parrot-haunted palms that lean in over the water to form green tunnels. Houseboats, their elegant superstructures sitting atop the wooden hulls of ancient cargo vessels, ply the waters alongside battered waterbuses used by traders carrying supplies to remote villages and swarms of children going to school.

INDIA

Kochi ●
● Kerala's Backwaters

SRI LANKA

What is it about a channel of water – natural or man-made – that elevates it into a place of wonder? Is it the rippling light, the peaceful landscapes, or the diversity of plant and animal life along the banks? Or is it age-old traditions kept alive by waterside communities who depend on canals linking lakes and lagoons, such as along Kerala's backwaters or Ontario's Rideau Canal?

Or is it the cleverly engineered canals themselves, the earliest known examples of which were built in ancient Egypt? Locks were the great invention that allowed a canal to take a direct route across uneven terrain. Pound locks, consisting of a chamber with lock gates at both ends, were in use in medieval Europe. The Canal du Midi in France, which opened in 1681, was the first to use series of locks to tackle steep elevations, providing a template for the expansion in canal-building that occurred during the early Industrial Revolution.

BRITAIN'S CANALS

The five-lock ladder at Bingley in Yorkshire, on the Leeds and Liverpool Canal, opened in 1774. At 127 miles (204km), the Leeds and Liverpool is the longest canal in Britain. Altogether, Britain is criss-crossed by a total of more than 2,220 miles (3,540km) of threadlike canals. Once bustling with activity, they were the highways of the early Industrial Revolution. Usurped by railways and then roads, much of the network fell into disuse, but an enthusiastic campaign led to extensive restoration. Reminders of the past are everywhere along the canals, in centuries-old lock gates and aqueducts. A few traditional painted narrowboats survive and are now used mainly for pleasure boating. They have a cruising speed of 4mph (6km/h), so the pace of life is slow and wildlife flourishes along the tranquil canal banks.

KHAO SOK NATIONAL PARK

An ancient living Eden survives in a small corner of southern Thailand. One of Asia's unspoilt treasure houses of native flora and fauna, it is a real-life Jurassic park.

Khao Sok is a new destination for globetrotters, but it is also one of the Earth's ancient places. Nowhere else will visitors be greeted by the sign 'Beware Wild Elephants!' perched alongside a sheer rock wall, be eaten alive by leeches, shower with a spider the size of a hand, or sleep with a vivid green snake.

The Khao Sok National Park is a place of superlatives, for it lays claim to being the largest virgin rain forest in Thailand, a remnant of one of the oldest evergreen rain forests in the world stretching back as much as 160 million years. With the influence of the oceans on both sides – the Gulf of Thailand to the east and the

Scattered islands Limestone towers pierce the surface of Cheow Lan Reservoir, which was formed by flooding a valley in the park.

WHERE ON EARTH?

Khao Sok is in the Surat Thani province of Thailand, a 90-minute flight from Bangkok. By road, the park is off route 401, 75 miles (120km) from the city of Surat Thani on the Gulf of Thailand, and about 40 miles (60km) from Takua Pa on the west coast. It is 140 miles (230km) north of the main holiday resorts of Phuket.

Andaman Sea to the west – even during the ice ages there was sufficient moisture for the forest to flourish and the creatures here to survive. This long-term stability has given rise to an amazing diversity of plants and animals that is thought to rival that of South America's Amazon Basin.

Giant flowers, giant trees

On most days, the thick fog that envelops the park in early morning is burned off by the rising sun to reveal an enchanted land of sheer-sided limestone towers, pillars and crags. Gentle waterfalls cascade across glistening rocks, and mysterious caves lined with pipelike stalactites and stalagmites provide a home not only to colonies of chirruping bats but also swifts that build nests of solidified saliva, the main ingredient of bird's-nest soup. These swifts use echolocation to find their nests in dark caves.

The floral jewel in Khao Sok's crown, and the symbolic flower of Surat Thani province, is *Rafflesia kerrii*. Known locally as *bua phut* (wild lotus), it is

one of the world's largest flowers. Although the flower is spectacular to look at, it gives off a foul smell similar to decomposing meat, a crafty trick of the giant red bloom to attract fly pollinators, rather than bees. The plant lives parasitically on wild lianas and its flowers blossom for one week only. Rafflesia grows in the perpetual gloom of the forest floor, which perhaps explains why the flower is so big and bold.

Giant dipterocarps, named for their two-winged fruits, are the dominant trees on the Thai-Malay Peninsula. They reach 70m (230ft) tall and take 50–60 years to mature before flowering. They are one of the emergent rain-forest

Flower power The only visible part of the parasitic *Rafflesia kerrii* plant is its flower, which is up to 80cm (2ft 8in) across and smells like rotten meat.

species, so-called because they push out above the canopy layer, growing side-by-side with coconut palms, bamboos, lianas and several species of fig. These include the sacred fig, or Bodhi tree, under which the Buddha was said to have attained enlightenment; the weeping fig, the official tree of Bangkok; and the notorious strangler fig that spreads in a lattice around the trunk of a host tree, eventually squeezing the life out of its host in the never-ending battle for light in the forest.

Forest voices

At about 5:30am or thereabouts, the forest canopy starts to resonate with the voices of the dawn chorus as the entire landscape comes alive – barbets, cuckoo-shrikes, francolins and bulbuls. The singers are not all birds; around

6am, the eerie and mournful territorial song of the white-handed gibbon dominates the forest. By the time the sun is up, the birds and gibbons are joined by the chatter of troops of monkeys, including the striking spectacled langurs and the dusky leaf monkeys.

Langurs are easy to spot: they have long tails, dark body hair with light patches on the chest and the top of the head, and white rings around the eyes. They feed on leaves and fruits in the treetops for a couple of hours in the early morning and again in the late afternoon. The biggest surprise are their babies, which are a bright orange colour.

In the carpet of mosses and ferns on the forest floor live centipedes the length of a forearm, with a painful bite to match, and some of the biggest scorpions

on Earth. Record-breaking snakes are here, too, including several species of cobra: the king cobra, which grows up to 5.6m (18ft) long, is the world's longest venomous snake. Other giants include the reticulated python, the world's longest constricting snake, measuring up to 10m (33ft) in length.

At night, golden tree frogs and thousands of buzzing insects take over the jungle chorus, while fireflies flicker in the trees, bulge-eyed slow lorises peer out from behind branches and huge, colourful atlas moths, with wingspans of 30cm (1ft), adorn tree trunks as they rest from the frantic search for a mate.

Water, water, everywhere

Exceptional rains maintain the rain forest. Influenced by the northwest monsoon from the Pacific and the

Native primate The white-handed gibbon varies in colour from black to light brown and is named for its distinctive white hands. It also has a white facial ring.

southwest monsoon from the Indian Ocean, Khao Sok is the wettest place in Thailand, with an annual rainfall of 3.5m (11.5ft), the heaviest rains falling between May and November. All that water feeds into rivers and waterfalls.

Hiking trails follow rivers that flow to the centre of Khao Sok and a vast body of standing water, the Cheow Lan Reservoir, a man-made lake, where visitors lodge in floating raft houses, oblivious to the drowned villages beneath the surface. The views of

the karst landscape from the Cheow Lan Reservoir are unrivalled. Isolated limestone islands resemble clenched fists thrust into the sky. Some of these rock projections are covered with trees that grow down to the water's edge; others are mere slithers of rock with vertical faces that plunge down into the emerald waters. Even at midday, wisps of mist float across the tips of the sculptured strata. Where the rock has been eroded by water, it resembles the trickle of molten wax from a candle.

Animal and bird event

The forests around Cheow Lan are prime habitat for Asian elephants, gaur, sunbears, tapirs, mouse deer, bamboo rats and the rare clouded leopard, the supreme climber of the big cat family. In the trees are flying lizards and myriad birds: 18 separate species of woodpeckers, including small groups of great slaty woodpeckers, the world's largest; ruddy kingfishers with unusual rusty red plumage, a bright red beak and a yellowish breast; Asian palm swifts that glue their nests to the undersides of palm leaves; and great and helmeted hornbills, two species that are under threat due to poaching because the hard casque on their bill can be carved like ivory.

Human impact

Khao Sok National Park has had a chequered history. People are thought to have lived in the area for at least 50,000 years, but were not recorded until the 19th century, when refugees

> ### MADE FROM THE SEA
> About 225 million years ago, the limestone rocks of Khao Sok were a coral reef on the floor of a shallow sea. It is thought that they were part of a reef five times the length of Australia's Great Barrier Reef. The limestone sediments were pushed up at the same time that the Himalayas were formed, about 66 million years ago. Today, some mountains are almost 1,000m (3,300ft) in height, three times that of the limestone hills in nearby Phang Nga Bay.

from a Burmese war hid in the forest. The new community felled many trees. Most of the permanent residents were wiped out by an epidemic in 1944. A few survivors moved away, and the derelict village that remained was named Ban Sop, or 'village of the dead'.

The forest had time to recover, but its erratic history of human settlement continued. In the 1960s, a trunk road was built linking the east and west coasts, which allowed access for tin miners and loggers. By the 1970s, the true ecological worth of Khao Sok was acknowledged and the mining and logging slowly ceased. In the late 1970s, rebel students camped in the mountains to avoid being caught by the army. It was fortuitous that neither the students nor the military had much impact. The forest breathed a sigh of relief once again.

Deadly waters

In 1980, Khao Sok was designated a national park but also the site for the Rachaprapha Dam hydro-electric power project. This required a vast area of the park to be flooded to create the Cheow Lan Reservoir that feeds into the dam. Ahead of the flooding, gestures were made towards relocating the wildlife, but most of the affected animals died when their irreplaceable habitat was destroyed. Five villages were also evacuated and flooded. The loss of habitat and species was a serious setback, but again the forest proved resilient and wildlife populations are building once again. Rangers now patrol the region, and the government supervision of tour operators ensures that a balance is maintained between nature and human activity.

Elephant safari Visitors to Khao Sok can get closer to wildlife if they explore the jungle by elephant than if they had gone on foot.

best of the rest...

PROTECTED RAIN FORESTS

■ **Dzanga-Ndoki National Park** in the Central African Republic has the most spectacular rain-forest clearing - Dzanga Bai, meaning 'village of elephants'. Hundreds of forest elephants congregate to dig nutritious minerals from the sandy soil. Bongos and sitatungas (two species of antelope), hogs and gorillas come, too, and the park itself has the highest density of western lowland gorillas in Africa.

■ Brazil's **Jaú National Park** is the largest forest preserve in the Amazon. It encompasses the River Jaú and its

tributaries. These are 'blackwater' rivers that are stained the colour of tea by the moving mass of decomposing leaves. Amazonian manatees, giant otters and river turtles are found in the rivers, while harpy eagles, jaguars, bush dogs and endangered spider monkeys live in the adjacent forest.

■ **Loango National Park** in Gabon is described as 'Africa's Last Eden'. It is an idyllic habitat, where the rain forest comes right down to the ocean shore. Elephants, buffalo, hippos, gorillas and even leopards venture out of the forest and onto the white sandy beaches. Some animals even bathe in the sea - the 'land of surfing hippos'. It is the leading example of a protected African rain-forest lagoon.

KRAKÓW

Buyers jostling for the best deal, the chatter from street cafés rising in the air and centuries of history clinging to ancient monuments – what else could it be, but the quintessential medieval market square?

WHERE ON EARTH?

Kraków lies in southern Poland, not far from the Slovak border and approximately 150 miles (250km) south of Warsaw. There is an international airport 7 miles (11km) to the west of the city, which is also well connected by train. Much of the old town is pedestrianised and easily accessed by public transport.

Baltic Sea

GERMANY   POLAND   ●Warsaw

Kraków

CZECH REPUBLIC

SLOVAKIA

With a history steeped in trade, the arts and academia, Kraków is one of Poland's oldest cities. It was the country's capital until 1596, when the royal court moved to Warsaw, and so has more than its share of majestic monuments. Wawel Royal Castle, once the seat of Poland's kings, occupies a low outcrop above a bend in the Vistula River. Next door stands the magnificent Gothic Wawel Cathedral, where Pope John Paul II was ordained as a priest in 1946. Church, state, scholarship and science – all are richly represented in the unique architectural heritage of this city. But the feature that encapsulates Kraków's identity and the tone of its old town, defining what is truly distinctive about the place, is the huge medieval market square – the biggest in Europe – right in the heart of the city: the Rynek Główny.

In honour of commerce

The city's main square has been the focus of the community for well over 700 years. Built specifically for commerce, it has hosted a market from the very beginning, though these days the stalls sell flowers, jewellery, gifts, postcards and guidebooks rather than the exotic imports and everyday staples of former times.

Kraków's residents have always been as interested in enjoying the square's atmosphere and gossip as in doing business. Generations of Cracovians have come here to take in the scene – to stroll and sit, to eat and drink, to talk and flirt, to revel and to riot. Cafés, restaurants and bars line all four sides of the square. In summer, customers sun themselves at outdoor tables or dive into beer cellars to seek the shade. In winter, the weather may be colder, but the mood is just as warm: New Year celebrations seem to last for weeks. Today, as in medieval times, carnival reigns in the week leading up to the start of Lent, with people partying before the yearly fast. Inevitably, the square is the focal point of festivities as the merrymaking crowds mill around the foot of the Adam Mickiewicz Monument, oblivious to the patriotic poet's austere gaze.

But it hasn't always been convivial fun here. Throughout Kraków's history, the Rynek Główny has been the stage on

> **" Generations of Cracovians have come here to take in the scene – to stroll and sit, to eat and drink, to talk and flirt, to revel and to riot. "**

which important events have been played out. The square, like much of the city that stands today, began its life in the extensive rebuilding that followed the sacking of Kraków by the Mongols in 1241 and again in 1259. It was from here that, at depressingly frequent intervals throughout medieval and early-modern times, angry crowds sallied forth to vent their frustrations on the city's Jews. It was also here, several centuries later, that scores of civilians were killed when troops violently broke up a demonstration by striking workers in 1923. On the positive

Vast open space Measuring approximately 200x200m (650x650ft), and with its origins in the 13th century, the Rynek Główny remains Europe's largest medieval town square.

side, in 1794 military leader Tadeusz Kościuszko took an oath to lead his people in the struggle against Imperial Russia and the kingdom of Prussia, who had both annexed parts of Poland. The uprising failed, but it inspired the Poles in their fight for liberty and for what Kościuszko called 'the universal freedom'. The movement has continued to be an inspiration to patriots over the years.

Building prosperity

The Rynek Glówny is rightly renowned for its architecture. It is enclosed by rows of handsome terraced townhouses, or *kamienica*, most of which date back to the 15th century or even earlier. Among them are four medieval mansions that were put

The Sukiennice Continuing to function much as it has for 400 years, Kraków's indoor market also houses an important art museum on its upper floors.

together and given a Baroque facade by a 17th-century nobleman. The resulting Krzysztofory Palace became Kraków's Historical Museum in the Communist era and has remained so ever since.

If there is a single building that can claim special synonymity with the city's history and identity, it is the long, arcaded Sukiennice, or cloth hall, running across the middle of the square. There has been a cloth hall of some description in the square since the beginning of the 14th century, when a makeshift roof was raised

across two facing rows of stalls. A more permanent structure burned down in 1555. Its replacement was built in the Renaissance style, but with Gothic touches that hark back to medieval times. Look closely at the parapet wall running round the roof of the Sukiennice and you will see that the carved ornamental features are not classical flourishes – as they at first appear to be – but grotesque, typically medieval gargoyle-like faces.

There is no disputing the grandeur of the cloth hall. Built to function as the city's trading centre, the Sukiennice was also intended to impress as a symbol of Kraków's pride and prestige, its enterprise and ambition. More specifically, the building was an acknowledgement of the honour owed to trade and industry in a city whose prosperity was based on commercial success. Kings and dukes had their palaces – why not craftsmen and merchants? Not to live in, but for doing business in; a place where they could display their wares and do the deals that underwrote the affluence of the Kraków community as a whole.

The cavernous interior of the Sukiennice offered the perfect space in which tradesmen from the city and from the world beyond could meet, walk and talk, and show off their wares out of the reach of wind and rain. Outside, long arcades (added during extensive renovations in the 19th century) open directly onto the square, providing protection to the market stalls.

best of the rest...

CITY SQUARES

■ **Naqsh-e Jahan Square** in Isfahan, Iran, was built in the early years of the 17th century, when the Safavid Dynasty was at its height. It is a serenely beautiful space with stunning mosques and palaces on every side. At its northern end is an entrance to the Isfahan Bazaar - one of the oldest markets in the Middle East.

■ Bustling **Jemaa el-Fna** in Marrakech, Morocco, is a delight by day, but it comes into its own as evening falls. Then, the food stalls open and street entertainers - from dancers and musicians to fire-eaters and storytellers - come out in force.

Jemaa el-Fna, Marrakech

■ Just about every historic town in Europe is centred on a picturesque square, but for a rival to Kraków's try Prague's Old Town Square, **Staromestske Namesti**. Perhaps the most intriguing sight is the elaborate astronomical clock on the town hall, built in 1410 and the first of its kind in Europe.

■ Despite its imposing title, the **Plaza de la Independencia** in Quito, Ecuador, feels intimate by comparison to other city squares, like a friendly city park. With a fine cathedral on the west side, a presidential palace on the north side and other colonial gems, the square has as its centrepiece a memorial column for the martyrs of the independence struggle. Most of all, though, this is a place for walking and talking, with trees and shrubs providing colour and shade.

By the mid-16th century Kraków's merchants had earned the right to be well housed. They had helped to turn the Polish capital into a major market centre. In particular, they had made it a hub for the long-distance trade in textiles. Woollen fabrics woven in and around Kraków were brought here to be loaded onto mule trains heading west into Silesia and Germany and east to the Danube and the Black Sea region – where European merchants could meet up with Saracen traders who had contacts along the Silk Route to the Far East.

The arterial east-west route intersected at Kraków with another major trading route that led north up the valley of the Vistula River to the Hanseatic ports of the Baltic coast and south through Slovakia and Austria to the Adriatic Sea and Italy. In addition to textiles, locally produced livestock, timber, salt, grain, furs and metals were all exported along these routes. Returning merchants brought with them many luxuries – oil and wine from southern Europe; manufactured goods such as armour and jewellery from the north; exotic silks and spices from the east. And while the region's craftsmen, merchants and farmers flourished, the Polish Crown and Kraków's government also thrived as everything was subject to taxation and customs duty.

Of bricks and bugles

A magnificent town hall once stood beside the Sukiennice. Built from stone and brick, it epitomised the wealth of the community that built it. The Gothic tower is all that remains of the 13th-century structure, but it is sufficient to give visitors a sense of the medieval city's self-confidence. St Wojciech's Church dominates the southeast corner of the square. Partially rebuilt in the Baroque style in the 17th century and given a stuccoed facade, the church looks much younger than it actually is. In fact, it dates from the 10th century.

In the northeast corner of the square stands the Gothic masterpiece, St Mary's Basilica. Built from brick, it may look strange to visitors accustomed to the symphonies in stone that can be seen in France or England – in cathedrals such as Notre Dame, Chartres or Salisbury – yet brick was very much the norm in northern Europe. Its use in Kraków is a reminder of the long-standing trading relationship that the city enjoyed with northern Germany and the Hanseatic states. The church has a quirky, asymmetrical

aspect – two slender towers stand side by side, one slightly shorter than the other – which has helped it to transcend its status as a local landmark and turned it into an iconic image for the Polish diaspora around the world. Every Pole recognises the five-note bugle blast that is sounded four times on the hour every hour (once to each point of the compass) from a windowed chamber high up in the taller of the two towers. The call at noon is broadcast on the radio nationwide. The custom commemorates the courage of a trumpeter who, tradition has it, tried to sound a warning of the Mongol attack in 1241, but was cut off when an arrow hit him in the throat.

St Mary's Basilica This church on Rynek Główny is particularly famed for its wooden altarpiece, carved in the late-15th century by Bavarian sculptor Veit Stoss.

A heroic tale, yet history is as much about the everyday experiences of ordinary people as it is about high deeds and epic adventures. This is the chronicle that the Rynek Główny implicitly records. It is stirring to imagine Poland's kings processing through the square in all their pomp, but it's just as evocative to think of their subjects congregating here over the years. To walk here and soak up the atmosphere, or sit quietly at one of the many cafés, provides the opportunity to reflect on a scene that has scarcely changed for centuries.

LALIBELA

A group of churches hewn out of solid rock around 800 years ago continues to lure pilgrims to a remote part of the Ethiopian highlands.

The patchy scrub and scattered trees do little to soften the rough edges of the jagged crags and rocky ridges of the Amhara hills, and the churches near the village of Lalibela make the effect seem starker still. There is something supremely awe-inspiring about a structure that has been carved out of the landscape, literally sculpted from the native stone.

Some of the churches are concealed in deep pits, others stand in quarried-out caves. Light pierces the dark interiors through intricately carved windows in the shape of Maltese and Roman crosses, squares and semicircles, illuminating the decorative mouldings, pillars, carvings of saints and wall paintings within. A network of tunnels and passageways with galleries and crypts link groups of neighbouring churches, creating a cool, shady world. Lalibela is a major pilgrimage site of the Ethiopian Orthodox Church, and each church has a resident monk.

Festive procession Ethiopian Orthodox followers take part in the Timkat festival, which celebrates the baptism of Christ, at the Church of St George.

WHERE ON EARTH?

Lalibela is a large village in northern Ethiopia, around 400 miles (650km) north of Addis Ababa. Approximately 2,500m (8,200ft) up in the hills of the Amhara region, the site is most easily reached by air from the capital, rather than by car or the two-day bus trip over unsurfaced roads.

[Map showing: SAUDI ARABIA, Red Sea, ERITREA, YEMEN, Lalibela, DJIBOUTI, Gulf of Aden, Addis Ababa, SOMALIA, ETHIOPIA]

A holy city

The Lalibela churches are said to have been built at the end of the 12th century by a saintly king of the same name, who saw the project as a spiritual re-creation of Jerusalem, to which he had recently made a pilgrimage. King Lalibela's efforts to realise the sacred vision had, it is suggested, been lent a special urgency by the loss of the earthly Jerusalem to Muslim forces led by Saladin in 1187.

The story rings true – at least in the sense that so extravagant a flight of architectural fantasy must have been conceived in response to some spectacular stroke of spiritual or imaginative inspiration. Archaeologists caution, however, that such massive works would have taken many decades – perhaps centuries – to construct. They could not all have been completed during Lalibela's reign but must have taken shape slowly under subsequent rulers of the Ethiopian Zagwe Dynasty.

Curious monoliths

A simple cross cut out of the ground, the Church of St George (Bet Giorgis) stands around 30m (100ft) tall, its roof flush with the surrounding ground. It could hardly be said to have been built at all: rather, its creators excavated a deep trench around a central core, from which they then whittled the fully formed church. Solid as its construction is, it has an almost tangible air of mystery – approaching on foot, it remains hidden until you are almost on top of it.

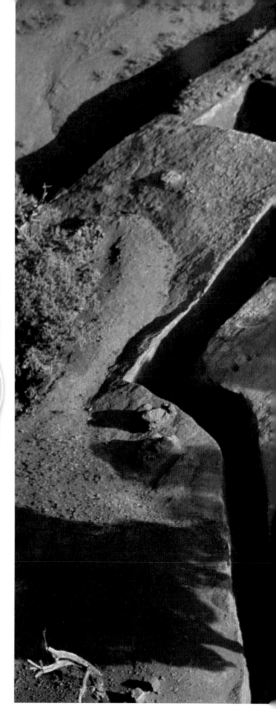

Sunken cross The peculiar construction of St George's Church is strikingly apparent from the air – it might have been stamped out by a giant pastry-cutter.

If its elaborately arched doors and windows lend St George's something of an Islamic look, the massive Saviour of the World (Bete Medhane Alem), with its rectangular plan and columned walls, suggests the ancient symmetry of a classical temple. It is thought to be the largest monolithic church in the world. St Mary's (Beta Maryam), with an array of delicately carved windows, is possibly the oldest church here. Its central pillar, square in shape, is said to have been touched by God himself in Lalibela's presence: it stands now for the unity of all the Christian faiths. In all, Lalibela has 11 monolithic churches, great and small – each an architectural treasure and every one unique.

best of the rest...

ROCK-HEWN ARCHITECTURE

■ The **Göreme Valley** in Turkey's Cappadocia region looks like another world. Over millions of years, uneven erosion of the soft volcanic tufa rock has produced strange 'fairy chimeys' – needle-like pinnacles of stone – across the landscape. Many of these have been hollowed out for homes, storerooms or churches.

■ A number of churches around **Matera**, Italy, have been created by excavating in the soft local rock. While some are little more than hollowed-out caves, others are elaborately built and richly decorated.

Göreme Valley

■ A community of more than 2,000 people live in dwellings dug out of the sides of deep pits at **Matmata**, in Tunisia – not until the 1960s was this community 'discovered' by outsiders. At the heart of each home, the open excavation serves as a sunny courtyard; doors lead into the artificial caverns, which provide the family with underground accommodation. In some places, the caverns are linked by connecting tunnels.

■ The monastery of **Geghard** in Armenia was originally known as Ayrivank, the 'monastery of the cave'. So indeed it was when St Gregory the Illuminator founded it in the 4th century, but it was progressively extended into the surrounding hillside. Many of the rock surfaces are elaborately carved.

■ Near Varna, in Bulgaria, an early cave-monastery of the 5th century was gradually extended and improved: by the 13th century **Aladzha Monastery** was impressive in both scale and sophistication.

LEPTIS MAGNA

Sandwiched between the Mediterranean Sea and the bright blue sky of North Africa stands Leptis Magna, a lasting monument to the power and ambition of the Roman Empire.

The Roman world was vast, extending from Scotland to Syria, from Mauritania to Moldova. Inevitably, the Romans left behind a fair few ruins when the empire finally fell: fortifications, temples, aqueducts, bridges, roads, irrigation systems, harbours, villas and quite substantial cities. Wherever they went, the Romans built cities – for theirs was, pre-eminently, an urban civilisation.

There may be more significant Roman ruins – other sites boast extraordinary treasures, some are impressively situated – but this ruined city on the coast of Libya has these and more. To walk among its ruins in the evening, with only night birds and a deep, silent sea as witness, to see the arches and columns coloured by the sunset and feel the marble flagstones underfoot, is to experience an epiphany that goes beyond historic interest or aesthetic pleasure. It is, quite simply, awesome. As the whole astonishing scene sinks in, it is apparent that when people speak of the Roman achievement, this is what they mean.

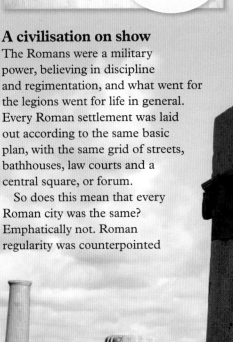

WHERE ON EARTH?

Leptis Magna is on the Libyan coast, east of the port of Homs and 60 miles (100km) east of the capital, Tripoli, which has an international airport linking Libya to Europe. Tourists are currently warned against visiting Libya due to political instability and should check the latest advice before travelling.

A civilisation on show

The Romans were a military power, believing in discipline and regimentation, and what went for the legions went for life in general. Every Roman settlement was laid out according to the same basic plan, with the same grid of streets, bathhouses, law courts and a central square, or forum.

So does this mean that every Roman city was the same? Emphatically not. Roman regularity was counterpointed

by and adapted to the vagaries of natural topography and climate, making each settlement unique. But Leptis Magna is in a class of its own.

The Romans cannot take credit for the natural majesty of the setting, where the Wadi Lebda reaches the Mediterranean Sea. Neither did they do more than

improve the superb natural harbour that forms around the bay. They could not even claim to have been responsible for founding the city when they first occupied North Africa at the start of the 2nd century BC. The Phoenicians, sea traders originally from Lebanon, had established a settlement here more than 800 years earlier.

It is hard to resist the thought that as the Romans established themselves in Leptis, they must have intuited the opportunity that the place presented

to them. Did they sense that this was a setting in which they could set out their stall and make their pitch to posterity? If the Romans had been minded to build a monument that encapsulated their imperial achievements, they could hardly have found a more fitting way of doing it than here.

Civic pride

Leptis Magna's function as a seaport is clear to this day from the way it is laid out: the Forum (the open area that

formed the civic heart of all Roman cities) is just a stone's throw from the harbour. Beside the forum stood the Curia, the seat of government for Leptis Magna and its hinterland; a temple to Hercules was also constructed here. Another temple – also to Hercules – was built on a level platform above the

Roman marketplace The market has features not found at other Roman ruins. Along with typical shop porticoes, there are two central circular stalls and equipment used to measure out goods.

harbour and was the first sight that approaching vessels had of Leptis.

The original forum and nearby buildings would have been bare and plain, but these were soon replaced by more splendid structures endowed by local magnates. Civic consciousness was seared into the Roman soul: the Roman citizen defined who he was through his public profile. Men of substance displayed their wealth and civic commitment by vying with one another in their generosity.

The Romans did not venture beyond the coastal plain, but even so Africa was the richest and most beautiful province of their empire. Blessed in its climate and fertile in its soils, it became the empire's breadbasket, vineyard and olive press. The Sahara was an impassable barrier but, paradoxically, it was also a highway that brought traders from the south.

The province flourished, and Leptis Magna led the way. By the time of the first Roman emperor, Augustus (63 BC–AD 14), the city was famous for its splendour. It had an open-air theatre, its terraced seating set into the contours of a hillside and its decorated stage backed by slender marble columns. The marketplace provided an august setting for conducting mundane business. Elegant porticoes surrounded the market square and divided it into sections for the sale of different goods: from olive oil to exotic animals, from salt to slaves, all manner of goods were traded here. On the eastern edge of the city stood the amphitheatre, where gladiatorial shows were staged, and the circus, which hosted chariot-racing. The former seated 16,000, the latter 25,000, making them among the biggest stadiums in the whole of the empire.

Mosaic of the gladiators This scene forms the edge of a larger mosaic at Villa Dar Buc Ammera. The early-morning gladiatorial shows featured fights between animals, such as the bull and bear tied together at top left.

If local magnates made munificent gifts to their cities, their emperors were not exempt from the same obligation: they also needed to win friends and influence people. Such was the spirit of Hadrian's donation of public baths and *palaestra*, or gym, in AD 126.

Severus's city

In AD 193, Septimius Severus ascended the imperial throne. He was a local boy, born in Leptis Magna to an Italian mother and North African father. As a soldier, Severus rose steadily through the ranks. Conquered nations were expected to assimilate into the Roman way of life. At the same time, the ruling classes were often indifferent to racial differences across the empire: foreigners of talent could expect to be treated with respect. Born in AD 146, Severus was a successful general by 191. After a

period of turbulence culminating in the assassination of Emperor Commodus, Severus's soldiers called on him to assume power.

Leptis basked in the reflected glory of the new emperor. Between his desire to show that he had not forgotten his African roots and that of wealthy Romans keen to curry favour, Severus's hometown found itself showered with gifts, including the sumptuously columned forum. The emperor himself presented the Severan Basilica at the northeast end of the forum. In 203, a triumphal arch was erected to mark the emperor's official visit, and a stunning temple of nymphs was endowed. The *nymphaeum* enclosed a semicircular ornamental fountain resembling a miniature theatre.

On the back of this economic boom, the population of the city grew. New immigrants streamed into Leptis and fortunes were made by new patrician clans. Townhouses and tenements went up year after year. The city sprawled westwards and villas sprang up along the coast. In the town centre, temples, public

buildings and the early forum were renewed. A grand processional way was constructed to connect the civic centre with the harbour.

Decline and fall

On Severus's initiative, the port was refurbished. This, ironically, was to be the city's downfall. There had always been a problem with silt in the harbour, which was supposedly cured when the harbour was modified. An upstream dam was built to divert the *wadi* and its alluvial deposits, and the harbour walls were extended. Unfortunately, they now projected so far out that they cut across a muddy coastal current, causing it to flow back into the harbour and dump its silt there. To add insult to injury, an earthquake destroyed the dam, pushing the river back to its former course.

After that, matters went downhill. Leptis Magna remained a regional centre, but its status as a major seaport was lost. In 439, the German Vandals arrived, having pushed all the way down through Roman Spain and crossed the Straits of Gibraltar before moving eastwards across North Africa. They took Leptis, but by this time it was no great prize.

The city was sacked again in 523 by Berber raiders. They left Leptis Magna in much the state that we see today. The hot, dry air has preserved the ruins; so has the drifting sand that covered them. With no pressure to redevelop either the city or its port, it remained a backwater. Where other Roman ruins were built over or pulled apart for stone, Leptis Magna has been left alone, a haunting monument to past glories.

Natural site The amphitheatre was built in a natural depression by the sea. The best seats were on the southeastern side, which received a cool sea breeze.

LOUVRE MUSEUM

Housed in a former royal palace, the Louvre contains a wealth of art treasures of astonishing quality, accumulated over hundreds of years of assiduous collecting and recently revamped with eyecatching panache.

French painting was the driving force of Western art for at least 250 years, from the days of Nicolas Poussin at the court of Louis XIII to the Cubists in the early 20th century – and Paris was always the hub. At the heart of this unfolding history was the Louvre, first as a royal palace commissioning the great artists of the day, then as a residence for artists and a gallery. And all the while, it was accumulating an extraordinarily rich and varied collection of works around which the history of Western art has been constructed. The Louvre today houses scores of the world's most famous and frequently reproduced paintings.

The collections in the Louvre extend far beyond well-known paintings and sculpture from recent centuries. As a museum it contains outstanding displays of sculpture and other artefacts from the ancient world, including archaeological trophies from Mesopotamia and Egypt, and world-famous pieces of Greek and Roman sculpture, such as the *Venus de Milo* and the *Winged Victory of Samothrace*. This great cultural bank, now presenting an astounding 35,000 works of art and artefacts, remains to

this day a source of inspiration to artists from around the world as well as a bastion of French national pride.

Scandale!

Set around a long courtyard, the Cour Napoléon, in a vast U-shaped group of neoclassical buildings, by the 1970s the Louvre was beginning to look tired – a wonderful collection of art, but spread over miles of rambling galleries, hard to navigate and hard to maintain. The entrance area was always crowded with visitors trying to find the sections of the museum that they wanted to see. The last major renovation had taken place in the 1880s. A large proportion of the collection was held in storage, and the administration facilities were so poor that the museum was likened to a 'theatre without a backstage'. Much of the northern wing, along the Rue de Rivoli, was occupied by government ministries. So, when the socialist leader François Mitterrand was elected president in 1981, he made the renovation of the Louvre a priority among his *grands projets*.

What followed was almost a decade of controversy and debate. In the view of outraged opinion, into the very heart of this treasured national institution a

Guardian spirit This huge alabaster sculpture of a human-headed winged bull guarded the royal palace of the Assyrian city of Khorsabad in the reign of Sargon II (721–705 BC). It was excavated in 1843.

Blending old and new In its brief time as the main entrance to the Louvre, the glass Pyramid has become almost as much an icon of Paris as the Eiffel Tower. Its uncompromising triangles have breathed new life into an old institution.

Chinese-American architect called I.M. Pei was being allowed to drop an alien spaceship: a glass pyramid that bore absolutely no relationship to its surroundings. Critics decried it as yet another example of modernism corroding the fabric of tradition. I.M. Pei's design was, to many Parisians, a *scandale*.

To others it was a stroke of genius. And after the new Pyramid entrance opened, on October 14, 1989, many more people came round to this opinion. By being so different from its neoclassical surroundings, the Pyramid, and its three satellite pyramids, brought a new sense of lightness and space to the huge

and rather gaunt Cour Napoléon. The technical quality of the new structure shone out: the diamonds and triangles of super-thick glass, held together in an aluminium frame, had been specially developed by the Saint-Gobain factory to match both the exacting requirements of security and the demands of I.M. Pei for colourless transparency.

Above all, the Pyramid was an ingenious solution to the problem of access that had bedevilled the old Louvre. It provides a central entrance to a new and spacious underground area from which visitors can fan out into the three main wings where the exhibits

are displayed – Richelieu to the north, Denon to the south and Sully to the east. Now the Louvre had first-class logistics to match its world-class collection.

Royal palace

The history of the Louvre is closely entwined with the history of Paris itself and with the French royal family. The first building on the site was a fortress built in 1190 by King Philippe II (known as Philippe Auguste, who reigned 1180–1223). Remains of this early structure can still be seen beneath the Cour Carrée.

Under Charles V (reigned 1364–80) the Louvre became a royal residence,

a *palais*, and so it remained until the 19th century, gradually expanding and developing in the styles of each successive era. The oldest surviving room is the Salle des Caryatides, built in 1550 for King Henri II (reigned 1547–59), and named after the Greek-style female figures that support the upper gallery; it is in the Lescot Wing, overlooking the Cour Carrée. After Henri's death, his widow Catherine de' Medici built the Palais des Tuileries, which formed the western wing of the Louvre complex. Destroyed by fire in 1871 during the Paris Commune and demolished in 1883, the Palais survives only in the name of the gardens, the Jardin des Tuileries.

Royal collectors

With the royal family came patronage of the arts. King François I (reigned 1515–47), who turned the Louvre into a Renaissance palace, was a collector of contemporary Italian art and patron of Leonardo da Vinci, who arrived from Italy as an old man and lived and died at Amboise on the River Loire, site of another royal residence. Leonardo brought with him an unfinished portrait. Now known as the *Mona Lisa*, it has

Star of the show Leonardo da Vinci's *Mona Lisa* is the Louvre's most famous possession, drawing large crowds all day, every day.

become the most famous work not just in the Louvre but in the whole world.

The French royal family continued to build in sumptuous style and needed artists to paint ceilings, wall panels and

portraits. They were also avid collectors of art. The Louvre collection began, therefore, as the royal collection. Under King Henri IV (reigned 1589–1610), the Louvre became home to artists attached to the French court; they lived here with their families and were provided with studios. Musicians and poets were also housed here.

In 1682, Louis XIV, the 'Sun King', moved his court to his new and spectacular palace of Versailles, to the west of Paris, and the Louvre became increasingly devoted to the arts. Jean-Honoré Fragonard, François Boucher and Jacques-Louis David were among the many famous painters who took up residence. But with royal attention focused elsewhere, the palace began to fall into disrepair.

During the French Revolution the fortunes of the royal artists became precarious. When Louis XVI and his queen, Marie-Antoinette, were brought to Paris from Versailles and placed under

Rubens gallery In 1621 Marie de' Medici, widow of Henri IV, commissioned the Flemish artist Peter Paul Rubens to create 24 large and fanciful paintings about her life. They are now housed in this dedicated gallery.

house arrest in the Palais des Tuileries, the revolutionaries set up a guillotine right outside in the Place du Carrousel. Here, in April 1792, Nicolas Jacques Pelletier, a thief, became the first-ever Frenchman to be executed by guillotine – a machine then considered a symbol of progress because of its speed at killing. In August 1792, it was the turn of Araud II de La Porte, minister to Louis XVI. The following year the guillotine was moved to the Place de la Concorde. The royal art collection, meanwhile, was sequestrated by the new republican state, and swelled enormously as the estates and possessions of the aristocracy were confiscated. In 1793, the Louvre was opened as a public art gallery under the name of the Musée Central des Arts, its huge collection displayed for all to see.

After Napoleon seized power in 1799, and gradually assumed the trappings of an emperor, he gave the Louvre a facelift. Rebranded the Musée Napoléon, the Louvre now acquired the spoils of his conquests, including important collections of sculpture and artefacts from the ancient world, in particular the Egyptian collection. To celebrate his military victories, in 1806–8 Napoleon built the Arc de Triomphe du Carrousel at the Louvre to serve as a grand entrance to the Tuileries palace.

One of the few artists who survived this dramatic transfer of power was Jacques-Louis David – admired by both Louis XVI and Napoleon, whom he flattered and glorified shamelessly. David's *The Coronation of Napoleon* is now one of the highlights of the museum's collection of French painting. In 1806 the tradition of housing artists in the Louvre ceased.

After the final defeat of Napoleon, many of his spoils of war were returned to their rightful owners. Nonetheless, in ensuing decades the Louvre's collection, under new royal patronage, continued to grow with around 20,000 donations.

A major attraction

Paris was the hotbed of artistic progress throughout the 19th century and into the 20th, as trends shifted from the Neoclassicism of David and Jean-Auguste-Dominique Ingres to the Romanticism of Eugène Delacroix and Théodore Géricault, then on through Realism, Impressionism, Post-Impressionism, Fauvism and Cubism. Young artists flocked to Paris to learn from the masters and attend the annual Salon exhibitions. At the Louvre, they

could study the work of international masters of the past: sculpture from ancient Greece and Rome, and painting and sculpture by the great Renaissance artists from across Europe – celebrated in works such as *The Madonna of Chancellor Rolin* by Jan van Eyck (Flanders), a self-portrait by Albrecht Dürer (Germany), *The Dying Slave* by Michelangelo (Italy), five paintings by Leonardo, the largest Leonardo collection in the world (including *The Virgin of the Rocks* as well as the *Mona Lisa*), *The Wedding at Cana* by Paolo Veronese (Italy), Rembrandt self-portraits (Dutch), *The Lacemaker* by Vermeer (The Netherlands), and the huge and controversial *The Raft of the Medusa* by Géricault.

Ghosts of the royal palace The sumptuous summer apartments of Anne of Austria, queen consort of Louis XIII, provide a suitable setting for the Louvre's collection of Roman sculpture.

At times, the fame of the Louvre's collection has attracted the wrong kind of attention, directed in particular towards its most celebrated possession: the *Mona Lisa*, known at the Louvre as *La Joconde* after the name of the possible patron, *La Giaconda*. In 1911, the painting was stolen. The poet Guillaume Apollinaire came under suspicion, and he in turn implicated Pablo Picasso – but both were exonerated when, two years later, the real culprit was discovered: Vincenzo Peruggia, a Louvre employee of Italian origin, who had walked out with the painting under his coat. He wanted to return Leonardo's masterpiece to Italy, but was caught when he tried to sell it to the Uffizi Gallery in Florence.

In 1956, a visitor to the Louvre threw acid at the painting, damaging the lower part, and later that year another visitor hurled a rock at it. A protective shield of bullet-proof glass has since saved the *Mona Lisa* from a flying cup lobbed at it in 2009.

Expansion and dispersal

As part of the redevelopment that introduced the Pyramid, new galleries were created in the north wing, including a covered area in the Cour Marly housing two large and famous statues of rearing horses and their horse-tamers. Called the Chevaux de Marly, they were sculpted in Carrara marble in 1743–5 for Louis XV, originally to adorn the park entrance at his Château de Marly. They were moved to the Place de la Concorde during the French Revolution, and then – for their protection – to this new site in 1984.

The renovation programme has continued ever since. In 2006 the Musée des Arts Décoratifs, located in the northwest wing on the Rue de Rivoli, reopened after ten years of renovation. Although a separate institution, it overlaps with the Louvre not only in sharing a site, but also in the content it displays: exquisite jewellery, clocks, tapestry and furniture, much of it drawn from royal

Dropping in A spiral staircase takes visitors from the Pyramid entrance to the subterranean Hall Napoléon, which gives convenient access to the galleries.

collections and produced using many of the same supreme artistic skills.

Some collections that were once in the Louvre have been moved elsewhere. A large anthropological collection was rehoused in the Musée du Quai Branly, which opened in 2007. The cut-off date for paintings in the Louvre is 1848, and many French paintings dating from between 1848 and 1915, notably by the Impressionists and Post-Impressionists, are now on display at the Musée d'Orsay, which opened in 1986.

That said, the Louvre still has one of the largest and most comprehensive collections of paintings in the world, covering all the major European schools, with – naturally enough – the world's greatest collection of French art. Today the whole collection is divided into eight departments distributed over four

Small but SPECIAL

COURTAULD GALLERY

This is a supreme museum on a pocket-sized scale. Occupying a corner of the palatial Somerset House, in central London, it comprises a series of 11 rooms on two floors. It is not just that it presents a roll-call of the greatest names of Western art (Pieter Bruegel the Elder, Lucas Cranach, Michelangelo, Albrecht Dürer, Leonardo da Vinci, Peter Paul Rubens, Francisco de Goya, the French Impressionists, Edgar Degas, Vincent van Gogh, Paul Cézanne and Pablo Picasso, to list a few) – but every work is of the highest quality. Many are world famous, such as van Gogh's *Self-Portrait with Bandaged Ear*, Edouard Manet's *Bar at the Folies-Bergère*, and Paul Gauguin's *Nevermore*. There are also exquisite examples of sculpture and of decorative art - furniture, ceramics and metalwork. The industrialist and philanthropist Samuel Courtauld (1876-1947) established the collection, along with the Courtauld Institute, an internationally respected school and research centre for art, architecture, curation and conservation.

floors. Paintings are split into three main groups: French (the largest), Italian and Spanish, and North European (German, Flemish and Dutch). Sculpture (excluding that of the ancient world) covers European work from the Middle Ages to the mid-19th century, focusing primarily on the highly accomplished work of French sculptors of the 17th and 18th centuries, but also including works by Italian sculptors such as Michelangelo and Canova.

The Department of Prints and Drawings displays a selection from its vast collection of around 150,000 items by artists such as da Vinci, Nicolas Poussin, Watteau, David, Géricault and Delacroix. Decorative Arts presents precious objects such as crowns and sceptres, devotional sculpture, stained glass, tapestry, bronzes, Sèvres porcelain and exquisite inlayed furniture by André-Charles Boulle, along with the furnished apartments of Napoleon III (nephew of Napoleon I and emperor of the Second Empire). The Islamic Art department has decorative sculpture, tile work and painted miniatures.

The extensive antiquities collection covers 9,000 years of sculpture, jewellery, pottery and glassware displayed in three departments: Egyptian; Greek, Etruscan and Roman; and Eastern.

The Louvre Museum today is easily the world's most popular museum in terms of visitor numbers, receiving 8.5 million every year. That exceeds the second most visited, the British Museum in London, by more than 2.6 million. This is not simply because it has one of the greatest collections of art in the world: it has also created one of the best environments in which to see art, in a subtle and triumphant marriage of the old with the new.

best of the rest...

MUSEUMS AND GALLERIES

■ One of the world's great international treasure troves of cultural artefacts, the **British Museum** in London was also one of the first major public museums, opening in 1759. It contains numerous artefacts of world renown, including the Rosetta Stone and the Elgin Marbles. Virtually all cultures are represented, from the ancient Mesopotamians and Egyptians to the Vikings, Aztecs and Native American Indians.

■ Housed in the Winter Palace of the Tsars in St Petersburg, Russia, the **Hermitage Museum** contains a collection of more than 3 million items, including outstanding works of Western art from classical antiquity to Raphael and Leonardo da Vinci (the *Benois Madonna* and the *Madonna Litta*), from Peter Paul Rubens and Rembrandt to Vincent van Gogh, Paul Gauguin and Henri Matisse.

■ Founded in 1870, the **Metropolitan Museum of Art** (The Met) in New York now has more than 2 million works, with paintings by Caravaggio, El Greco, Vermeer, van Gogh, Paul Cézanne, Gauguin and many others. It also has major collections of historic artefacts from all over the world, including musical instruments, weapons, armour and costumes, and archaeological finds, notably the Temple of Dendur from Roman Egypt.

■ Opened in 1819, Spain's **Prado Museum** in Madrid contains around 17,000 paintings, sculptures, drawings and prints. Not only are great Spanish painters represented, such as El Greco,

Rembrandt's *The Night Watch*, Rijksmuseum

Diego Velázquez and Francisco de Goya, but also the Dutch, Flemish and Venetian schools, with paintings by Brueghel, Rogier van der Weyden, Hieronymous Bosch, Rubens, Anthony van Dyck, Titian, Tintoretto and Paolo Veronese.

■ The Dutch national museum in Amsterdam, the **Rijksmuseum** first opened in 1885. It is noted for an unparalleled collection of Dutch paintings, particularly works by Vermeer, Frans Hals and Rembrandt.

■ The **Uffizi Gallery** in Florence, Italy, follows the story of Western art from Roman antiquities and medieval altarpieces to the great Renaissance paintings of Sandro Botticelli, da Vinci and Raphael and on to later international works by Rembrandt, Goya and Jean-Baptiste-Siméon Chardin.

■ The **Vatican Museums** in Rome present art treasures accumulated by the popes over many centuries, including some of the best examples of Greek and Roman sculpture, Renaissance art and ancient Egyptian antiquities - not to mention Michelangelo's Sistine Chapel and the Stanze della Segnatura decorated by Raphael.

Temple of Dendur, Metropolitan Museum of Art

MACHU PICCHU

Imperial residence, ancient observatory or sacred ground? Mysteries abound in these ruins high above the Peruvian rain forest. The truth is long gone – lost with the Incas and the passing of time.

The quintessential lost city, Machu Picchu lay undisturbed by all but locals for nearly 500 years before its rediscovery in 1911. Yale professor Hiram Bingham found the ruins with the aid of a local Indian boy, setting off a global publicity blitz and a frenzy among archaeologists and explorers desperate to uncover other lost cities in the Andes, the Amazon and elsewhere.

'It fairly took my breath away. What could this place be?' wrote Bingham.

Historians are still not certain. Without doubt – given its architecture, location and age – Machu Picchu is an important Inca site. But given the fact that the Spanish conquistadores never found it and that the original builders were

WHERE ON EARTH?

Machu Picchu is 70 miles (110km) north of Cusco in the Peruvian Andes. Cusco has the nearest airport, with daily flights from Lima and other major cities in Peru. Getting to the ruins entails a train from Cusco to Aguas Calientes then a bus, or intrepid trekkers can walk the strenuous Inca Trail.

long gone by the time Bingham arrived, the city's precise function remains unknown.

Unsolved mysteries

There are all sorts of theories, of course. It may have been an astronomical observatory, or the royal estate of Pachacuti (the Inca emperor at the time it was built). It could have been a place of worship. Or the mountaintop metropolis may simply have been a place of refuge.

Nobody is even sure exactly when Machu Picchu was built. Most researchers date its original construction to the mid-15th century, roughly 65 years before the conquistadores arrived in Peru. They estimate that the city was abandoned (for reasons unknown) some time around the middle of the 16th century.

Dizzy heights Inhabited for little more than a century, Machu Picchu stands 2,430m (7,970ft) above sea level on a mountain ridge above Peru's Urubamba Valley.

Indigenous people living in the area no doubt knew about the old ruins up on the mountaintop. There is also evidence that late-19th century German treasure-hunters and American missionaries may have known about, or even visited, the site. But it was Bingham who took Machu Picchu from cloud-covered obscurity to world fame. With an interest in Inca ruins aroused by a previous trip to the region, Bingham and local guides set out from Cusco in July 1911. As the story goes, the party had to cross a raging whitewater river on a rickety wooden bridge and machete their way through thick jungle before coming upon the ancient ruins with the aid of a Quechua boy from a nearby village.

Bingham's 'straight-out-of-Hollywood' archaeological adventure story, the enduring mystery of what this city might have been and the spectacular Andes location on an emerald-coloured crest perched high above the rain forest, are what make Machu Picchu such a compelling place to visit, and the best lost city on Earth.

The city ruins

In the century since its rediscovery, about one-third of Machu Picchu's ruins have been reconstructed. There are around 140 structures in total and more than a hundred sets of stone steps, plus an extensive stone plumbing and irrigation system that transported water to individual homes and agricultural areas. The architecture is typically Inca: large, rectangular stones with square edges and smooth, polished faces fitted together without masonry, the joints so precise and so fine that it is impossible to slide a knife blade between the stones.

Among the city's landmarks is the Temple of the Condor, a natural rock formation that Inca stonemasons reshaped into a giant condor with outspread wings as if about to take flight. The Temple of the Sun, dedicated to the Inca sun god Inti, was probably the city's most important place of worship. According to legend, the temple's Window of the Serpent facilitated the passage of wild snakes into the shrine.

Elsewhere there is a mass tomb or mausoleum where the remains of more than a hundred people were discovered by Bingham. He estimated that around 80 per cent of them were female, but contemporary examination has revealed a more even split between the sexes. The structure also contains a step-like

altar and niches that were presumably used for ceremonial purposes. Another important relic is the Intihuatana, also known as the 'hitching post of the sun', a stone structure that Inca priests may have used to make astrological forecasts or examine the stars.

Although the population may never have reached more than a thousand souls, ancient Machu Picchu must have had its criminals and social delinquents, because the ruins also house what is thought to have been a prison complete with small stone cells and a dungeon. Cascading down the lush mountainside

Plunging terrain A stone-carved altar stands in the Temple of the Sun, protected within a semicircular wall. Beyond it are narrow, vertiginous terraces where crops were grown.

on either side of the city are meticulously constructed stone terraces where people cultivated maize, potatoes, beans and other crops.

The national reserve that surrounds and protects Machu Picchu is noteworthy for its flora and fauna, a combination of High Andes and upper Amazon species. Alpacas are frequently seen grazing the ruins, and those with a keen eye may see rabbit-like viscachas scampering through the stones. Among other creatures that call the area home are the highly endangered spectacled bear, pampas cat and ocelot, the huge Andean condor and the cock-of-the-rock bird with bright-red head and crest.

In tune with nature

In 1993, Machu Picchu became a World Heritage Site listed as 'the most amazing urban creation of the Inca Empire at its height'. The listing also cited the city's stonework as an outstanding example of the use of a natural raw material in architecture that is totally appropriate to its surroundings.

Ironically, the most photogenic feature of the ruins was hewn by natural forces rather than the hand of man. A sheer peak called Huayna Picchu towers more than 300m (1,000ft) above the city, draped in vegetation and often shrouded in cloud. It looks impossible to scale without modern climbing equipment, yet the Inca chiselled a narrow path leading up to temples, terraces and lookout points. Although no one knows for sure, legend holds that a high priest and temple virgins lived at the top. Writing in 1949, British author Christopher Isherwood was clearly

impressed by the Incas' mastery of the heights of Huayna Picchu. Writing on his return, he said that they 'must have been able to climb like flies'.

Whatever the answers to the mysteries of Machu Picchu, more than 300,000 people a year now make the pilgrimage to experience the spirit of this place for themselves. Many would agree with the

Hitching post of the sun Priests are believed to have used the post as an indicator of the two equinoxes: on those days of the year, the sun stands directly above the rock, casting no shadow.

words of Hiram Bingham: 'In the variety of its charms and the power of its spell, I know of no place in the world that can compare with it.'

best of the rest...

LOST CITIES

■ **Akhetaten**, created during the 14th-century BC reign of the monotheistic pharaoh Akhenaten, was occupied through Roman times and the early Christian era before its abandonment. Now called Amarna, the ruins were discovered by Napoleon's Corps de Savants during the French occupation of Egypt in the late 18th century.

■ Prominent German archaeologist Robert Koldewey is credited with rediscovering ancient **Babylon**. Although other Europeans had excavated parts of the site during the 19th century, it was Koldewey's marathon dig of 1899-1917 that identified the Iraqi site (then in the Ottoman Empire) as the famed biblical city. Among Koldewey's finds were remains of the Hanging Gardens, the Marduk ziggurat and the elaborately decorated Ishtar Gate.

■ Even the South Pacific has its lost city. **Nan Madol** was the capital of an ancient civilisation on Pohnpei island in Micronesia. Comprising nearly a hundred artificial islands fashioned from coral and linked by canals, the city was founded around AD 1200 and was occupied until the early 17th century. A Russian maritime expedition came across Nan Madol in 1828.

■ **Sigiriya** citadel was carved out of a Sri Lankan mountaintop in the 5th century AD and flourished as a Buddhist monastery for

Sigiriya

nearly a thousand years. The fortified eyrie was abandoned and lost to history until its accidental rediscovery by a British major, Jonathan Forbes, in 1831.

■ One of the largest cities of the Mundo Maya, **Tikal** thrived from AD 200 to 900. When the Spanish arrived six centuries later, the metropolis had faded back into the Central American rain forest. Continuing accounts of a lost city in northern Guatemala led the government to organise a local expedition, which celebrated the rediscovery of Tikal in the 1840s.

■ The ancient city of **Troy** was no more than a legend until 1866, when British amateur archaeologist Frank Calvert identified a large mound in northwestern Anatolia as its most likely site. In the decade that followed, German archaeologist Heinrich Schliemann proved that theory with excavations that unearthed a sequence of bygone cities built one on top of another.

MANÚ NATIONAL PARK

Peru's largest national park is a birdwatcher's paradise, with more feathered species than any other protected area in the world.

Manú National Park is part of the Manú Biosphere Reserve, an area about half the size of Switzerland covering three different biomes from the high Andes to lowland tropical forest. It has a greater level of biodiversity than any other national park in the world. In a single hectare of forest near the Cocha Cashu research station, there are more than 200 types of trees, with a single tree supporting up to 43 species of ant. Thirteen types of monkey live here, and more than 1,000 bird species, 10 per cent of the world's total and absolute heaven for birdwatchers.

High in the Andes is the puna tundra with its yellow ichu grass, home to the magnificent Andean condor, the world's largest flying bird, which lives by scavenging. In the foothills are the cloud

WHERE ON EARTH?

Manú National Park is in southeast Peru. It is largely inaccessible by road, and most visitors arrive by boat along the Manú River. Some fly from Cusco to a small airstrip near the river, a journey of about 45 minutes, and proceed by boat. Access to the park is strictly controlled and visitors must use a recognised tour operator.

Clay lick A flock of red and green macaws at the Tambo Blanquillo clay lick, where they eat mineral deposits to supplement their diet of seeds and fruit.

forests, their trees festooned with lichens, bromeliads and orchids. Bejewelled hummingbirds and bright orange male cocks-of-the-rock compete for attention with, at sunset, the lyre-tailed nightjar, its tail feathers streaming behind it. In the lowland rain forest, vividly coloured parrots and macaws dart among the trees, while herons, egrets and kingfishers search for food along the riverbanks.

A pandemonium of parrots

One of the noisiest avian events occurs each morning by the rivers and lakes. At dawn, blue-headed and mealy parrots drop down to clay licks in the eroded riverbank, from which they obtain sodium. Later on, the macaws arrive. If there is a quorum, they gather at the clay lick amid much squabbling. Up to 200 birds visit at any one time, with activity peaking in the breeding season, when the birds take clay back to their chicks. The clay licks are dangerous places as they attract predators. The macaws only visit if there are plenty of fellow eyes to watch for danger. One of those dangers – the

best of the rest...

BIRDWATCHING SITES

■ At the peak of the spring migration each May, **Cape May** on the US east coast offers 200 species of birds on a single day. Teams of bird-spotters compete in the 24-hour World Series of Birding fundraising event.

■ Each winter, 10,000 cranes from at least seven different species come to the fields of Arasaki on Japan's island of **Kyushu** where, in a glorious avian spectacle, they perform their elegant courtship dances.

Rift Valley

■ Thousands of flamingos gather at the soda lakes of East Africa's **Rift Valley** to feed and breed. African fish eagles, hyenas and olive baboons try to catch unwary birds.

powerful and highly manoeuvrable harpy eagle – attacks from the sky.

On the river, black skimmers trail their long bottom bills through the water to snag fish, while in an overhanging tree a female hoatzin bird, with electric-blue, punk-style plumage, supervises her chick. At any hint

of danger, the chick throws itself into the water, clambering back out using wing claws reminiscent of a pterodactyl. Sharing the forests with these colourful creatures are indigenous tribes surviving in harmony with their fragile natural environment and hoping to be left alone by visitors.

MATTERHORN

This isolated peak has become an icon of the Alps, with a history of mountain-climbing achievements to match.

Pick one mountain that truly soars and it has to be the Matterhorn, a shard of rock that shoots relentlessly up from base to peak. At 4,478m (14,690ft), it is not the highest Alpine peak, that distinction goes to Mont Blanc, but it is visually the most dramatic. Its twisted pyramid stands alone, shaped by a million years of erosion, with only the sky as a backdrop. Its four sheer sides are aligned to the compass points, giving it distinct north, east, south and west faces. Topped by its crooked peak, the Matterhorn is easily the most recognisable mountain in the world.

Climbing legends

A peak like this presents an irresistible challenge to climbers. In the pioneer days of mountaineering, competing teams raced to reach the top. As the Matterhorn is on the Swiss–Italian border, this became a patriotic issue, with French and British climbers adding to the mix. The Englishman Edward Whymper made six attempts before achieving the goal on July 14, 1865, beating his Italian rivals by just three days. But Whymper's triumph came at a cost: on the descent, four members of his team fell to their

WHERE ON EARTH?

The Matterhorn straddles the border between Switzerland and Italy. Matterhorn is its German name – it is known as Monte Cervino in Italian, Mont Cervin in French. Zermatt is the nearest town on the Swiss side, Breuil-Cervinia on the Italian side. Both towns are accessible by train.

deaths. Since then, every route to the top has been explored; the difficult north face was the last to be conquered, in 1931.

Being prone to rapid weather changes and regular rock falls, the Matterhorn is one of the most challenging and dangerous peaks in the world, yet hundreds of people still climb it each summer, most of them via the Hörnli ridge between its north and east faces. And climbers still die attempting the Matterhorn – adding to a toll of more than 500 deaths since 1865.

Double glory The Matterhorn's east face is reflected from the still waters of the Riffelsee. The Hörnli ridge, which is outlined on the right-hand side, is the usual climbing route.

best of the rest...

MOUNTAINS

■ **Kilimanjaro**, at 5,894m (19,366ft) the highest mountain in Africa, rises from the African savannah through mist-shrouded rain forest, desolate moorlands and alpine deserts before ending in a flat, snow-covered top.

■ A flat, vertiginous plinth called the **Preikestolen** (Pulpit Rock) presents a natural balcony 604m (1,982ft) above sea level with astonishing views up and down Norway's Lysefjord and its mountainous hinterland.

■ At 8,850m (29,035ft), **Mount Everest** on the border of Nepal and China is the world's highest mountain. Kala Patthar, a rocky crest in Nepal, provides trekkers with a complete view from Everest's base camp to the peak. The summit has been reached every year since 1977.

Mount Everest

MENIN GATE

With classical dignity, this bold memorial stands as a poignant reminder of the tragedy of war. Tens of thousands of names are inscribed here, just some of the millions of men who died.

In medieval times, Ieper – or Ypres, to give the city its French name, by which it is known in the English-speaking world – was a wealthy Flemish trade centre, like Bruges and Ghent. Specialising in woollen textiles, it was famous for its grand 13th-century cloth hall, the Gothic Lakenhalle. Like many Belgian towns, it quietly prospered through the industrialisation of the 19th century. But in 1915 it descended into a vortex of destruction, and today the name Ypres resonates with some of the bloodiest episodes of World War One.

The Western Front

At the outbreak of the war, German forces attempted to sweep through Belgium to attack France and eliminate the threat from the west. But Belgian forces put up stiff resistance and then retreated to the coast behind the River Yser, breaking the dikes to flood the landscape. Ypres lay on high ground just to the south of this flood zone, so now it became the gateway to the French ports of Dunkirk and Calais, which the

WHERE ON EARTH?

The Menin Gate stands on the eastern side of the small city of Ieper in the province of West Flanders, Belgium. Ieper is 75 miles (120km) west of Brussels, and 45 miles (70km) southeast of the French port of Calais. Visitors to the city can tour the area, visiting a number of battlefield memorials on the Western Front.

English Channel
Dunkirk ● BELGIUM
Calais ● Ieper ● Menin Gate (Ypres) ● Lille
FRANCE

Germans needed to take in order to cut off British supply routes.

In October 1914 the German armies clashed with British, French and Belgian forces on a D-shaped ridge of higher ground – known as the Ypres Salient – to the east of the town. Both sides dug in and four years of grim trench warfare ensued, punctuated by five periods of deadly activity that are collectively called the Battles of Ypres. The third and most devastating of these, lasting from July 31 to November 6, 1917, is also known as Passchendaele: it alone claimed the lives of half a million men.

The Germans were desperate to take Ypres. With their armies more or less surrounding it on three sides they were able to bombard it with huge shells from their 42cm (16.5in) Big Bertha howitzers. Gradually Ypres was pulverised. Nevertheless, the city remained in British hands, and through the ruined streets of 'Wipers', as they

Remembrance A poppy parade is held here on November 11, when wreaths are laid and thousands of poppy petals are released from the roof to float down among the silent crowd.

called it, tens of thousands of British and Commonwealth troops marched to the Salient, many of them never to return.

Homage to the unknown

World War One cost the lives of almost 10 million servicemen and a further million civilian casualties occurred through military action. The Allies on one side and the Central Powers (Germany, Austria-Hungary and the Ottoman Empire) on the other had colonies and

TO THE ARMIES
OF THE BRITISH EMPIRE
WHO STOOD HERE
FROM 1914 TO 1918
AND TO THOSE OF THEIR DEAD
WHO HAVE NO KNOWN GRAVE

PRO
REGE

connections around the globe. Africa, the Balkans, northern Italy, Turkey, the islands of the Pacific and the world's oceans all saw action. But by far the greatest number of casualties were in northern Europe on the Eastern and Western fronts, with perhaps 7 million deaths on the Western Front alone.

After the war, the Allies chose not to repatriate the bodies of the dead, but to create memorials and cemeteries near to where they fell. There are about 160

British and Commonwealth cemeteries around the Ypres Salient alone. The Germans repatriated their dead after the war, but one of their cemeteries near Ypres has remained, at Langemark, where around 44,000 soldiers are buried. There are also two French and one Belgian cemeteries near the Salient.

Of the British and Commonwealth soldiers killed in the Ypres Salient, 90,000 were missing, presumed dead. Either they could not be identified and

Lest we forget Crowning the eastern arch of the Menin Gate memorial is a lion, national symbol of both Flanders and Britain.

were buried as 'known only unto God', or they fell and were buried beneath the shell-churned soil of the battlefield. In order that these 'dead who have no known grave' should be properly commemorated and honoured, after the war the Imperial (now Commonwealth) War Graves Commission asked Sir

Reginald Blomfield – one of the chief British architects of memorials in the years following the end of the war – to design a suitably imposing monument. The site chosen was the Menin Gate (Menenpoort), on the eastern side of Ypres, through which the men had passed on their way to the front.

Restraint and sobriety

Bloomfield chose a classical design of stone and brick in the form of an elongated triumphal arch – yet subtly devoid of triumphalism. The decoration is restrained. Carved stone reliefs of garlands and wreaths decorate the outer walls. A simple stone sarcophagus draped with a flag crowns the west-facing arch; a lion lies on top of the eastern arch. Both were the work of the Scottish sculptor Sir William Reid-Dick. But the real emphasis at the Menin Gate memorial is on the names of those who gave their lives.

Through the centre, running west to east, is the barrel-vaulted Hall of Memory, with an elegantly coffered ceiling pierced with circular windows to let in light. Lining the walls are Portland stone panels bearing the names of the fallen, arranged by regiment and in order of seniority. Flights of stairs lined

with more name panels lead to galleries with yet more panels. A total of 54,896 names are inscribed here and the effect is powerful: they clamour in the silence – so many lives cut short. No other memorial to the dead captures the same balance between deep mourning and honour.

Yet the Menin Gate fell short of fulfilling its task of memorialising all those who fell at Ypres as there was not enough room. A decision was made to list all those who had died up to August 15, 1917 – the first three years of the war – at the Menin Gate. The remainder, a further 34,957 names, appear

Continued respect The Last Post has sounded daily at the Menin Gate since 1928. The only break in this tradition came during the German occupation in World War Two.

on the Memorial to the Missing at Tyne Cot Cemetery, 5 miles (8km) east of Ypres. Here, amid the 12,000 graves in what is the world's largest Commonwealth cemetery, the names are carved into Portland stone panels lining a memorial designed by Sir Herbert Baker.

Last Post

While Ypres – reconstructed almost brick for brick after World War One – today buzzes with small-town life and the constant flow of visitors to the World War One sites, there is always a hypnotic calm to the Menin Gate, induced perhaps by the subdued elegance of the architecture. It demands honour and respect. This is in vivid contrast to the scene here between 1914 and 1918. When General Charles Harington, a combatant at Ypres, witnessed the opening ceremony of the memorial in July 1927, he could not help picturing 'the casualties incurred nightly by the endless stream of transport men, their horses and mules – on their nightmare journeys through that Menin Gate... Each gateway a bottle-neck, registered to an inch by the enemy guns.'

The sacrifice of the British and Commonwealth troops has been honoured by the people of Ypres ever since. For almost a century now, crowds have gathered here at 8pm every evening to listen to buglers of the Ypres Volunteer Fire Brigade as they play the Last Post.

Small but SPECIAL

ROYAL ARTILLERY WAR MEMORIAL

Beside the busy traffic at Hyde Park Corner in Central London, three bronze World War One soldiers in full combat dress stand in solemn

contemplation against a plinth crowned by a large howitzer carved out of Portland stone. A fourth soldier lies dead, covered by his cloak. This is the memorial to the 49,076 casualties of the Royal Regiment of Artillery, designed by the sculptor Charles Jagger, himself a decorated veteran of the war. When the memorial was unveiled in 1925, it caused great controversy. Previous war memorials commemorated the dead in a heroic light, or in dignified, classical abstraction, as at the Cenotaph in Whitehall. Jagger, by contrast, had chosen to depict the grim reality of war. Many critics condemned the memorial, but others championed its honesty. After seven years of numbed silence, Britain was beginning to come to terms with the true horror of World War One, and here was a monument that eloquently voiced this altered perspective.

best of the rest...

WORLD WAR MEMORIALS

■ In World War One, the Western Front trailed southwards through northeastern France. Here, about a million men from both sides lost their lives in the Battle of the Somme in 1916. At the **Thiepval Memorial**, 72,191 missing British and South African soldiers are commemorated in a high, arched monument of red brick and stone. This is also a memorial to Anglo-French cooperation: British and French flags fly aloft, while 300 British and 300 French war graves – many containing unidentified soldiers – stand in neat ranks below.

■ In World War One, the Canadian Expeditionary Force fought their most famous battle on Vimy Ridge, in northern France, in April 1917. This is now the site of the **Canadian National Vimy Memorial**, a large monument

Thiepval Memorial

Canadian National Vimy Memorial

of bright limestone walls and two tall stone pylons. A scattering of 20 sculpted stone figures, representing the virtues and mourners, signal distress, isolation and solemnity. The most famous work of the Canadian sculptor and architect Walter Seymour Allward, the memorial commemorates Canadian casualties of the war, including 11,285 who have no known grave.

■ At least 1.1 million people died at the largest of the German Nazi extermination camps in Poland, now preserved as the **Auschwitz-Birkenau Memorial and Museum**. A shocking reminder of the genocidal policies that the Nazis directed against political prisoners, Russian prisoners of war, gypsies, homosexuals and, above all, European Jews,

Auschwitz-Birkenau Memorial and Museum

the numbing statistics are made personal through the human detail of the exhibits: piles of shoes, labels on suitcases, and tonnes of human hair shaved from women's heads before gassing.

■ Atrocities of World War Two have been memorialised at the village of **Oradour-sur-Glane**, in the Limousin region of west central France. Here, on June 10, 1944, shortly after the D-Day landings in northern France, German SS troops assembled the villagers on the pretence of checking their identity, then machine-gunned the men in barns and burnt the women and children in a church. The village was then torched; 642 people died. The motive was reprisal for the reported capture of an SS soldier by the French Resistance. The village was never rebuilt, nor demolished: the haunting shells of the ruined homes and burnt-out cars have been left as they stood on that day.

■ On August 6, 1945, three US B-29 bombers appeared in the sky over the Japanese city of Hiroshima. Moments later, the first-ever atomic bomb to be used in war exploded over the city, killing some 70,000 people instantly; a further 70,000 died in the aftermath. The **Hiroshima Peace Memorial** offers the gaunt remains of a domed exhibition hall, built in 1915; because it stood directly beneath the blast, it was one of the few buildings left standing. Since 1966, it has been preserved as a lasting reminder of the utter devastation of nuclear war.

MESA VERDE

A flat-topped mountain in Colorado shelters a settlement of ancient cliff dwellings. The thriving society that occupied them was adept at community living and accomplished in the arts.

Perched high above the ground and housing large numbers of people, the cliff dwellings of the southwestern United States are the high-rise apartments of a thousand years ago, impressive not just because of their precipitous perches on canyon or mesa walls, but also for the complexity of the architecture and the sophisticated logistics involved in constructing them. The greatest of them all are the soaring stone and adobe dwellings of Mesa Verde in southwest Colorado.

The national park that embraces the 2,600m (8,600ft) high Mesa Verde contains no fewer than 4,700 archaeological sites, including around 600 cliff dwellings created by the Ancestral Puebloan people between AD 550 and 1300. The majority of dwellings have between one and five rooms – large enough to accommodate a single or extended family. But the largest, such as the one known as Cliff Palace, were virtual villages in the sky with more than a hundred rooms that housed

Prime location Like many dwellings in the area, Cliff Palace was built in an alcove in the cliff face. Space was limited and buildings used every nook and cranny available.

perhaps hundreds of residents. The mesa's immense proportions and extreme seclusion prevented outsiders from discovering the ruins until the 1880s. Almost at once they realised what an extraordinary site they had come upon.

Despite decades of research, little has been discovered about the Ancestral

Puebloans (sometimes called the Anasazi) who developed Mesa Verde. Centred on the Four Corners region of Colorado, Utah, Arizona and New Mexico, the civilisation first took root around 12,000 years ago. It is easy to see why they chose this place: plenty of wood, fresh water and game; flat areas of land for farming; cooler temperatures than the sweltering desert all around; and protection from enemies.

Construction skills

In the early years, building was fairly primitive, with most people living in caves or pit houses. But the residents of Mesa Verde moved on from simple pole-and-adobe construction, which used poles plastered with mud, to sophisticated stonemasonry. Most of the dwellings were created during the Classic Period (AD 1000–1300) and were occupied for little more than a hundred years. Many rooms had stone floors and adobe-plastered walls decorated with painted designs.

Spruce Tree House has 130 rooms, making it the third largest of the Mesa Verde dwellings. It shows the sturdiness of the original construction and the extent to which the rock alcove protected the inhabitants from the weather. The structure has needed little restoration since it was first excavated in 1908.

Cliff dwellings included *kivas*, underground ceremonial rooms where the spiritual life of the community was played out. Cliff Palace has more than 23 kivas, which were entered via a wooden ladder through a hole in the roof. A hole in the middle of the mud-brick floor (called the *sipapu*) was a

Inside a kiva These subterranean rooms may have been used for community crafts, such as weaving, as well as for religious rites.

symbolic entrance to the underworld. The flat kiva roofs provided spaces for other communal daily activities.

Top of the town

Mesa Verde's ancient residents also built structures on the flat mountaintop, including agricultural terraces for

WHAT'S IN A NAME?

The prevailing name for the people who built the Mesa Verde cliff dwellings and similar structures throughout the southwest is the Ancient Puebloans. From the Spanish term *pueblo* for 'village', the name reflects the fact that the native people encountered by early Spanish explorers lived in permanent settlements rather than being nomadic.

Another name for these people, coined shortly after Mesa Verde was discovered by Americans, is Anasazi, which means 'ancient ones' or 'enemy ancestors'. The term is not popular with contemporary Pueblo Indians because it is perceived to be derogatory, deriving from another Native American group, the Navajo, who invaded and settled former Puebloan lands.

Village in midair The view from Cliff Palace reveals its remote mountain location. The overhanging cliff provided shade and protection from the elements.

growing corn, beans and other crops, masonry towers, religious buildings and stone dams to create reservoirs for drinking water and irrigation. Largest and most complex of the religious sites is the Sun Temple; researchers think that the Puebloans used the indented stone basin in one of the corners as a sundial.

The aptly named Far View Complex, to the north of the modern visitor centre, is the largest of the villages that developed on the mesa top prior to the advent of large cliff dwellings. The remains of around 50 villages, where several hundred people may have lived at a time, are scattered around. Among these remains are the Pipe Shrine House, which has a spiral pattern inscribed into one of the sandstone blocks in its south wall.

Protecting the dwellings

By the end of the 13th century, Mesa Verde had become a ghost town. Sometime between 1270 and 1300 – for reasons that are still a mystery – the residents began moving to new homes in the desert of northern Arizona and New Mexico. There is much speculation on the causes of this mass evacuation. Droughts and crop failures occurred in the region in the late 13th century, but researchers also think that political and social problems – and, perhaps, the pressure of a growing population – led the Ancestral Puebloans to abandon their sky-high homes.

The Mesa Verde cliff dwellings had been empty for nearly 600 years when

American ranchers and reporters came across them in the 1880s and described them to the outside world. Swedish aristocrat and amateur archaeologist Gustaf Nordenskiold excavated more than 600 artefacts, including pottery items and tools. But when he shipped them back to Europe – which he could do as there were no laws to prevent such pilferage – an outraged American public began lobbying the government to protect the ancient treasures of the southwest.

Mesa Verde's most energetic advocate was writer Virginia McClurg, who gave lectures, raised money, organised

Built to last The thick walls of the Sun Temple on top of the mesa consist of a double brick wall with rubble filling the cavity. The cavities have now been covered with a concrete skin to prevent deterioration.

petitions and wrote to the White House urging official protection for the Colorado mountaintop. Perseverance paid off when President Theodore Roosevelt signed the 1906 bill making Mesa Verde a national park – the first dedicated solely to human rather than natural endeavour. That same year, the US Congress passed the federal Antiquities Act to safeguard artefacts and ancient sites on all public lands.

best of the rest...

AMERICA'S CLIFF DWELLINGS

■ Hundreds of cliff dwellings are scattered throughout the American southwest, many of them now designated as national monuments under the aegis of the National Park Service. Nearly as spectacular as those at Mesa Verde are the ruins of the **Canyon de Chelly**, tucked away down red-rock gorges in the middle of the Navajo Indian Reservation in northern Arizona.

■ **Chaco Canyon** in northwestern New Mexico thrived around the same time as Mesa Verde as a cultural, economic and administrative hub. The closest thing to a city in the region, Chaco had a high level of

community organisation, with far-reaching trade ties and monumental architecture that includes the largest buildings in North America prior to the 19th century.

■ One of the easternmost of the Ancient Puebloan sites is **Bandelier**, which sits near the Rio Grande in central New Mexico. Its cliff dwellings were occupied through the early Spanish period, but residents eventually abandoned their high-rise homes for pueblos in the river valley.

■ **Ute Mountain Tribal Park** in Colorado, adjacent to Mesa Verde, is a Native American reserve with hundreds of archaeological sites, including significant cliff dwellings such as Eagle Nest House. Visitors are only allowed into the park with a Native American Ute guide.

Chaco Canyon

MILFORD SOUND

Over millions of years, glaciers carved the scenery of New Zealand's Fjordland National Park. At its heart is Milford Sound, a fjord of serene beauty, surrounded by snowy peaks and sheer cliff walls.

The spectacular fjord known as Milford Sound was created more than two million years ago by the powerful grinding and scouring action of glaciers descending from the snow-capped peaks of surrounding mountains. It extends for 10 miles (16km) and reaches 350m (1,150ft) deep in places. The near-vertical grey-

Mile high Towering 1,692m (5,551ft) above the water, Mitre Peak earned its name because its shape resembles a bishop's mitre.

WHERE ON EARTH?

Milford Sound is one of 14 fjords in Fjordland National Park on New Zealand's South Island. The island's main air hub is Christchurch, 470 miles (755km) away. Weather permitting, spectacular flights from Queenstown to Milford by fixed-wing aircraft or helicopter take around 35 minutes.

NEW ZEALAND
● Wellington
Milford Sound ● Christchurch
Queenstown

black rock faces, scored by glaciers, are streaked with green in places, indicating copper, elsewhere by white quartz. Cool temperate rain forests of mosses, ferns and beech trees cling to the lower slopes.

Milford's natural bounty

Cruising the waters of Milford Sound is like a geography lesson come to life. Moisture-laden westerlies cross the Southern Ocean to dump annual rainfall of more than 7m (23ft) here. Brooding clouds cloak the surrounding peaks for more than 200 days a year, turning into silvery cascades before your eyes. Four big waterfalls hurtle permanently into Milford Sound, but the number can quickly increase to hundreds after heavy rains as temporary waterfalls that last

for a few days are fed by the rain-soaked moss in the forests above.

Fur seals sometimes bask on the rocks around Copper Point, as do birds such as the kea, New Zealand's only alpine parrot. Bottlenose dolphins often frolic in the sheltered waters. Also, below the tannin-stained layer of fresh water that flows into the sound, the sunless submarine environment encourages aquatic life more usually found at far greater depths, such as black coral.

Mythical origins

When British explorer Captain James Cook sailed up the rugged coastline in 1770, he missed the entrance to Milford Sound. Instead it was found by European sealers, including Welshman John Grono, who named it after his hometown of Milford Haven in 1822. Maori already visited to fish and hunt birds at the entrance to what they called Piopiotahi. In Maori mythology the inlet was carved out with an adze by the god Tu-Te-Raki-Whanoa who wanted to reach inland. He never completed the task, but he did create a perfect haven from the stormy southern seas.

Photo opportunity A tourist vessel gets as close as it can to Bowen Falls, the Sound's tallest permanent waterfall, which plunges into Harrison Cove.

best of the rest...

FJORDS

■ Part of the Patagonian wilderness area in southern Chile, the **Aysen Fjord** (also spelled Aisén) is 40 miles (65km) long. The glacier-carved inlet offers snow-capped peaks, fishing, kayaking, trekking and abundant wildlife, including dolphins.

■ A narrow track through a wild and empty glen leads from the Glencoe Road to the head of **Loch Etive** in Argyll and

Bute. Carved by glaciers during the last Ice Age, the loch is 18 miles (30km) long. Its mirror-still waters extend through some of Scotland's most enchanting scenery to connect with the beautiful Firth of Lorn on the Atlantic coast.

■ Canada's 340-mile (550km) **Saguenay Fjord** is part of the Park National du Fjord-du-Saguenay in Quebec and links the Gulf of St Lawrence and Atlantic Ocean with the Saguenay region. Once used by fur trappers and explorers, it has become a playground for visitors: in summer, cruise boats mingle

with kayaks; in winter, ice-fishing cabins are set up on the ice. Freshwater and seawater species mingle along much of its length, giving Saguenay the greatest biological diversity of any fjord on the planet.

■ The **Sognefjord** is Norway's longest and deepest – popular with visitors for its magnificent waterfalls, the Jotunheimen mountain range and blue-ice glacier. It is up to 1,308m (4,291ft) deep and extends inland more than 124 miles (200km). It is easily accessible by boat from Bergen or Oslo.

MONASTERIES OF METÉORA

Sandstone rock pinnacles rising dramatically from the Plain of Thessaly in northern Greece provided an unassailable retreat for hermits and monks devoting themselves to lives of austerity and prayer.

S et against the backdrop of the rugged Pindus Mountains, a refuge for bears and eagles, Metéora is simply awesome in its natural magnificence. The grey sandstone pillars soar 550m (1,800ft) from base to summit, sculpted over 60 million years by the erosion of wind and rain. The rock formations seem improbable enough, but perched on top of the sheer cliffs are six gravity-defying monasteries, reaching to the heavens.

Alone together at Metéora
It was in the ninth century AD that this remote forest of rock towers first began to attract hermits of the Orthodox Christian Church. The early anchorites, or religious recluses, took shelter in caves in the rock, often sharing their primitive homes with wild goats. Initially, the hermits lived in isolation, dedicating themselves to solitary prayer and meditation, but as their numbers increased they became less reclusive.

WHERE ON EARTH?
The Metéora monasteries are about 250 miles (400km) northwest of Athens – roughly a five-hour drive. There are also buses and trains from Athens to the nearby town of Kalambaka, from where visitors can take a taxi. Visitors to the monasteries must dress modestly (tops with sleeves; knee-length skirts or long trousers).

MACEDONIA
ALBANIA
GREECE
Monasteries of Metéora
Aegean Sea
Athens

> **"** According to legend, Athanasios was borne to the site of his new monastery in the claws of an eagle. The building materials had no such convenient transport. **"**

Gradually a loose monastic arrangement, known as a skete, emerged in which the religious individuals associated in groups, sharing a place of worship and offering mutual support.

The skete stopped short of being a full religious community and the monks were still essentially anchorites. Their purpose was private contemplation and they cooperated as a way of furthering that end. Elsewhere in Europe, monasteries were centres of agriculture and industry, knitted tightly into secular society as a whole, important engines of local economies and the nuclei for significant urban centres. But the Orthodox monastery remained a place apart from the world.

Pinnacle of prayer Dating from the 15th century, the Agia Triada (Holy Trinity) monastery claims the most dramatic setting in Metéora. It featured in the 1981 James Bond movie, *For Your Eyes Only*.

The first true monastery at Metéora was Mégalo ('Great') Metéoron, created in 1334. In this year, Athanasios Koinovitis, later known as St Athanasios the Meteorite, arrived at the head of a band of Christian followers migrating from the Orthodox monastic centre at Mount Athos. It was Athanasios who christened the site Metéora, Greek for 'in the sky', and conceived the outlandish project of building a monastery on top of the sandstone outcrop.

There were no paths or steps to the summit of the rocky mountain. According to legend, Athanasios was borne to the site of his new monastery in the claws of an eagle. The building materials had no such convenient transport, and were either carried on monks' backs up a precarious system of ladders or hauled by ropes up sheer rock faces. The Church of the Transfiguration was finished by 1356, but the other monastery buildings were not completed until 1372.

Metéora as metaphor

As the base for a working monastery of the Western European type, this site would have been hopelessly impractical. Medieval monasticism in the West was, by this time, following the 'Benedictine Rule'. While recognising the value of individual contemplation, St Benedict saw the monastery as a community, consecrated to a collective effort to help each other towards a spiritual goal. Hence the emphasis on group worship, shared meals and physical labour. Ploughing and harvesting the fields, raising livestock, keeping bees, brewing, wine-making – these all glorified God.

Up here, in contrast, the Greek monks were completely cut off. Even getting down from their religious eyrie was a dangerous business. But Athanasios was

Glory on a rock At the heart of Varlaam monastery is the *katholikon* (main chapel), built in the 1540s using materials hauled up from the plain and richly decorated with frescoes and gilded icons.

motivated by a spiritual ideal. Living high upon a rock eminence lifted the monks above the world the better to contemplate heaven. Mere symbolism, it might be said, but symbolism has always been important to the spiritual quest.

Most religious cultures have seen a strong analogy between the ideas of physical ascent and transcendence of a 'higher' sort: mountains and mysticism have always gone together.

ICON PAINTING

Painted either on panels or as frescoes on the walls of churches, icons play a vital role in Orthodox worship and have been produced for more than a thousand years. Depicting sacred images, such as Jesus, Mary, saints, angels and the Christian cross, the icon artists sought to create a bridge between the human and the divine experience. Every element of the image, from the gestures of the figures to the colours and materials used, is fixed by tradition, yet individual painters infuse each image with impressive emotion and spirituality.

The notion has had its place in the Judaeo-Christian tradition ever since Moses went up Mount Sinai to receive the Ten Commandments.

Mount Sinai had since become the site of a monastery, and it was there in the 7th century that St John Climacus wrote *The Ladder of Divine Ascent,* a treatise on spiritual salvation which became an inspiration for Orthodox Christians. Climacus set out his scheme for spiritual development as a series of steps, each one taking the soul a little higher, a little closer to the heavenly goal. While it might be true that the arduous climb to Metéora brought the believer closer to heaven only in a metaphorical sense, it was a metaphor with prestigious antecedents and a powerful influence on the Orthodox mind. The symbolic effort of cutting himself off from the world gave the monk the perfect mental preparation for his contemplative task.

Out of harm's way

There were other, more practical reasons why the remote site chosen by Athanasios made sense in a world that was becoming more unpredictable and perilous. For a thousand years Greece had been part of the Orthodox Byzantine Empire, but in the mid-14th century bands of Ottoman Turks were pressing into the country from Asia. To

SKELLIG MICHAEL

A climb of 618 steps, ascending over 180m (600ft), brings you to the clochans, the beehive huts, and other stone-built remains on Skellig Michael. These are the survivors of one of Europe's most remarkable and remote monastic communities. A wave-lashed outcrop off southwest Ireland, Skellig Michael (also known as Great Skellig) is now home to a noisy population of seabirds, but in the 7th century monks lived and prayed here. The dwellings and ancient walls are well preserved and open to pilgrims and visitors, but the surrounding choppy seas mean that the site is only accessible for short visits during the summer months.

Simple life Within the circular towers of Mégalo Metéoron are the monks' living quarters. The only decoration is iconographic artwork and religious symbols.

site your religious community in an inaccessible location made sense in the face of this alien threat.

Over the following two centuries, Ottoman intrusions grew into a full Turkish takeover of Greece, and the Christian Byzantine Empire was destroyed. Against this background of catastrophe for the Greek Orthodox Church, monastery building on the craggy heights of Metéora flourished: 24 independent monasteries were eventually founded there, of which six survive. The most spectacular was Agia Triada (Holy Trinity), completed in 1475, with sheer cliffs on all sides plunging to the valley. The monastery of Varlaam, built between 1541 and 1548, was second to Mégalo Metéoron in size and perhaps superior in the richness of its decoration. The life of the monks in these vertiginous retreats was inconvenient, to say the least. Mégalo Metéoron was accessible only by climbing ladders flimsily secured to the rock face. At Varlaam, which stood atop a sheer cliff almost 400m (1300ft) high, monks were raised and lowered in a net suspended from rope cables that reputedly were only replaced after they had snapped.

Moving forward

Despite these difficulties, the monasteries did not just survive, they positively prospered, farming extensive areas of land in the valley and keeping flocks of goats and sheep. Becoming a little more like their Western European counterparts, the monks started to look outwards, their trading contacts encouraging a wider interest in the world. They were anything but 'worldly' by normal standards, yet their horizons expanded as their economic means grew.

By the 16th century, the finest icon painters of the time were being brought from as far away as Crete to transform the interiors of the monastery churches into richly coloured jewels of Byzantine art. Varlaam can boast some of the finest work by the Theban-born Frangos Katelanos, a leading light of the School of Northwestern Greece.

Theophanis Bathas-Strelitzas is these days celebrated chiefly for his work in Russia, but he created the stunning wall-paintings in the *katholikon* (main chapel) of the Monastery of St Nicholas Anapausas. Theophanes of Crete, as he is more commonly known, was responsible for an important series of frescoes in the Mégalo Metéoron, too. They represent something of a high point in the Greek art of the time. But they also, and more literally, recall the Roman persecutions of the early Christians in startlingly graphic detail, providing a clue to the mindset of the communities who commissioned them. The monks flourished, but they felt beleaguered; their isolation was voluntary, but they were physically marooned in a rapidly changing world.

In addition to the Holy Trinity, Metéoron and Varlaam, the other monasteries that survive today are Rousanou, St Nicholas Anapausas and St Stephen, with no more than ten individuals living in each. The buildings have been remodelled over the centuries and they sustained significant damage during World War Two, but those who visit the site as a place of modern pilgrimage still experience the transcendence of its founding fathers.

best of the rest...
MONASTIC RETREATS

Monk at a Lake Tana monastery

■ No rocky walls or rolling waves cut off **Heiligenkreuz Abbey** from the outside world; just the gentle landscape of the Vienna Woods and the self-sufficiency of a monastic community that has followed the traditional Cistercian rule – of obedience, hard work, prayer and periods of silence – ever since the abbey's foundation in 1133. Over the centuries, monks from Heiligenkreuz have played a full and active part in the life of the Roman Catholic Church in Germany, but at the abbey itself all is serenity and calm.

■ Founded in 1958, the **New Camaldoli Hermitage** is a modern reaffirmation of the ancient Benedictine Rule. The hermitage has a stupendously scenic setting high up in the Santa Lucia Mountains above the Big Sur coast in California. The Camaldoli monks are extremely hospitable: visitors from Los Angeles, San Francisco and far beyond come here to the monastic retreat to find personal peace and inner calm.

■ There are few retreats farther from the world than the **Lake Tana Monasteries** at Bahir Dar in Ethiopia. More than 1,800m (5,900ft) up in the Amhara Mountains, at the source of the Blue Nile, are 20 churches and monasteries scattered over the islands of Lake Tana. The monasteries have stunning wall-paintings, rich vestments, sacramental vessels, manuscripts and other treasures. Daga Istifanos is said to have briefly housed the Biblical Ark of the Covenant. The monasteries reflect local building traditions and techniques. They are round in shape and each one consists of an inner sanctuary surrounded by inner and outer ambulatories, with magnificent paintings decorating the walls.

MONET'S GARDEN

Light and colour bring Impressionism to life at Giverny, the garden where Claude Monet shaped nature with such artistry that it became his inspiration for hundreds of paintings.

WHERE ON EARTH?

The village of Giverny is in the Haute-Normandie region of France, near the small town of Vernon 50 miles (80km) northwest of Paris. From Vernon, well-groomed paths cover the 2-mile (3km) walk to the gardens. Visitors can also hire bikes from cafés near the train station. A variety of day trips to the gardens can be made from Paris.

When the painter Claude Monet spotted Giverny from a train window while travelling from Normandy to Paris, what he saw was a sad, empty house in an abandoned garden. But this was exactly the place he had dreamed of, the perfect house for an expanding family, just one hour northwest of Paris. So in 1883, at 43 years of age, Monet with his second wife, Alice, and their eight children moved from Vertheuil on the River Seine to Giverny. At last Monet had not just an inspiring

Monet in his garden The artist stands on the Grande Allée, highlighting a view that was the inspiration for many of his paintings.

environment in which to paint, but one where he could orchestrate a continuous sequence of blossoms and foliage throughout the year. The artist planted, weeded and transplanted until this outdoor studio, its ever-changing subjects now thriving, was to his satisfaction. By 1901, no fewer than five gardeners were needed to tend the garden.

Floral magnificence

The long, pink-stuccoed house with green shutters served as both an anchor and a backdrop for the floral display of the Clos Normand. Divided by the

Grand Allée, a central path 3m (10ft) wide, and several smaller pebble paths, the 1.2ha (3 acre) Clos Normand is the principal garden at Giverny – essentially a meadow stretching across the front of the house and down to a country lane. Here, Monet planned long, rectangular flowerbeds that ran parallel to each other from the top to the bottom of the garden, so filling the entire meadow with flowers for bouquets.

Walking back towards the house under trellised arcs of roses, whatever the season, one marvels at the way Monet choreographed the progression of colour, paying attention to height, season and foliage, all to complement the tones of the house. By paying particular attention to the way early-morning mist created veiled colours, as well as to the sharp silhouettes and shadows cast by the midday sun, Monet incorporated the power of light in the garden's overall scheme.

The water garden

Once the flowerbeds had been planted and painted from many perspectives, the artist turned his considerable energies to creating a water garden. In 1891, across the country lane from the Clos Normand, Monet diverted the Rû – a tributary of the River Eure – to make a pond. Winding and intersecting paths were designed around the water to create a greater sense of space in this new garden.

It is here that Monet's beloved *nymphéas* – delicate pink and white blossoms resting on broad lily pads – appear to float among the clouds as reflections interplay with sky and water. The artist planted a Japanese wisteria, still rambling along an iron arbour today, to frame the pond. Clusters of yellow iris edge the composition in early summer, accenting the arc of the Japanese bridge. This graceful note is just one element of Japanese art found at Giverny: in the house, Monet's collection of Japanese prints – including

many by the 19th-century master Katsushika Hokusai – line the hallway, yellow dining-room and staircase.

Loving restoration

Following Monet's death from lung cancer in 1926, his son Michel inherited Giverny and his stepdaughter Blanche looked after the property, but after World War Two it fell into a state of neglect. After Michel's death in 1960, it passed to the French Académie des Beaux-Arts, and in 1977 Gérald van der Kemp was appointed curator. With

Floral splendour A profusion of colours based on Monet's paintings fills the long beds of the Clos Normand and rose trellises span the Grand Allée.

IMPRESSIONISM

In the second half of the 19th century, Monet and a group of painters, including Pierre-Auguste Renoir, Alfred Sisley and Berthe Morisot, began to work out of doors in order to capture moments of changing light. It was Monet's hazy-brilliant painting of a seaport, *Impression, Sunrise*, that earned the group their name after a scathing review of their first exhibition in 1872.

The Impressionists' passion for subjects bathed in natural light was a daring move at the time, creating a bridge into the revolutionary 20th century. Monet's own passion for capturing the effects of light and atmosphere, seen especially in his

paintings of his Clos Normand (below), led him to produce series of paintings of subjects such as haystacks, willow trees and cathedrals in different conditions.

generous financial support from a group of American and French donors, as well as advice from people who had visited during Monet's lifetime, Van der Kemp oversaw the restoration of the garden.

By then, the lily pond had silted over, so a new water source was found and the Japanese bridge was rebuilt. Using Monet's paintings as the only guide to the original garden, roses and irises were replanted in the Clos Normand flowerbeds, while interiors were repaired and the famous chrome-yellow dining-room repainted. Today, if one stands in this bright room, looking out across the Clos Normand, one can almost hear the hum of Monet's voice with his family and friends, such as Edouard Manet, Pierre-Auguste Renoir and Guy de Maupassant, as they exchange ideas over a long lunch.

Lasting influence

Today, much of Giverny's charm lies in its original spirit – still palpable – as a family garden. It is easy to imagine children chasing each other along the pebble paths, or playing with kittens beneath the rose trellises, or heading off with nets to try their luck with fish in the pond across the lane.

But there is more to this story, for this exceptional garden brings into focus an

Spring blooms Tulips, aubretia, pansies and forget-me-nots were among the garden's early-flowering plants, along with cherry and crab-apple blossoms.

era of transition in painting as well as in garden design. The garden at Giverny became a mecca for both garden and art lovers for many years. To this day it remains a destination for artists and gardeners looking for inspiration in its masses of iris and brilliant poppies in

spring and in the on-going dance of pink cosmos, purple autumn asters and golden helianthus. The garden at Giverny is more than an artist's statement: it marks a time of great cultural change and remains a living record of Claude Monet's vision.

Created to inspire Its design based on Japanese gardens, Monet's lily pond eventually became his principal subject.

best of the rest...

GARDENS

■ The **Abbey Gardens** on Tresco in the Isles of Scilly display 232 subtropical plants from 80 countries. The garden's unique setting, created in 1834 around a medieval priory ruin, is carved out of a rock slope.

■ The Renaissance **Giardini di Boboli** in the grounds of the Pitti Palace offer sweeping views over the rooftops of Florence in Italy. Designed in 1549 for the Spanish wife of Cosimo di Medici, the walkways and vistas are enhanced with Roman sculptures as well as figures from the 16th and 18th centuries.

■ French painter, Jacques Majorelle, planned the 5ha (12 acre) **Jardin Majorelle** in Marrakech, Morocco, during the 1920s. Following extensive restoration in the 1980s, more than 300 native North African plant

Keukenhof

species now feature amid the garden's weaving paths and water features. Majorelle's signature blue still sparks both the architecture and fountains of this botanical wonderland.

■ A spring destination for fragrance and vibrant colour, **Keukenhof** gardens in Holland appeal to those seeking contemporary as well as historic aspects of Dutch horticulture. Rare 17th-century daffodils and 16th-century tulips

from the Hortus Bulborum in Leiden feature in the historical section.

■ Established in 1913, the **Kirstenbosch National Botanical Garden** in South Africa features a great diversity of natural flora set against the forest backdrop of the eastern slopes of Table Mountain.

■ The **Ryoan-ji** garden, northwest of Kyoto in Japan, is a fine example of the Zen dry garden tradition that dates back to the Muromachi period (1392-1568). Arranged in a long rectangle, stones carefully set on a base of lichen are surrounded by fastidiously raked gravel in precise, waved lines. It is a calm space for meditation.

■ An opulent garden in the centre of Shanghai's old city in China, the **Yuyuan** dates back to the Ming dynasty. The stunning 12m (40ft) high rockeries, a zigzag bridge and an inner garden are all best viewed in the early spring as cherry trees bloom.

NAZCA LINES

Etched into the hard-baked desert of southern Peru are a series of vast images whose purpose is one of the world's most compelling mysteries.

Whether you believe the Nazca Lines were made by visiting aliens or ancient human civilisations, these giant geometric and animal forms, which can only be properly understood when seen from the air, are stunning in their scale, quantity, complexity and state of preservation.

Drawings in the desert

More than a thousand lines, geometric figures and animal forms are rendered on a wide desert plain known as the Pampa de San Jose. They cover an area 37 miles (59km) long and 1 mile (1.6km) wide. Trapezoids and triangles are the largest works, and the Lines also include spirals and circles, and sets of parallel lines, the best known being the Runway. Eleven animal forms are recognisable, including a hummingbird, monkey, pelican, condor, spider and whale. The most celebrated figure – and the nexus of all the theories that swirl around the site – is the 'Astronaut', a giant, cartoon-like humanoid figure etched onto a hillside.

Some of the straight lines run for a few miles, while the largest formations are more than 200m (660ft) in diameter. They were made by pushing aside the dark stone covering the desert surface to expose the lighter soil beneath. In the dry, windless desert conditions, the Lines have remained uncovered.

Science fiction

During an expedition in search of ancient irrigation systems in Peru in 1939–41, American historian Paul Kosok revealed the existence of the Nazca Lines to the

Monkey business The monkey figure, which measures 93m (305ft) by 58m (190ft), is surprising as monkeys are not found in this desert region.

WHERE ON EARTH?

The Nazca Lines are near the city of Nazca in southern Peru, about 290 miles (465km) by road south of the capital, Lima. Buses run from Lima (eight hours) and from the town of Ica (three hours). Tour operators offer trips over the Lines in light aircraft stationed at the tiny Nazca airport.

COLOMBIA
ECUADOR
PERU
BRAZIL
Lima
Ica
Nazca Lines
Pacific Ocean
BOLIVIA
CHILE

outside world. One of his colleagues, the German mathematician Maria Reiche, then spent the best part of five decades recording and interpreting the geoglyphs. But it was Erich von Däniken, author of the paranormal, who turned the mysterious artworks into internationally known figures in his 1968 book *Chariots of the Gods*. He postulated that the lines marked landing strips for the spaceships of extra-terrestrial visitors from long ago.

Modern researchers believe that the works were made by the ancient Nazca civilisation that thrived in the area between 200 BC and AD 600. But speculation continues about the purpose of the Lines. Reiche thought they formed an astronomical calendar. Others endow the Lines with religious significance, suggesting that people walked along them as part of religious ceremonies. The most recent theories speculate that the Lines

The Hummingbird A complex pattern of lines scratched into the top of a plateau make up the form known as the hummingbird. It covers an area similar in size to a football pitch.

were associated in some way with sources of water in the desert.

The same artistry that could have created the Nazca Lines is also evident on local ceramics excavated from ancient Nazca cemeteries. Vessels show both realistic and stylised depictions of plants, animals and deities. It is possible that the Nazca people created their vast desert images by scaling up smaller drawings and plotting them on the ground.

Although theories abound, the purpose of the Nazca Lines continues to be a mystery. History will keep its secrets, but the Lines will remain for millennia.

best of the rest...

GEOGLYPHS

Brazil's **Acre Geoglyphs** are recent discoveries. More than a hundred earthwork images have been exposed by deforestation in the Amazon rain forest in Acre state. The perfectly rendered figures include circles, squares, rectangles and octagons.

Lost in the Mojave Desert until a pilot noticed them in 1932, California's **Blythe Geoglyphs** include more than 50 humanoid figures and a huge maze made around a thousand years ago.

Uffington's White Horse

The **Marree Man** is a human figure etched into the South Australian desert discovered by Trec Smith in 1998. Objects buried nearby suggest that it is a modern creation, but the artist is unknown. It is also called Stuart's

Giant after the famed Outback explorer. At 2.6 miles (4.2km) tall and nearly as wide, it is the largest geoglyph in the world.

Uffington's **White Horse** is the second-largest chalk figure in Britain and possibly the oldest, dating from 800-700 BC. Its designers may have used a mathematical scale to render the image on the chalky soil.

Satellite mapping and aerial photography revealed the **Works of the Old Men** in the Arabian Desert, Jordan, in 2011. The wheel-shaped stone images were originally spotted by British pilots in the 1920s, but then forgotten again.

NEUSCHWANSTEIN

'Mad' King Ludwig II of Bavaria built castles the way other monarchs might commission carriages or paintings. His crowning creation was the Schloss Neuschwanstein, the fairy-tale castle that inspired Walt Disney.

Seen at dawn across its Alpine valley, the castle appears to float on air. Here an Arthur might have held his court; to such a place might Parsifal have come in his quest for the Holy Grail. Neuschwanstein is utterly gorgeous and at the same time outrageous: a medieval monument built in relatively modern times; a royal whim followed through at colossal cost and on a gigantic scale.

King Ludwig II was extremely shy and eccentric and this superb structure was the most grandiose expression of his architectural passion. Today, 120 years on from its construction (it was never quite completed), Schloss Neuschwanstein still exudes a dreamlike regal dignity from its mountaintop.

Paradoxically, it lives up to the idea of a medieval castle more than many real-life examples ever did. Ravishingly beautiful, it rises sheer from its dramatic craggy setting, its pinnacled towers rhyming with the pine trees below and the distant Alpine peaks beyond.

WHERE ON EARTH?

Neuschwanstein Castle stands high on a hillside above the village of Hohenschwangau, not far from Füssen, Bavaria, near the Austrian border. The closest international airport is 80 miles (130km) away, in Munich. The castle is easily reached by road and rail. There is even a horse-drawn carriage.

GERMANY   Munich ●

Neuschwanstein ●

LIECHTENSTEIN   Innsbruck ●
  AUSTRIA

SWITZERLAND   ITALY

Monumental legacy

Ludwig's obsessions were not so unusual for a man of wealth, education and imagination living in the second half of the 19th century. His grandfather, Ludwig I, had rebuilt Munich, work which was continued by his father Maximilian II. Ludwig II was in part inspired to build castles by a visit to Versailles and other great French palaces. He longed to bring a touch of this glamour to his own country, and he set about the task with gusto.

Using his own personal fortune, rather than dipping into state coffers, he began altering and building a series of castles. Neuschwanstein was to be his cliff-top hideaway, a fantasy evoking medieval myth and a setting for the works of composer Richard Wagner. Ludwig himself was quite explicit in suggesting the castle's direct inspiration by – and allusion to – Wagner's works. The castle's keep and courtyard were intended to recall those of the Castle of the Grail in *Lohengrin*; the Singers' Hall within was supposed to be the 'Minstrels' Hall' from *Tannhäuser*.

While Neuschwanstein is medieval in its copious use of intricate wood-carving, tapestries and wall-hangings, this romantic masterpiece was also to be the last word in modern comfort. It had opulent furnishings, carpets and all mod cons: electric bells to summon servants; central heating; hot and cold running water in the bedrooms; even telephone lines so the king could keep in touch with the outside world. Although the interior was never finished (the main building alone had more than

200 rooms), enough was completed to show what Ludwig had in mind.

Ludwig's architectural ambitions led to him borrowing heavily and powerful ministers in government, after vetoing some of his plans, eventually had him certified insane and deposed. But today his creations – and Neuschwanstein, in particular – are among the biggest money-earning tourist attractions in Germany. Ludwig II remains a popular figure in the collective Bavarian memory and as time has shown he and his schemes were not so mad after all.

Fairy-tale inspiration So fantastical was Ludwig's creation that the Disney Corporation used it as the model for Sleeping Beauty's Disneyland palace.

best of the rest...

FANTASY HOMES

■ **Tsarkoe Selo**, south of St Petersburg, Russia, was the summer home of Catherine the Great. In the 1780s, she had a 'Chinese Village' constructed here, complete with pagodas, pavilions and a palace in the oriental style.

■ Roman temple, Renaissance cathedral, Moorish mansion - California's **Hearst Castle** is all of these things and more. And all built in the 1920s and 1930s using brick and concrete, for the newspaper magnate William Randolph Hearst.

Knights' tales Occupying an entire floor in the east wing of the castle, the Singers' Hall is decorated with murals depicting scenes from medieval legends.

Hearst Castle

NGORONGORO CRATER

East Africa in miniature, the world's largest unbroken volcanic crater has it all – savannah grassland, lakes, springs and the 'big five'.

WHERE ON EARTH?

The Ngorongoro Crater is in the highlands of northeast Tanzania, about 110 miles (180km) west of Arusha, the nearest town with an international airport and gateway to the safari circuit. The area around Ngorongoro is part of the Serengeti ecosystem with the plains of Serengeti National Park to the northeast.

UGANDA
KENYA
Lake Victoria
Nairobi
SERENGETI NATIONAL PARK
Ngorongoro Crater ● Arusha
TANZANIA

Wildlife sanctuary Herds of zebra and wildebeest feed on Ngorongoro's grasslands.

Dark, steep walls surround the vast natural amphitheatre that is the Ngorongoro Crater. The residents of this huge, pastel-coloured bowl include 25,000 large mammals, the densest concentration anywhere in the world, along with the greatest number of large predators in the whole of Africa. Here, wildebeest, zebra and gazelles live cheek-by-jowl with lions, leopards, cheetahs and hyenas in a self-contained and partly isolated ecosystem of savannah, woodland, river, swamp and lake.

The big five

The crater walls are up to 600m (1,960ft) high and the crater itself is more than 11 miles (18km) across, four times the size of Manhattan. So many animals are packed into this relatively small space that visitors are almost guaranteed to see the 'big five', a term originally used by big-game hunters to describe the most difficult animals to hunt on foot – lions, leopards, black rhinos, elephants and Cape buffalo.

Ngorongoro is more than 2,000m (6,500ft) above sea level so the climate is often unexpectedly cool. October to December can be sunny and warm, but June to August can be downright cold, especially at night, when the temperature on the crater's rim can drop below freezing. Thunderstorms rock the crater during the short rainy season in November, and again during the long rains in April and May. There is almost always water in the crater, even during the dry season, so droughts (which occur from time to time) are normally not as serious a problem here as in other parts of Africa.

The slopes on the eastern side of the crater receive the most rain and are cloaked in verdant montane forest, while the drier western slopes support grass and bush, and a scattering of towering euphorbia trees, among which the diminutive dik-dik antelope and the rare mountain reedbuck reside. Mineral-rich soils support a lush, short-grass plain

CRATERS AND CALDERAS

Although called a 'crater', Ngorongoro is strictly speaking a 'caldera', a huge crater that formed when a massive volcano erupted and then collapsed on itself two to three million years ago. The volcano is thought to have been about 18,000m (59,000ft) high, and was part of the volcanic activity associated with the formation of the East African Rift Valley. Nearby Ol Doinyo Lengai – the mountain of God – is still actively erupting.

in the centre of the caldera floor, where herds of zebra, wildebeest and gazelle graze alongside eland and kongoni antelopes. In the eastern section, tussocks of longer grasses provide food for African buffalo and hiding places for serval, a medium-sized, spotted cat with a small head, big ears and long legs.

A patch of thorny acacia fever tree and fig tree woodland forms the magical Lerai Forest in the southwest of the crater. Its name is derived from the Masai word for the tall fever trees with their distinctive greenish-yellow bark. In the early morning they seem to float on a wispy mist, while brightly coloured, iridescent sunbirds flit between the branches; large 'tusker' elephants churn up insects for expectant cattle egrets; vervet monkeys and baboons search for seeds; and, in the shadows, a secretive leopard might appear for a moment, disappearing once more as it merges with the dappled green and brown foliage.

Wildlife communities
The Lerai Forest is fed by the Lerai Stream, which in turn flows into Lake Makat, meaning 'salt', one of Africa's smaller soda lakes. In the drier times of

year, the lake is little more than a stark white salt pan, but in the wet season thousands of lesser flamingos arrive to feed on the blue-green algae that grow in its alkaline waters.

Freshwater springs emerge around the foot of the crater walls. Ngoitokitok Spring, on the eastern side, feeds the large Gorigor Swamp, one of two swamps in the crater (the other is Mandusi Swamp). The swamps are the favourite haunts of hippopotamuses, as well as of many species

What's in a name? The black rhinoceros above is not that different in colour to the white rhinoceros, also native to Africa. More accurate descriptions include hook-lipped (black) and square-lipped (white rhino).

of water birds, including the occasional party of regally attired crowned cranes, white storks, and swallows that fly in from Europe to overwinter here.

The area between the Lerai Forest and Gorigor Swamp is black rhino territory. Native to central and eastern Africa, these

best of the rest...

AFRICAN WILDLIFE PARKS

■ The **Serengeti National Park** - the name Serengeti means the 'endless plain' to the Masai people - hosts one of the greatest mass migrations of wildlife on the planet. Millions of wildebeest, zebra

Serengeti crocodile

and Thomson's gazelle, along with topi and eland, embark on their annual circuit of the Serengeti's savannahs, riverine forests and acacia woodlands in an unending search for food and water. Predators - lions, leopards, cheetahs and hyenas - often watch for the herds from rocky outcrops, but the greatest danger comes when the animals must cross crocodile-infested rivers.

■ In the northern part of their Serengeti migration, wildebeest tackle the Mara River in Kenya's **Masai Mara National Park**, itself a continuation of the Serengeti ecosystem. Here, some of the largest Nile crocodiles in Africa intercept the herds. The result is a food bonanza not just for the crocodiles but also for griffon vultures, which time their breeding to coincide with the annual glut of dead wildebeest. The birds fly a round trip of 185 miles (300km) between the hunting

sites and their nests in the Gol Mountains at the northern end of the Ngorongoro Conservation Area. And what the crocodiles don't kill often fall prey to lions. The Mara, meaning 'mottled' on account of the patchy vegetation, is noted for its lions, especially the Marsh Pride.

■ In South Africa's Eastern Cape Province is the **Kwandwe Private Game Reserve**, a pristine, malaria-free wilderness straddling the Great Fish River. The 'big five' are here, together with a number of local specialities. Kudu, springbok and grysbok are active during the day, while aardwolf, aardvark and the rare spotted porcupine appear at night. *Kwandwe* means 'place of the blue crane', South Africa's national bird, and a healthy population of this very rare bird can be found here, a clear indication of the reserve's conservation success.

animals are exceptionally rare, and the Ngorongoro Crater has one of the finest populations. They spend the night in the forest, then, in the morning, venture onto the grassy plain to feed before the sun gets too high in the sky, when they retreat back to the trees for the rest of the day.

The rhino population has been decimated by poachers, who kill these magnificent creatures for their horns. From a pre-1970s population in the crater of about 110, the number dropped to just ten survivors. With armed rangers now watching rhinos around the clock, poachers are less of a problem, but rhino numbers increase very slowly due to their long gestation period.

Humans are not the only threat to the black rhino population. Hyenas kill the newborn calves and elephants compete with rhino mothers for food. Tick-borne diseases also take their toll, while disturbance from tourists is another factor in the slow rate of recovery. Even so, according to the Frankfurt Zoological Society, which studies them, 35 black rhinos live here today, four calves having been born during 2011.

Freedom of movement

Although the steep walls create a natural enclosure, the animals of Ngorongoro are not trapped in the crater. Some of the zebra and wildebeest leave during unusually wet periods, and bull elephants come and go, fighting it out on the nearby Serengeti plains for the right to mate and returning to Ngorongoro for rest and recuperation.

> **" Native to central and eastern Africa, black rhinos are exceptionally rare and the Ngorongoro Crater has one of the finest populations. "**

Large irritable bulls, with huge tusks and flapping ears, regularly confront visitors on the roads in and out of the crater.

Lions tend to stay put, living in family groups called prides. In 1962 the lions met their nemesis in the form of a small insect. A drought in 1961 was followed by rains the following year that continued even through the dry season, and the crater was overrun by a plague of stable flies. These biting insects drank so much blood and caused so many infected sores

among the lion population that numbers drastically dwindled. From a population of about 70, just eight survived by hiding from the flies in hyena burrows or up trees. In the following years numbers picked up and by 1999 there were 68 lions in the crater. A recurrence of drought followed by extensive rains in 2000 and 2001 saw the deaths of 604 large mammals. Buffalo, wildebeest and zebra took the brunt of fatalities, but five rhinos and six lions also died. With little new blood entering the population from outside, inbreeding among the lions is becoming a real problem for the crater's four prides.

Cradle of humankind

Humans and their forebears have lived in and around the Ngorongoro Crater for at least four million years. Evidence of this can be found about 18 miles (30km) to the north of the crater in a steep-sided ravine known as the Olduvai Gorge. This name is both a misspelling

Master of his universe The male lion is large, well fed and does not take kindly to strangers – he will see off any other male who tries to muscle in on his pride.

202

and a misunderstanding. It was adopted in 1911 when German entomologist Wilhelm Kattwinkel thought his Masai guide was giving him the name of the gorge but was, in fact, describing the vegetation. Since 2005 the area has been officially known as Oldupai Gorge from the Masai word for 'wild sisal', a plant with natural healing properties that grows there.

It is here that archaeologist and naturalist Louis Leakey (1903-72) and members of his family dug for fossils of early humans and their close relatives, collectively known as 'hominids'. They discovered several distinct hominid species more than a million years old. Some were of the genus *Australopithicus*, meaning 'southern apemen', while others were thought to be the progenitors of humankind, such as *Homo habilis*, or 'handyman'. At nearby Laetoli they discovered footprints left by individuals thought to have walked upright on the Earth around 3.7 million years ago.

Early modern humans, *Homo sapiens*, lived here about 17,000 years ago. They were hunter-gatherers, much as the Bushmen are today, but about 3,000 years ago they were replaced by pastoralists and farmers – first the Iraqw and Datoga people, and then the semi-nomadic Masai. Among the fig trees growing in the Lerai Forest are a number of 'sacred' specimens planted on the grave of a Datogan chief who met his death in a battle with the Masai more than 200 years ago.

Small but SPECIAL

VIRUNGA NATIONAL PARK

Established in 1925, the Virunga National Park (formerly Albert National Park) in the Democratic Republic of the Congo is Africa's oldest. Wars and civil unrest in the recent past have damaged its wildlife, but now the park is undergoing a renewal. It was set up to protect the critically endangered mountain gorillas, along with forest elephants, okapi and chimpanzees. Even through the worst of the region's troubles the gorilla population has more than doubled thanks to the dedication of its rangers.

The park has a multiplicity of habitats, ranging from alpine forests to lowland swamps, and tropical savannah to eternal snow. It is one of the few places in Africa where visitors can trek to a glacier - in Uganda's Rwenzori Mountains, known more romantically as the 'mountains of the moon' - or climb up and camp on the rim of an erupting volcano, Nyiragongo, whose crater is sometimes filled by a lava lake and whose molten lava is so fluid it races down the slopes of the volcano at speeds of up to 60mph (100km/h).

Lake Makat The Ngorongoro Conservation Area supports large numbers of the lesser flamingo. While the birds like to feed at Lake Makat in the crater, many of them breed further north, at Lake Natron.

In 1892 Austrian mapmaker Oscar Baumann was the first European to enter the crater. At the time, this part of what is now Tanzania was German East Africa. Not long afterwards, in 1899, two German brothers set up two farms about 7 miles (12km) apart on the crater floor, where they grew sisal and wheat. They also killed many wildebeest, canning and shipping the tongues out of the country. After World War One they were forced to leave when the English became rulers of this part of Africa.

In 1954 everyone living in the crater was evicted, and in 1959 the Ngorongoro Conservation Area was inaugurated. Even so, today the Masai are permitted to take their livestock to salt licks around Lake Makat, their red *shukas* billowing in the breeze and their spears reflecting

the sun. They must leave the crater by nightfall, along with the tourists.

The first lodge to be built on the crater rim appeared in 1935, and in recent times more have sprung up, each with spectacular views. Access to the crater is controlled to maximise visitor numbers while minimising disturbance.

Explosive past and present

Ngorongoro is not the only volcanic crater here. Within the Ngorongoro Conservation Area there are several smaller, less visited calderas. In the highlands to the northeast of Ngorongoro, the Olmoti Crater has a floor of grass tussocks where Masai livestock graze alongside eland, buffalo,

bushbuck and reedbuck antelopes. The 3.7 mile (6km) wide Empakaai Caldera has an 85m (280ft) deep soda lake, unusually deep for an alkaline lake, with flamingos, cape teal and black-winged stilts. These two calderas are the remains of extinct volcanoes, but a third crater about 50 miles (80km) from Ngorongoro, called Ol Doinyo Lengai, is still active. During 2007 and 2008, a series of eruptions rocked the 2,962m (9,718ft) high mountain. Ol Doinyo Lengai is the only active volcano on Earth that sometimes produces natrocarbonatite lava, which emerges at the comparatively low temperature of 510°C (950°F) – about half that of the basalt lavas from volcanoes such as those on Hawaii. By day, the fluid lava resembles a mudflow; at night it glows orange. And when the lava solidifies, it sparkles in the sunlight.

Vulnerable species Despite a 1989 ban on hunting elephants for their ivory, poaching continues and the African bush elephant remains an endangered species.

OLINDA

A rich blend of colonial architecture and thriving Brazilian culture combine in this jewel of a city overlooking the Atlantic Ocean.

It may not be as well known as other Iberian outposts scattered across the planet, but Olinda in northeastern Brazil outshines the competition with its meticulously preserved architecture and vivacious cultural life. The city traces its roots to 1535, when Portuguese military leader and aristocrat Duarte Coelho Pereira founded a small settlement on a hillside here, making it the second-oldest city in Brazil after São Vicente in São

Baroque splendour One of many religious landmarks in the city, the Convent of San Francisco is noted for the carved wooden ceiling in its Church of Our Lady of the Snows and for the beautiful tilework in its cloisters.

Paulo state. By the early 17th century it had grown into the capital of the Pernambuco region and was a hub of the Portuguese sugar-cane industry.

Warfare in Europe led to a Dutch invasion and occupation of northeastern Brazil from 1630 to 1654. The invaders chose Recife with its better harbour as their stronghold and later burned Olinda to the ground, destroying many of the original buildings.

Rebirth and longevity

When the Portuguese returned, they rebuilt Olinda into an even more splendid city, meshing buildings that had survived the inferno with new ones in the Baroque style. Most prominent are the churches, convents and seminaries, their interiors richly decorated with carved wood, gilding, sculptures and painted tiles. Landmarks include Carmo Church, the oldest Carmelite church in Brazil, Olinda Cathedral and the Convent of San Francisco. Strewn along the narrow cobbled streets are hundreds of houses from the same period. Painted bright colours, their pretty facades are decorated with wooden window shutters and wrought-iron balconies. Conservation efforts started in the 1970s and the strict renovation rules have preserved the architectural integrity of the old town.

Although it lost much of its political and commercial clout when Recife was made the state capital in 1827, Olinda continued to prosper as a cultural, religious and intellectual centre and today is home to almost 400,000 people. A highlight of the city's unique cultural life is the annual carnival in the week preceding Lent. Unlike the glitzy affairs in Rio de Janeiro and elsewhere, Olinda's carnival adheres to tradition: scores of small musical groups perform and giant puppets are paraded through the streets to the samba beat.

best of the rest...

IBERIAN COLONIAL ARCHITECTURE

■ Guatemala's oldest European city, **Antigua** has endured earthquakes and volcanic eruptions to emerge as the most splendid Hispanic survivor in Central America. Founded in 1527 it was one of the first Spanish cities in the Americas and has been wowing visitors ever since. Aldous Huxley, normally not prone to hyperbole, said of it 'there is much that is charming, much that is surprising ... picturesque and romantic in the most extravagant 18th-century style'.

La Merced Church, Antigua

■ Set along Cuba's secluded south coast, **Trinidad** basks in the Caribbean sun, its pastel palaces, Baroque churches and cobblestone squares restored in recent years to pristine condition. The city was born in 1514, making it even older than Antigua, and it seems little changed from Baroque days, a relic of colonial times that survived the Cuban Revolution.

■ Surrounded by moats and thick stone walls, Manila's ancient **Intramuros** area huddles between the harbour and the high-rise towers of the Makati business district. Seat of Spanish power in the Far East for more than 300 years, the city was started by conquistador Miguel López de Legazpi in 1571. Largely destroyed during World War Two, Intramuros has been brought back to life over the past 30 years with the restoration of its colonial churches, plazas and townhouses.

PANTANAL

In the centre of South America, rivers flow into an immense landlocked delta where each year floodwaters rise, then recede again, creating an ecosystem unrivalled for its wildlife.

The Pantanal is the largest wetland in the world. It is ten times bigger than the Florida Everglades – in fact, it is bigger than the entire state of Florida – and represents 3 per cent of all the world's wetlands. Its name comes from the Spanish *pantano*, or *pântano* in Portuguese, meaning 'swamp', 'marsh' or 'bog'. But these terms do not do justice to the mosaic of savannah, forest, swamps and lagoons that form one of the most biologically rich environments on Earth.

The Pantanal is essentially a broad, flat basin that tilts slightly from east to west. Its rivers and streams feed into the mighty Paraguay River, but the quantity of water flowing through varies between the wet and dry seasons. It is this seasonal change that gives the Pantanal its unique character.

WHERE ON EARTH?

The Pantanal is south of the Amazon and east of the Andes; two-thirds is in Brazil, the rest in Bolivia and Paraguay. Cuiabá is a hub for the northern Pantanal, while Campo Grande is a gateway in the south. Access by river is via Caceres on the Paraguay River, or by the rickety-bridged Transpantaneira road.

BRAZIL
BOLIVIA
• Cuiabá
● Pantanal
● Campo Grande
CHILE
PARAGUAY
ARGENTINA

Seasonal flood

During the wet season, between October and March, rain falls on the Cerrado, a huge tract of tropical woodland and savannah to the east of the Pantanal, and tumbles over an escarpment in spectacular waterfalls that cascade into the Pantanal basin. Coupled with more localised rain, these torrents swell the

Pantanal crocodile A caiman suns itself beside a slow-moving river. Caimans prefer to hunt at night, feeding on fish, birds and small mammals.

Paraguay River, which backs up and bursts its banks, turning about 80 per cent of the Pantanal into wetland. The local caimans, members of the alligator family, make the most of the spill, lining up along the riverbanks with their mouths agape, ready to grab any fish that are washed their way.

The wet season is the main feeding, growing and breeding time for the Pantanal's many fish species. As the water spreads, it is enriched with nutrients, leading to an explosion of freshwater plankton and aquatic invertebrates, and fish travel across the flooded plain to take full advantage of the glut.

The floodwaters can raise the water level by as much as 5m (16ft). Land animals congregate on higher ground, with predators and prey making strange bedfellows in their bid to escape the

flood. The top carnivore in the food chain is the elusive jaguar; in fact, the Pantanal is one of the few places in South America where visitors have a good chance of spotting one.

Seasonal drought

In the dry season, between April and September, everything changes. Water-dependent creatures search for residual pools, so peccaries and feral pigs find themselves at the water's edge, sharing space with capybaras, the world's largest rodent. Capybaras grow to 1m (3ft) in

length and resemble large guinea pigs. They wallow in water during the day to keep cool and rid themselves of biting flies.

In the pools, stranded catfish and eels are packed together like sardines in a can, providing a feast for flocks of herons, egrets and storks – especially jabirus and wood storks, which maximise their catch with the minimum of effort by jabbing at the water, catching a fish every time. Some of the larger lagoons have floating meadows of water hyacinths and giant water lilies. Wattled jacanas, which have huge feet, clamber from plant to plant across the lagoon searching for insects, and snail kites swoop down to feed on molluscs and other invertebrates. Below the surface lurks another of the Pantanal's giants, the anaconda, the world's heaviest snake and a formidable predator that is capable of swallowing a capybara whole.

Visitors drop in

Each year an influx of world travellers arrives. The Pantanal attracts migrants from three major flyways across the Americas, the birds either overwintering

Seasonal floodplain In the dry season the floodwaters subside, leaving meandering rivers and lakes surrounded by lush vegetation.

here or dropping in to refuel on their journey. Ospreys come in from North America, for instance, along with sandpipers, golden plovers and black-necked stilts. Wood storks arrive from Argentina to the south, and flycatchers from the Andes to the west.

Taking into account migrating and resident birds, researchers have identified more than 656 species in the Pantanal.

Bringing up babies The Pantanal has the largest population of resident jabiru storks in South America. They nest high in trees along the riverbanks.

In addition, the area is home to 95 types of mammal, 162 reptile species and at least 263 species of fish. It is likely, because of the density of the ecosystem, that even more plants and animals are yet to be discovered.

It is not just the number of species that is exceptional in the Pantanal, but the sheer quantity of animals. Researchers have estimated, for example, that more than 10 million caimans reside here, the largest concentration of crocodilians in the world, and more than 500,000 capybaras. The Pantanal is one of the best places in the world to see jaguars, giant otters, giant anteaters, giant armadillos, maned wolves and marsh deer, all endangered or vulnerable species. The Amazon receives more media attention for its biodiversity, but the Pantanal is the most exceptional place to see wildlife.

Animal harmony
Birds sing, insects buzz, frogs chirp, macaws squawk, piping guans rattle and the occasional yodel of the southern screamer pierces the air, but the overwhelming sound is the lowing of cattle. Around 98 per cent of the Brazilian section – two-thirds of the Pantanal – is privately owned and cattle ranching is a vital industry. There is little state protection. The Pantanal Matogrossense National Park covers just 520 of the Pantanal's estimated 77,000 sq miles (1,350 of 200,000km²), while the Taiama Ecological Station protects just 42 sq miles (110km²) of wetland.

Yet cattle ranching and wildlife have coexisted side by side here for more than two centuries. The ranchers look after their land and everything that lives on it. Some ranches, or *fazendas*, include designated wildlife reserves and finance conservation projects such as nest-boxes for rare hyacinth macaws and programmes for giant otters. The flood season is the key. The floods exclude cattle from the grasslands for part of the

Jaguar homestead The Pantanal's jaguars are the biggest in the world. Their strong jaws enable them to tear through the tough hides of caimans.

year and encourage rich growth in the dry season. As a result the grasslands are not overgrazed, allowing the Pantanal to remain one of the world's supreme reservoirs of life.

best of the rest...

WETLANDS

■ **Banc d'Arguin National Park** on the coast of Mauritania is an extraordinary place. Shorebirds from northern Europe, Siberia and Greenland overwinter here, and thousands more come to breed at the edge of the desert, between the Sahara and the Atlantic Ocean. The local Imraguen fishermen, whose name means 'the ones who gather life', continue to fish sustainably, and are one of the few peoples in the world who fish grey mullet cooperatively with wild ocean dolphins.

■ North America's **Bosque del Apache** is a spectacular wildlife refuge on the Rio Grande, New Mexico, where sandhill cranes, snow geese and many species of ducks spend the winter. Surrounding farmland provides them with supplementary food, and water levels are manipulated to ensure conditions are the optimum for birdlife. In summer, the place is deserted because all the birds have flown.

■ The **Danube Delta** on Romania's Black Sea coast is Europe's largest area of continuous marshland and second-largest river delta. It is an important wetland on the migratory route between central and Eastern Europe and the Mediterranean and Africa and attracts large numbers of birds. Cormorants, white and Dalmatian pelicans breed here in summer.

■ **Doñana National Park** in southwest Spain is an important European wetland, home to Spain's largest colony of imperial eagles and Iberian lynx, and a refuelling stop for birds migrating between Europe and Africa. There was once a

Lechwe in the Okavango Delta

delta here, but a huge sandbar blocked the streams and so the Guadalquivir River now has only one outlet to the sea. The sand has been blown into large dunes behind which are the marshes, or *marismas*, where flamingos are seen in summer.

■ The **Niger Inland Delta**, the Macina, is an area of wetland in central Mali. Here, the Niger River, the third-longest river in Africa, breaks up into a system of channels, marshes and lakes in the semi-desert Sahel, south of the Sahara Desert. Thousands of waterfowl overwinter here; cormorants, ibis, spoonbills and black-crowned crane use it as a nesting site. One of the only remaining large mammals is the rare African manatee, which lives in the river.

■ Botswana's **Okavango Delta** is the world's largest inland delta. The Okavango River discharges into a vast, flat basin in the Kalahari Desert. It is a great oasis within an arid land that becomes a temporary home for 200,000 mammals, including elephants and wild dogs, which move to the delta in winter. The most populous mammal is the lechwe, an antelope that can run in knee-deep water.

PARO TAKTSANG

Perched almost impossibly on a rocky ledge above the Paro Valley is a group of Buddhist temples in one of Bhutan's most sacred sites.

In the 8th century, the legend goes, Guru Rinpoche, the founder of Tibetan Buddhism, arrived in the Paro Valley on the back of a flying tigress. Landing on the Copper-Coloured Mountain, he meditated in a cave for three months before setting out to spread Buddhism across the valley. The site became a place of pilgrimage for Buddhists from across the Himalayas, and in 1692 the first main temples were built. Called Taktsang, or Tiger's Nest, the monastery – painstakingly restored after a fire in 1998 – now has more than a dozen shrines and temples and accommodates a small group of monks. Other monks live in nearby retreats, some remaining in solitary meditation for several years.

Place of pilgrimage

Seen from the main gate, a thin ribbon of white walls and pagoda roofs are squeezed up against the cliff face, linked only by steps and passages cut into the rock and rickety bridges. The occasional small terrace offers the visitor relief from the vertiginous path and the reward of spectacular views of the Paro Valley far below.

Temples jostle for space. Inside, the walls are covered with murals depicting

WHERE ON EARTH?

Taktsang is about 6 miles (10km) north of the town of Paro in western Bhutan, not far from the capital, Thimphu. There is an international airport nearby. Visitors need to join an organised tour to enter the country. A festival is held in the Paro Valley every spring in honour of Guru Rinpoche.

Jigme Dorji National Park
Paro Taktsang
Punakha
Torsa Strict Nature Reserve
Paro
Thimphu
BHUTAN

gurus and gods gazing through clouds of incense among gilded statues and altars piled high with offerings of flowers and fruit and butter sculptures. Among them are Guru Rinpoche and his consorts, the Copper-Coloured Paradise, the God of Long Life and the God of Wealth. Devotees peep through the grille into the holy cave, known as Pel Phuk, in which Guru Rinpoche lived and meditated, where now butter lamps flicker in the dark and images of the Bodhisattvas are just visible. Now and then, the deep chanting of monks echoes along the walls, punctuated by cymbals and gongs.

On the edge of the precipice Temples cling to the cliff face alongside sacred caves high above the valley.

best of the rest...

BUDDHIST MONASTERIES

■ The **Namgyal monastery** at Dharamsala in the Indian state of Himachal Pradesh is the private monastery of the exiled Dalai Lama and his followers. The complex includes his residence and several temples. Monks study Tibetan traditions, including religious rituals, debates, meditation and sacred dances.

■ At the foot of the Stok Mountains, south of Leh, **Hemis** is one of the largest monasteries in Ladakh, famous for its summer festival of religious dances.

■ On a lonely hill in the Indus Valley, the 15th-century **Thikse**, in Ladakh, has ten temples and a collection of rare books. Most stunning is the giant statue of the Future Buddha, sitting in the lotus position and gleaming with jewels.

PETRA

Once a bustling hub on two busy trade routes, Petra fell into obscurity for 700 years, abandoned in its rock canyon. Its rediscovery revealed a unique city carved into rose-red stone.

N o city in the world claims a more dramatic approach. Suspense and anticipation build as visitors – on foot, donkey or mule, or in horse-drawn traps – thread through the shadows of the winding rock cleavage known as the Siq ('the shaft'). In places, the mile-long (1.6km) passage is only 5m (16ft) wide, and the outlandishly weathered sandstone walls crowd in as they rise 200m (660ft) up out of sight. Altars, tombs, pillars and inscriptions carved into the walls whisper of what is to come, and expectations rise sharply. Suddenly the end appears. Beyond, spotlit from the open sky, is the stately facade of an impossibly grand and beautifully preserved classical building sculpted out of glowing rock.

To the right the dry valley of Wadi Musa snakes westwards through a canyon more than a mile (1.6km) long. Upwards of 800 ruins cling to the cliff faces,

Dramatic entrance The Treasury comes into view gradually as visitors approach the city along the narrow gorge known as the Siq.

WHERE ON EARTH?

Petra is in southern Jordan, 160 miles (260km) south of the capital, Amman. The hotels in Wadi Musa serve the tourist trade, as do the Bedouin-style camps nearby. International flights to Jordan arrive at Amman and Aqaba. Spring and autumn are the best seasons in which to visit to avoid the summer heat.

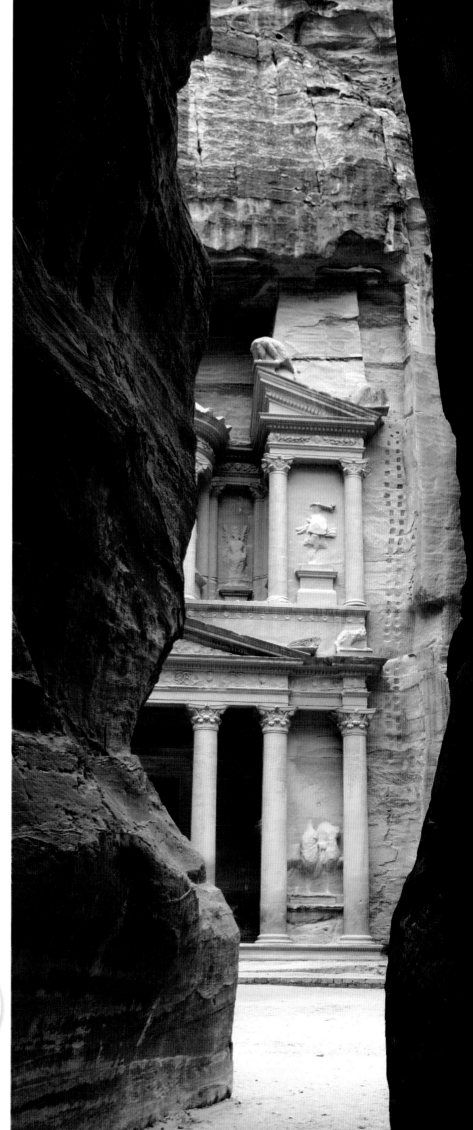

fronted by columns, pediments and architraves, pierced by doors and windows. Inside, cool, dark rooms, echoing and cavernous, plead mutely to tell their tale. Many are tombs with descriptive names – Silk, Urn, Corinthian and Royal – and they once held the skeletons of people who had animated the city.

Half as old as time

Records of ancient Petra are virtually non-existent barring rare references by authors of classical antiquity, such as Strabo and Pliny the Elder. The name simply means 'stone' in Greek. For centuries Petra was known only to the Bedouin, who grazed their goats on the sparse scrub and used the buildings for winter shelter and to store fodder. Then, in 1812, a 27-year-old Swiss explorer, Johann Ludwig Burckhardt, simply stumbled on it.

Burckhardt was on a mission to cross the Sahara Desert from east to west in an Arab caravan. Near the Dead Sea in southern Jordan, he heard tantalising reports of lost ruins and persuaded a local man to act as his guide, saying that he wanted to sacrifice a goat at the altar of Aaron (brother of Moses), whose supposed tomb stands on the nearby Jabal Haroun (Mount Aaron). The area is associated with the story of Moses after the Israelites' flight from Egypt – Wadi Musa means 'Valley of Moses' and the main water source for Petra is called Ain Musa (the Spring of Moses). In order to reach the altar, on August 22, 1812, Burckhardt was led down the Siq to the unseen city.

The discovery of a complete, ancient city was a major breakthrough, and Burckhardt suspected that it might be Petra. He had to conceal his excitement because he was travelling disguised as an Arab and he might betray himself if he showed interest in pre-Islamic ruins. He took surreptitious notes and, eventually arousing suspicion, was obliged to carry out his sacrifice.

Burckhardt died in Cairo in 1817, but on the basis of his reports a stream of intrepid Europeans travelled to Petra. They included the British watercolourist David Roberts in 1839, the pioneer sociologist Harriet Martineau in 1846, and the painter and writer Edward Lear in 1858. European visitors spread word of the magical lost city. 'A rose-red city – 'half as old as Time!'' wrote the poet and theologian John William Burgon in 1845, having never even been there. The phrase stuck. Edward Lear's chef

> 66 The hues of youth upon a brow of woe, Which men call'd old two thousand years ago! Match me such marvel, save in Eastern clime, A rose-red city – 'half as old as Time!' 99
>
> JOHN WILLIAM BURGON
> *PETRA* (1845)

Giorgis used the more prosaic terms of his profession to describe the marbled and striated colours found in the rock in Petra: 'Oh master,' he exclaimed, 'we have come into a world where everything is made of chocolate, ham, curry-powder, and salmon.'

Ancient trade routes

Gradually, the history of Petra was pieced together. It had been a trading city since the 4th century BC, located at the crossroads of two trans-continental routes: a north–south route from the Red Sea to Damascus and Central Asia, and an east–west route from the Mediterranean to the Arabian Gulf and Indian Ocean. Caravans passed through with gemstones, gold, silver, cotton, ivory, sugar, spices, perfumes and incense –

frankincense and myrrh. Petra also tapped into trade along the Silk Road that brought luxuries from China.

The entire Dead Sea region was controlled by the Nabataeans. Poachers turned gamekeepers, they were essentially nomads known for raiding camel caravans who found it more profitable to offer paid protection to traders. Petra was the Nabataean capital, chosen in part for its water supply, which came from springs and flash floods. Water was stored in underground cisterns around the city. In addition, the city's mountainous location allowed the entrances to be defended.

Rock-hewn arena The amphitheatre was originally designed by the Nabataeans for just 300 spectators. The Romans increased its capacity to 8,000.

214

A head for heights The magnificent scale of the Treasury, carved directly into the rock, is clear when viewed from above. The visitors at ground level are dwarfed by the elaborate facade, which displays Greek influence as well as Nabataean deities.

By the 1st century BC, the Nabataean kingdom ran west to the Mediterranean and north to Damascus and Philadelphia (today's Amman). This was the period when Petra's grandest buildings were created, and a distinct style emerged blending Greek, Roman, Egyptian and Assyrian influences – a measure of the city's reach. A particularly impressive feature is the rock-cut, Greek-style amphitheatre with rows of expertly chiselled stone seats, later enlarged by the Romans to accommodate up to 8,000 spectators.

At this time, the Romans were pressing to control the region using proxy kings, such as Herod of Judea. The Nabataeans were forced to become political tributaries; then, when the Nabataean King Rabbel II died in AD 106, the Romans assumed direct rule. Petra took on the aspects of a Roman city, with a forum (market place) and a paved and colonnaded main street leading to the sacred precinct. Water was piped in from distant hills for baths and fountains.

The only evidence of dwellings are the imprint of foundations in the valley floor, but it is thought that Petra once sustained a population of between 20,000 and 30,000. It prospered for another century or so, but when the Romans built a new paved road from Tyre to the Gulf via Palmyra, 250 miles (400km) to the north, trade through Petra dwindled. A massive earthquake in AD 363 destroyed most of the city, yet it staggered on into the Christian era of the Roman and Byzantine empires. Petra has the remains of a large 5th to 6th-century Byzantine church, complete with 70m² (750sq ft) of mosaic floors depicting animals and personifications of human virtues.

Pharaohs and crusaders
After the 7th century, Petra seems to have become an isolated Christian community surrounded by a Muslim world. During the First Crusade, around 1100, it was evacuated by the Crusader leader Baldwin, who took the title of King of Jerusalem. The crusaders used Petra as a base, referring to it as the Valley of Moses. This reinforced the myths around Petra's connection to

Moses and the legend that Moses was pursued here by Egypt's pharaoh. The building that greets visitors at the end of the Siq is known as Al-Khazneh al-Faroun, the Pharaoh's Treasury. The pharaoh, encumbered by too much gold, is said to have hidden it in the stone urn that crowned the facade. The temple in the sacred precinct is known as Qasr Bint al-Faroun, House of the Pharaoh's Daughter. In reality, the Treasury probably served as a royal tomb, perhaps of the Nabataean King Aretas IV. The House of the Pharaoh's Daughter was likely to have been a temple dedicated to the Nabataeans' male god, Dushara.

After the Crusades, Petra was abandoned. The Bedouins preserved the names of the buildings, not all of which were entirely fanciful. The largest of all the rock-carved buildings –

two-thirds of a mile (1km) away into the hills – is called Al-Deir (the Monastery), in recognition of its Christian use. It was originally built by the Nabataeans, probably as a royal tomb or temple.

Refound
Petra is certainly not a lost city now. Well established as a tourist venue of world rank, it receives up to 6,000 visitors a day. The Treasury has featured in several films, attaining international fame in 1989 in *Indiana Jones and the Last Crusade*. But Petra's unique mountain setting still restricts access, just as it did 2,000 years ago, and visitors have to contend with the physical challenge of reaching it. This, combined with the drama of reaching the end of the cavernous Siq, reinforces its sense of history untouched by the modern world.

best of the rest...

ANCIENT TRADE-ROUTE CITIES

Samarkand in Uzbekistan was a key stop on the Silk Road, which ran from China to the Mediterranean world. The Registan Square is enclosed by grand 15th-17th century *madrassas* (Islamic schools), with arches, domes and minarets. The city contains the tomb of the mighty warlord, Tamerlane.

West of Samarkand is **Khiva**, also in Uzbekistan, on a spur of the Silk Road feeding into Russia. Behind crenellated ramparts lies the Itchan Kala (Old Town), which contains the Kunya Ark fortress and the Juma mosque, with 212 carved pillars. The Tosh Khovli palace is famed for its beautiful harem.

Samarkand

Timbuktu in Mali was the destination of explorers searching for a fabled city said to be roofed in gold. It was on a Saharan trade route sending gold and salt to the Mediterranean, but the city was past its prime when the French explorer, René Caillié, finally got there in 1827.

Vikings traded along the Dvina and Dnieper rivers that link the Baltic and Mediterranean seas. The Latvian capital, **Riga**, was at the head of this route and later rose to fortune within the Hanseatic League, a powerful alliance of European trading cities.

PHONG NHA CAVE

A world of spectacular river-hewn limestone chambers and miles of labyrinthine passageways lies hidden deep underground beneath the dense evergreen rain forests of north-central Vietnam.

Cavers, potholers, spelunkers, speleologists, indeed everybody who enjoys squeezing through claustrophobically narrow passageways to see grand natural halls and other fantastic features beyond, has long recognised Phong Nha as the ultimate underground experience, arguably the best cave system in the world.

Almost a mile (1.6km) of Phong Nha is open to the general public and lit by artificial lights that bathe the rock formations in a magical psychedelic glow. All visitors accesss the cave by boat from the Son River. Inside there is an underground lake, several broad fine-sand beaches, and unusual stalactitite and stalagmite formations, many of which have been named for

Underground waterway The only way into the Phong Nha cave system is by boat. The small boats carry up to ten people and collect visitors from the nearby village of Son Trach, 20 minutes downriver.

WHERE ON EARTH?

Phong Nha and its neighbouring caves lie in Quang Binh Province, sandwiched between Laos in the west and Vietnam's north-central coast in the east. They are about 300 miles (500km) south of the Vietnamese capital Hanoi, 160 miles (260km) north of the port of Da Nang, and 30 miles (45km) from the fishing town of Dong Hoi.

their appearance, such as the Lion, the Buddha and the Angel Cavern. The Royal Court is named for its extraordinary resemblance to a seated king and his attendants, complete with elephants on either side of the throne.

Yet this is just the start of Phong Nha. In the absolute darkness, far beyond the razzmatazz of the parts open to the public, the main cave system stretches for more than 5 miles (8km) encompassing 14 huge chambers, each one connected to the next by an underground river. In this caver's cave, hundreds of tantalising side passages and wondrous caverns branch off in all directions, some with roofs as high as 40m (130ft) above the cave floor.

An ancient landscape

The caves are found in Vietnam's thickly forested Phong Nha-Ke Bang National Park, which together with Hin Namno Nature Reserve in neighbouring Laos,

is the largest and oldest major karst region in Asia. The area is composed of ancient limestone, along with shales and sandstones, the oldest strata being about 400 million years old. As in all karst landscapes, the limestone has been dissolved and eroded by water and is riddled with caves – more than 300 on the Vietnam side alone. More than 20 have been mapped by Vietnamese survey teams, and since 1991 members of the British Cave Research Association have been exploring some of the major cave systems in the park.

Phong Nha means 'cave of teeth', a reference to rows of stalactites that once grew near the entrance, but which were destroyed by US military action during the Vietnam War. The Viet Cong used the cave as a military store and hospital, and evidence of the conflict is visible all around in the form of water-filled bomb craters that local people have adopted as fish ponds. People were using these caves long before that conflict. During the 9th and 10th centuries, the eastern Cham people, from the ancient kingdom of Champa (modern southern and central Vietnam), kept shrines within the cave. Visitors can still view remnants of their altars.

Limited access

While the cave system is nearly 5 miles (8km) in length, there are some 27 miles (44km) of known chambers and passageways. People enter by boat from the Son River, which flows through the cave system as the Nam Aki River and exits 12 miles (20km) to the south, making it one of the longest underground waterways in the world. The broad, low cave entrance is at the base of sheer grey limestone cliffs, and once inside the boatman switches off the motor and rows into the cave to land passengers on a subterranean beach. From there, the cave can be explored on foot.

The grotto with the Cham characters on the walls, known since the 1990s as Bi Ky Grotto, is the largest chamber open to the public. Its ceiling is about 30m (100ft) high, but the cave formations are

Light show Many of the spectacular rock formations in Phong Nha are picked out and highlighted with coloured lights.

blackened by smoke from fires that were lit when the grotto was used by the Viet Cong as a hospital ward.

Although the public caverns and more remote tunnels and passageways were surveyed and mapped as recently as the 1990s, their size and splendour have long been recognised. The earliest known written account dates back to 1550, when Duong Van Nga, a minister in the Mac dynasty, included them in his geographical and historical records of the region. And in the late-19th century, the French Catholic priest Léopold Michel Cadière, who wrote extensively about Vietnam, declared them to be 'the number one cave in Indochina'.

Local rival

Phong Nha is a river cave. A second cave complex in the region – the older Tien Son Cave – is a dry cave set in the mountainside just above Phong Nha. It was discovered in 1935 by a man looking for firewood, and today it is reached by a stairway with 600 gruelling steps from a spot close to the entrance to Phong Nha. A 10m (30ft) deep hole 400m (1,300ft) from the entrance to Tien Son

is something of a hazard for visitors, but the stalactites and stalagmites are said to conjure up visions of fairy tales, hence the cave is often referred to as the Fairy Cave. One stalagmite has been nicknamed the Leaning Tower of Pisa. Overhead, the cave ceiling glistens with sparkling gold and silver-coloured veins. Some of the cave formations are said to 'sound out', or ring, when struck by hand. Part of Tien Son has now been installed with walkways and artificial lighting, enhancing its many attractions

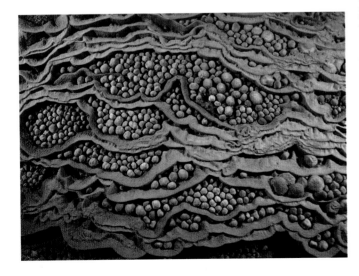

Rock gems It is rare for cave pearls to grow bigger than the size of a marble, but some found in Hang Son Doong are as large as grapefruits.

for the general visitor, but experts still say: 'if you only see one cave in your life, Phong Nha is the cave to see'.

New record-breakers

Despite this, a number of new discoveries in the area are beginning to threaten Phong Nha's pre-eminent position. The first is Thien Duong, or Paradise Cave, discovered in 2005 by a British-led team. Located about 9 miles (15km) from Phong Nha, it is at least 19 miles (31km) long, making it the longest dry cave in Asia. It has exceptionally beautiful stalactite and stalagmite formations, including tall white glass-like pillars, organ pipes and shapes that resemble tigers, elephants, fish and

Ancient formations Many of the caves in the Phong Nha-Ke Bang National Park were carved by the Chay river, a process that took many millions of years.

figures representing the Vietnamese gods of happiness, fortune and longevity. An arch at the entrance is said to be the mountain genie who guards the cave. Parts of Thien Duong are open to the public, and at about 20–21C (68–70F) the temperature is always cool there.

The same caving team also explored Hang Son Doong, or Mountain River Cave. It was discovered by Ho Khanh, a local hunter, who as a youngster had hidden in the cave during air raids in the Vietnam War. He had quite forgotten the cave's location until the caving team went with him to search for it in the thick, almost impenetrable bamboo forests. It took three expeditions – and a six-hour trek from the nearest road – to find it.

Once inside, the team came upon an immense cavern, the largest known single underground chamber in the world. Measuring more than 2.5 miles (4km) long, 180m (590ft) high and up to 200m (650ft) wide, it is so big that an entire block of 40-storey skyscrapers could fit inside and there would still be space for clouds to form above them.

Hang Son Doong is the guardian of extremely rare, giant cave pearls – stone spheres that form from drops of hard water. Two areas of collapsed roof have let in the jungle, which grows in the cave in isolated pockets, like Arthur Conan Doyle's lost world. The plant species growing here are similar to those in the surrounding forest. The expedition members light-heartedly named these pockets the Garden of Edam and Watch Out for Dinosaurs. The puns continue

with a stalagmite resembling a dog's paw called the Hand of Dog. In addition, the cave features algae-coated and water-carved rock terraces, thundering waterfalls that turn on and off like taps, tall, phallic-shaped stalagmites, and a 60m (195ft) high overhanging muddy flowstone formation, resembling a petrified waterfall and named the Great Wall of Vietnam.

Hang Son Doong and Thien Duong are not the only new record-breakers. Other gigantic caves in the region include Hang Khe Ry, site of one of the world's

longest river caves at nearly 12 miles (19km); the 9-mile (15km) long Vom Cave (part of the Phong Nha system), home to the abyss known as Tang hole, the deepest hole in Vietnam; and Hang Hen, which has a cave passage 140m (460ft) wide and 100m (330ft) high.

With the help of the Hanoi University of Science, the British team is to continue the exploration. There are many more secrets waiting to be discovered in the Phong Nha-Ke Bang National Park. As one keen caver remarked: 'We've just been scratching at the surface.'

best of the rest...

NATURAL CAVES

■ **Eisriesenwelt**, meaning 'world of ice giants', is a limestone cave that extends for 26 miles (42km) inside the Hochkogel Mountain, 25 miles (40km) south of Salzburg in Austria. It is the world's largest ice cave, the first 1,000m (3,300ft) of the cave system being covered with ice. Thawed snow drains into the cave, where it refreezes to form many different ice formations, among them the 25m (80ft)

high Great Ice Wall, Hymir's Hall, the dome-shaped Frigga's Veil and the Ice Palace. The ice is present all year: in winter ice-cold air blows into the cave, freezing the dripping water, and in summer cold air blows out of the cave so the ice does not melt.

■ Slovenia's Reka River flows first through a 2.5 mile (4km) long gorge and then disappears in spectacular fashion into the **Skocjan Caves**, at the 165m (540ft) deep Velika Dolina (sinkhole). It then flows underground for 21 miles (34km), through one of the world's deepest underground canyons – a subterranean

'Grand Canyon' – and a series of enormous chambers, including Martel's Chamber, one of the largest in Europe, to reappear at Monfalcone near the Adriatic coast.

■ The world's deepest known cave is **Krubera-Voronya** or 'crows cave' in the disputed territory of Abkhazia on the eastern shores of the Black Sea. To date, Ukrainian cavers have reached a point 2,191m (7,188ft) below the entrance, and at 1,980m (6,495ft) they found four previously unknown species of tiny insects called springtails – the world's deepest underground invertebrates.

■ **Mammoth Cave** in Kentucky, USA, is the world's longest known cave system. It is more than 390 miles (630km) long, with the discovery of new passageways and chambers increasing that figure year on year. Bats occupy the cave, along with cave crickets that wave exceptionally long antenna, two species of blind fishes, eyeless shrimps, pure white crayfish and spotty cave salamanders. The name 'mammoth cave' does not refer to the elephant-like mammoth, but to the enormous size of the system: no mammoth remains have ever been found here.

■ Until the discovery of Hang Son Doong, the world's largest known cavern was Deer Cave in the Gunung Mulu National Park in Sarawak, Malaysia. In nearby Nasib Bagus ('good luck cave') **Sarawak Chamber** vies with Hang Son Doong for the title of largest single chamber. Eight jumbo jets positioned nose-to-tail could fit comfortably in Sarawak Chamber; Britain's largest cave - Gaping Gill in Yorkshire - would fit in the cave's entrance.

Eisriesenwelt

POKHARA VALLEY

In the shadow of Annapurna lies this lush Himalayan valley, its serene lake and traditional villages set against the dramatic mountain backdrop. It is the closest reality comes to the fabled Shangri-La.

'In all my travels in the Himalayas, I saw no scenery so enchanting', wrote the first outsider to reach Pokhara in 1899. Few travellers today would disagree because no other valley can claim such a dazzling Himalayan backdrop, shooting upwards to more than 8,000m (26,000ft) in under 18 miles (30km). Glinting glaciers and snowy peaks stretch for 90 miles (140km) along the northern horizon, crowned by three of the world's highest peaks: Dhaulagiri to the west, Manaslu to the east and, in the central range, Annapurna I, the closest and the first 'eight thousander' ever climbed. But the most dramatic mountain is Pokhara's own, called Machhapuchhre, the 'Fishtail', for its two-pointed summit, which rises to almost 7,000m (23,000ft). The local people consider it sacred so no one is allowed to set foot on its summit. A British expedition in 1957 is the only one to have approached the summit. Its

WHERE ON EARTH?

The Pokhara Valley is 125 miles (200km) west of the Nepalese capital, Kathmandu. Pokhara city has a regional airport with internal flights from Kathmandu. Government buses, tourist buses and private minibuses also run between the two cities, the journey taking anywhere between 4 and 10 hours.

ANNAPURNA CONSERVATION AREA

NEPAL

Seti Gandaki River

Phewa Lake   Pokhara

Pokhara Valley

members turned back, as agreed, within 50m (165ft) of the top.

Looking up at the wind-sculpted ice cap of Machhapuchhre, it is easy to see why it's called the abode of the gods. Down in the valley the land is lush and green, blessed by a sub-tropical climate that is pleasantly tempered by the mountains. Flowering cacti and poinsettia grow among citrus groves and banana plants, while ancient pipal and banyan trees spread welcome shade. Summer brings the monsoon, obscuring the views as thunderous clouds and raging torrents wash the land clean, ready for the next harvest. By October, the sky is blue again, and the Himalayas gleam fresh above the valley.

The Pokhara Valley is the result of mountain-building and glacial activity that brought flows of debris down from the slopes of Annapurna. Boulders and gravel deposits dammed the rivers, drowning the land at the foot of the mountains. Phewa Lake is all that remains of the flood, silting up in places as the landscape forever changes, shaped as it is by fast-flowing rivers, man-made dams and mountains continuing

High trail A mule train crosses one of the mountain gorges around the Pokhara Valley. Mule trains have long provided a vital link between remote villages and today are also used on trekking routes.

their upward thrust. For trekkers, the lake is sheer bliss, a place to rest and wonder at the view. Known as the 'jewel among the peaks', it is the second-largest lake in Nepal – about 2.4 miles (4km) long and just under a mile (1.6km) wide – perfectly positioned to reflect Pokhara's mountainscape. When a gust of wind sends ripples across the surface, reflections vanish for a moment, then the magic returns: fluffy clouds and snowy tops shimmering in the placid water. Sails and rowing boats glide past the shore, laundry dries in the meadows, and on the northern bank rugged ochre-coloured rocks glow in the sun.

On the south shore, forests reach down to the water's edge, which is fringed with meandering coves, terraced slopes and hamlets. In the early morning, fishermen paddle across the water in skiffs. The lake swarms with a multitude of fish that, in turn, attract up to 43 species of waterbird. Egrets,

Productive land Rice fields sit alongside the shoreline of Lake Phewa, which provides an ample supply of fish for local fishermen.

kingfishers and Indian herons are seen alongside ringed plovers and bronze-winged jacana. In summer, cotton pygmy geese appear, and coots and ducks nest in the reeds, including endangered Baer's pochards and comb ducks.

At weekends, pilgrims head for the island temple of Barahi in the middle of the lake laden with garlands of marigolds and live cockerels and other offerings for sacrifice to Ajima, the boar-headed

> **"In all my travels in the Himalayas, I saw no scenery so enchanting."**
>
> ANONYMOUS JAPANESE MONK,
> THE FIRST OUTSIDER TO VISIT POKHARA, 1899

manifestation of Shakti, the goddess who destroys evil. Holy men meditate and incense rises from the shrines, while pigeons gather on the pagoda waiting for pickings. Boats move in a silent flotilla as colourful saris flutter against the canvas of snow-capped mountains. On the ridge above the southern shore, the huge Peace Pagoda gleams brilliant white, like a Buddhist observatory. This massive

stupa was built in the 1990s by Japanese monks and offers spectacular views of Annapurna, Phewa Lake, Pokhara city and the surrounding villages.

Pokhara city

The wheel was virtually unknown in Pokhara right up until 1961: the locals say it arrived as part of an oxcart, brought by aeroplane from the capital, Kathmandu. Today, there are few wheeled oxcarts but there is no shortage of bicycles, motorbikes, cars, buses and tinselled rickshaws. Yet, in this town with four rivers and open space, life is relaxed. Holy cows wander the streets. and the sound of jingling bells could signal a mule train bringing goods from Mustang or sheep and goats being herded to market.

The trade route from India to China has lost its appeal, but in the 1970s European and American travellers brought new life to the valley. Although trekkers now outnumber the mystics, Pokhara city has managed to keep much of its charm. It has luxury hotels that rub shoulders with traditional buildings

with orange-coloured walls of decorative brickwork and carved windows. The bazaar buzzes with stalls selling baskets and pottery, copper pots, silver earrings, cotton clothes and anything else travellers might need. Mobile kitchens and shoeshine boys ply their trade along the lanes, among teashops in quiet gardens, guesthouses that promise good karma and a sprinkling of temples and shrines. The oldest temples include the 200-year-old Bhimsen, a two-storeyed pagoda known for its erotic carvings, and the 17th-century Bindabasini, perched on a hill and a lively hub of Hindu devotion. Outside town, Lord Shiva is worshipped in the dimly lit Mahadev Cave, where a stone statue of the seven-headed cobra of Hindu myth guards the shrine and the chilling waterfall gushes from above.

The valley's porous rock has led to the formation of river-worn potholes and caves. One of the most mysterious has been created by the White River (Seti Gandaki), which flows across the middle of the city but is rarely seen as it roars through a gorge so deep and narrow that the bottom is out of sight.

Rural life

There are no records of the first settlements in the Pokhara Valley, but history tells of the 24 ancient kingdoms of Nepal. In the 18th century, Nepal's Gorkha ruler, Prithvi Narayan Shah, unified the country. Pokhara was brought

into the fold, but retained its ethnic identity, expressed with music and dance at festivals to celebrate the harvest or family events. Rural Nepalese cling to their roots in the lowlands and nearby hills. They are farmers and traders, honey gatherers, craftsmen and lodge keepers.

Glimpses of rural life come a-plenty along the stony trails by the lake and in the hills. At a Tibetan refugee village, red-robed monks chant to the rhythm of long horns and drums. At Ghandruk there is not a road in sight but mazes of stepped alleyways and stone cottages with women sitting outside to weave. There are flower gardens, vegetable plots and terraces carved like stairways to heaven. High above the rice fields

Buddhist Peace Pagoda Three different paths lead up to the pagoda. The site offers superb views of Pokhara city and the Annapurna mountain range.

and papaya trees, rhododendrons bloom in the spring, and lakes and waterfalls glisten, framed by the Himalayas.

Perched on a ridge above the city, the village of Sarangkot is renowned for its splendid views. On one side is the entire Pokhara Valley, with Phewa Lake turning from silver to blue according to the sky; on the other are the sweeping snowfields and glaciers of ten Himalayan peaks. Soon after dawn, the range glows in shades of pink and gold, but Machhapuchhre steals the show, appearing almost within arm's reach.

best of the rest...

MOUNTAIN VALLEYS

■ Straddling the French-Spanish border in Catalonia, **Cerdanya** is a land of flower-strewn pastures and farms, lakes, gorges, rivers and natural springs framed by some of the highest peaks in the Eastern Pyrenees. It is sparsely inhabited and boasts 3,000 hours of sunshine a year. Ski slopes, rambling trails and spas are top attractions but most memorable is the ride on the narrow gauge Yellow Train, climbing to 1,593m (5,226ft).

■ At around 3,000m (10,000ft), the **Indus Valley** in northern India is stark and beautiful. Tiny oases of willows and poplars nestle below the glaciers and eternal snows. The barren slopes below glow in mineral-rich colours, fringed with dark rocky crags

and white sands, mirrored in the icy blue waters. Beyond the confluence with the Zanskar River, the valley is increasingly wild, with just a sprinkling of isolated hamlets draped in marigolds and Buddhist flags.

■ In the foothills of the Atlas Mountains, close to Marrakech in Morocco, the **Ourika Valley** is a quiet valley where verdant oases and red mud villages glow among flowering cherry and almond trees. There are herb gardens and roses, traditional Berber pottery drying by the roadside and rickety bridges crossing the fast-flowing river. Snow-capped mountains peep on the horizon and at the end of the road, a steep rocky trail leads to a series of refreshing cascading waterfalls.

■ The sub-tropical valley of **Punakha** in Bhutan claims the country's most inspiring *dzong* (Bhutanese monastery), poised auspiciously

at the confluence of two rivers. All around are rice terraces, guava trees and chir pines where crickets sing together. At 1,250m (4,000ft), myriad butterflies flutter along the trails among showers of wild peach blossom. The water is milky blue, the air crystal clear and up in the hills you can catch a glimpse of Jomolhari, Bhutan's second highest peak.

■ In a National Scenic Area of the Scottish Highlands, the steep-sided valley of **Glencoe** rises from Loch Leven to the vast heathland of Rannoch Moor. Sedges, grasses, mosses, ferns and fungi grow without interference, as do delicate alpine flowers that bloom in early summer. Golden eagles hover around ridges and peaks and deer, red squirrels and otters share the glen with rare Scottish wild cats. Tales of ancient clan feuds linger in the valley, but today only the sound of waterfalls disturb the peace.

POTALA PALACE

The world's highest palace was the historic winter residence of the Dalai Lama, spiritual leader of Tibet, raised to the heavens on a craggy hillside in the centre of the capital, Lhasa. Dating from 1645, the Potala Palace is a unique concentration of Tibetan culture. The exterior has the muscular profile of a fortress, with massively thick, inward-leaning walls rising through some 13 storeys of steps and flat-roofed terraces to a soaring summit topped by *dhvaja* (cylinder banners). Inside, a honeycomb of 1,000 rooms includes halls and chapels containing thousands of religious paintings and statues, carved and bejewelled shrines, and precious gold stupas holding the sacred remains of past Dalai Lamas – the focus of pilgrimage to this day.

As the official homes of royalty and heads of state, palaces are the architectural embodiment of power and prestige. Their names – Buckingham Palace in London, the Elysée in Paris, the White House in Washington, DC – are often used as synonyms for the person or role that resides there. The very best palaces are unforgettable icons, imprinting an image of unique scale and

style. They have never been just homes, but were - and in some cases still are - centres of government, teeming with officials, administrators and visitors. As such, they are highly structured communities in which everyone knows their function in the service of the leader. The architecture is designed to reflect this, with rooms laid out in a sequence that culminates in the audience chamber or throne room. The two palaces here symbolise power in very different ways, one a pinnacle of spiritual striving, the other a paean to worldly success.

PALACE OF VERSAILLES

When King Louis XIV of France began remodelling the royal hunting lodge at Versailles, 10 miles (16km) west of Paris, in 1668, he was embarking on a project to create the greatest, most extravagant palace in Europe. Suites of sumptuous state rooms, with the Hall of Mirrors – 73m (240ft) long and hung with 357 mirrors – at their heart, created a dramatic progression towards the royal apartments. The formal gardens, laid out with lakes, statues and fountains, are the largest palace gardens in Europe. All spoke of the glory and power of the Sun King. Building continued under Louis XV and XVI and for a century Versailles led European taste in architecture and fashion. Nowhere rivalled its ambition and magnificence – or cost. The rooms have been restored to give a vivid impression of Versailles in its full glory.

RHINE VALLEY

The River Rhine is one of the world's most fabled waterways, not just for its long and rich history, but also for its unusual geology.

The Rhine rises in the Swiss Alps and flows to the North Sea, and since prehistoric times it has provided a major corridor for the movement of people, goods and ideas between southern and northern Europe. What is referred to as the Rhine Valley runs between the cities of Basel and Bonn. The upper section is a huge rift valley, called the Rhine Graben, that formed around the time that the Alps were raised. The lower section, the Middle Rhine, was created by the simultaneous action of a powerful river grinding down through the bedrock in a landscape that was gradually being uplifted, resulting in a narrow, twisting gorge with sheer walls that average 130m (425ft) in height.

Romantic appeal

The gorge stretches from Bingen to Koblenz and has come to symbolise the romance of the Rhine in literary accounts and paintings. Small towns and villages dating from medieval times are strung along the riverbank, overlooked by the remains of hilltop castles that once guarded trade along the river and surrounded by the vineyards that produce some of Germany's finest

Commanding position Burg Katz sits above the medieval town of St Goarshausen. Just beyond, the river curves around the Lorelei Rock.

WHERE ON EARTH?

The Rhine Valley runs along the western side of Germany and the northeastern corner of France. Various hiking and biking trails thread their way through the valley. Its primary gateway and largest city is Frankfurt, which lies in the valley bottom along a tributary called the Main.

wines. Among the landmarks are Burg Katz and Burg Maus, the Cat and Mouse castles, and the walled town of Oberwesel with its cobblestone streets and Gothic churches. Here, too, is the fabled Lorelei Rock, whose legendary siren was said to be the reason why so many ships have been wrecked at this narrow, sharp bend in the river.

In part, the enduring fame of the valley is owed to the Romantic writers and painters who flocked here in the early 19th century. Lord Byron set the tone in 1816, waxing lyrical about the ruined castles as reminders of an age when Europe represented chivalry and noble causes rather than dictators and destruction. 'Ye glorious Gothic scenes!' he wrote of the riverside bastions. 'The brilliant, fair and soft – the glories of old days.'

best of the rest...

RIVER VALLEYS

■ The **Nile Valley** is the world's longest river valley, stretching for more than 4,000 miles (6600km) between Lake Victoria in Uganda and the Mediterranean. It embraces vast swamps, Saharan sands and several ancient civilisations.

■ Pakistan's **Indus Valley** stretches from the border with India to the Indian Ocean. Its riverside was far more populated in bygone times, when it cradled early urban centres such as Harappa and Mohenjo-daro along the banks.

■ Populated for at least 10,000 years, the dramatic **Jordan Rift Valley** of the Middle East marks the sharp divide between modern-day Jordan, Israel and the Palestinian West Bank. Among its features are the Jordan River, Sea of Galilee and Dead Sea.

Nile Valley

ROMANIA'S PAINTED CHURCHES

Art and architecture are perfectly fused in these gorgeously decorated Orthodox monastic churches in a corner of what is now northeastern Romania.

A huge canvas Voronet was built in the Romanesque style, with small windows and large expanses of wall. Frescoes cover every nook and cranny of the exterior.

WHERE ON EARTH?

Romania's painted churches are to be found in a cluster in Moldavia in the northeast of the country, some 220 miles (350km) from Bucharest, not far from the border with Ukraine. The province of Moldavia is not to be confused with Moldova, the modern nation, though the people share the same roots and are neighbours.

UKRAINE
MOLDOVA
Romania's painted churches
Odessa
ROMANIA
Bucharest
Black Sea
BULGARIA

It was conceived in celebration: Voronet monastery, at Gura Humorului, was begun in 1488 by Stephen III, 'the Great', of Moldavia to thank God for a victory over the Turks at nearby Vaslui. All Christendom had joined in the rejoicing, but the Orthodox believers of the East had been especially ecstatic, seeing Stephen's victory as the salvation of their Church.

Just a generation earlier, in 1453, the Ottomans had occupied the ancient Byzantine capital of Constantinople, and had been attempting to extend the boundaries of their empire westwards ever since.

Fabulous frescoes

Stephen's monastery had to be special. Its main chapel, or *katholikon*, consecrated to St George, has three apses topped with domes and half-domes; the overall effect is reminiscent of clustered conch shells. Though there are signs that the architect was aware of the Gothic revolution taking place in western Europe (pointed arches are used for windows and internal vaults), he remained true to Romanesque principles.

St George's was bedecked within with beautiful murals representing the complete narrative of Christ's Passion, a breathtaking masterpiece of late-Byzantine art. More striking still was the riot of fresco work that adorned every surface of the church's exterior walls. These works are not just stunningly conceived but ebulliently coloured with a sumptuous palette.

Toma's vision

Stephen's monastery set a trend. During the decades that followed, a series of new Orthodox monastic houses was founded across the region, each one vying with the last in painted splendour. Among the first was one at Humor, just a few miles from Voronet. Built by Stephen's son Petru Rares, this monastery was dedicated in 1530. Little is known of the artist who decorated its church beyond his name, Toma of Suceava, and

his taste for a rich red-brown that gave his work extraordinary warmth and fervour. Particularly arresting is the scene showing the Virgin Mary intervening to save the ancient city of Constantinople from a siege by the Persians (who are, confusingly, presented in the dress and style of 15th-century Turks).

Toma was also responsible for the finest of the frescoes at Moldovita – another of Petru Rares' foundations from the 1530s. Ravishingly colourful creations, these are at the same time ambitiously large-scale works. Outstanding are Toma's harrowing *Last Judgment* and a wonderfully complex

Vibrant colours Voronet is sometimes called the Sistine Chapel of the East. The intense blue is known as Voronet blue. Overleaf: Part of the exterior of the Church of the Annunciation at Moldovita.

representation of the Tree of Jesse, showing Christ's royal lineage, and a second version of the Siege of Constantinople.

Steps to salvation

Further to the east, at Sucevita, the last great monastery was built, starting in 1583. Its frescoes were not created until the beginning of the 17th century. Pride of place here goes to a stupendous *Ladder of Virtue*, showing the steps by which the believer can hope to make his or her ascent to Heaven. Many allegorical works are lifelessly schematic, but here the excitement of the drama is palpable. Intrepid souls teeter across a vertiginous gulf, cheered on from above by ranks of angels and distracted by demons from below. Some make it to the other side; others stumble and fall into the abyss.

How was the church at Sucevita to be protected? Its fortified construction – a solid, square curtain wall enclosing an open courtyard in which the chapel, living quarters and workshops were all built – betrays a certain vulnerability. Even in the 16th century, Moldavia's painted churches were very much in the frontier zone between warring states. This makes their survival in such good condition all the more remarkable.

best of the rest...

REMARKABLE LOCAL CHURCHES

■ Simple, even austere in its appearance, the village church at **Kilpeck**, Herefordshire, stands out as a marvellous example of the Romanesque architecture of England's Norman Age. Built in imitation of those seen in the Roman ruins that abounded across Europe in the early Middle Ages, the rounded arches used in the Romanesque style were comparatively weak, so windows had to be small and walls massively solid to take the strain. Kilpeck's squat construction contrasts with the soaring lines of later churches built in the Gothic style, but its stone carvings are enchantingly beautiful - and decidedly mysterious.

Church of the Transfiguration, Kizhi

■ The island of Kizhi in Lake Onega, northwestern Russia, boasts not one but two stunning wood-built churches erected in the 18th century. The larger **Church of the Transfiguration** has 22 onion domes.

■ Norway's medieval stave churches were built using similar techniques to the communal longhouses - and, for that matter, the clinker-built dragon longships - of Viking times. Log frames with walls of overlapping planks typically give such stave churches a boxy look, but inside they have a spacious, airy feel. **Urnes Stave Church**, in Luster, along the coast to the north of Bergen, is among the finest surviving examples.

ST PETERSBURG

Tsar Peter the Great's new coastal city satisfied his hunger for a modern capital that was a 'window on the West'. Distinctly European in style, the city was a triumph of ambitious urban planning.

The midnight sun turns the summer skies above St Petersburg into a kaleidoscope of colours from pinks and mauves to blues and muted greys. Sometimes the sky is a soft and silken white, as though the blazing sun of noon were still shining across the city, but the whole scene had been draped in the finest gauze.

Up here at latitude 60°N, the winters are dark and harsh, yet summer's evenings are long and light. A single continuous day lasts all the way from mid-May to mid-July. Throughout that time, though clearly declining as the afternoon gives way to evening, the sun never quite makes it below the horizon. Even at midnight, this great city of almost five million souls is bathed in a tranquil sunset. In these long summer nights, orange streetlights twinkle in the endless twilight, making the trees along the embankment beside the River Neva seem to glow. The light plays on

WHERE ON EARTH?

St Petersburg stands at the mouth of the River Neva, where it flows into the Gulf of Finland, an eastern extension of the Baltic Sea. The international Pulkovo Airport is 10 miles (16km) to the south of the city centre. It can also be reached by ferry from Estonia and Finland or by high-speed train from Moscow.

FINLAND
Helsinki • • St Petersburg
Baltic Sea
ESTONIA
RUSSIA
LATVIA

the green-and-white walls of the Winter Palace on one side of the river, and on the churches crowding the skyline on either side, glinting off gaudily painted and gold-leafed onion domes. Across the shimmering waters, the Peter and Paul Fortress appears anchored like a ship, its apparent mast the slender, pointed spire of the city's great Cathedral of Sts Peter and Paul.

White nights, scarlet sails

These 'white nights' are the time when St Petersburg comes alive and have always been welcomed with excitement by the city's people. In modern times, spectacular festivities have been organised. With its carnivals, concerts, street theatre, open-air ballet, plays and pageants – even mock sea battles staged

Winter Palace The fourth incarnation of the tsar's city residence, on an adjacent site to that of Peter the Great's original, is now part of the Hermitage Museum.

on the Neva – the White Nights Festival brings visitors from every corner of the world. Its best-known event is the Scarlet Sails celebration, a unique evening of fireworks, music, dance and general revelry named after a popular novel of the 1920s. Alexander Grin's *Scarlet Sails* is a love story set at sea – hence the accent on waterborne activities, and the climactic appearance of an old-style fully-rigged ship with scarlet sails.

Russia's coastal capital

Named in honour of its founder's patron saint, the city was planned and constructed in the early 18th century by Tsar Peter I, the Great, to be the showpiece of the nation. The honorific 'the Great' was self-bestowed, but it is hard to imagine any contemporary daring to contest it – or subsequent historians disputing that it was justified. No ruler did more to drag his country into the modern age.

For centuries, the state of Russia had taken shape around Moscow, its historical capital hundreds of miles from the nearest coast or international border. By building a new capital on the Baltic coast, Peter hoped to show a backward Russia his vision for the future and to prove to the rest of Europe that Russia was no longer to be disdained.

Peter was an admirer of all things Western, but this did not prevent him from picking quarrels with his neighbours – notably in 1700 with Sweden, then the main military power in the Baltic region. The 21-year Great Northern War reflected Peter's resolve not only to make Russia great but to reorientate his nation geopolitically: winning access to the Baltic Sea would provide a 'window on the West'.

By 1703 he was in a position to found a fort on an island at the mouth of the River Neva, looking out across the Gulf of Finland in the Baltic Sea. Just short of a decade later, in 1712, Russia had a new capital on what had been the marshy flats of adjacent islands and on either bank of the river. It tilted Russia's political axis – from now on, it would be an outward-looking state. Not only did it open a window to overseas trade and culture, but it also announced Russia's arrival as a naval power.

White Nights Festival Various arts events run from May through to July. The Scarlet Sails celebration coincides with the end of the school year in June.

St Petersburg was also an assertion of European civilisation and culture. An entirely new city, it was conceived along the most up-to-date Western lines, with wide boulevards and sweeping terraces of stone-built houses. Its setting on the River Neva was dramatic, its spacious vistas punctuated by palaces and churches: the overall effect could hardly have been more impressive. With its civilised modern amenities, including street-lighting, paved sidewalks and public parks, the new city was Peter's architectural manifesto.

Creating the Venice of the North

The Tsar had appointed his second-in-command, Prince Aleksandr Menshikov, to oversee the construction work, but the important expertise for the project was brought in from abroad. The Peter and Paul Fortress was the work of the Swiss-Italian architect Domenico Trezzini, who was to set his stamp on the city as a whole. His original intention was that St Petersburg would be the 'Venice of the North', laid out across a grid of canals: in the event, many of the canals were built as streets, but Trezzini's grid-system was preserved.

In 1716 overall charge was passed to a Frenchman, Jean-Baptiste Alexandre le Blond. He moved the focal point of

THE MODERNISER

Having become tsar of Russia in 1682, Peter I was not content merely to rule. He secured his first important military victory in 1696, seizing the Black Sea port of Azov from the Turks, signalling Russia's emergence as a military power and identifying the country with the cause of the Christian West. Building on this triumph, Peter set out on a tour of western Europe, visiting factories, workshops and shipyards. Once back in Russia he began to make substantive changes, bringing in large numbers of foreign craftsmen and scientists and promoting education. He sought to modernise Russia in every way he could – by building a modern navy on Western models and by introducing reforms into Russian institutions, such as the army, the civil service and the Orthodox Church. In just 40 years, he succeeded in hauling his country out of the middle ages and into the 18th century.

the developing city across the river to Vasilievsky Island, where he constructed public buildings, palaces and parks, including the luxurious Menshikov Palace for Alexander Menshikov, Governor General of St Petersburg under Peter the Great. Le Blond's hope was that Russia's new capital would have an elegant oval ground plan within its strongly fortified walls, though the full realisation of this vision was to prove impracticable. Even so, the spirit of his thinking was captured to astonishing effect. Gardens, open spaces, avenues, tree-lined embankments: for Le Blond the spaces between his buildings were just as important as the buildings were themselves. It is largely to Le Blond that the city owes its modern feel of airy openness.

Beauty and cruelty

St Petersburg's gracious townscape did not come without human cost: it was raised up on the mass graves of thousands of Russian serfs and Swedish prisoners-of-war who were worked to death in unspeakable conditions in its

construction. In this too, the city was a fitting symbol for a determined tsar who pursued his modernising goals without regard to human suffering.

Peter died in 1725 and the city, at least in its original form, did not survive him for long. He was succeeded by his wife Catherine I and his son Peter II and then, in 1730, by Empress Anna, another keen builder. In 1736 a series of devastating fires swept through the city. Again and again that year, and into the following one, whole residential neighbourhoods went up in flames. A cruel logic was at work once more, allowing Peter's 'modern' city to expand at the expense of human life and security. The neighbourhoods that burned down were crowded with timber-built homes that had sprung up around the peripheries of Peter's idealised vision of a city, attracted by its new prosperity. Some people suspected that the Empress Anna secretly

Trezzini's canals A number of canals survive, flowing through St Petersburg alongside the rivers of the Neva delta. They are crossed by more than 60 bridges.

ordered her agents to start the fires to remove this blight. There is no doubt that she took advantage of the catastrophe, building grand new neighbourhoods with spacious boulevards and handsome squares and gardens, and shifting the city's centre across the Neva to the east.

A turbulent 20th century

St Petersburg's more recent history has also been one of turbulence. Discontent in Russia grew gradually through the 19th century. In 1905, peaceful demonstrators in St Petersburg were cut down in their hundreds by Tsar Nicholas II's cossacks on a 'Bloody Sunday' that set the tone for many years to come.

In 1914, the capital's name was Russianised to Petrograd with the outbreak of World War One. Ten years later, it changed again in honour of the leader of the 1917 Communist Revolution – the city was known as Leningrad until 1991. It was here that Lenin led the October Revolution, bringing the Bolsheviks to power and setting up the Soviet state. Communism brought cruelties of its own, especially after Lenin's death when Joseph Stalin came to power and inaugurated his reign of terror through the 1930s.

If it was hard to see how the sufferings of the Soviet people could conceivably be deepened, Adolf Hitler found a way when he invaded the USSR in 1941. From September that year, his German forces subjected Leningrad to a merciless siege. Despite the efforts of rescue teams,

who braved blizzards and enemy fire to bring supplies in across the frozen Lake Ladoga, the residents could not be fed adequately – or, ultimately, at all. Dogs, cats and other pets were eaten, then rats; eventually, as human corpses piled up, there were reports of cannibalism among a population crazed with hunger. The Red Army lost a million men in Leningrad's defence and as many civilians starved to death or were killed in the fighting before the Germans were dislodged in January 1944, after 872 days. Leningrad was awarded the title of 'Hero City', though that didn't give its people any protection when Stalin resumed the persecution that he had started before the war.

Last resting place The tomb of Peter the Great lies within Sts Peter and Paul Cathedral, whose golden spire rises above the city's other buildings.

Today, looking out across the River Neva and seeing St Petersburg stand so serene, such horrors may be easily forgotten. But the sense of history here is striking even so. This prestigious planned city may be just three centuries old, but it is a monument to the eternal truth that historical prestige often comes at a cruel cost and that human plans do not necessarily work out as intended. Not that this would have worried Peter the Great: his vision had been accomplished and the city stands as his memorial.

best of the rest...

OLD PLANNED CITIES

■ The Tuscan town of **Pienza** was a rambling, shambling place like any other Italian village when Enea Silvio Piccolomini was born there in 1405. Later, as Pope Pius II, he had the place razed to the ground and rebuilt it as the ideal Renaissance town.

■ The old town of **Cartagena**, on Colombia's Caribbean coast, is a pretty little corner of 16th-century Spain on the other side of the Atlantic. Encircled by a 2-mile (3km) wall meant to keep out marauding pirates, its houses and churches are laid out across a grid of streets. In 1533 all the wooden buildings burnt down, so a law was introduced allowing only buildings of stone, brick or tile to be constructed.

■ In 1755, an earthquake followed by a tsunami and raging fires levelled **Lisbon**, the capital of Portugal, at that time one of the largest cities in the world. Following the tragedy, a new city of wide avenues and large squares emerged. Prefabricated buildings with flexible wooden frames were laid out along

Cartagena

widened streets so that the new city would, to some extent, be earthquake proof. They are among the earliest anti-seismic buildings in the world.

■ The burning of **Washington DC** by British troops during the War of 1812 spurred the USA to resume an ambitious programme of urban planning. Immediately after the war, many buildings were restored, including the presidential mansion, which was painted white for the first time. Later developments included the construction of wide avenues radiating from central circles and city squares with fountains, along lines originally designed by the French military engineer, Pierre Charles L'Enfant, in 1791.

SAN GIMIGNANO

Dizzying views from the Torre Grossa reveal one of the best-preserved medieval towns in Tuscany. Prominent and puzzling, San Gimignano's numerous high towers are the product of bitter family feuds.

The 'Manhattan of Tuscany' is how San Gimignano is often described. It's a tongue-in-cheek association, as the town is not like Manhattan in any way, except that from a distance its 14 towers can look rather like skyscrapers. The nickname might have been more appropriate, if anachronistic, in medieval times, when no fewer than 72 towers rose from San Gimignano's streets. Most have since been pulled down because they were unsafe, unused or simply unwanted reminders of a brutal bygone era.

Medieval skyline Its buildings clustered on the crest of a low hill, San Gimignano retains much of its medieval shape. The town's distinctive profile is a landmark for miles around.

A saintly town

Founded by the Etruscans in the 3rd century BC, then expanded by the Romans, San Gimignano took its name from the 4th-century St Germain, Bishop of Modena, who is credited with saving the region from the Huns by miraculously conjuring up a dense fog to blanket his town. In medieval times, San Gimignano prospered from its location on the so-called Via Francigena, the road of the French, a pilgrimage route to Rome that ran through Italy, Switzerland, France and all the way to Canterbury in England. Pilgrims from all over Europe came through San Gimignano on their way to and from St Peter's holy city,

WHERE ON EARTH?

San Gimignano is in the province of Siena, in the region of Tuscany, northern Italy. The nearest airports are at Florence, 23 miles (37km) to the northeast, and Pisa, 35 miles (56km) to the northwest. San Gimignano has no railway station, but there are bus links from Poggibonsi station 6 miles (10km) to the east.

capital of the Roman Catholic Church. The people of San Gimignano provided food and lodging, while various Church organisations offered spiritual sustenance and hospital care for the sick.

San Gimignano later became a pilgrimage site in its own right through its home-grown St Fina. In 1248, at the age of ten, Fina was struck down by a paralysing illness. Resigned to her fate, she lay on a wooden table and prepared to meet her maker. She stayed so long in this position – five years – that her decaying body became fused to the wood. Towards the end, she had a vision in which the spirit of St Gregory the Great (Pope Gregory I, 590–604) predicted that she would die on March 12, 1253, which she duly did.

When Fina's emaciated remains were peeled away from the planks, white violets were found to be growing in the place of putrefaction. Her remains were placed in a chapel in the cathedral (now a collegiate church, but still San Gimignano's principal church), and further miracles associated with her body were reported. In 1479, the Florentine painter Domenico Ghirlandaio decorated the walls of her chapel with scenes

from her life. Her feast day, March 12, has been celebrated every year in San Gimignano since 1481.

Power struggles

As northern Italy emerged from the Middle Ages into the Renaissance, individual towns and cities increasingly became focal points of power, and their

Mayoral residence The Palace of the Podestà, or mayor, flanks the Cathedral Square. Its Rognosa Tower, built around 1200, is one of San Gimignano's oldest.

citizens demanded ever greater autonomy from feudal overlords. In 1199, San Gimignano broke away from the bishops of Volterra to become an independent city-state governed by a group of citizens.

From 1207, the town was gradually fortified with a ring of city walls, large sections of which, along with three city gates, have survived to this day.

Against the backdrop of medieval prosperity, the town's leading families built tall square towers above their palaces – the higher the better – in part to provide defensive strongholds and lookout posts, but also as symbols of power and prestige. The interiors of the towers were usually very simple, in many cases consisting of a series of landings connected by ladders. San Gimignano was not alone in this habit: Italian cities such as Florence and Bologna also bristled with towers. Bologna still has 20, one of which, the Torre degli Asinelli rises to 97m (318ft) – almost twice the height of any in San Gimignano.

At this time, northern Italy was on the fault line between two rival power blocks: the Pope in the south and the German-dominated Holy Roman Empire in the north (which included much of the territory in northern Italy that Charlemagne had acquired in the 8th century). This rivalry in Italy evolved into political divisions. In general, the Holy Roman Empire represented old values and power structures, whereas the opposition, supported by the Pope, was formed largely of the emerging merchant classes and promoted free trade and

independent cities. Within Italy, the supporters of the Holy Roman Emperor were known as the Ghibellines, and those supporting the Pope were the Guelphs. Their names are said to derive from two powerful German families who were divided by similar allegiances: Waiblingen was a castle of the Hohenstaufen family, which supplied a dynasty of Holy Roman Emperors, while the rival Welfs were dukes of Bavaria.

Local setting Bartolo di Fredi's *The Separation of Abraham and Lot* is part of his 14th-century fresco cycle in the Collegiate Church. The scene is from the Old Testament, but the background has a Tuscan appearance.

Renaissance treasure house The plain exterior of St Augustine's Church belies the Renaissance treasures within, including frescoes by Benozzo Gozzoli.

For some 300 years, northern Italy was tormented by the rift between the Guelphs and the Ghibellines. Also, after 1289 internal feuds began among the Guelphs as the Pope tried to incorporate independent towns and cities into the Papal States. San Gimignano itself was split in bitter rivalry: the Ardinghelli family were Guelphs and the Salvucci family were Ghibellines. Both clans built towers as defensive strongholds and refuges from the outbreaks of deadly violence that erupted onto the streets.

In 1300, eight years before he began writing *The Divine Comedy*, Italy's greatest Renaissance poet, Dante, came to San Gimignano from

Florence as a negotiator for the Guelph League. His visit is commemorated to this day by the Sala di Dante, a room in the Palazzo Comunale (town hall).

From pilgrims to tourists

In 1348 a visiting pilgrim brought the Black Death to San Gimignano. As elsewhere across Europe, this plague drastically reduced the population, causing an economic and social crisis. In 1353, a diminished San Gimignano was forced to ally itself to Florence and the town never fully recovered its upward trajectory. No more towers were built. But as the Renaissance peaked in the 15th century, San Gimignano underwent a final flourish and was able to invite leading Florentine artists – such as Benozzo Gozzoli, Ghirlandaio and Piero del Pollaiuolo – to decorate its churches.

From the 15th century onwards, San Gimignano entered several centuries of gentle slumber as a market town. Even by 1580 all but 25 of the towers had been demolished. Otherwise the fabric of the town remained largely untouched by the pressures of industrialisation and modernisation, creating a legacy that is the focus of a thriving tourist trade today.

Visitors flock to see the Renaissance art in the churches and in the town hall's civic museum. Most of all, they come to savour the charms of the medieval streets and squares that cling to the hilltop – all of which can be viewed from the top of the Torre Grossa.

Hotels and restaurants jostle for space with shops selling souvenirs and local produce, such as the almond cake called *mandorlato*, and the white wine called Vernaccia di San Gimignano, celebrated since the Renaissance. If San Gimignano throngs with too many visitors, it is worth remembering that it was the tourist trade that built the town in the first place, in the days when tourists were called pilgrims.

Medieval skyscraper At 54m (177ft), the town hall's Torre Grossa is the tallest tower. The Collegiate Church is beside it on the Cathedral Square.

best of the rest...

HILLTOP TOWNS

■ Packed onto a huge rock outcrop, the stone houses of **Al-Hajjarah**, near Sana'a in Yemen, rise to five or six storeys. Views from their flat-roofed tops look down to the fertile, terraced valley below.

■ Perched on a cliff edge overlooking the valley of the Rio Guadalete, inland from the Atlantic port of Cadiz, **Arcos de la Frontera** takes its name from its frontier position between Christian and Moorish lands in 13th-century southern Spain. The stone of the Gothic church of Santa María de la Asunción and the castle, originally built by the Moors, contrast with the white houses that cluster tightly around them.

■ In southern France, dramatically sited hilltop villages are known as *villages perchés* (literally, 'perched villages'). One of the most celebrated is **Gordes**, in the department of Vaucluse, east of Avignon. Narrow cobbled streets wind up past houses of honey-coloured stone to the 16th-century castle on the crest.

Arcos de la Frontera

■ Another famous *village perché* is **Éze**, in the south of France. Set on a high, conical rock overlooking the sea between Nice and Monaco on the Côte d'Azur, it has served as a refuge and lookout post since ancient times. Today the village is cherished for its dense maze of alleys and stairways, punctuated here and there with bougainvillea and cypress trees, and with stunning coastal views at every turn.

■ **Ragusa**, in southern Sicily, sits atop a limestone hill with a deep valley on either side. The city is divided into two parts. The oldest is Ragusa Ibla, which the Greeks and Romans took from the Sicels in 258 BC. Destruction by an earthquake in 1693 led to the creation of Upper Ragusa, across a ravine and linked by bridges. Both are noted for their elaborate Baroque churches.

SAN TELMO

This atmospheric district of Buenos Aires resounds to the heady beat of the tango, the faded grandeur of its colonial architecture providing the perfect palette for a flourishing contemporary arts scene.

Born out of the confluence of the diverse groups that settled Argentina, Buenos Aires is a city of contrasts. The barrio of San Telmo contains all the multiple facets that make up the city's cultural heritage, and no other neighbourhood encapsulates the history and character of Buenos Aires in quite the same way. Spanish colonial and French classical buildings stand side by side, punctuated throughout with Italianate architectural details. The opulence of the district's 17th-century mansions, built when the barrio was one of the original neighbourhoods of Buenos Aires, has given way to the shabby chic that characterises San Telmo today.

The birth of the tango

A yellow fever epidemic in 1871 forced the barrio's aristocratic families to move out of San Telmo, and their grand old houses were subdivided into rooms for the subsequent influx of new immigrants. It was in the courtyards of these *conventillos*, or tenements, that

Weekend browsing Plaza Dorrego's Sunday market spills into the neighbouring streets, including La Defensa, and sells everything from candles to chandeliers.

the tango was born – a fusion of the musical influences of far-off homelands, incorporating lyrics that spoke of the hard life of the poor working class.

Both an art form and a lifestyle, the tango became the pride of San Telmo, and the barrio's centuries-old cobbled streets continue to buzz with its seductive rhythms and movements. The visual elegance of the dance inspired by this music is demonstrated by the couples who perform directly on the street or on small, improvised dance floors, illuminated at night by intricate wrought-iron lanterns. The dancers' graceful fluidity and controlled ardour create a captivating show. Impromptu audiences

gather to watch the duos, who dress in the fashions of the 1930s and 1940s – the golden age of tango: the men in fedoras and lace-up shoes, and the women in high heels, always with straps to keep them from slipping off during the dance's characteristic long strides.

San Telmo's street life

To walk along San Telmo's main street, La Defensa, towards the Plaza Dorrego, the heart of the neighbourhood, is to get a glimpse into the city's past while experiencing all the vibrancy of its present. Old-timers' bars coexist with hip cocktail bars, chic cafés jostle with the traditional *parrillas* where they grill the grass-fed beef that is part of Argentina's national identity.

On Sundays, a huge antiques market and street fair takes place in the Plaza Dorrego, with craft booths, artists, tango orchestras and street performers from mime artists to musicians. Shoppers searching for antique jewellery, vintage clothing, sterling silver heirlooms and other treasures sift through the profusion of items for sale, each one a small part of Buenos Aires' past. Families crowd the parrillas for the traditional Sunday meal of *asado*, a selection of beef, pork, chicken and various types of sausage, giving off the smoky, savoury aroma of grilled meat.

As day gives way to evening, the vendors begin to pack up their wares and the street performers vacate the plaza. In their place, restaurant tables start to appear as people enjoy the early evening light and sip an aperitif – perhaps the orange-flavoured Hesperidina, unique to Argentina, or a glass of the country's famous red wine from the western Mendoza vineyards. At night, the plaza takes on a different ambience again as the host to a *milonga*, or open tango dance, where

Quiet interlude Antique collectors can browse in the cool, shaded courtyard of the Pasaje La Defensa – a calm contrast to the bustle of the streets outside.

❝Of all the elements that embody the Argentine spirit, the tango – San Telmo's signature dance – is the most iconic.❞

some of the city's best dancers come to show off their moves. Sometimes the night's festivities include the *chacarera*, a whirling folk dance from the rural regions of northern Argentina.

A vibrant arts scene

The same creative nature that inspires ongoing interpretations of the tango is evident in San Telmo's art scene. From street art to galleries and museums, the energy and flair that characterise the music and life of the barrio are reflected in both its outdoor wall murals and in shows at public and private venues.

Bold shapes, primary hues, futuristic styles and contemporary themes define much of the art that covers walls that were once pasted over with posters. A stroll along neighbourhood streets reveals an ever-changing display of stencil art, graffiti and quirky, cartoon-inspired tableaux, all of which manifest San Telmo's legacy of transformation.

Galleries occupy a variety of buildings ranging from converted warehouses to restored 19th-century buildings, including the Pasaje La Defensa, an Italianate mansion that became a tenement and is now home to a gathering of antique stores and art galleries. Its vintage black-and-white harlequin patio tiles and intricate iron balcony railings are evocative of a gilded era whose traces continue to imbue the barrio with an air of faded elegance.

Several galleries provide platforms for innovative young artists, showcasing video and digital art alongside more traditional forms. Some galleries along the eclectic Calle Venezuela art district further engage the senses through sound and tactile installations.

Major museums

The lively art activity in San Telmo make it an ideal setting for the Museo de Arte Moderno de Buenos Aires, housed in the 1918 British American Tobacco Company building in the heart of the community. The renovated structure

retains the original exposed brick facade, but its heavy, iron-studded wooden doors belie the ethereal white light and impression of limitless space inside, with a staircase that seems to float from floor to floor. A permanent collection of 7,000 artworks includes pieces by Piet Mondrian, Wassily Kandinsky and other modern masters, as well as Argentina's Julio Le Parc and Antonio Berni.

Another major collection is on display at the National History Museum in Lezama Park. This 30-room Baroque mansion contains 50,000 items. Among them are furnishings, documents and personal belongings of former president Juan Perón and his wife Eva and other significant political and military leaders from the country's past.

Milonga events Couples of all ages take part in open tango shows. Young dancers improvise alongside older couples performing traditional salon-style routines.

Lezama Park is possibly the site of the founding of Buenos Aires. Rich in history, today it is a sprawling green space with classical-style sculptures, towering casuarina trees, flowery purple jacarandas and a fragrant rose garden. A slave market was held here in the 18th century and it became the property of a patrician family in the 19th century. Beyond the walls of the museum building, the denizens of the park form a microcosm of San Telmo's populace – from young lovers on benches to old men bent thoughtfully over chessboards – which seems little changed for centuries.

best of the rest...

OLD CITY QUARTERS

■ Throughout its history, the most outstanding characteristic of New York's **Greenwich Village** has been its departure from the social and cultural norms of the rest of the city. From its days as the 17th-century Dutch village Greenwijck to its incarnation as the birthplace of the Beat movement, this divergence in spirit and attitude has attracted and nurtured some of the most creative thinkers, artists and writers of several generations. Its narrow streets - sometimes curved and frequently running at odd angles - evolved before the newer streets of Manhattan were laid out in the grid system, and this still gives the neighbourhood a different feel from the rest of the city. The Village has mostly kept the old street names, too, some of them, like

Coyoacán

Greenwich Village

Bleecker and MacDougal, having become symbols of a bygone time when Jack Kerouac, Lenny Bruce, Bob Dylan and other fertile minds of the 1960s populated the cafés and clubs below 14th Street.

■ Once a village on the outskirts of Mexico City, the *colonia*, or neighbourhood, of **Coyoacán** was not part of the city until the late 1920s. The tree-lined streets with their colonial homes, artists' studios and museums, transport visitors to an earlier time. The central plaza is a hub for artisans and vendors, becoming a fair on weekends, filled with artists, craftsmen, performers and a festive crowd of onlookers. A few blocks from the plaza is the Blue House,

once home of the artist Frida Kahlo. Nearby is the house, also open to the public, where Leon Trotsky lived in exile from Stalinist Russia and where he was assassinated in 1940.

■ The small quarter of **Anafiotika**, tucked under the massive hill of the Acropolis in Athens, Greece, seems to be an island in the city. In 1841, Anafiotika was colonised by craftsmen from the Cyclades island of Anafi. Using rocks that had tumbled down from the Acropolis, the migrants built houses in the style of their island homes. Steep, meandering streets wind past whitewashed houses, bright bougainvillea, pots of aromatic herbs and cats stretched out in the sun. Two churches mark the boundaries of Anafiotika: Agios Georgios, with its flower-filled courtyard, and Agios Symeon, with a copy of a miraculous icon from Anafi.

■ The ancient Jewish quarter of Seville, the barrio known as **Santa Cruz**, is set apart from the rest of the city by its tranquillity, architecture and antiquity. The old houses are so close together, and the cobblestone streets so narrow and labyrinthine, that the combination creates sheltering shade and welcome respite from the blazing sun of southern Spain. Every so often the streets open out into flower-filled plazas, scented with orange blossoms, that create an urban oasis.

Santa Cruz

SANA'A

Unchanged for centuries, the Old City of
Yemen's capital is a labyrinth of traditional
hand-crafted tower houses wrapped in a
lattice of ornate decoration.

Every nation in the world has its
indigenous architecture, based on
local materials and meeting the
demands of the prevailing weather, but
few have stayed with traditional methods
into modern times, especially in the
cities. Sana'a is a glorious exception.
While other urban centres have given
way to external influences and the
commercial pressure to renew, Sana'a's
Old City has continued unchanged.

For centuries, Yemenis have boldly built
upwards rather than outwards, creating
prototype skyscraper cities. Stone floors
and thick walls of brick or rammed earth,
pierced by small wood-framed windows,
create cool, shaded interiors that protect
from the fierce summer sun and occasional
winter downpours. Elaborately carved
wooden doors face onto narrow streets
that form deep canyons of cooling shadow,
while the upper floors and flat roofs are
cooled by breezes that brush the skyline
five, six, seven storeys above street level.

WHERE ON EARTH?

Sana'a lies at the centre of Yemen's simple road
network 95 miles (150km) inland from the Red Sea as
the crow flies. Some governments
strongly advise against travel
to Yemen at present due
to political unrest in
the country combined
with potential dangers
posed by terrorism
and kidnapping.

The high-rise homes of Sana'a were
built by hand, and have subsequently
acquired lopsided, organic additions to
match a family's needs. Each building
is decorated with individually designed,
lace-like geometric patterns, applied with
white stucco around window frames and
across facades, with no other purpose
than to beautify. In Old Sana'a, every
home has its own personality, and the
city has a beguiling human scale.

best of the rest...

ETHNIC ARCHITECTURE

■ The houses of the **Batak Toba** tribe
in North Sumatra represent the most
distinctive of Indonesia's indigenous
architectural styles. They are built on stilts,
have steeply sloping, boat-shaped roofs and
are decorated with intricate wood carvings.

A Hakka walled village

■ China's **Hakka** walled villages comprise
circular or square fortresses that date
back over 500 years. Also known as 'tulou',
the fortresses were built to protect Hakka
migrants from northern China from their
southern enemies. The thick outer walls
enclose several storeys of domestic
dwellings around a courtyard. There are
370 walled villages in the provinces of
Fujian and Jiangxi. Some tulou are isolated,
but others are clustered, such as those at
Chuxi Tulou in Fujian.

■ Pueblos are the adobe (mud-built)
villages of the Pueblo people of southwest
USA, found mainly in New Mexico. **Taos
Pueblo** is the most famous - a village
of flat-roofed, multi-storey dwellings,
divided by a fast-flowing river and with a
picturesque mountain backdrop.

Cradled in the Haraz mountains, at an
altitude of about 2,300m (7,500ft), Sana'a
is one of the world's highest capital cities.
It is also one of the oldest continuously
inhabited cities in the world, dating back
to 500 BC – although local tradition
places its origins even further back, in the
time of Shem, one of Noah's sons, who is
said to have founded the city as the Flood
receded. This mountain setting makes the
surrounding landscape surprisingly green
and moderates the hot desert climate.

Two ancient and important trade
routes crossed here, placing Sana'a on
the map as a commercial hub and a

centre of power. The city was an early convert to Islam: its Great Mosque, first built in about AD 705, is one of the oldest in the world. It was then ruled by a succession of competing caliphs – of Baghdad, Egypt and Ottoman Istanbul, as well as its own Zaydi imams.

Living history

This history is evident in the modern city. Locals wear traditional Arab dress: the men in white *thawb* robes, with a cloth *keffiyah* wrapped like a loose turban on their heads, and perhaps an ornamental curved dagger in their belt. In public,

women shroud themselves in the black, burka-like *balto*. Beneath the stone arches of the Salt Market (Suq-al-Milh), brilliantly coloured spices from across Asia are arranged in piles, alongside stalls selling bread, silverware, copper and pottery, while the air is punctuated with fragrant wafts of frankincense.

Sana'a's Old City was originally defended by massive walls of clay, as still seen today in the fortifications at the Yemen Gate (Bab al-Yemen). Minarets pierce the skyline above mosques that contain the tombs of revered imams. And in the bustling tower houses, families

Sun city The evening sun casts a warm glow over Sana'a's densely packed buildings. The stucco decorations showcase the skills of local craftsmen.

gather in the shade of the sparsely furnished upper rooms late into the evening. As soft light filters in through the stained-glass windows, they settle down on cushions and carpets to pass the time and discuss the issues of the day, sipping sweet tea and chewing leaves of mildly narcotic *gat*. More than 6,500 of these houses remain in Sana'a, along with around 100 mosques, all justifiably protected as architectural treasures.

SANTORINI

This idyllic Greek island has been shaped by volcanic activity. Its picturesque villages make the most of a rocky but beautiful setting left by a violent eruption almost 4,000 years ago.

At one time Santorini was called Kalliste, 'the most beautiful one'. The views from its cliffs are nothing short of spectacular, especially of sunsets seen from the village of Oia, which the locals claim are the best on the planet. The sunsets alone make Santorini the most stunning island in the Mediterranean, and it all comes down to the Earth's explosive dynamics.

Santorini's main town, Fira, is perched on 300m (980ft) high, almost vertical cliffs that form the rim of a vast, flooded caldera created by one of the biggest volcanic explosions ever known. The town and nearby cliff-edge villages are labyrinths of immaculate, tightly packed whitewashed buildings, cobblestone streets and winding paths, churches with bright blue cupolas, windmills,

neoclassical mansions and cave-like houses dug directly into the rock. Far below Fira at the base of the cliff, a cable-car or donkey ride away, is the old harbour at Ormos, its terraces, cruise ships and fishing boats resembling tiny toys.

The previous capital was Skaros, a medieval fortress town built around a vertical crag of red and black rock on

a headland to the northwest of Fira, where it was free from raiding pirates and invaders. Islanders claim that the castle was never conquered during its 600 years' existence, but repeated earthquakes finally forced the inhabitants to move from this place of relative safety. The capital was eventually moved to Fira in the 18th century. Today, the town of Skaros has largely gone and Skaros Rock is bare. Only a small chapel survives.

The highest point on Santorini is Profitis Ilias (a name common to many Greek mountains), with a fortress-like monastery at the top. The building is a creamy-white colour during the day, but glows terracotta as the sun goes down. Its bells are set into a buttressed bell tower, and the adjoining monastery

Skaros Rock The fortress town of Skaros, once a thriving settlement, is now in ruins. Just the chapel of Agios Ioannis Apokefalistheis survives intact.

'Dug-in' dwellings Houses, some of them carved into the volcanic rock, jostle for space in the village of Oia, which claims the best sunset views in the Mediterranean.

contains precious icons and bibles. The terrace below the monastery gives a commanding view of the island and the surrounding Aegean Sea – and those celebrated sunsets.

Where the earth moved

Santorini and the neighbouring island of Therasia, together with the privately owned Aspronisi and some smaller uninhabited islands, are all that remain above the sea of a huge dormant volcano. They form a broken rectangle that marks the rim of the flooded caldera, 7.5 miles (12km) long, 4.3 miles (7km) wide and 600m (2,000ft) deep. Santorini's red, brown and green cliffs and the string of cliff-top villages enclose three sides of the lagoon, Therasia and Aspronisi form the fourth side, leaving gaps in the southwest and northwest corners that allow ships to pass through. The beaches are not on the caldera side of the islands, where the water is deep, but on the outer slopes. The colour of the sand or pebbles depends on the underlying rock, giving rise to distinctive black, red and white beaches.

In spring, the hillsides are carpeted with swathes of brightly coloured flowers, but any ground that is not too steep is cultivated. Fields of grapes growing in baskets on the ground, along with Santorini's very own fava beans, capers, cucumbers, watermelons and tomatoes thrive in the rich volcanic soil.

Water is scarce, so crops depend on sporadic rain in winter and dew during the rest of the year.

Local cooks use their homegrown produce in a distinctive Santorini cuisine, and for such a small island Santorini has an unusual wealth of culinary specialities. There is fava, a bean dip with onion and lemon, served with a red sauce and capers in summer and fried with pork or kaborma in winter. Tomato keftedes are mint-scented tomato balls, and there are juicy white aubergines and chloro, a homemade goat's cheese, its production a closely guarded secret. Even the local wine is recognised for its superior quality.

Daily life has remained unchanged for centuries. The agricultural and religious calenders are closely intertwined with communal festivals. The feast of St John the Baptist falls on June 23, when the evening sees the tall May wreaths publicly burned in Santorini's tiny villages. Adults and children alike jump over the fire for good luck.

Fiery beginnings

Santorini is named after the 5th-century cathedral of St Irene, whose ruins are at the base of Mesa Vouno, a rocky outcrop near the town of Perissa. About 200m (650ft) up Mesa Vouno is a chapel called Panagia Katefiani, from *katefio* (refuge). In 1650 local people took refuge in the chapel during the 'Time of Evil', when the submarine Kolumbo volcano 5 miles (8km) northeast of Santorini pushed above the surface in a violent eruption, killing many of the island's population and much of the livestock. Today, Kolumbo bubbles away beneath the seabed, emerging through hydrothermal vents (underwater hot springs).

Small but SPECIAL

ISOLA BELLA

Isola Bella is a tiny island near the cliff-side town of Taormina, on the eastern shore of Sicily. Known as the 'Pearl of the Ionian Sea', it is joined to the mainland by a single strip of sand. It was once the private property of Lady Florence Trevelyan (1852-1907), who commissioned its only house and gardens, stocked with exotic plants, including cycads, great white bird-of-paradise, pines and dragons' blood trees. Seabirds and peregrines are common, as are migrants who stop on the way to and from Africa. The native flora is of Mediterranean maquis plants, together with Ionian sea lavender and Taormina cornflower. The surrounding waters are teeming with fish, feathered nudibranchs, stark red sea anemones, and octopus. The island is now a nature reserve run by Catania University, with its own natural Grotta Azzurra.

Neon glow Nea Kameni is a fusion of volcanic cones thrown up from the Santorini caldera. Volcanic gases colour the seawater and rocks bright orange.

Santorini is in the South Aegean Volcanic Island Arc, created by the collision of the African and European tectonic plates. In around 1613 BC, the island exploded in one of the biggest volcanic eruptions in recorded history. A Minoan Bronze Age settlement at Akrotiri on Santorini dating from the third millennium BC was buried in pumice, like Pompeii many centuries later, although in Santorini's case people may have had warning because no human remains have been found at the site.

The ash plume reached 22 miles (35km) high, dumping debris on islands to the northeast. A tsunami thought to have been up to 150m (490ft) high hit neighbouring islands and devastated Minoan coastal communities. Historians have suggested that the eruption may have contributed to the collapse of the Minoan civilisation centred on Crete, and was Plato's inspiration for the myth of Atlantis.

Legacy of a big bang

Geological evidence shows that the volcano had exploded regularly and cyclically prior to the cataclysmic event of 1613 BC. The eruptions were violent; each time, the crater caved in and seawater inundated the caldera. Then magma would build up again, leading to another eruption. The process repeated until the biggest eruption of all blew off the top of the volcano. The remaining caldera collapsed in on itself and the sea rushed in, leaving the broken caldera rim above water.

Two small volcanic islands inside the caldera, Palea Kameni and Nea Kameni, ('old burnt' and 'new island'), provide a reminder that Santorini, though dormant, could just be resting before another eruption. Nea Kameni, which has two craters and active sulphur vents, had a minor eruption in 1950. Palea Kameni has hot springs and mud baths and spews orange-coloured, sulphur-rich thermal water into the lagoon.

In the first part of 2012 Santorini and the surrounding area experienced a higher than normal number of earthquake swarms (sequences of small earthquakes over a short space of time). The islands are monitored closely by geologists, however, and there is no indication that another volcanic eruption is imminent.

best of the rest...

IDYLLIC MEDITERRANEAN ISLANDS

■ Set in the Tyrrhenian Sea, on the southern edge of the Gulf of Naples, the exquisite island of **Capri** was a holiday resort even in Roman times. Ancient Roman ruins can still be seen, along with other picturesque delights: the Marina Piccola ('little harbour'), the high promenade of the Belvedere di Tragara, the Grotta Azzurra sea cave with its brilliant blue waters, and the towering Faraglioni - three limestone sea stacks, one of which has its own subspecies of wall lizard.

■ Carloforte is an Italian fishing town on the volcanic island of **Isola di Santa Pietro**, 4 miles (7km) off the southwest coast of Sardinia. High, steep rocky cliffs with caves and small beaches dominate the north and west of the island. The town's medieval church, Chiesi dei Novelli Innocenti, is said to have been built to commemorate the drowning of shipwrecked passengers during the so-called Children's Crusade of 1212. Historians now believe the victims of the fated ship were not children, but dispossessed peasants fleeing from northern Europe.

■ **Stromboli** is a volcanic island off the north coast of Sicily, home to three charming fishing villages - San Bartolo, San Vincenzo and Ginostra - and one of Italy's three active volcanoes. Stromboli has been in almost continuous eruption for more than 2,000 years, with activity as recently as August 2011. Visitors

Capri

come to watch nature's night-time fireworks - incandescent volcanic explosions that have earned the island the name 'Lighthouse of the Mediterranean'.

■ **Ponza** is Italy's closely guarded secret. Few tourists come here, only Italians. The island is steeped in history: three caves with ancient fish tanks and traps mark the Grotta di Pilato, where Pontius Pilate reared eels for Roman nobility. A Roman tunnel connects Ponza town with the island's largest beach, Spiaggi di Chiaia di Luna. The Grotta della Maga Circe, is an essential grotto for fans of Homer's *Odyssey*, for Ponza is said to be the inspiration for the mythical island of Aeaea, home of the sorceress Circe, where she detained Odysseus on his way to Ithaca.

■ **Ibiza** represents the Balearics at their best: not just azure skies and searing sun, but centuries of old-world charm. Since it was founded by the Phoenicians more than 2,500 years ago, Ibiza Town has been constantly redeveloped but never spoiled: there is no more atmospheric little harbour to be found anywhere in the world.

SHWEDAGON PAGODA

Gleaming on a hilltop overlooking Yangon (Rangoon) is one of the most lavish, expensive and revered structures ever built.

There was a time when Burmese monarchs competed to contribute the most gold to Shwedagon's glimmering stupa. Queen Shinsawbu started the tradition in the 15th century when she gave her own weight in gold – 40kg (90lb) – to be pounded into gold leaf and used to cover the pagoda. Her son-in-law King Dhammazedi outdid her by giving four times his weight in gold. And the practice continues to this day: pilgrims buy packets of gold leaf to fix to the temple's Buddha statues.

Rudyard Kipling called Shwedagon a 'beautiful winking wonder that blazed in the sun'. Somerset Maugham saw the temple as 'sudden hope in the dark night of the soul of which the mystics write'. Even without the gilt, the Shwedagon temple complex, with more than a hundred pavilions, stupas and other buildings, would be an impressive architectural achievement.

Golden tower

According to legend, the temple was founded 2,500 years ago, but historians now believe it was first built between the 6th and 10th centuries AD by the Mon civilisation. It was enlarged during the

WHERE ON EARTH?

Shwedagon Pagoda lies on the revered Singuttara Hill in Yangon (Rangoon), the capital of Myanmar (Burma). Yangon International Airport (Mingalardon Airport) is the main gateway, with direct links to other Asian capitals. Visitors are advised to dress modestly.

MYANMAR (BURMA) · Shwedagon Pagoda · Yangon · Andaman Sea

Forest of spires The main central pagoda towers above 64 smaller stupas, prayer halls and Buddha statues around its base.

14th and 15th centuries, reaching its present size in the 18th century.

The main stupa, which houses eight strands of the Lord Gautama Buddha's hair, soars to 99m (325ft) high. It has an octagonal base, a bell-shaped dome covered in gold leaf, and a tapering spire that incorporates the *nga-pyaw-bu* ('banana bud') and the *hti* ('umbrella crown'). The spire is covered with 21,000 gold plates and studded with more than 5,000 diamonds, 2,000 rubies, assorted emeralds, topaz and sapphires and 420 silver bells that tinkle in the wind. At the tip is a 76-carat diamond.

Although Shwedagon's main focus is Buddhism, the temple has always provided a focal point for Burmese social and political movements. The seeds of Burmese independence from the British Empire were sown here, and a monument commemorates a student protest against the British in 1920.

Places for prayer Shwedagon has many smaller shrines, some of which were created by local families.

best of the rest...

GOLDEN TEMPLES

■ The **Harmandir Sahib** (Golden Temple) is the most sacred Sikh shrine. Set in a lake of holy water in the Indian city of Amritsar, the temple is reached by a marble causeway.

■ The **Jin Dian Temple** is the pride of Kunming, in China's Yunnan province. Built of bronze, it blazes gold in the evening sun.

■ Japan's **Kinkaku-ji**, in Kyoto, is set in a lush garden. The upper two storeys of the shrine are covered in gold leaf.

■ Bangkok's Temple of the Emerald Buddha includes the **Phra Sri Rattana Chedi**, a stupa said to house relics of Gautama Buddha. The exterior is covered in gold mosaic.

■ The Hindu **Sripuram Golden Temple** near Vellore in India, completed in 2007, is covered in 1,500kg (3,300lb) of gold foil.

STAFFA AND THE GIANT'S CAUSEWAY

Nature, myth and history come together in two matching rock formations that face each other across the Irish Sea.

As vessels laden with visitors round the last promontory on the approach to Staffa, a small uninhabited island in the Inner Hebrides, the boatmen cut the engines. A hush descends, broken only by the cries of seabirds and the lapping of waves, and visitors take in their first view of Fingal's Cave. Stone colonnades crowd in on either side of an imposing portal, as though a strange cathedral had been carved out of the cliffs. Pillars, perfectly hexagonal in shape, rear up in ranks, their improbable exactness emphasised by the rugged contours of the rocky island that forms their pediment above. Visitors entering on foot along the rocky ledge that leads into the cave gaze at the columned walls and arching roof above their heads.

Voyage of discovery

Though locals had long known of this rocky basalt outcrop, Fingal's Cave was discovered for the outside world in 1722 by the English botanist Joseph Banks. He had recently returned from accompanying Captain Cook on his first Pacific voyage, bringing back hundreds of specimens unknown to science. In Banks's day the Hebrides were a more exotic destination than they are now, and Fingal's Cave represented almost as much of a 'discovery' as New South Wales.

Legend and lava

Fingal was a nickname of the mythical Irish warrior-hero, Fionn mac Cumhaill, or Finn McCool. It is said he stood 15m (50ft) tall. Legend has it that Fionn, wanting to cross to Scotland, built a stone causeway from the coast of what is now County Antrim, where a similar formation of about 40,000 basalt columns extends out from the foot of the cliffs and disappears into the sea. Fionn's final stepping-stone was Staffa.

Geological science partly confirms the myth because the two groups of basalt

WHERE ON EARTH?

Staffa is 6 miles (10km) west of Mull in the Inner Hebrides, off Scotland's west coast. Fingal's Cave is on the island's southern tip. Access is by boat from Mull or from the mainland at Oban. Rough seas may prevent boats from landing. The Giant's Causeway is on the Antrim coast in Northern Ireland.

Natural order Ranks of hexagonal rock columns line the outer faces and walls of Staffa's many caves. The large opening at the far right is Fingal's Cave.

columns are believed to have formed from the same lava flow. When the lava cooled and contracted, vertical cracks opened up in the resulting rock, which hardened into columns. The volcano that produced the lava around 60 million years ago was probably more than 90 miles (150km) away, towards East Lothian, and has long since subsided. The basalt columns have been scoured away by successive glaciations and the action of the sea, leaving the two formations in splendid isolation.

Romantic appeal

After Banks, a stream of eminent visitors were drawn to Staffa, keen to see the island's columns and cave for themselves. The artist J.M.W. Turner, the poets John Keats and William Wordsworth, even Queen Victoria came to wonder at the natural beauty of this geological phenomenon. The *Hebrides Overture* by Felix Mendelssohn, better known as *Fingal's Cave*, was inspired by the sound of waves reverberating around the cave's cavernous interior, which made a lasting impression on the composer during a visit in 1829.

Banks himself was moved to quasi-religious reverence by what he found in Fingal's Cave: 'The mind can hardly form an idea more magnificent than such a space … Compared to this what are the cathedrals or the palaces built by men!' Banks was an enlightened scientist, but he also acknowledged the miraculous order that science could find in the Universe. To this spirit, Fingal's Cave became a true shrine.

Legendary walkway The tightly packed basalt columns of the Giant's Causeway form stepping stones down into the sea.

best of the rest…

BASALT MARVELS

■ If size were everything, the **Devil's Tower** in Wyoming would win outright. This monolith rises nearly 400m (1,300ft) from the flat American plains. Volcanic action forced the 'intrusion' of hard igneous rock up through softer sedimentary layers, although geologists cannot agree on the causes of the strange striations that run up the side of the massive rock tower.

■ The **Hexagon Pools** on the Israeli-Syrian border are overlooked by sheets of grey, polygonal basalt columns. The rocks have been acted on by shifting fault lines, which accounts for their twisted appearance.

■ Located off the south coast of Sicily, the **Cyclopean Isles** are a group of tiny volcanic islands associated with nearby Mount Etna. The black basalt formations have been slowly eroded by wind and seawater to form a variety of vertical columns and horizontal polygonal mosaics.

SUGARLOAF MOUNTAIN

A mountain like no other, right in the heart of Rio de Janeiro, provides a 360-degree view of the city surrounded by ocean and mountains.

One of the most photographed peaks on the planet, the mountain known as Pão de Açúcar, or Sugarloaf, towers 395m (1,295ft) above the entrance to Guanabara Bay in the heart of Rio de Janeiro. The views from its summit are spectacular – a vast panorama taking in the huge bay and beaches, the endless city, forested mountains and the vast South Atlantic. Equally spectacular are the views of the mountain from elsewhere in the city: the distinctive shape and sheer slopes of Sugarloaf's granite mass, and the unusual juxtaposition of rock and water, give the mountain its unique caché. If not quite geometrically perfect, it is close enough to seem unnatural.

The mountain got its name during the heyday of Brazil's sugar boom. Cane juice was boiled and refined into raw sugar that was packed into conical clay moulds for export to Portugal and elsewhere. These sweet heaps were called *pãos de açúcar*, or sugar loaves, a name that naturally lent itself to Rio's similarly shaped peak. In fact, Sugarloaf Mountain has played a key role in Rio's history. It was at the base of the mountain that military commander Estácio de Sá established the first Portuguese settlement on Guanabara Bay in 1565, during an expedition to expel French colonists. The fortress of São João (Fortaleza de São João) still stands

testimony to the struggles that have dominated Brazil's turbulent history. It is one of a network of colonial forts that has protected the bay for more than 400 years.

During the 19th century, European artists found the mountain a compelling subject, and their paintings popularised the landmark. Sugarloaf also provided a dramatic backdrop in films such as *Flying Down to Rio* (1933), *That Night in Rio* (1941) and *Moonraker* (1979), further adding to the city's reputation as a romantic port of call.

Bondinho ascent

The mountain's rocky mass consists of two summits soaring from the same base – Morro da Urca (Urca Hill), the lower summit, and Sugarloaf itself. It formed about 600 million years ago when this portion of the Brazilian coast took shape. Compared to other

Giddy height Sugarloaf Mountain cuts a distinct shape above Rio, with Guanabara Bay and the downtown area beyond. The cable-car terminus at the top is just visible.

granite monoliths, the mountain's flanks are nearly vertical and devoid of vegetation. It can be climbed on foot, but the most popular means of reaching the twin summits is a vertigo-inducing cable-car ride from the terminus at Praia Vermelha (Red Beach). Dubbed the 'Bondinho', the cable cars were

introduced in 1912, the first of their kind in Brazil and only the third cable-car system in the world. From ground level, the first part of the journey stretches 220m (722ft) up Morro da Urca, taking only three minutes. The second part of the journey, from Morro da Urca to the top of Sugarloaf, takes another three minutes. The glass pods dangle above the granite saddle that separates the twin peaks. The vintage cable cars on display indicate just how far cable-car technology has developed since those first thrilling journeys up the mountain.

REVERSE ANGLE

While the view from the top of Sugarloaf is breathtaking, the best way to photograph the humpback mountain itself is from other vantage points around Rio. The best sunrise and sunset shots are from Corcovado Mountain, the granite dome to the west that looks down on Sugarloaf. The best daylight shots are from the western side of Guanabara Bay, including the Morro da Viúva and Flamengo Beach. On the waterfront between these landmarks is the Porcao restaurant, which offers spectacular views of Sugarloaf from its terrace. One can also snap the peak from Copacabana Beach in the west. Another good outlook is from the top of Morro do Leme on the south side of Praia Vermelha, accessible from Avenida Atlantica at the east end of Copacabana.

The crowds thin out on the upper peak, especially along the intimate ecological trail on the ocean side, where secluded overlooks provide views to the distant horizon. Sheltered in the trees at the back of the mountain is a picnic area, where lizards sun themselves on the walkways and walls.

Panoramic spectacle

The views from Sugarloaf's summit are nothing short of spectacular. To the west stretch the golden curves of Copacabana and Ipanema, two of the world's most celebrated beaches, as well as Corcovado Mountain with its towering statue of Christ the Redeemer. To the north lies the crowded Flamengo district, downtown Rio and the city's domestic airport, some of the planes appearing so close to the mountain that you feel you can almost reach out and touch them. Due east is the entrance

to Guanabara Bay, the Niterói and Jurujuba suburbs, as well as the 16th-century Fortaleza de São João.

The lush Atlantic forests that cover much of Sugarloaf and Morro da Urca provide refuge for native toucans and parrots, as well as marmosets, the world's smallest primates, which frolic in the trees near the Morro cable-car station. The natural landscape was regenerated in the 1980s as part of the Operação Vegetação programme, which involved planting thousands of native trees, shrubs and flowers on both mountains.

Scaling the peaks

Sugarloaf Mountain was unclimbed until 1817, when the intrepid English nanny Henrietta Carstairs became the first person to reach the summit. To the chagrin of locals, she planted a Union Jack flag on top. The precipitous

City of contrasts Sugarloaf's 360-degree view includes, looking west, the long sweep of Copacabana Beach curving away to the left and Corcovado Mountain rising above the city on the right.

north wall was not scaled until 1972, when an Australian team overcame the ominous granite facade. Nowadays, the Sugarloaf offers many climbing routes with various degrees of difficulty and colourful names, such as Checkmate, Crazy Horse, Ace of Spades and Waldo. The mountain has become one of the world's most popular urban climbing destinations, and some people come just to watch as climbers test their skills on the monolith.

Climbing up the back of Sugarloaf is possible, but casual hikers are discouraged as it's a tough ascent even for experienced climbers. Once at the top you can't buy a ticket for the return cable car, so it's best to buy a one-way ticket at the base and take it with you. The lower Morro da Urca climb follows the Claudio Coutinho Trail, starting at the Praia Vermilho beach and winding up between the peaks.

Outstretched arms Standing on top of Rio's Corcovado Mountain, this statue of Christ the Redeemer is clearly visible from Sugarloaf Mountain.

CITY VIEW LOCATIONS

▨ **Alcatraz** island presents its own unique urban vista: a prison panorama of San Francisco and its Golden Gate and Bay bridges. From here, inmates had an alluring view of lost freedom.

▨ The **Gianicolo** (Janiculum, the Romans called it) has fine monuments of its own, but its greatest asset is the vistas it affords of other sights. Stand up here on a summer's evening and you can see the Italian capital ablaze in the glow of sunset, a city of shining walls and rooftops and glinting domes.

▨ In 2000 the **London Eye** opened to celebrate the new millennium with spectacular views of the British capital. The world's tallest Ferris wheel, the structure rotates sedately to reach 135m (443ft) above the River Thames. The journey takes 30 minutes in glass-enclosed capsules that afford bird's-eye views of Parliament, Big Ben and other London landmarks.

▨ Viewed across the scudding wake of the **Staten Island Ferry**, Manhattan seems like a raft afloat. This routine commuter ride is a sublime experience for the visitor in New York. The Twin Towers may be gone, but a new World Trade Center now dominates a scene that remains as iconic as it ever was.

▨ In addition to the view from the Eiffel Tower, Paris offers an enticing hill view from the crest of **Montmartre**. Tourists can see Parisian life unfold from the terraces in front of the Sacré Cœur church, or scale its grand dome for a higher view.

▨ Hong Kong's **Victoria Peak** is named after the reigning monarch when Britain first ruled the island. Reached via the red-and-white Peak Tram or a long, winding drive, the Peak affords a sweeping view of Hong Kong Harbour, the Kowloon Peninsula, the island-spangled South China Sea and Pearl River Delta.

SVANETI

As if Svaneti's villagers weren't high enough in their remote mountain homeland, they built and lived in fortified five-storey towers. Many of their ancient tower-houses still stand.

Rising to a height of more than 5,190m (17,000ft), Mount Shkhara in the Greater Caucasus Mountain Range is one of the highest peaks in Europe. Unless, of course, you think the mountain is in Asia – for geographers disagree over what route the continental border takes through the mountains of the Caucasus. In fact, the entire area between the Black Sea and Caspian Sea is characterised by ambiguity – cartographical, geological, cultural and linguistic.

The Caucasus region belongs both to Europe and Asia – and to neither. Ecologically, it follows its own rules. The lower valleys have a temperate, almost Mediterranean, climate; in the mountains, a more northern climate dominates. Above 3,000m (9,850ft), Arctic conditions prevail, with snow, glaciers and permafrost (frozen subsoil); even below this height, down to 2,000m (6,000ft), Siberian-style mixed pine and fir forests cloak the slopes. The wildlife is just as diverse: northern species, such as lynx, and southern ones, such as leopard, share this wilderness.

In the shadow of Shkhara

The wildlife of the Caucasus shares its home with an extraordinary variety of peoples. Dozens of languages are spoken across the region by more than 50 distinct ethnic groups. None is more remarkable than the Svan, who live ringed in by high mountains in the upper valleys of the Enguri, Rioni and Tskhenistskali rivers, in the Georgian province of Svaneti. Beyond the Bezengi Wall – a group of peaks in which Mount Shkhara is the highest point – lies Russia.

The Svans are ethnographically Georgian, having been completely cut

Defendable homes In medieval times each house in Svaneti villages had a tower for protection against attacks and natural disasters such as landslides.

WHERE ON EARTH?

Svaneti is in northwest Georgia, about 300 miles (500km) from the capital, Tbilisi. The airport is at Mestia, which has regular flights to and from Tbilisi. In summer, quicker flights are available on Georgian military aircraft between Georgia's second city, Kutaisi, and a rough landing field in Mestia.

off from their Russian neighbours to the north. Not that communications with the rest of Georgia are much better. Svaneti is cut off by snow for half the year. And during the remaining months, flash floods and rockslides make travel hazardous along the precipitously steep and poorly surfaced mountain roads.

Remoteness has had its advantages. Since Byzantine times, the region has been beyond the reach of government control. But if the people were free from officialdom, they also went without protection – in a region whose forests were roamed not only by wolves but also by groups of bandits. In addition, villagers had to defend themselves from each other as blood-feuds were a feature of life in Svaneti. The Svan's home was his castle, and families lived in fortified compounds that were dominated by tower-houses standing 25m (80ft) tall.

Tower towns

Once there were hundreds of tower-houses across the length and breadth of Svaneti. Their overall design did not change for a thousand years. Wider at the base, giving them the strength to resist avalanches and landslides, the five-storey towers generally tapered towards the top, which incorporated a lookout post that was a last-ditch refuge from attack. For windows, the upper floors had arrow slits, which narrow

towards the outside of the wall. In winter, the family hunkered down on the ground floor with their livestock, using the upper levels to store forage and equipment; in summer, the family occupied the cooler upper floors.

Today, across much of the region, these traditional tower-houses have been demolished or abandoned, allowed to slip inexorably into disrepair, homes to nesting hooded crows. But even in a ruined state they are impressive – a melancholy human imposition on one of the world's most spectacular landscapes. Viewed from ground level, these towers seem to challenge the sky; seen from above, from hillsides carpeted in summer with an unrivalled array of wildflowers, the towers look like natural rock chimneys rising out of the craggy mountain landscape.

Higher up the valley, a greater quantity of original architecture remains. At Ushguli, to the southeast of Mestia, near the head of the Enguri River, the landscape bristles with medieval tower-houses that are part of living, thriving local communities. Strictly speaking, Ushguli is made up of four separate villages: Chasgazi,

Zhibiani, Chubiani and Murqmeil. Chasgazi is still unspoiled, with more than 100 tower-houses.

Land of the Golden Fleece

Did Jason journey to Svaneti with the Argonauts to fetch the famous Golden Fleece? In the Greek myth, Jason's uncle, Pelias, demands this prize in payment for the throne he has usurped from Jason's father. A magical ram's fleece of purest gold, this alluring treasure is in the possession of Aeëtes, King of Colchis (to this day, Georgia's coastal plain is known as Kolkhida).

As Pelias knew, storms in the Black Sea were the least of the challenges presented by this dangerous mission – but Jason had the backing of the goddess Athena. It was at her bidding that Jason called his warriors and set them to work building a ship. The vessel was called the *Argo* – hence the name Argonauts under which Jason's heroic party put to sea.

After many adventures, they landed in Colchis at the mouth of the River Phasis – believed to be the Rioni River of today. They made their way upriver into the wilds of what could have been Svaneti, and there found the fleece hanging from

Old and new Medieval stone towers stand side-by-side with modern brick buildings in the village of Ushguli. The snow-covered craggy slopes of Mount Shkhara rise up behind.

a branch in a sacred grove guarded by a dragon. Jason captured it with the help of Aeëtes' daughter Medea, a beautiful but sinister sorceress who showed him how to defeat the dragon and escape. She then eloped with Jason, murdering her own brother and casting his butchered body into the sea behind the *Argo* to distract her pursuing father. When Jason abandoned her for Glauce, Princess of Corinth, Medea took revenge by giving the bride a poison-imbued gown. Glauce put on the dress and the poison killed her.

Svaneti culture has its own femme fatale. The Georgian hunting goddess, Dali, was said to make her home by Mount Ushba, northwest of Mestia. She was an enchanting temptress who took forest men as her lovers – but murdered them if they so much as breathed a word.

Fortresses of faith

Times change – even in Svaneti. Pagan deities, such as Dali, are consigned to legend and the Svan have been Christians for 1,500 years. But their Orthodox faith has adapted to conditions in which the sword has been more prevalent than peace. Hence the churches are fortified as strongly as the houses. Some were incorporated into the larger tower-houses of feudal rulers, effectively becoming private chapels. The church of Lashkdash in Chasgazi is a fine example.

Churches were built for strength more than style, yet the Svan still wanted to worship in an atmosphere of grace and beauty. Too much use of jewels, gold, silver and stained-glass was inadvisable in a country where raids by bandits were a constant danger, so they relied on wall paintings to set the spiritual mood. Those in Chasgazi's Matskhvar (Church of the Saviour) are justly famed. Dating from the end of the first millennium, they offer scriptural scenes and episodes from the lives of the saints, filling the

Orthodox worship There are still about 70 churches in use around Svaneti, with well-preserved treasures, such as icons and gold crosses.

interior with vibrant colour. While these murals belong to the Eastern Orthodox tradition in subject and style, they have a freshness and fluidity often lacking in iconography from this era. Unlike the Western fresco technique of working on wet plaster, the church's rough interior masonry was coated in a layer of plaster that was allowed to dry before scenes were painted onto it. Paintings and other items salvaged from Svaneti's crumbling churches, from illuminated manuscripts to wood carvings, are kept in Mestia's Museum of History and Ethnography.

A culture of continuance

The real heritage of the Svan never took such tangible form. Song, dance and celebration have always been their main forms of self-expression – treasures that no invader could carry off. The Svan developed mesmerising, intoxicating folk dances and polyphonic songs that are as popular today as they ever were.

Meanwhile, daily life goes on, too. There are flocks of sheep and goats to tend, cheeses to be made, and livings to be scratched from the stubborn soil. Farmers grow barley and potatoes, but much of their effort goes into growing animal fodder for the winter, when the surrounding slopes are under snow. They may dwell in ancient monuments, but the Svan people live for today – as they always have – and for the unforgiving winter that is never more than a few weeks away.

best of the rest...

MOUNTAIN SETTLEMENTS

◼ The rugged villages of Morocco's **Atlas Mountains** include Telouet, southeast of Marrakech. This *kasbah*, or fortified centre, stands at 1,800m (6,000ft) and once commanded the caravan route for camel trains coming north from the Sahara Desert to Marrakesh, with its famous souk. The fortifications, though crumbling, still remain. All told, there are more than 1,000 fortified villages in the mountains: the Berber tribes up here lived as bandits and were constantly at war. Justly celebrated is the fine kasbah of Aït Benhaddou, a village south of Telouet, whose earthen buildings remain intact.

Ladakh

◼ Rising to 800m (2,600ft), Le Puy-en-Velay and Ambert in France's **Auvergne** region derive their essential character from their mountain setting. These historic towns developed as staging posts for traders, and their remoteness has kept them unspoiled. The neat, well-organised settlements of upland France and Italy contrast with the wildness around them – that is their charm.

◼ At altitudes between 1,200 and 1,800m (4,000-6,000ft) above sea level, the villages of Italy's **Dolomites** nestle beneath blue skies and jagged, snow-draped mountain peaks. They include picturesque centres such as Cortina d'Ampezzo at the head of the Valle del Boite, a popular skiing resort, and the villages of Arabba and Selva in the Sella mountain group.

◼ **Ladakh**, the Land of High Passes, in Kashmir, is in a region contested by India and Pakistan. Many of Ladakh's inhabitants feel drawn to neither of these claimants, and are fiercely independent, both as mountain dwellers and as Buddhists. Culturally and linguistically, they have more in common with the Tibetans, their neighbours to the southeast. The Ladakhis live by stock-rearing and subsistence agriculture.

SYDNEY HARBOUR

This intricate natural harbour provides one of the most spectacular settings for a city in the world, and is home to two of Australia's most recognisable icons: Sydney Harbour Bridge and Sydney Opera House.

Captain Arthur Phillip of the British First Fleet claimed it to be 'the finest harbour in the world' when he first set eyes on Port Jackson in 1788, and quickly decided that Sydney Harbour was a better choice for settlement than Botany Bay further south. And many others agreed with him. 'So inexpressibly lovely', according to the Victorian novelist Anthony Trollope, 'that it makes a man ask himself whether it would not be worth his while to move his household goods to the eastern coast of Australia.'

The sheer size and extent of the waterways and coastline alone give Sydney its stunning cityscape. Leading in from the Tasman Sea through the famous Sydney Heads, Port Jackson – the waterway containing North Harbour, Middle Harbour and Sydney Harbour – extends over an area of 21 sq miles (55km²) and the estuary stretches a further 12 miles (19km) inland. Sydney Harbour is the longest

Natural harbour Popular Manly Beach, in the foreground, faces the ocean. The Harbour and city stretch away beyond it. The Harbour Bridge is just visible in the distance.

displaced and pushed inland or along the coast, but their heritage is preserved in more than 4,000 petroglyphs scattered around the coastline, including the rock art of Watsons Bay and North Bondi.

A city emerges

The Harbour has huge historic and cultural significance as the place where the first Europeans were settled 'Down Under' in 1788. The Sydney Cove settlement was named after Thomas Townshend, First Viscount Sydney, British Home Secretary of the day. After a shaky start, the colony rapidly outgrew its initial penal beginnings, taking shape around Sydney Cove (Circular Quay), Farm Cove and Cockle Bay (Darling Harbour) on the southern shore of the Harbour. Sydney grew rapidly during the 19th century, having become an important commercial centre and port.

By the start of the 20th century, a vibrant Sydney vied with Melbourne for the title of Australia's foremost city. The construction of the Sydney Harbour Bridge, which opened in 1932, ensured that Sydney became the better known of the two. The Bridge's iconic status was reinforced in the aftermath of World War Two, when it became a highly recognisable feature seen by the large numbers of displaced people who arrived by ship to begin a new life in Australia. It is still the world's widest long-span bridge.

Perched on Bennelong Point, a spit of land named after the senior Eora man Woollarawarre Bennelong, the Sydney Opera House opened in 1973.

arm of Port Jackson and contains many bays and beaches, along with a collection of picturesque islands and historical fortifications. Port Jackson's coastline measures nearly 200 miles (320km), as it winds in and out of coves and inlets that lead off in every direction. Metropolitan Sydney is tightly wrapped around the complex shoreline of Sydney Harbour, taking full advantage of the stunning harbour views and coastal lifestyle.

valley of the Parramatta River to create Port Jackson. Several Aboriginal tribes occupied the shoreline, among them the Eora, Wangal, Gadigal and Cammeraygal peoples, who were living in the area when the British arrived. They were soon

Natural beginnings

Although the landscape around Sydney Harbour began forming about 225 million years ago, the Harbour itself is quite recent. It formed between 18,000 and 6,000 years ago as sea levels rose following the last Ice Age, drowning the

Cultural icon When it opened in 1973, the Opera House instantly became a symbol of Australia's cultural progression. It houses an opera theatre, concert hall, drama theatre and restaurants.

US architect Louis Kahn said of it, 'The sun did not know how beautiful its light was until it was reflected off this building'. Danish architect Jørn Utzon's shell or sail-like forms have subsequently replaced the Harbour Bridge as Sydney's most famous landmark.

Sydney's economic strength and quality of life have continued to attract new residents. The 2011 census put the population at 4.4 million, among whom the most common ancestries apart from Australian were English, Chinese, Irish, Scottish, Italian, Lebanese and Greek. About 18 per cent described themselves as Asian Australian.

Bays and coves

With ferries constantly on the move and huge cruise ships moored along Circular Quay, Sydney Cove has always been the Harbour's busy heart. But other inlets and bays around the Harbour have their own legacies. Once a commercial haven for wool and coal exports, Darling Harbour, on the west side of the Bridge, has been transformed into a tourist, convention and exhibition centre and is home to the floating Sydney Aquarium and the National Maritime Museum.

Australian aviation was born along the calm shores of Rose Bay on the southeastern side of the Harbour. At the turn of the 20th century, pioneer aviator Lawrence Hargrave created huge cellular kites and flying machines at his Rose Bay home, and in 1938 the bay became Sydney's seaplane terminal.

Completed in 1915, Wooloomooloo Wharf on Wooloomooloo Bay is the largest wood-piled structure in the

New Year celebrations Each year, fireworks light up the night sky above the Harbour Bridge and Opera House to usher in the new year.

world. The area has become a hub of upmarket bars, gourmet eateries and occasional celebrity residents, such as actor Russell Crowe. The Spit, on Middle Harbour, is a main crossing point between the city and the north shore over the landmark Spit Bridge. Built in 1958, it is one of the few working drawbridges left in Australia.

On Sydney Harbour, boats form a constant feature, but never more so than at the start of the annual Sydney to Hobart Yacht Race, a four-day ocean race from Sydney to Tasmania, crossing the treacherous waters of Bass Strait. Hundreds of spectator craft gather on

the Harbour and along the shore and thousands of people line vantage points along the waterfront to watch the fleet sail out through the Heads.

Wildlife haven

Despite two centuries of urban development, Sydney Harbour continues to host an incredibly varied array of fauna. More than 550 fish species are either permanently or seasonally resident in the Harbour, including big-belly seahorses, poisonous lionfish, scorpion fish and Port Jackson sharks. During their winter migration, humpback whales have been spotted by the Harbour Bridge, and southern right whales also visit during migration.

Waterfront wildlife is just as diverse and the region supports many native species. Elusive fairy penguins may be spotted in Manly Cove, water dragons bask on the sandstone at Obelisk Bay and white-bellied sea eagles swoop to catch fish along the upper reaches of Middle Harbour. Lyrebirds and sugar gliders make their homes in the gullies of Garigal National Park. The ubiquitous grey-headed flying foxes can be seen around Sydney at sunset, while green and golden bell frogs live on the shore by Sydney Olympic Park.

The natural beauty and richness of Port Jackson is protected by three reserves. Sydney Harbour National Park embraces a dozen different shoreline areas around Sydney Harbour and the

Waterside view Giraffes feed at Taronga Zoo on the north side of the Harbour against the familiar backdrop of the Sydney skyline and Opera House.

Heads, as well as historic islands such as Fort Denison and Goat Island. Lane Cove National Park protects the valley on the upper reaches of the Lane Cove River estuary. And Garigal National Park stretches north from Middle Harbour to the Hawkesbury River and beyond. For all its sprawl, Sydney today is a city at home in its beautiful surroundings, and the Harbour remains its most precious natural asset.

best of the rest...

CITYSCAPES

■ In the early 21st century, **Dubai** has emerged out of nowhere in the sands of the Arabian desert to become the quintessential modern city. Although some may claim it lacks the cultural and social maturity of older cities, it is the world's leading centre of modern architecture.

■ **Frankfurt** in Germany is a city of contrasts where traditional low-rise, high-density European architecture mixes and contrasts with cutting-edge skyscrapers such as the Commerzbank Tower.

■ **Hong Kong's** cityscape is evolving. The closing of Kai Tak Airport in 1998 enabled skyscraper building on both sides of the harbour, creating a canyon of steel, glass and neon with Victoria Peak and the Kowloon (Nine Dragon) mountains as dramatic backdrops.

Hong Kong

■ The **Manhattan** skyline is the original iconic cityscape: the forest of stylish skyscrapers ranges from Art Deco masterpieces, such as the Chrysler and Empire State buildings, to more recent monuments, including the United Nations headquarters. The lost Twin Towers are being replaced by the 541m (1,776ft) Freedom Tower.

■ The **Shanghai Bund** waterfront sprawls along the west bank of the Huangpu River in China. The area's trademark Art Deco style buildings are from the 1930s, when this was the heart of the city's international district. On the opposite bank, the Pudong district offers a futuristic architectural vision.

BEYOND COMPARE

TAJ MAHAL

Described by the Indian poet Rabindranath Tagore as 'a solitary tear suspended on the cheek of time', the Taj Mahal is the crowning jewel of Indo-Islamic architecture.

The Taj Mahal is, quite simply, one of the world's most stunning buildings. This white marble mausoleum in the city of Agra has become the premier cultural icon of India; endlessly photographed, its image is familiar all over the world. Yet people seeing the reality for the first time still gasp at its breathtaking beauty. To architects, the Taj Mahal is the finest surviving example of Mughal architecture (a blend of Indian, Persian and Islamic), unsurpassed in its harmonious proportions and fluidity of decoration. To the rest of the world, it is an enduring monument to love, built by a grief-stricken man after the death of his most beloved wife.

WHERE ON EARTH?

The Taj Mahal is in Agra, in the state of Uttar Pradesh, 125 miles (200km) from Delhi. Service to Agra's Kheria Airport is seasonal, so it is advisable to travel by train, then take a taxi. The Taj Mahal is best seen as part of a trip that includes Agra's other famous sites - the Red Fort and Fatehpur Sikri.

A labour of love

The Taj Mahal was constructed in the 17th century by the Mughal emperor, Shah Jahan, in honour of his favourite wife, Arjumand Banu Begum, better known as Mumtaz Mahal (meaning Chosen One of the Palace), who died giving birth to their 14th child in 1631. Devastated by her sudden death, Shah Jahan set out to create an eternal monument to her memory – indeed, the name Taj Mahal, which means 'Crown Palace', is a derivation of her name. The result was a true labour of love that took 22 years to complete.

Though his name is now inextricably linked to love, Shah Jahan was as ruthless as any of his ancestors, dispatching four of his brothers on his way to the throne. And he brought his imperial power to bear in constructing his most famous legacy. A team of 22,000 workers – sculptors, stonemasons, carvers, painters, calligraphers, inlayers and others – was recruited from Europe, the Middle East and Asia. At first it was a job of brute strength, bringing the translucent white marble blocks 120 miles (190km) from Rajasthan: 1,000 elephants were used in transporting the materials. Then 28 kinds of precious and semi-precious stones – including onyx, amethyst, lapis lazuli, turquoise, jade and mother-of-pearl – were brought from Russia, Persia, Afghanistan, China and Tibet to decorate his fabulous creation rising in Agra.

The building work was completed in 1653, although decorative additions continued to be made until 1657. The inscriptions on the gateways, mosque and tomb were the work of the renowned calligrapher, Amanat Khan. The chief architect remains unknown, although he is believed to have been Ustad Ahmad Lahauri, an Indian of Persian descent. The overall concept is said to have been the brainchild of the Shah himself, who had apparently loved designing palaces since childhood.

Paradise regained

Although it is the mausoleum's central dome that stays in people's minds, the Taj Mahal has five main components – the main gateway, garden, mausoleum, mosque and the mosque-mirroring *jawab* (mirror building). In all it covers 17ha (42 acres) of grounds sloping in terraces down towards the River Yamuna. In accordance with the principles of Mughal architecture, the five elements were designed as a unified entity and no subsequent alterations were allowed.

Southern view The dome, designed by Ismail Afandi, cleverly bulges out before tapering back in, transferring its heavy load directly downwards.

The Islamic view of heaven is ever-present in the buildings and gardens. The gateway at the southern end of the complex (the original entrance) is adorned with calligraphic verses from the Koran inviting the faithful to enter Paradise. Designed to a precise grid according to the Mughal *charbagh* (four-garden) style, the gardens are divided into quadrants by waterways, representing the Islamic Gardens of Paradise where rivers flow with water, milk and honey. The four 'rivers' are intended to converge at a central marble tank representing Kawthar, the Koran's celestial pool of abundance. In practice, only the north–south courses contain water, and they create a perfect reflection of the Taj Mahal that has become an enduringly popular image.

Central space

The focus of any visit is the central mausoleum. Set on a square platform 7m (23ft) high, this massive white marble structure has four almost identical facades, each with a wide central arch and smaller, peaked arches to the sides.

Red and green Enshrining the Taj Mahal is a superb mosque (*masjid*) to the west. Elegant cypress trees underline the subtle symmetry played out between the red sandstone and green gardens.

TAJ MAHAL LOVE STORY

When the young prince Khurram (1592-1666), favourite son of the Mughal Emperor Jahangir, met Arjumand Banu Begum, descended from Persian nobility, he was instantly dazzled by her beauty and was determined to marry her. They were betrothed in 1607, when he was 15 and she 14, but had to wait for another five years to marry, until the court astrologers found an auspicious date for the wedding.

After they were married, the prince, finding his wife 'elect among all the women of the time', gave her the title of Mumtaz Mahal, 'Jewel of the Palace'. For the next 19 years the couple were inseparable, with Mumtaz, despite her many pregnancies, often travelling with her husband on his military campaigns. The prince took two other wives, but according to court chroniclers, his feelings for Mumtaz 'exceeded by a thousand times what he felt for the others'. In 1627, when he succeeded to the throne as Shah Jahan, his trust in her was so great that he gave her his imperial seal, the Muhr Uzah.

In 1631 Mumtaz Mahal accompanied her husband on a military campaign to the Deccan and died at Burhanpur while giving birth to their 14th child. Devastated by her death, the Shah went into mourning for a year and built the Taj Mahal in her honour. On its completion, her body was transferred from Burhanpur to Agra.

In 1658 Shah Jahan fell ill and was deposed by his son Aurangzeb, who put him under house arrest in Agra Fort, where he ended his days in the company of his daughter, Jahanara Begum. After his death, in 1666, his body was laid to rest alongside that of his wife.

The magnificent central dome reaches a height of 73m (240ft) and is surrounded by four slender minarets. Steps lead up to the main tomb (visitors remove their shoes before starting the climb), and only as the visitor comes closer does the grand scale of its decoration become evident. Arabic calligraphy fringes the soaring archways, which, along with the walls, are embellished with exquisite examples of the decorative inlay technique of pietra dura ('hard stone'), in which precisely cut pieces of precious and semi-precious stones are fitted together to form geometric and floral designs. Lapis lazuli, jade, crystal, turquoise and amethyst are used to spectacular effect to create images of vases of flowers and tiny, delicate representations of flowers of paradise that curl and intertwine.

Inside the mausoleum is an octagonal inner chamber in which the marble cenotaphs of Mumtaz Mahal and Shah Jahan lie side by side, enclosed by a delicate filigree screen. Muslim tradition forbids elaborate decoration of graves, so the actual tombs are underneath the chamber in a plain crypt that is rarely open to the public. Any disappointment in not seeing these tombs is made up for by the superb inlay work on the false tombs on display, which is among the best in India. In places, as many as 35 different types of precious and semi-precious stones – including coral, turquoise, garnet and malachite – have been used to create individual flowers, with up to 60 fragments used on a single leaf or petal.

Symmetry and symbolism

The Taj Mahal is a masterclass in harmony and symmetry, and everything is pleasing to the eye. In the interests of balance, the central mausoleum is flanked to the west by a mosque and to the east by a *jawab* ('an answer' – a building mirroring the mosque), both built from red sandstone.

Despite its massive proportions, the mausoleum appears light and airy. The dazzling white marble is offset by the colours of the inlaid precious stones and the black jasper used for the calligraphy, just as the dome is offset by the four minarets, which in turn reflect the four-plan garden.

Jewelled flowers Flowers are sculpted in marble or recreated with precious stones to produce incandescent images.

Mumtaz's cenotaph is decorated with the 99 names for Allah; other calligraphic inscriptions identify and praise her. On the top of Shah Jahan's commemorative tomb is a symbolic pen box and writing tablet, the typical funerary accoutrements of the supreme male ruler. In the crypt below, the bodies of the emperor and his spouse are buried with their faces towards the holy city of Mecca, with the husband on his wife's right side.

In a stroke of genius, the calligraphy running throughout the building is written in a slightly larger script on the higher panels to reduce the skewing effect when it is viewed from below. A charming etching of the calligrapher's own signature appears at the base of the dome inside the mausoleum: 'Written by the insignificant being, Amanat Khan Shirazi.'

Some features of the Taj Mahal are so exquisitely designed and crafted as to approach the mystical, leading scholars to ponder on the Taj Mahal's hidden symbolism. The garden and Koranic references are clearly meant to represent Paradise, but there are many other spiritual allusions. The colour of the Makrana marble used for the mausoleum changes in the sun and in moonlight. According to the time of day, it can appear red, soft grey, yellow, cream or dazzling white. Many modern scholars believe that the effect of the changing colours is no accident, rather that Allah is being represented in the form of light since he cannot be depicted as a person. Studies have been made of the acoustics inside the main dome, which has a reverberation time of 28 seconds – in order, perhaps, for the recited words of the Koran to linger in the air.

More controversially, the rediscovery of an ancient Sufi document once owned by Shah Jahan's father that includes a diagram exactly mirroring the Taj Mahal has led many to believe that the tomb was planned in advance as a reproduction of God's throne, and that, far from being a romantic, Shah Jahan was an egotist

Monument to love The false tombs of Shah Jahan and Mumtaz Mahal lie in the highly decorated inner chamber. The smaller tomb is that of Mumtaz.

with delusions of grandeur. Whatever its real origins, Shah Jahan was said to have been so delighted with the building that he had the architect beheaded to ensure that no other building would ever rival it.

Later in his life, he planned to build a black mausoleum for himself on the other side of the River Yamuna. It was to have been every bit as magnificent as the white Taj, and the two were to have been connected with a bridge of solid silver.

Scholars may come and go as they debate the Taj Mahal's merits and mysticism, but this sublime monument, this masterpiece of Indo-Islamic architecture, will continue to amaze, entrance and delight for many generations to come.

the best because...

■ The Taj Mahal is the finest example of Mughal architecture in the world.

■ It is designed to represent an earthly form of Islamic paradise and is a masterpiece of symmetry and harmonious visual proportions.

■ Its translucent marble changes in appearance throughout the day, from red and soft grey, to white and gold.

■ It is inlaid with thousands of precious and semi-precious stones.

■ It is full of coded references and theological symbolism.

TEOTIHUACÁN

No one knows for certain who built this great city in the Valley of Mexico, or why its people abandoned it. Giant pyramids and vibrant symbolic murals are tantalising clues to a thriving ancient civilisation.

WHERE ON EARTH?

Teotihuacán lies about 30 miles (45km) north of Mexico City and is easily reached by taxi, bus or car from the Mexican capital. Visitors should be prepared to do a lot of walking – and step climbing if they intend to scale the pyramids. The ruins are mostly toured as a day trip from Mexico City.

MEXICO
Gulf of Mexico
Teotihuacán
Mexico City
Pacific Ocean

O f all the great archaeological marvels that have been unearthed in Mesoamerica – an area in Central America stretching south from mid-Mexico to Costa Rica – the one that continues to astonish above all others is Teotihuacán. In addition to having the largest intact ancient pyramid in the western hemisphere, the site displays the ruins of what was once the most populous city in the Americas. Big questions remain about who built the city, how it was used – and what brought about its downfall.

City of artistry and religion

In around 500 BC, the population in this part of the Valley of Mexico began to grow and develop into an increasingly

complex society. The earliest buildings at Teotihuacán have been dated to around 200 BC, but the leap from settlement to ceremonial city began in the 1st century BC when work began on the Pyramid of the Sun. Construction took around 200 years and was followed by the smaller Pyramid of the Moon. At its peak from AD 300 to 600, Teotihuacán had between 100,000 and 200,000 inhabitants, making it the largest and most powerful city in Mesoamerica.

Very little is known for certain about the ancient Teotihuacános. We do not know what they called themselves or their monumental buildings and can only guess at the intricacies of their culture and traditions. But in addition to their striking architecture, they left behind a rich artistic heritage, including murals that are among the largest

❝This ancient city's name, Teotihuacán, is of Aztec origin, derived from a Nahuatl term meaning 'birthplace of the gods'.❞

and finest of their kind to have been discovered anywhere in the Americas.

The Teotihuacános traded up and down the length of what is now Mexico and Central America, especially in the hard, black obsidian that was plentiful in their valley. The city became rich enough to build massive structures and develop a sophisticated artisan class.

Teotihuacán must have had a highly organised political structure and probably a powerful military. But the city's most important role seems to have been as a religious centre, for the city's religious buildings take pride of place along the Avenue of the Dead, the site's main thoroughfare. Scholars believe that the avenue probably remained a pilgrimage centre long after the city's decline, a

theory that partially derives from the Aztec veneration of the site some 800 years later. The Aztecs based one of their creation myths in Teotihuacán, which they believed to be the birthplace of the Sun, the Moon and the Universe, and actively worshipped here.

A fate unknown

By the arrival of the Spanish in the early 16th century, Teotihuacán was long abandoned by its original inhabitants. Given that the Teotihuacános had no written language, there was only Aztec folklore to explain who they were and what the sprawling ruins were all about. Archaeologists have yet to decipher many of the city's secrets, including why it was abandoned around AD 700.

Pyramid of the Sun Soaring to 65m (213ft) above the Avenue of the Dead, this 2,000-year-old pyramid is one of the iconic structures of ancient Mesoamerica.

272

Some have postulated that the city was sacked and burned, either by outside invaders or during a local rebellion against the Teotihuacán elite, but ecological factors may be a more likely explanation: the city's demise corresponded with a period of climate change and prolonged drought in the region. Overpopulation and depletion of natural resources have been put forward

as further possibilities. Whatever the reason, Teotihuacán was in free fall by the early 8th century and other city-states in the Valley of Mexico were on the rise.

Architectural legacy

Teotihuacán's major buildings are arrayed along the Avenue of the Dead, a cobblestone thoroughfare that stretches

Lunar temple The Pyramid of the Moon at the northern end of the Avenue of the Dead was completed in around AD 300.

about 2 miles (3km) from north to south. The name derives from the Aztecs and their belief that the dozens of earthen mounds along the avenue were tombs rather than temple platforms. Recent discoveries have proved them right: burial sites have been unearthed at several points along the avenue. Among them are the remains of animals and humans that appear to have been buried alive. This would suggest that they were sacrificial victims of ceremonies that took place when the structures were either started, finished or expanded.

The Avenue of the Dead runs perpendicular to the principle axis of the Pyramid of the Sun, which is itself determined by the position of the setting Sun on spring and autumn equinoxes. The interior of this huge pyramid is mainly rubble (an estimated 2.5 million tonnes of it), the exterior smoothed out with adobe bricks, stones and plaster that at one point must have been richly decorated. In ancient times there was a temple on the flat-topped summit that disappeared long ago.

Modern scientific instruments have failed to find any substantial chambers or spaces inside the structure, although in 1971 a mysterious lava-tube cave

was discovered beneath the Pyramid of the Sun. Some think this underground chamber may have been a royal tomb, while others postulate that it was a religious shrine representing the birthplace of mankind or the womb of the Great Goddess who was the city's paramount deity. Visitors with a head for heights can ascend 248 steep stone steps to the pyramid's summit for a panoramic view of the ruins and beyond.

The nearby Pyramid of the Moon can also be scaled for an impressive view straight down the Avenue of the Dead. Excavations are ongoing here, with new tombs discovered beneath the structure as recently as 2007. Flanking the plaza in front of the pyramid are a number of smaller temples and the exquisite Palace of Quetzal-Mariposa. Reconstructed in the 1960s, the palace has some of the site's finest murals, including those of the mythical butterfly-bird that gives the structure its name.

Further south along the Avenue of the Dead is a large compound called La Ciudadela (the Citadel), which features miscellaneous buildings set around a large central plaza. Foremost of these is the Temple of Quetzalcoatl, the feathered serpent, known for its stone carvings and remnant murals. As at the pyramids, burial sites have been discovered at the

four corners of this temple, containing the remains of people who may have been sacrificed when the temple was dedicated.

A door to the past

The first surveys and excavations of the site were made during the worldwide upsurge in archaeology in the 19th century. By then, the ruins were covered by debris, dirt and vegetation. Between 1905 and 1910, pioneer Mexican anthropologist Leopoldo Batres led a team that investigated and restored many of the site's most important structures. Excavation and restoration continued through the 20th century,

Symbolic art In this mural, one of several in the Atetlco Palace west of the main site, a jaguar in a feathered headdress devours a human heart.

culminating in the discovery of the Palace of Quetzalmariposa and the cave beneath the Pyramid of the Sun.

Today the archaeological park features two museums showcasing finds made at the site: a main collection housed in a modern building behind the Pyramid of the Sun and the Beatriz de la Fuente Museum of Teotihuacán Mural Paintings. New finds were being made as late as the 1990s as the city slowly but surely revealed more of its secrets.

best of the rest...

MESOAMERICAN SITES

■ **La Venta** at Tabasco in Mexico was a centre of the Olmec culture. An impressive ceremonial complex with open plazas, an earth-built pyramid, seven massive basalt altars and four giant stone heads was established here more than 3,000 years ago.

■ Overlooking modern Oaxaca City in southern Mexico are the ruins of **Monte Albán**. Created by the Zapotec, the city was founded around 500 BC and occupied for 1,200 years. Most of the major structures – including ball courts, an observatory and several pyramid-like platforms – are arranged around a large central plaza.

■ On the plains east of Oaxaca are the ruins of **Mitla**, a city that reached its zenith after Monte Albán's decline (AD 700-800). Mitla's claim to fame is its astonishing decoration,

in particular its intricate mosaics. Scholars disagree on the origins and function of the site. Many believe that it was developed by the Zapotec as a ceremonial centre. The geometric artwork leads others to postulate that it may have been a Mixtec metropolis.

■ The great Mayan city of **Chichén Itzá** in Mexico holds many secrets. Most scholars agree that it became a large and powerful metropolis

Chichen Itzá

between AD 800 and 1000, yet they disagree when it comes to explaining the city's history. Many of the primary buildings have been reconstructed, including the Observatory, the elaborately decorated Temple of the Warriors and the Kulkulcan pyramid.

■ An even larger Mayan city was **Tikal** in northern Guatemala. The site encompasses hundreds of structures, including massive pyramid-temples. More than 400,000 people may have lived there at its height. Tikal's golden age came between AD 200 and 900, and there is strong evidence that its inhabitants traded with Teotihuacán and other urban centres in central Mexico.

■ Another spectacular Mayan site in Mexico is **Palenque** in the rain forest of western Yucatán. It flourished at roughly the same time as Tikal as a trade centre between the southern highlands, northern Guatemala and the Yucatán, and its unique architecture reflects the influence of all three areas.

TERRACOTTA ARMY

Thousands of life-size warriors stand to attention in the tomb of China's first emperor, having kept vigil for more than 2,000 years.

On March 29, 1974, near the city of Xi'an in Shaanxi province, farmers digging for water came upon a scattering of pottery fragments and bronze weapons. Archaeological excavations began soon afterwards, and the first pit uncovered was opened to the public in 1979. The world gazed in wonder at the discovery: row upon row of life-size terracotta warriors. This was just the beginning of what is now China's largest on-site museum.

Imperial legacy

The vast tomb complex was meticulously planned to ensure an afterlife worthy of the first emperor of China. In 247 BC 13-year-old Ying Zheng ascended the throne under the direction of his mother and regent Lu Buwei. Assuming full power at the age of 22, Ying Zheng

WHERE ON EARTH?

The Museum of Qin Terracotta Warriors and Horses is located 22 miles (35km) east of Xi'an, in the Shaanxi province of central China. Xi'an has an international airport within easy reach of the city. Buses to the museum operate from various locations in Xi'an, and shuttle buses run between the museum and the tomb.

Beijing

Terracotta Army
Xi'an

East China Sea

CHINA

Waiting in line Ranks of warriors guard the tomb of Emperor Qin Shi Huang. In Pit 1 around 1,000 figures have so far been excavated.

promptly crushed a rebellion led by his mother's intimate servant, exiled his regent and set out to conquer the remaining six states of ancient China. By 221 BC, his goal achieved, he proclaimed himself Qin Shi Huang, first emperor of his newly created Qin Empire.

Keen to bring the affairs of state under central control, the new emperor abolished the feudal system. Imperial laws were set in stone in every corner of the land; roads and palaces were built; weights and measures, currency and script were standardised; and new defences were erected – the first Great Wall. Meanwhile, Confucian writings – considered a threat – were destroyed and followers of Confucius murdered. Farming reached an all time low as a huge labour force was conscripted to the emperor's service.

Yet above all, Qin Shi Huang was obsessed with death. They say that he started building his tomb on ascending the throne and spent untold resources searching for the secret of eternal life. According to legend, the Immortals lived on mystical mountains in the middle of the sea and the emperor sent thousands of boys

Life models The figures all have different facial features and headgear and may have been modelled on actual warriors.

Fine detail Once the clay figures had been fired, details were painted on in vivid colours, though only a few figures still have traces of colour.

and girls to investigate. They never returned. He died, aged 50, while touring the empire. His death was kept secret while succession plots were hatched. The plotters had their way but the Qin imperial dynasty was overthrown following a peasant's revolt just 15 years after it had begun.

The emperor's tomb

The chosen site for the imperial burial mound was at the foot of the evergreen Mount Li, an auspicious place according to *feng shui* principles. The emperor would be in good company, close to the graves of former kings, placated by the soothing river, the cool breeze and the rolling hills with their vast reserves of jade and gold. Rising originally to 115m (377ft), though now eroded, the great earth pyramid took almost 40 years to complete – with work continuing after the emperor's death – and employed up to 720,000 labourers at the busiest times. Deep inside was an imperial palace, divided into halls and chambers where walls and ceilings depicted scenes from Heaven and Earth. Mercury representing the rivers flowed mechanically towards a sea glistening with golden boats.

The tomb itself will not be opened, say the authorities, until secure ways are found to preserve and protect its

content. Apart from the emperor's remains, it may contain unimaginable treasures. However, within the inner enclosure of the underground palace, archaeologists have uncovered two important pits: one housing two sets of painted bronze chariots and horses; and, in 2000, the civil official pit, with fragments of terracotta figures with painted faces. Each one carried an 'eraser knife' to scratch off mistakes inscribed on wood or bamboo (paper had not yet been invented). Other pits were unearthed within the mausoleum outer wall, including the pit of stone armour and helmets, the stable pit,

the pit of terracotta acrobats and the pit of rare birds and animals. Reconstructed elements from each can be found in the museum.

The warrior pits

Roughly a mile (1.5km) east of the mausoleum, the three warrior pits cover an area of 22,000m² (5.4 acres), containing around 8,000 terracotta soldiers and horses. They stand with their backs to the tomb to protect their emperor. The pits are currently 5–7m (16–23ft) deep and the figures are arranged in military formation in trenches divided by earth-rammed walls. The wooden roof once covering the pits was concealed by fibre mats and soil. Today the pits are enclosed in weatherproof halls where archaeologists are still at work.

Pit 1, the largest and first to be excavated, is almost twice the size of a football pitch and houses the main body of the army. Around 1,000 figures are on display, with an estimated 5,000 awaiting excavation or restoration. The army is in battle order, facing east, the direction of conquered states, except for a single row of guards protecting the sides and rear. The vanguard consists of 204 soldiers in three rows, followed by 30 horse-drawn chariots and soldiers. Originally the frontline warriors carried crossbows and bows, those behind held halberds, spears and similar weapons. Some of the warriors wore armour.

Just 20m (65ft) to the north, the L-shaped Pit 2 was designed to support the main army, with 1,300 figures arranged in different forces. More than 300 archers occupied the northeast wing, kneeling or standing, all facing east. To

---

best of the rest...

ANCIENT TOMBS

■ Around 62 BC, King Antiochus I built his own tomb-sanctuary on top of Mount Nemrut in the kingdom of Commagene, now in southeast Turkey. The sanctuary, **Nemrut Dag**, was surrounded by statues up to 9m (30ft) high, representing the king, lions, eagles and gods. At some later point, most of the statues toppled over and the heads remain scattered on the ground. A stone lion bears images of planets and stars, indicating that the site was also of astronomical importance.

■ **Newgrange** in County Meath, Ireland, is a 5,000-year-old passage tomb. Aligned with the megalithic Brú na Bóinne complex, it is a large

Nemrut Dag

grass-covered mound rising to a height of 12m (40ft), with a long passage leading to the chambers. The site was in use through much of the Neolithic period and at some point was enclosed by timber and stone circles. Triskele carvings of three interlocking spirals can be seen on the entrance stone.

■ On the west bank of the River Nile near Luxor, Egypt, over 60 pharaohs from the 18th to 20th dynasties were laid to rest in what has become known as the **Valley of the Kings**. Cut into limestone cliffs or scree slopes, the tombs consist of corridors leading to one or more antechambers and sunken sarcophagus rooms.

the south were found the scanty remains of wooden chariots, while more chariots, infantry and cavalry occupied the centre. The northern area was reserved for the cavalry, each man standing in front of his horse and equipped with a bow. Remnants of wooden rafters once supporting the roof are still visible.

Pit 3, the smallest, has 68 figures, one chariot and four horses in a U-shaped compound. Most experts agree that this was the command centre. Figures unearthed here carried small ceremonial weapons, known as *shu*, thought to be the hallmark of guards of honour.

Fine craftsmanship

Chinese pottery figures long predate the Qin dynasty, but this project was on an unprecedented scale and required a high degree of technology. The figures weighed between 110 and 300kg (240 to 660lb), with an average height of 1.8m (5.9ft), and were fired at temperatures higher than ever before, reaching 1,000C (1,800F). Local clay was mixed with quartz to improve its appearance and strength,

Skilled construction Horses or men, the same technique was used to create all the figures: solid pottery legs supported a hollow body and a head that had been cast in a two-piece mould.

then body parts were made separately and assembled, with facial features added later.

Rank and duty can be identified on the figures. Ornate armour and sashes denote officers, a charioteer is distinguished by armoured sleeves, a cavalryman by a helmet with chin strap, tight chest armour and loose clothing below the waist. Horses also have features relating to their position: a short tail for a chariot horse, keeping it safe from the harness, or a fine saddle for a cavalry horse.

Display cases in the museum hold some of the best figures. Among them is a general with shoulder plate, fish-scale armour, sideburns and groomed moustache; a standing archer with his hair coiled up

in a bun, feet apart ready to shoot; and two richly decorated bronze chariots and horses. This is a world away from those first pottery fragments that propelled the Qin dynasty into the modern age. Here on view is unique craftsmanship, high technology and complex military structure. After 2,200 years, Qin Shi Huang's longed-for immortality would seem secure.

One of a pair The two bronze chariots excavated at the tomb, with bronze horses and riders, are thought to be the vanguard of a long procession.

TREVI FOUNTAIN

THE ULTIMATE FOUNTAIN?

The Latin origin of the word 'fountain' simply meant a spring or source, but collection points at the ends of ancient Rome's aqueducts were elaborated with sculpture. This practice was revived in the Trevi district when an old Roman aqueduct was restored during the Renaissance, after a thousand years of disuse. Over the next 300 years, various plans for a fountain were devised, culminating in a glorious feast of Baroque marble sculpture designed by Nicola Salvi and completed in 1762. Against the backdrop of a neoclassical palace, Oceanus, the god of water, stands in his seashell chariot being pulled by horses and Tritons, while the water tumbles and foams over natural-looking rocks into a deep pool. This cherished icon features in classic films such as *La Dolce Vita* and *Roman Holiday*, and visitors throw in coins in the hope that this will ensure their return to Rome.

ITALY

Rome
• Trevi
Fountain

Tyrrhenian Sea

Water is the essence of life, and to play with it is to celebrate the glory of one of nature's most vital yet mundane gifts. The Romans created elaborate fountains by constricting the downward flow of water using a narrow outlet: with enough water and pressure, fountains could perform any effect, from gentle cascades to high jets. Fountains usually soothe and invite reflection, but in medieval

and Renaissance gardens concealed fountains could be switched on and off at will to drench – and hopefully amuse – unsuspecting guests. In Islamic gardens, they were reminders of the God-given bounty of water and symbols of a well-ordered society. At the Palace of Versailles, an array of fountains symbolised the king's power over France and man's control over nature. Fountains are, in other words, a form of expression, and in recent years 'musical fountains' – incorporating computer technology, lights, laser imagery and music – have taken this concept to new heights.

DUBAI FOUNTAIN

The world's most spectacular and sophisticated 'musical fountain' was inaugurated in Dubai, United Arab Emirates, in 2009. There is no elaborate sculpture here: instead the entire effect is produced by the water itself, blasted into the sky in sequence by hundreds of jets and shooters, carefully coordinated with lights and a variety of music – opera, classical, pop, Arabic. Because the nozzles can move, the water swings and sways, often resembling massed dancers. During night-time shows – illuminated by 6,600 lights and 25 projectors – the soaring spouts of water rising up to 73m (240ft) high, accompanied by the boom of the shooters, could be mistaken for fireworks. In essence, the installation is simple: five circles of jets set along two curves, totalling 275m (900ft) in length. But the effect is utterly dramatic.

TRUNK **BAY**

It is hard to argue with beach aficionados who delight in the soft sands and turquoise waters of Trunk Bay. A cloak of coconut palms backed by primary rain forest completes the island idyll.

Perched on the north shore of St John island, Trunk Bay is often cited as the world's most glorious and unspoiled beach. Contrary to popular belief, the bay is not named after its ubiquitous palm trunks fringing the beach, but for the leatherneck turtles that nest there. The Danes – who were the colonial power ruling the western Virgin Islands until 1917, when the islands were sold to the United States of America – thought that the lumbering sea creatures resembled leather travel trunks.

Trunk Bay lies within the boundaries of the Virgin Islands National Park, established in 1956 to protect the indigenous flora, fauna and scenery of St John island. Prior to that, the beach was in private ownership, but philanthropist Laurance S. Rockefeller purchased much of Trunk Bay and donated it to the US National Park Service. The bay is now the park's most popular visitor attraction.

Coral foundations

The fine white sand is created by an offshore coral reef made up of staghorn, elk, brain, finger and many other coral species. Meandering through this underwater garden is a snorkel trail, one

WHERE ON EARTH?

Trunk Bay is on the north side of St John in the US Virgin Islands. Without an airport, the island can be reached only by ferry or private boat. From the dock in Cruz Bay, it's an easy 3-mile (5km) drive along Route 20 (North Shore Road) to Trunk Bay. There are campsites and hotels scattered across the island.

Trunk Bay
ST JOHN
Cruz Bay

US VIRGIN ISLANDS

of the first of its kind, with 15 underwater plaques identifying common fish and corals found along the route.

The area behind the beach is well worth exploring for its lush vegetation, including the noni (*Morinda citrifolia*), nicknamed the painkiller tree because its whitish-yellow fruit is used in herbal medicine. More than 140 species of birds have been recorded in the park, including two species of Caribbean hummingbird and the bananaquit. The only native mammal is the bat, which is a key player in pollination and the dispersal of seeds.

Picture perfect St John is the smallest and prettiest of the sunny US Virgin Islands, with world-class white sandy beaches.

best of the rest...

PALM-FRINGED BEACHES

■ The Seychelles has many palm-fringed strands, but the most captivating is **Anse Source d'Argent**, with its hulking granite boulders and pink sand. The first Europeans to visit thought it was the Garden of Eden.

■ South America's best beaches are on the islands off Venezuela, in particular **Playa Parguito** on the Isla Margarita. Towering palms

offer shade to beach-side restaurants and the waves are ideal for surfing.

■ **Waikiki** is the world's most photogenic beach: the classic shot is the volcanic bulk of Diamond Head framed by swaying palms. This Hawaiian hot spot was where Elvis learned to surf, and its annual festival for Hawaiian slack-key guitar still rocks beneath the palms.

■ **White Beach** on Boracay Island in the Philippines offers weary travellers pure white sand on which to relax and unwind.

TUBBATAHA REEFS

This striking coral landscape is the stuff of the best adventure stories, complete with giant clams, moray eels and shipwrecks. Divers checking in to 'Shark Airport' will not be disappointed.

Tubbataha Reefs are at the heart of the Coral Triangle, a biodiversity hot spot in southeast Asia that encompasses coral-rich tropical waters between the Philippines in the north, Borneo in the west and the Solomon Islands in the east. Evolution has run riot here. Marine biologists call it the 'Amazon of the seas', and Tubbataha Reefs are the jewels in its watery crown.

Known for huge schools of colourful reef fish, large marine predators and coral walls where the reef drops almost vertically down into deeper water, the Tubbataha Reefs are recognised as having the best diving sites not only in the Philippines, but in the whole of southeast Asia. Evocatively named sites – such as Sea Fan Alley, Gorgonian Channel and Shark Airport – enjoy exceptional water quality, with visibility exceeding 40m (130ft) on a good day. The demand to visit this underwater paradise is so great that most live-aboard diving boats – the only way to get to this remote spot is by boat – are booked up years in advance. Access is strictly controlled.

Barren at the surface

Tubbataha's two coral atolls and the nearby Jessie Beazley Reef, an even more remote coral cay, are protected by the Tubbataha Reefs National Marine Park.

WHERE ON EARTH?

The Tubbataha Reefs are in the middle of the Sulu Sea, 80 miles (130km) south of the Philippine island of Cagayancillo and 110 miles (180km) southeast of Puerto Princesa, capital of the island of Palawan and main gateway to the marine park. The reefs are accessible only by sea, a 10-hour journey from Puerto Princesa.

PHILIPPINES
PALAWAN • Puerto Princesa
Sulu Sea
Tubbataha Reefs

The atoll of the oval-shaped northern Tubbataha Reef is 10 miles (16km) long and the triangular southern reef is 3 miles (5km) long. Between them lies a 5-mile (8km) wide, deep-water channel. Each atoll was once a fringing reef around an active volcano, but eruptions ceased and the sea eroded the volcano tops. The corals then grew upwards through the water in the rims of the submerged craters, each reef encircling a central sandy lagoon, the former crater floor.

There are no permanent human inhabitants here, and indeed there is very little to see at the surface. There are a couple of sandy islets, both with grasses and one with trees – coconut palm, sea almond, *Pisonia* and *Argusia*, so characteristic of coral islands – where sea turtles haul out to deposit their eggs and seabirds nest or put down while on migration. There are nesting great crested terns and brown boobies, along with rare passage migrants, such as Christmas Island frigate-birds and Chinese egrets. Parts of the reef flats are exposed at low tide,

Reef resident A two-barred goatfish uses the pair of sensitive barbels under its chin to search for food on the reef.

along with a few rocks and numerous sandbanks. There is a lighthouse to warn of the reef's presence, the rusting hulk of a wrecked ship and a ranger station on stilts in the middle of nowhere. And that's it. The action is all below the surface, and what a place it is.

Underwater glory

Beneath the waves in this otherwise unremarkable location are exquisite, multi-coloured coral gardens. Though

far from the biggest reefs in the world, Tubbataha is home to more than half the world's hard and soft coral species, along with enormous barrel sponges and giant clams. Huge Napoleon wrasses, some up to 2m (6.5ft) long, swim effortlessly over the coral slopes. Blacktip reef sharks dart about in the shallows and shoals of ray-finned barracuda wait for prey to pass by.

Moray eels lurk in coral crevices, and blue-spotted rays and whitetip

reef sharks rest on the sand – indeed, Tubbataha has the largest population of whitetip reef sharks in the world. A wealth of small creatures are found here, too: colourful shrimps that operate drive-through 'cleaning stations' for larger fish; slender pipefish that seem to vanish in front of your eyes; pineapple

A diver's paradise Tubbataha's short diving season runs from the end of March until June, when the seas are relatively calm and water clarity is at its best.

Coral landscape Among the soft corals found at Tubbataha Reefs are gorgonian sea fans – colonies of tiny polyps in fanlike formations. Their bright-coloured structures can spread over several metres.

sea cucumbers with tiny fish living in their nether regions; garden eels that disappear into the sand at the slightest hint of danger; and delicate feather duster worms that look exactly as their name suggests.

Underwater wonderland

Divers lucky enough to visit this vibrant aquatic world will find myriad reef fish, some with vivid colours and bizarre patterns, others with flashing silver scales, and all with engaging names – sweetlips, snappers, fusiliers, trevallies, Moorish idols, surgeonfish, butterflyfish, angelfish, damselfish, clownfish, puffer fish, unicorn fish, squirrelfish, cornetfish, trumpetfish, rabbitfish, boxfish, triggerfish, fire gobies, and rainbow runners. The underwater parade seems endless.

Among the most exciting dives are those along the perpendicular coral walls, some extending to a depth of 50m (165ft). Here, whip corals and gorgonian sea fans replace the hard corals, and sand trickles down from above like the flow from a waterfall. Grey reef sharks patrol the drop-off into the abyss, tawny nurse sharks hide in caves in the wall and silvertip sharks rocket up from the depths to investigate anything that smacks of being a tasty meal.

A convergence of currents here brings in a continual stream of nutrients and clean water, and being one of the few structures in the middle of the Sulu Sea, the reefs attract the ocean's giants. Whale sharks – the world's biggest fish – and manta rays are regular visitors, along with tiger sharks, hammerhead sharks, jacks and tuna. Sperm whales also sometimes put in an appearance.

The reefs offer resting and feeding sites for two species of sea turtle. The first is the critically endangered hawksbill turtle, which feeds on sponges. The second, the green sea turtle, can be found close to the lighthouse, where it is attracted to seagrass meadows – flowering plants related to water lilies that grow in shallow seawater.

Paradise almost lost

The Tubbataha Reefs were once a favourite spot for local fishermen. Sailing to the atolls in their flimsy, one-person craft, small numbers fished the area sustainably for many years. Then, during the 1970s and 1980s, larger numbers of fishermen arrived – many without permits. They used motorised boats and larger vessels to increase the size of catches; some resorted to dynamite to kill fish in the reef, or used a poison that dazed them. Inevitably, these methods damaged the fabric of the reef. Matters came to a head when a company proposed establishing commercial seaweed farming in the region. Action was needed to protect the reef. In 1988, under intense international pressure from scuba divers and conservationists, the Tubbataha Reefs got the state protection they needed as the country's first National Marine Park. Today, an armed guard is stationed there around the clock to deter illegal fishing; impounded craft close to the ranger station are proof of their effectiveness.

Thanks to these efforts, the reef has recovered and few signs of fishing damage can now be seen. Thriving once more, as they had for centuries, the reefs support nurseries for fish and coral larvae, and have become an important breeding centre. And because of their remote location, the reefs are not exposed to direct pollution from the land. Tubbataha is vibrant and healthy once more.

> **"** Research shows that the Tubbataha Reefs are a major breeding centre today, probably seeding the entire Sulu Sea. **"**

best of the rest...

CORAL REEFS

■ At 160 miles (260km) long, the **Belize Barrier Reef** is the world's second-largest coral reef. Marine biologists have still to record all the creatures that live here – it is estimated that 90 per cent of them have yet to be discovered. One of the barrier's strangest features is the almost perfectly circular Great Blue Hole at Lighthouse Reef, a collapsed and submerged cavern about 400m (1,300ft) across.

Belize Barrier Reef

■ At the northern tip of the Red Sea some coral reefs are accessible directly from the shore without the need for boats. On the foreshore of Eilat, Israel's southernmost town, is the 1,200m (3,900ft) long **Coral Beach Nature Reserve**, where tropical marine life is within the reach of almost anybody. One of its features is a walkway to the outer reef, where even the most inexperienced snorkellers can enter the water, drift along the shore in the current and observe the creatures living there.

■ Clearly visible from space, Australia's **Great Barrier Reef** is the largest living structure on the planet. It stretches more than 1,240 miles (2,000km) along the Queensland coast, a kaleidoscope of coral gardens packed with a huge diversity of resident marine life. It is also an international hub where wildlife arrives from far and wide – minke and humpback whales from the Antarctic, seabirds from the Asian mainland and tiger sharks and sea turtles from

distant reefs in the Indo-Pacific region. The climax of its year is the mass spawning of corals, which creates an extraordinary upside-down 'snowstorm'. Each species of coral spawns at the same time, on the same night, in sexual behaviour that is synchronised to the phases of the moon.

■ The most southerly tropical coral reef is at **Lord Howe Island**, a volcanic remnant between Australia and New Zealand, which is at the crossroads of five major ocean currents in the Pacific Ocean. The most northerly reefs in the Atlantic Ocean surround the **Bermuda Islands**. Bathed by the warm Gulf Stream, they are seeded with coral-reef animals from the Caribbean. And in the Pacific the world's most northerly tropical coral atoll is the remote **Kure Atoll** in the northwestern Hawaiian Islands, a nesting area for hundreds of thousands of seabirds and an important pupping and resting site for the critically endangered Hawaiian monk seal. All of these reefs have one thing in common in that they are close to the so-called Darwin Point, the latitude at which reef growth is equal to reef destruction. Any further south in the Southern Hemisphere or north in the Northern, and tropical corals cannot grow.

Planet Rock, Madang Barrier Reef

■ Another exciting and spectacular dive site centres on **Magic Passage** and **Planet Rock** off the north coast of Papua New Guinea. The passage cuts through the Madang Barrier Reef, where shoals of chevron barracuda hang in the current along with fat starfish the size of dinner plates. Planet Rock is about a mile (1.6km) offshore, and only accessible in very calm weather. All the reef fish and sharks are here, including large schools of hammerhead sharks that rest here by day then head into deeper waters to feed at night.

■ A Conservation International survey in 2001 revealed that the coral reefs of the **Raja Ampat Islands**, located off the West Papua province of Indonesia, probably have the greatest marine biodiversity of any place in the world's oceans. More than 1,300 fish species are recognised, along with 600 hard coral species, and new species are being discovered every day.

Coral Beach Nature Reserve

ULURU

For more than 20,000 years, humans have stood in wonder before this immense red monolith in the Australian outback. It is an extraordinary geological formation that, for many, holds deep spiritual significance.

Although visitors may be familiar with the image of Uluru, also known as Ayers Rock, nothing can prepare them for the rush of spine-tingling awe when the massive, rust-coloured natural monolith comes into view. Rising abruptly from the sandy plain to a height of 348m (1,142ft), the rock is 1.5 miles (2.4km) long. Astonishingly, what people see is only the tip of a buckled sandstone slab that extends 4km (2.5 miles) underground. Earth movements over the last 600 million years first compressed the layers of rock, then turned them on end so that horizontal strata became vertical furrows.

Heart and soul

In the belief system of the Anangu Aboriginal people, Uluru was formed by ancestral beings such as the Mala (rufous hare wallaby), and the Kuniya and Liru (poisonous snakes) during the Creation time. Every crevice, fissure

WHERE ON EARTH?

Uluru, which is in the Uluru-Kata Tjuta National Park, lies 335km (208 miles) southwest of Alice Springs on the southern edge of the Northern Territory; it takes about five hours to get there by road. There are also flights to Ayers Rock airport from Cairns, the Gold Coast and most of Australia's state capitals.

AUSTRALIA
Alice Springs
Uluru

Southern
Ocean

and eroded scar on Uluru's ridged and pitted flanks is evidence of the ancestors' activities. Deep grooves on the rock show where snake woman slithered, while boulders nearby are her eggs. Potholes on the rock face are the footprints of fleeing Mala men.

The Anangu ask that visitors do not climb the rock. In fact, there is much to be discovered by taking the 6.5-mile (10.6km) Base Walk. There, fed by run-off from the heavy, but infrequent, desert storms, are deep waterholes shaded by lush vegetation that support a surprisingly rich ecosystem.

Traditional life

The animals and plants around Uluru have supported native communities for thousands of years. The natural habitat has provided food and drink, medicine and tobacco. It has also supplied the Anangu with materials for fuel, building, art and religious rituals.

Bush food, or tucker, includes tjanmata (bush onion), arnguli (bush plum) and ili (native fig). Sweet nectar is claimed from the kaliny-kalinypa (honey grevillea bush) and honey-gorged tjala ants. Meat is sourced from malu (red kangaroo), tinka (sand goanna) and ngintaka (perentie lizards). Bird and lizard eggs, along with grubs, provide extra nutrition. However, some of the hundreds of tree, plant and shrub species in the National Park are highly poisonous.

Rusting sunsets

The changing colours through the day are one of Uluru's best-loved features. Oxidation, or 'rusting', of the feldspar and iron in Uluru's arkose sandstone produces the distinctive colour, and this mineral composition also causes the changing colours through the day. At dusk it glows bright red, then fades to orange, terracotta and purple. At sunrise, the same spectacle happens in reverse.

the best because...

■ Uluru is a place of deep spiritual significance, possibly the world's oldest sacred site. Significant events in the Anangu story are commemorated here with traditional ceremonies.

■ It is the largest monolith – single mass of stone – on the planet.

■ It is on a scale so grand that it can be seen for more than 60 miles (100km) across the flat Australian plains.

■ From sunrise to sunset, the rock's colour continually changes from deep purple, through pinks and oranges, to blazing red, then back again.

■ The waterfalls that tumble off Uluru during rare desert rains fill waterholes that sustain a rich ecosystem around the mighty rock.

SALAR DE UYUNI

Bolivia's vast, white salt flats stretch from horizon to horizon, a surreal landscape. Yet even here, people and animals scratch a living.

Salar de Uyuni is the world's largest salt pan, a vast white plain of cemented salt that covers 4,085 sq miles (10,580km²), an area almost as big as Jamaica. The pan sits 3,656m (11,995ft) above sea level and is part of the Altiplano, the high plateau in the South American Andes.

At first glance the salar looks dead flat, but modern GPS observations have revealed bumps in the salt up to 40cm (16in) high. The bumps lie above dense rocks buried deep below the surface, the salt rising over the rocks rather as water bulges almost imperceptibly over a seamount on the ocean floor. So, Salar de Uyuni has hills, ridges and valleys – but they are measured in millimetres, rather than metres.

Islands of life

The salar was once part of a giant prehistoric lake that dried out to leave the salt flats, and areas still flood in the wet season from December through to February. On a still day, the shallow water forms one of the biggest natural mirrors on Earth, reflecting the sky through the dry, clean air.

In the dry season the salar appears devoid of life, but a keen observer might spot a lizard chasing flies between the ridges of salt, or a tiny carnivorous mouse that has a penchant for lizards.

Most animals are found on isolated 'islands' of volcanic rock that provide oases for wildlife and tourists. The islands support forests of 12m (40ft) tall cacti and stunted trees and bushes, and some of the larger outcrops have their own animal communities.

Isla Incahuasi (Inca House), for example, has several species of small birds, such as sierra finches and hummingbirds. Clambering over the rocks are mountain viscachas, chinchilla-like rodents with long, fluffy tails, warm fur and cushion-soled feet for a firm grip. Andean mountain cats and culpeo foxes travel between the rock outcrops and puna hawks swoop down to catch prey including, if the visitors do not disturb them, those endearing mountain viscachas.

Salt harvest A worker uses the traditional method to harvest salt, scraping surface salt into small mounds so that water can evaporate.

The wet season Flamingos breed here during the wetter months, along with plovers and avocets. Overleaf: In the dry season, Salar de Uyuni's rocky islands are surrounded by a parched, cracked surface.

Precious but perilous

Salar de Uyuni contains vast mineral wealth, but exploitation at present is modest. Salt production is in the hands of a workers' cooperative in the small settlement of Colchani. In places, the salt is no more than a thin crust over lithium-rich brine, yet the government has so far resisted foreign interest in lithium extraction, preferring to keep it local.

The town of Uyuni exploits another resource: tourists. Without a guide, Salar de Uyuni is a dangerous place – there are few landmarks and no fresh water in the centre – but a guided trip from Uyuni out onto the spectacular salt flats has become a must for visitors to Bolivia.

best of the rest...

SALT FLATS

■ **Bonneville Salt Flats** in northwest Utah, USA, is the home of land-speed records and was a favourite destination for drivers seeking to set or break them. In 1965 Sir Malcolm Campbell took *Bluebird* to 301.129mph (484.620km/h), the first absolute land-speed record set on the 'Bonneville Speedway', a section prepared each summer for such record attempts. The salt flats formed after the last Ice Age, when the vast Lake Bonneville receded. Having been about 300m (980ft) deep at its peak, the lake eventually left a layer of salt that is 1.5m (5ft) thick near the centre.

■ The **Etosha Pan** in Namibia, southwest Africa, is a dried lakebed for most of the year. Its desiccated mud, divided into roughly hexagonal shapes, is covered by salt that is coloured green in places from the blue-green algae that grow when the pan has a thin layer of water in the wet season. Very little lives here

Etosha National Park

all year, but if the rains come, so do tens of thousands of flamingos and pelicans to breed. Many creatures, including elephants, zebra, white rhino and lions live in the surrounding savannah.

■ A great mystery surrounds **Lake Eyre** in central Australia. The lake – in fact, for most of the time a huge salt pan – may not fill with water more than once or twice in a decade. Yet when the rains arrive, water birds – especially pelicans – abandon a life at the coast and head hundreds of miles inland to the parched outback and Lake Eyre to breed. How the creatures know that the lake has water, and therefore an abundance of food, is the subject of ongoing research, but for now remains a biological puzzle.

VARANASI

The sacred city of the Hindu god Shiva, Varanasi on the River Ganges is the spiritual heart of India and one of the most important Hindu pilgrimage sites in the world.

As day breaks over the River Ganges, the dim shapes of boatmen move across the water touting for passengers. The steeply stepped stone ghats leading down to the river teem with life as people come in their hundreds to wash away their sins at the start of the day. Smoke wafts over the water, and a faint scent of rosewater mixes with that of sandalwood. It is just another morning in Varanasi, the holiest of all Hindu cities.

WHERE ON EARTH?

Varanasi is in the state of Uttar Pradesh in northern India. It sits almost midway between Calcutta 460 miles (740km) to the southeast and Delhi 495 miles (795km) northwest. It has good bus connections from the airport and is served by two railway stations: Varanasi Cantonment and Mughal Sarai.

Varanasi · River Ganges
INDIA · Mughal Sarai

Centre of the Hindu universe

To Hindus, the Ganges is a sacred river and any town or city on its banks is auspicious. But Varanasi has a special sanctity for it is here, according to legend, that one of the chief Hindu deities, Shiva, came to live with his consort Parvati. To the most devout, the city is known as Kashi, the Luminous, or City of Light, referring to Shiva's first manifestation as a pillar of light.

The position of this great city in the Hindu religion is unrivalled. It stands at the centre of the Hindu universe, at the crossroads between the sacred Himalayan cave of Amarnath in Kashmir in the north and the southern tip of India at

Ancient city Above the bathing ghats on the river bank in the centre of Varanasi, temples, shrines, palaces and modern buildings jostle for space.

Kanyakumari, and between Puri on the east coast and Dwarka on the west coast. Situated next to an ancient ford, it is also considered one of the holiest *tirthas*, or 'crossing places', where the heavenly and earthly worlds meet.

Varanasi is the eternal pilgrimage destination of Hindus. Every devout follower hopes to come here at least once in his or her lifetime to bathe in the holy waters of the Ganges. To live here is to be with the gods, and to die here is to gain *moksha*, or eternal absolution. Revered by Buddhists, Jains and Hindus alike, it has attracted pilgrims and students of the Vedas throughout its history.

Past and present

One of the oldest living cities in the world, Varanasi has had a connection with spiritual and religious life since the second millennium BC,

Way to heaven While some devotees bathe, others pray standing waist deep in the water and facing the rising sun.

when it was already a seat of Aryan religion and philosophy. In the 6th century BC, it was the capital of the kingdom of Kashi, and Buddha, it is said, gave his first sermon at nearby Sarnath. Despite three centuries of Muslim rule, the city remained a centre of Hindu activity and continued to attract pilgrims in their thousands. The constant influx of visitors led to it becoming an important trading post, and it is still a major centre of silk production.

The ghats

Despite the addition of many modern buildings, the hub of everyday life is still the old city, which, with its narrow, maze-like streets, has all the chaotic charm that regular visitors to India have come to expect. But it is the continuous chain of ghats descending into the river on the elegant west bank that is the focus for the millions of Hindu pilgrims who come here. For them, the sanctity of Varanasi is inextricably bound up with the Ganga Ma, or Mother Ganges, which in Hindu mythology was once a river in heaven that Shiva allowed to cascade to Earth through the tresses of his hair. They regard the Ganges as *amrita*, the elixir of life that brings purity to the living and salvation to the

dead; bathing in its waters, they believe, will release them from suffering and wash away their sins.

Varanasi has about a hundred ghats spread along a 4.5 mile (7km) stretch of the river. Dotted with palaces, pavilions, temples and terraces, each has its own name and symbolic significance, such as the Dhobi (laundrymen's) Ghat, where people wash clothes every day at sunrise. Some are crumbling; others, such as the Man Mandir Ghat, with its magnificent 18th-century observatory, retain traces of their former splendour. Most are marked with a lingam, a phallic symbol of Shiva, and all occupy a special place in the religious geography of the city.

Traditionally, the ghats form part of a holy route by which devotees trace the city's perimeter, praying at shrines along the way. The devotees are accompanied by a *panda* (priest) and must recite a *sankalpa*, a statement of resolve at each stage of the journey. One of the most popular routes is the Panchartithi Yatra, which runs north to south taking in the five *tirthi* ghats of Assi, Dasaswamedh, Adi Keshava, Panchganga and Manikarnika Ghat.

Devotees begin bathing in the Ganges at sunrise. Men, women and children come in family groups to begin their prayers, accompanied by Brahmin

Ritual bathing People crowd along the banks of the Ganges among the umbrellas of the pandits or scribes. Family members of all ages bathe together.

priests offering *puja* (devotion); others practise meditation or yoga. Some totally immerse themselves in the water once or several times. Others hold out cupped hands to the sky to make water offerings to the sun, as they cleanse away their sins. This is religious devotion en masse, yet it is also a part of day-to-day life that can take on the air of a social occasion. Children play in the water while their mothers do the laundry. Masseurs ply their trade, *sadhus* (holy men) sit smoking their long chillum pipes, and *pandits* (experts in the Hindu scriptures) open up their umbrellas and settle in for the day, as everyone catches up with the local news. Impromptu cricket matches have even been known to start.

Death on display

For Hindus, to die in Varanasi is to gain *moksha*, instant absolution and access to heaven with liberation from the cycle of life, death and reincarnation. So for centuries, people have come here to live out their final days; others bring the ashes of their dead to cast upon the Ganges. The public cremations on the riverbank are a source of fascination for visitors, but the ceremonies are strictly private and photography is forbidden. Most cremations take place at Harishchandra and Manikarnika Ghats, known as the 'burning ghats'. Cremation grounds are usually considered inauspicious and are located on the fringes of cities, but Varanasi is an exception. This great city of Shiva is regarded as the *mahashamshana*, or 'great cremation ground', for the corpse of the whole universe.

The cremation ceremony is relatively simple. The corpse, wrapped in cloth, is carried to a pyre on a bamboo stretcher, and different grades and quantities of firewood, sandalwood, ghee (clarified butter) and other funeral paraphernalia are offered, depending on the means of the family of the deceased. A priest performs last rites, then the chief mourner sprinkles ghee on the pyre and is handed a torch to set it alight – an intensely emotional moment for the family. When the burning is complete, the family douse the smouldering pyre with Ganges water, then gather the remains in an urn and empty it in the river.

Temples and festivals

As befits a city with such strong religious and spiritual associations, Varanasi is home to around 2,000 temples. Some are on the ghats, but most are scattered around the city. Holiest of all is the 18th-century Kashi Vishwanath, or

Golden Temple, which contains a *Jyotirlinga*, a shrine where Shiva is shown in his first manifestation as a pillar of light. There are only 12 such shrines in India, and Hindus believe that just to glimpse a *Jyotirlinga* is a soul-cleansing experience.

In the annual Mahashivratri, one of the most important religious festivals in the city, the Kashi Vishwanath Temple is the final destination of a procession devoted to Shiva, though people visit all nearby temples to the god and offer prayers in large numbers. The festival continues late into the night and includes scripture

Evening worship Each day at sunset, priests perform *Ganga Aarti*, a ceremony in which light is offered to the River Ganges, accompanied by prayers and song.

recitals, fasting, offerings of flowers and fruit to the statues of Shiva and songs sung in his honour.

Along with the Ganga Mahotsav festival – a five-day celebration of the Ganges – Mahashivratri is an important part of the religious calendar in Varanasi, and is conducted in a mood of gaiety and euphoria. In this extraordinary city, life and death are held in perfect balance, and each is embraced with joy.

best of the rest...

PLACES OF PILGRIMAGE

■ The 9th-century temple of **Borobudur** in Java, Indonesia, is the largest Buddhist structure in the world. Its ascending terraces symbolise the three levels of Buddhist cosmology. Pilgrims begin at the lowest level, representing the world of desire, and follow corridors and stairways up to nirvana (Heaven) at the top.

■ The **Golden Temple**, or Harmandir Sahib, in Amritsar in the Punjab is the holiest shrine, or *gudwara*, of the Sikh religion and a pilgrimage centre for Sikhs from all over the world. The most famous and sacred part of the temple complex is the Divine Temple (Hari Mandir), a gold-plated building decorated with verses from the Guru Granth Sahib (the Sikh holy book).

■ **Kunisaki Peninsula**, Japan, is a mountain area of Buddhist shrines that was once an important centre of Shugendo, the earliest form of Japanese Buddhism. It is one of the few places where monks still practise '*mine-in*', a traditional way of praying while walking sacred mountain paths.

■ The birthplace of the prophet Mohammed and location of the Kaaba, a shrine holding the sacred Black Stone, **Mecca** in Saudi Arabia

Golden Temple

is Islam's holiest city. Non-Muslims are forbidden to enter it. All Muslims should attempt the pilgrimage to Mecca, known as the hajj, at least once in their lifetime. Millions of people do so each year.

■ In the Galicia region of northwestern Spain, **Santiago de Compostela** is one of the Christian world's most important pilgrimage sites. The city's cathedral, said to hold the mortal remains of St James, is the destination of the pilgrimage route, the Way of St James. Thousands of people - pilgrims and non-pilgrims - walk the route each year.

■ The **Temple of the Sacred Tooth** in Kandy, Sri Lanka, houses a tooth said to have come from Buddha. Monks worship daily in the temple's inner chamber and perform a weekly symbolic bathing of the relic.

VENICE

At once fragile yet resilient, this floating city has survived for more than 1,000 years on the flood-prone shores of the Adriatic. This paradox has done much to create the city's unique spirit.

WHERE ON EARTH?

The capital of the region of Veneto, Venice is in northeast Italy, with good road, rail and air links to the rest of Italy and to Europe. The city is connected to the mainland by a causeway that goes to Piazzale Roma at the top of the Grand Canal – the last point at which cars can be used.

Vincenza
Padua · Venice
ITALY
CROATIA
Adriatic Sea

In the 6th century, Venice was no more than a series of small fishing settlements on a lagoon in the Adriatic Sea, inhabited by people from the mainland who came to this marshy wilderness to escape the invading Goths. Six hundred years later it had grown into a powerful republic with its own constitution and leader, the doge. By the 16th century it had conquered Byzantium, colonised the whole of

Waterside view Across the lagoon from the waterfront of San Marco district is the island of San Giorgio Maggiore and its church designed by Andrea Palladio.

northeastern Italy and held a monopoly on Mediterranean trade – a position it was to enjoy until its decline in the 18th century. Since the end of the Venetian Republic in 1797, this island city has re-invented itself as a subject of fascination for people the world over. Endlessly photographed, filmed and written about, Venice is now one of the world's greatest tourist

Lasting glory The Doge's Palace sits alongside the Campanile, with St Mark's Square and Basilica behind. The two columns on the waterfront to the left of the palace were once the official gateway to the city.

attractions. More than 20 million people come here each year, drawn by its magnificent history, its beauty and its unique setting.

A city of landmarks

Venice sits in a lagoon as part of an archipelago of 117 islands, the only city in the world built entirely on water. To create land fit for building, the early Venetians had to reinforce and extend the waterlogged islands with thousands of closely packed wooden piles driven into the mud of the lagoon. Over this went foundations of waterproof Istrian limestone.

The city itself is made up of six districts, or *sestieri*, connected by more than 150 canals and 400 bridges. The focal point is Piazza San Marco (St Mark's Square), a grand colonnaded piazza with cafés and shops once described by Napoleon as 'the finest drawing room in Europe'. Many of the city's landmark buildings are here and in the adjoining Piazzetta: St Mark's Basilica; the Campanile (bell tower),

Golden interior Scenes from the Bible, including events from the life of Jesus, are retold in mosaic form within the richly decorated Basilica of St Mark.

the tallest building in Venice at 98.5m (323ft); the richly decorated clock tower; and the Doge's Palace, the main seat of government in the days of the Venetian Republic. The rear of the palace is linked to the city prison by the Bridge of Sighs, so-called because prisoners are said to have sighed at their last view of Venice as they were marched to gloomy dungeon cells.

Visually and symbolically, the square is dominated by the five-domed Basilica of St Mark, a masterpiece of Byzantine architecture and looted Byzantine treasures reflecting the status of Renaissance Venice as a great power. Its dazzling interior, containing 4,000m² (40,000ft²) of golden mosaics, is one of the wonders of the Christian world.

The labyrinthine streets and alleys radiating from this central point in San Marco district link up to the other five districts of the city, each of which has its own character: Castello, the largest, encompassing the Arsenale, was once the largest naval complex in Europe; San Polo and Santa Croce are bustling working districts of narrow alleyways packed with shops, cafés and wine bars and including the world-famous Rialto Bridge and La Pescheria (fish market); chic, smart Dorsoduro encompasses the island and canal

of Giudecca; and Cannareggio to the north is the site of the world's oldest Jewish ghetto.

Sweeping through the six districts is Venice's famous central thoroughfare, the Grand Canal, a 2-mile (3km) long, looping waterway lined with more than 100 sumptuous Renaissance, Byzantine and Gothic merchant houses. Particularly noteworthy are the Ca' Pesaro, now a museum of modern and Oriental arts, and the Ca' Rezzonico – a museum of 18th-century Venice. The journey along the Grand Canal from the railway station to San Marco, now done by vaporetto rather than gondola, is still one of the all-time great experiences for any visitor.

A treasure house of art

Although Venice occupies only a relatively small area (2 sq miles/5km²), its wealth of artistic and architectural wonders outshines the cultural heritage of many sizeable nations. The 14th to 18th centuries, in particular, saw painters flock to Venice, drawn by the light of the lagoon – and by lucrative commissions from wealthy merchants, religious orders and *scuole*, charitable institutions whose wealthy members commissioned high art to embellish their premises.

Among the many artists who painted here were the Bellinis (Jacopo and his sons, Giovanni and Gentile), Veronese, Tintoretto (a native of Venice), Giorgione, Carpaccio and Titian, the great master of Venetian High Renaissance style, whose expressive use of light transformed Venetian painting – and, by extension, Western art itself. Many of their works are displayed in *scuole*, such as the Scuola Grande di San Rocco (a shrine to Tintoretto), major galleries such as the Accademia (with, among other masterpieces, Carpaccio's St Ursula cycle and Titian's *Presentation of the Virgin*) and in the many glorious churches that punctuate and define the cityscape.

The Gothic Frari church, founded by the Franciscans in 1340, has two Titian masterpieces, *The Assumption* and the *Madonna di Ca' Pesaro*. Santa Maria della Salute, built to commemorate the end of the 1630 plague, has works by Tintoretto and Titian. Overlooking the lagoon, the spectacular churches of San Giorgio Maggiore and Redentore, both designed by Venice's master architect Andrea Palladio, feature, respectively, works by Tintoretto and Veronese.

VENICE IN PERIL

It has long been known that the city of Venice is slowly sinking. Some reports claim that the process started around 1,000 years ago, even as the city was being built. In recent centuries, the gradual erosion of silt beneath the city's foundations, owing to the sheer weight of the buildings, combined with rising sea levels have made Venice ever more prone to flooding.

In particular, the annual tide peaks of the Adriatic Sea, known to the Venetians as the 'acqua alta', or high water, leave parts of the city close to the lagoon totally flooded. Important landmarks, such as St Mark's Square and many city walkways, can be under water for days. Over the

years, residents have become used to walking on duckboards.

In November 1966 Venice was hit by the worst floods in its history, when water levels rose by more than 2m (6ft) above the norm for that time of year. The event sparked international concern that one of the world's greatest treasures could disappear beneath the waves. After a major international appeal, the British Venice in Peril and American Save Venice funds were established, under the coordination of NATO, to protect the city. Projects undertaken since have included new tidal barriers to combat the flooding, along with a major restoration and cleaning of the city's buildings, statues and paintings.

These are the famous masterpieces of Venice, mentioned in all the guidebooks. But many of Venice's most rewarding experiences lie concealed along warrens of medieval streets, for even the humblest of the city's 200 churches will contain a gem of some kind.

Extraordinary and captivating

One of the great pleasures of Venice is simply wandering. For that we have to thank the city's unique layout – which has prevented the intrusion of cars, making Venice one of the few entirely pedestrianised cities in the world. Away from the crowds in San Marco, visitors on foot can lose themselves, sometimes literally, in the narrow alleyways that weave in and out of the city. Such rambles can lead to the discovery of a quiet square that contains a simple church with a beautiful painting, an unusual decorative well head or chimney, a tiny fresco above a doorway, or an interior that feels like a glimpse back into the 17th century.

Venice is more robust than it looks. Over the years, it has learned to adapt to the modern age, its palazzi converted into shops, hotels and apartments, its gondolas (other than for tourists) replaced by vaporetti, its warehouses transformed into museums. Along the way the city's relationship with the arts has embraced modernity. The Biennale (a major two-yearly contemporary arts exhibition), and the Peggy Guggenheim Museum featuring works by Pablo Picasso, Piet Mondrian and René Magritte, have established Venice as

" The 14th to 18th centuries, in particular, saw painters flock to Venice, drawn by the light of the lagoon... "

a great European centre for modern art, while the seaside resort of the Lido (the strip of land between Venice and the open sea immortalised by Thomas Mann in *Death in Venice*) has for years hosted the annual Venice Film Festival with all its glitz and glamour.

But when all is said and done, what we are left with is the city's signature element – water. In the absence of traffic noise, the canals and lagoon amplify the city's characteristic sounds of bells ringing in a hundred campaniles and the bow waves of boats slapping against ancient stones, while offering luminous reflections of the stunning cityscapes in their glimmering waters.

Whatever the season, this jewel-like city, the birthplace of Marco Polo, Tintoretto and Antonio Vivaldi, transports visitors into another world. A city where Vivaldi concerts are held in the very church he worked in (La Pietà), where gondolas float past the most beautiful Renaissance buildings in the world, where you can wander for days without seeing a car. Where else can so much art be enjoyed in such a compact area? And where else is glorious art outshone by its setting, as when the sun sets over Santa Maria della Salute in summer, or pierces the early morning mist over the lagoon in autumn? Unique, magical, entrancing – a city truly beyond compare.

Bridges and boundaries One of four bridges over the Grand Canal, the Rialto marks the boundary between San Polo and San Marco districts. It was completed in 1591, making it the oldest bridge on the canal.

VISBY

On a small island in the Baltic Sea stands a city adrift in time, a living memorial to a golden age of medieval prosperity and one of the best-preserved walled cities in Europe.

On May 13, 1525, a force from the city of Lübeck, now in Germany, landed on the island of Gotland without warning and took Visby by storm. Ransacking homes and destroying churches, the Lübeckers did their best to wreck the handsome and prosperous trading city and then withdrew.

Medieval legacy

Visby recovered, but its heyday was well and truly over. Today, although 18th-century houses and more recent public buildings exist, the city remains defined by its pre-eminence during the 12th and 13th centuries as a major European commercial centre. The shift in fortunes from trading hub, home to merchants from all over northern Europe, to Baltic backwater nevertheless has helped to preserve the city's architectural glory.

A formidable *ringmur* (ring wall) with 27 towers, built in the 13th century, encloses some 200 medieval buildings, including churches, guildhalls, merchants' houses and warehouses. St Mary's Cathedral, built in the 12th century and remodelled in the 13th with Gothic-style arches and vaulting, dominates the maze of cobbled streets,

Gothic flourishes Watchtowers along Visby's old city walls punctuate the skyline, as do the black-tipped spires of St Mary's Cathedral.

all angles and dog-leg turns, abruptly widening or narrowing for no apparent reason. The Old Pharmacy is typical of the medieval stone-built warehouses that crowd the hillside sloping down to the old port. Big vaulted rooms permitted bulky items to be stored and winch doors gave access to every floor. Stepped gables give the building a castellated look: it might be taken for a fortress, but this was a base for a merchant prince rather than an aristocratic lord.

Rise and fall

In the Middle Ages, when overland transport was arduous and inefficient, the Baltic waters provided an open highway. Merchants from Finland, Russia, Sweden, Latvia, Estonia, Lithuania and the northern German states transported timber, textiles, furs, amber, ivory, honey, beer, wine, unworked metals and weapons across the Baltic, as did trading partners from Norway, Scotland,

England and beyond. Visby was ideally situated as a way station, meeting place and market. By the 14th century, it was well placed to take the lead when the Hanseatic League came into being. An alliance of like-minded trading cities, the League grew into a powerful economic force, furnishing Visby with a trading network that extended from Russia to Iceland and from Norway to France.

Visby's pre-eminence did not go unchallenged. Lübeck also had ambitions to dominate the League. Growing rapidly in wealth and power, it was soon the greatest of the Hanseatic city states. By the beginning of the 15th century, competitive rivalry gave way to outright hostility, with regular quarrels in the councils of the League. Sooner or later Lübeck was bound to take action to remove what it had come to regard as an irritant. In 1525 it launched the attack on Visby that brought to a halt five centuries of enterprise and affluence.

best of the rest...
SMALL CITY GEMS

A spa city built on Roman foundations, **Aix-en-Provence** in France is famous for its fountains, university, music festivals, museums and galleries. Most of all, it is celebrated as the quintessential Provençal city, a market centre for a region that has gone its own rustic way for centuries.

The Romans gave **Bath** in England the facility for which it is named by enclosing the local hot springs, previously sacred to a Celtic goddess. The fashionable spa city of Jane Austen's novels still stands, its majestic Georgian squares and crescents set off by the enfolding Avon hills.

The spirit of the Flemish Renaissance is summed up in **Bruges**, a small Belgian city in which beauty and the bourgeois work ethic go hand in hand. Bruges is unmistakably industrious, with merchants' houses, a medieval Bourse and market square, as well as a cathedral and canals.

The Spanish city of **Cuenca** perches on top of a rocky outcrop between two ravines. A medieval wall guards the more gently sloping southern side. Crammed together for want of space, its so-called 'hanging houses' cling to the cliff top.

Straggling down from the Castle, **Edinburgh's** medieval Old Town has a distinctly Gothic feel. Below extends the Scottish capital's airy, elegant New Town, home to Enlightenment thinkers such as Adam Smith and David Hume.

Still an important seaport, **Savannah**, Georgia, was founded in 1733. It was the target of Unionist General Sherman's March to the Sea in 1864, during the American Civil War, but it was left relatively unscathed and has all the architectural elegance of the antebellum South.

Roman monuments, Romanesque buildings such as San Zeno's Basilica, the classical symmetries of San Anastasia's Renaissance church - **Verona** in Italy has repeatedly reinvented and re-imagined itself down the centuries.

VW TRANSPARENT FACTORY

The noise, dirt and smells of a typical factory are banished here. Instead there is a quiet, light-filled environment where luxury cars are assembled on the finest parquet floor.

WHERE ON EARTH?

The Gläserne Manufaktur – as the Transparent Factory is called in German – is located in Dresden, capital of the German state of Saxony. Due to its mild climate, rich heritage of Baroque architecture, and fine museums and art collections, Dresden is known in German as 'Elbflorenz' – Florence on the Elbe River.

Berlin

GERMANY   POLAND

Dresden ● VW
        Transparent
        Factory

CZECH REPUBLIC

Nothing is normal about this ultra-modern glass-walled factory. It was not, like most factories, built on an industrial estate on the outskirts of the city. Instead, it is close to the historic centre of Dresden in a tranquil setting on the edge of the city's central park and botanical gardens. And it is not just a factory; the complex is also used for TV recordings and concerts. The Dresden Opera even performed *Carmen* here when their concert hall was inundated by floods in 2002.

Temple of industry Spotlessly clean and almost silent, the production line is a far cry from the noise, dirt and bustle of most factories.

Designed by architect Gunter Henn, the factory was purpose-built to assemble Volkswagen's high-end luxury car, the Phaeton. It is as luxurious as the car that it produces. Light floods in through the glass walls – all 88,000m² (947,000sq ft) of them. The floor is Canadian maple parquet. Visitors enter through the lobby, known as the Orangery, a nod to the adjacent botanic garden. From there, they move on to the gallery with its unobstructed view of the assembly line.

Factory of the future

The heart of the Transparent Factory is the production hall with its 1-mile (1.6km) long oval-shaped assembly line that produces just 44 cars each day. The workers wear white uniforms and gloves. Robots move around the floor delivering parts. A factory or a futuristic laboratory? It is hard to tell from looking, but the clue is in the half-assembled vehicles moving almost silently from one workstation to the next. At some workstations, human workers toil; at others, robots do the heavy lifting, putting in windscreens and rear windows.

Building a factory close to a park and residential area raised many concerns: environmentalists worried that birds might fly into the windows and be killed; residents feared that the delivery of parts

Multi-storey showroom The glass tower (at right) rises 40m (130ft) into the sky. Up to 280 new cars can be stored on its 16 levels.

by lorries would lead to more traffic and noise on the roads. To protect the birds, an outdoor speaker system broadcasts bird sounds indicating that the territory is already taken. To deliver the 1,200 parts and 34 pre-assembled components that go into each car, a special tram was designed that uses the tracks of the existing passenger tram at night, significantly reducing the delivery traffic on the road. The trams arrive in the building's lower level.

The glass walls of this coolly elegant structure symbolise the transparency that Volkswagen wants to project in its dealings with customers. Visitors come simply to admire, but customers can also come to choose a car or to collect one. After lunch and a tour, the customer drives off from the factory of the future into one of Europe's most beautiful Baroque cities.

best of the rest...

MODERN FACTORIES

■ Foster + Partners used oak, steel and glass in the Faustino Group's new winery, **Bodegas Portia**. About 90 miles (150km) north of Madrid in Spain, each of the winery's three wings houses a different stage of production: fermentation in steel vats, ageing in oak barrels, and ageing in bottles. Trucks drive onto the sloping roof to drop the grapes directly into hoppers. Gravity does the rest. Nature helps keep the winery cool in summer: the wings where the wine ages are partly buried into the slope of the site. Sensors in the fermentation wing open vents when the carbon dioxide level is too high.

■ The RAPT Formation Center, known as the **Helicopter Building**, is the headquarters of the Paris Métro's maintenance department. Named for the solar-panel-clad rotor blades on its roof, the triangular four-storey building is surrounded by train tracks and factories. The grey concrete exterior is enlivened with portholes and, at ground level, bright orange caution stripes. The interior is playful, too, with spots of colour.

■ The **Aonni Mineral Water Plant** in remote Patagonia in Argentina sits between the shore and a tree-clad ridge. The plant's roofline is fragmented and the whole building looks like a glacier or like ice crystals. Natural light floods the interior and sustainable materials have been used throughout.

WIES PILGRIMAGE CHURCH

Festooned with painted whorls and gilt scrolls, the interior of Bavaria's Wieskirche is a miraculous confection of 18th-century rococo style, the ultimate religious expression of artistic and architectural joie de vivre.

Walking towards the hamlet of Wies, travellers might not guess that they are approaching an artistic miracle – such a small village and such an unprepossessing church. But such is the celebrity of the Wieskirche that few are caught totally unawares as they step inside. Even so, the first sight of the outrageous interior for a moment – quite literally – takes the breath away.

Rococo extravagance

What greets the visitor is a glowing symphony in stucco, an extravaganza in alabaster and marble. The interior here seems to have been iced like a cake, not built in plaster, wood and stone. Gold-leaf stems sprout in profusion from pillars and pilasters; even the organ pipes are crowned with a flourish of foliage and fleurs de lis. Statues of saints and cherubs look down from walls that the visitor is barely aware of, so completely are the transitions from

WHERE ON EARTH?

The Wieskirche stands in the foothills of the Alps, 3 miles (5km) to the southeast of the small town of Steingaden in eastern Bavaria, Germany. The church is one of many historic sites along the Romantic Road tourist route that runs through southern Germany between Würzburg and Füssen.

GERMANY Munich •
Wies Pilgrimage Church ●
• Füssen
LIECHTENSTEIN   AUSTRIA
SWITZERLAND   ITALY

wall to wall and wall to ceiling obscured by an explosion of ornamentation. Large, high-placed windows let light flood in to reflect off the gilded and painted stucco shells, bows, swags and scrolls around the upper parts of the church, the use of pastel colours increasing the effect of luminosity.

The painted ceiling seems almost to float free, borne aloft by flights of angels. Just visible, on the edge of Heaven,

The divine made visible Decoration, sculpture and painting come together in an exuberant expression of religious faith. The statue of the Scourged Saviour is incorporated into the elaborate altar design.

Christ is carried upwards with his cross, welcomed home by singing choirs and trumpeters sounding fanfares; elsewhere we see him seated in resurrected glory.

A church transformed

It was the celebrated Bavarian architect Dominikus Zimmermann of Landsberg, with the help of his brother, court painter Johann Baptist, who worked this creative miracle in commemoration of an alleged miracle. The community of Wies had a much prized wooden statue of the scourged Christ, and in 1738 a local family reported seeing real tears streaming down the statue's face. Zimmermann was commissioned to build a worthy home for this sacred object; by 1745, he was hard at work. The Pilgrimage Church of the Scourged Saviour, as it was called (for by now devotees were arriving from across much of central Europe to wonder at what had happened here), was completed in 1754.

The story of how a humble village church became an artistic treasure reflects the transformation of Roman Catholicism during the Counter-Reformation and the corresponding development of the Baroque style in religious architecture and art. The Counter-Reformation movement emphasised intensity of feeling over pious observance; the Baroque and its late manifestation, known as rococo, helped bring this about by using elaborate visual effects to stir people's emotions.

The Wieskirche is not to everyone's taste – some criticise its unrestrained ornamentation as excessive. But it was conceived as a gesture of defiance against the visual severity of Protestantism.

best of the rest...

BAROQUE BEAUTY

■ Not too far from Wies, **Melk Abbey** overlooks the River Danube in lower Austria. A medieval foundation, its abbey was rebuilt on an impressive scale in the Baroque style in the 18th century, with exquisite attention to ornamental detail.

■ The **Church of the Holy Cross** in the Italian town of Lecce is a spectacular example of Italian Baroque dating from the 17th century. The exterior is richly decorated with carved plant forms and grotesque figures. The interior is more restrained, yet has a large rose window above the main portal.

■ The 17th-century church of **Santa Maria della Vittoria** in Rome has a striking early Baroque facade. Among the treasures within is a statue by Gian Lorenzo Bernini, *The Ecstasy of St Teresa*, depicting a scene from the life of St Teresa of Ávila.

■ Designed by Sir Christopher Wren, **St Paul's Cathedral** in London exemplifies the more restrained English Baroque style.

■ The Baroque style successfully crossed the Atlantic: some of the finest examples are to be found in the churches and cathedrals of Mexico and Brazil. None is more exciting than the **Church of St Francis of Assisi** in Ouro Preto, Brazil, with an interior dripping with statues and gilded woodwork.

YELLOWSTONE NATIONAL PARK

This explosive landscape is powered by forces unleashed from within the Earth. The majority of the world's geysers are found at Yellowstone and are the key to its scientific interest.

Established in 1872, Yellowstone was one of the world's first national parks (the first being Bogd Khan Mountain National Park in Mongolia, founded in 1783). Yellowstone is still the most impressive, with more geothermal features – geysers, bubbling mud pots, sulphur-spewing fumaroles and multicoloured hot springs – than any other area on Earth. It also encompasses mountains, deep canyons, rivers, thundering waterfalls, petrified forests, a wealth of wildlife and dense forests that stretch as far as the eye can see.

Old geysers

More than 10,000 geothermal features are concentrated in Yellowstone Park, including two-thirds of the entire world's geysers. Aside from the many 'minor players', six major geysers spew out water and steam to a height of around 30m (100ft) every day. The most reliable is

Rainbow ring Grand Prismatic Spring pumps out 2,500 litres (550 gallons) of hot water every minute. The colours are created by mats of bacteria.

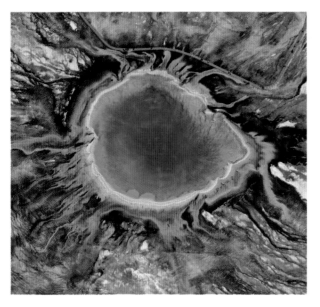

WHERE ON EARTH?

Yellowstone National Park lies mainly in the state of Wyoming, USA, extending into Montana and Idaho. There are gateway towns on all sides of the park, including Jackson Hole in the south. Flights arrive at airports at Cody and Jackson (Wyoming) Bozeman and Billings (Montana) and Idaho Falls (Idaho).

Old Faithful, which erupts on average every 90 minutes. Its column of steam once peaked at 56m (184ft) and its blast can last up to five minutes.

A white sinter (mineral) cone in the shape of a mini volcano surrounds Castle Geyser, which releases so much energy during its steam phase that it roars like a train. Riverside Geyser is unique in squirting at an angle of 60 degrees across the Firehole River, creating rainbows in the afternoon. The less predictable Steamboat Geyser is the current world record holder: it can reach a height of 90m (295ft) and erupt for up to 40 minutes, followed by steam venting for a couple of days. But Steamboat can go for days, months, even years without any activity at all.

Water features

The majority of geothermal features do not erupt, but instead flow quietly as hot springs, although some can be quite lively. Dragon's Mouth Spring is in a hillside cave where hot water sloshes around like a lashing tongue, hence its name. Some springs, especially those

on hillsides, turn to steam before they reach the surface, becoming the hottest geothermal events in the park. The steam emitted from Black Growler Steam Vent can reach a temperature of 138C (280F), while common geysers tend to be a more modest 95.5C (204F).

Fountain Paint Pots are a collection of bubbling mud pots whose mud is coloured white, grey or brown. Mud pots occur where rising steam causes mud to bubble like porridge, then burst and splatter. Some mud pots even turn into mud geysers and spurt mud 10m (33ft) high. Congress Pool seems undecided what it is: most of the year it is a quiet pool with pale blue water, but every so often it erupts, its water turning to dark mud that boils vigorously. The most colourful location in the park is Grand Prismatic Spring, which is the largest hot spring in the United States and the third largest in the world. At its centre the water is blue, but around the edge are bands of green, yellow, orange, red and brown. The colours are caused by mats of pigmented bacteria that live in the warm, mineral-rich water. The bacteria change with the seasons: in winter the mats tend to be green, while in summer they are orange and red. Bacteria also play a role at Mammoth Hot Springs, another Yellowstone highlight, where a series of travertine terraces are either coloured by bacteria or are pure white like cake icing. The overall effect is of a streaked waterfall frozen in time.

Super-volcano

The heat source for Yellowstone's geothermal activity is an immense body of molten rock below the Earth's surface. The Earth's crust here is no more than 40 miles (65km) thick, compared to an average of 90 miles (145km) under

Forceful blast White mineral deposits have created a cone around Castle Geyser. The surrounding waters are coloured by dense, heat-loving microorganisms.

most landmasses. Pushing up into the thin crust are bubbles of magma that intrude to within 4–10 miles (6–16km) of the surface, producing much higher temperatures below the surface than in other places. On most continents, the temperature rises by 0.6C (33F) for every 30m (100ft) below ground, but in Yellowstone's Norris Geyser Basin investigative drilling has revealed an increase of 68C (154F) per 30m and a temperature of 205C (401F) at a depth of only 80m (262ft).

The park sits in an immense volcanic caldera – the world's largest super-volcano. The Yellowstone volcano has blown its top several times in the past two million years and is still considered active. The last major event, which gave rise to the current

Scratching tree One of Yellowstone's grizzly bears sharpens its claws on a well-worn tree trunk.

caldera, occurred about 640,000 years ago. A 'big one' has occurred, on average, every 730,000 years, which would make the next one due in a mere 90,000 years.

Wildlife junction

North America's Continental Divide runs through Yellowstone, so the Snake River flows to the Pacific Ocean in the west while the Yellowstone River (a tributary of the upper Missouri) eventually flows to the Atlantic. On its way through the park, the mighty Yellowstone tumbles over the spectacular Yellowstone Falls into Yellowstone's Grand Canyon. It is the longest river without dams in

the 48 contiguous states of the USA. The biggest body of water in the park is Yellowstone Lake, North America's largest high-altitude lake.

About 80 per cent of the park is forest, the rest grassland. It is home to grizzly and black bears, coyotes and bald eagles. The predatory carnivores are wary of people, so it is usually the plant-eaters that are visible: bison graze peacefully, but put on a fair turn of speed when people get too close. The males fight during their seasonal rut in late summer. In September, elk bugle during their own ruts. Pronghorn antelope, the fastest long-distance runners in the animal kingdom, migrate across the park. Big-horn sheep live in the Gardner River Canyon and, taking a liking to tourists, cause traffic jams at the Dunraven Pass.

When wolves were reintroduced in 1995, the ecosystem quickly changed. Elk numbers dropped and the resulting reduction in grazing and browsing allowed aspens and willows to grow, creating habitats for beaver and moose. Even bears have benefited as they fatten up on the remains of wolf kills on emerging from hibernation.

With its varied landscape and wealth of wildlife, Yellowstone and its neighbouring wilderness areas constitute the largest and most intact temperate ecosystem in the Northern Hemisphere. They have become one of the foremost natural laboratories on Earth.

Long-time residents A bison feeds near Old Faithful. Yellowstone is the only part of the USA where bison have lived continuously since prehistoric times.

best of the rest...

GEOTHERMAL FEATURES

■ **Lady Knox Geyser**, at the Wai-O-Tapu geothermal area on New Zealand's North Island, erupts daily at 10:15am. The geyser is a 20-minute drive from Rotorua, nicknamed 'Sulphur City' on account of the sulphurous smell there. The geyser's 'Champagne Pool' is so-named for its bubbling carbon-dioxide omissions; its bright orange shoreline

Lady Knox Geyser

is caused by arsenic and antimony sulphides in the water. There are many other geothermal sites in the area, including the Pohutu Geyser in the Whakarewarewa Thermal Valley, which spurts water up to 30m (100ft), 20 times daily.

■ The **Valley of Geysers** on Siberia's Kamchatka Peninsula has been called one of the 'wonders of Russia'. In 2007 mud slides engulfed the valley, but the geysers survived. Until the 1940s, locals kept away from the area, believing evil spirits dwelt there, but

tourists now fly in by helicopter, the only way to get there.

■ Chile's **El Tatio** ('The Grandfather') is one of the world's high-altitude geyser fields. With 80 geysers, it is also the largest field in the Southern Hemisphere, and the third largest worldwide after Yellowstone and Kamchatka.

■ **Beppu** in Japan has nine hot-spring areas, the so-called 'Hells of Beppu'. It is said that the 2,909 springs produce the world's second-greatest quantity of hot water, some of it utilised in *mushiyu* (hot steam baths), *sunayu* (hot sand baths) and *doroyu* (hot mud baths). The most unusual spring is *jigoku*, 'Blood Pond Hell', a pool of hot red water.

ZENTRALFRIEDHOF
CEMETERY

More people have been interred in Vienna's central cemetery than in any other burial site in Europe. A walk through its peaceful park reveals eclectic styles and celebrity graves.

WHERE ON EARTH?

The Zentralfriedhof is in the Simmering district of Vienna, Austria. It is on tramline 71, which has given rise to the local euphemism that the deceased has 'taken the 71'. The 106 bus route has several stops inside the cemetery. Suburban trains (Vienna S-Bahn) also stop nearby.

CZECH REPUBLIC · SLOVAKIA · Vienna · Zentralfriedhof Cemetery · Bratislava · AUSTRIA · HUNGARY

Zentralfriedhof means 'central cemetery', but its location is not central at all. This extraordinary burial ground lies on the southern outskirts of Vienna, on a plot covering 0.75 sq miles (2km²). It was called 'central' because of its importance. In the 19th century Vienna was a fast-expanding imperial capital and its old graveyards were full. This vast cemetery, which has always been open to all religious denominations, solved the problem.

Controversial centrepiece The Karl Lueger-Gedächtniskirche is the largest of several churches and memorials surrounded by neat rows of graves.

It opened in 1874, and since then 3.3 million people – twice the current population of Vienna – have been buried there. With more than 330,000 graves, Zentralfriedhof is a wonderland of funerary art, with elaborate tombs and mausoleums arranged on a grid of tree-shaded avenues.

Initially, the Viennese were reluctant to bury their dead so far from home, so in a deliberate marketing ploy, the authorities brought in some big names from Vienna's star-studded world of music. Ludwig van Beethoven, whose body was exhumed in 1862 for study, was reburied here in 1888, 61 years after his death. The tomb of Franz Schubert, who died a year after Beethoven, was similarly relocated to Zentralfriedhof, as was Mozart's contemporary Antonio Salieri.

To the list of *Ehrengräber*, honour tombs, were added Johannes Brahms (died 1897) and Johann Strauss the Younger, the 'Waltz King' (died 1899). Arnold Schoenberg (died 1951) continues the roll call of famous composers in an eye-catching grave marked by a huge plain stone cube. A monument to Wolfgang Amadeus Mozart stands among the composers, although he is buried elsewhere.

Cultural melting pot

The Zentralfriedhof has always attracted controversy. The opening ceremony was held on November 1, 1874, All Saints'

Day, preceded by a private Catholic consecration of the site by the Cardinal and Prince-Archbishop of Vienna, who found it hard to accept that the cemetery would also include Jewish burials.

In 1908–10, a new church was built in the cemetery. It was the masterpiece of Max Hegele, a student of Otto Wagner, one of the founders of the Vienna Secession art movement. While the exterior combines Byzantine and

Musical neighbours Elaborate gravestones mark the tombs of Johann Strauss the Younger and Brahms in the Ehrengräber section.

neoclassical features, the interior sports exquisite Jugendstil (Art Nouveau) decoration. The church was originally called the Friedhofskirche zum Heiligen Karl Borromäus, after the 16th-century Italian Cardinal-Archbishop of Milan, Carlo Borromeo. In 1910 it became the mausoleum of a popular mayor, Dr Karl Lueger, and since then has become known as the Karl Lueger-Gedächtniskirche (Karl Lueger Memorial Church). An anti-Semite, Lueger's politics directly influenced Adolf Hitler and his presence at the heart of the cemetery continues to cause discomfort.

One of the Jewish sections of the cemetery was vandalised in the Nazi *Kristallnacht*, the night of Nazi attacks on Jews in Austria and Germany in 1938, but there are still 138,000 Jewish graves in the Zentralfriedhof. Culturally, the cemetery remains a broad church. There are dedicated sections for Roman Catholics, Jews, various Orthodox churches, Protestants, Muslims, Buddhists and Mormons. In 2000 a section opened for stillborn babies, and in 2009 another part was dedicated to those who donate their bodies to science for use by the University of Vienna.

Some 150 years after opening, the Zentralfriedhof still tends to the city's deceased citizens. About 20 funerals take place there every day.

best of the rest...

PUBLIC CEMETERIES

▪ The **Cementerio de La Recoleta** in Buenos Aires looks like a miniature city, its paths lined with elaborate vaults and mausoleums. Leading Argentinians buried here include Eva Perón.

▪ By the 19th century, London's graveyards were overflowing and seven new cemeteries were created, including **Highgate Cemetery**, which opened in 1839. Among the 53,000 tombs, vaults and statues in its wooded avenues are memorials to George Eliot, Douglas Adams and Lucien Freud. The most famous resident is Karl Marx.

▪ Funerary gondolas used to take the dead across Venice's lagoon to the **Isola di San Michele**, where a cemetery was established in 1807 under French occupation. Resident celebrities include Sergei Diaghilev, Ezra Pound and Igor Stravinsky.

▪ The **Merry Cemetery** in Săpânța, northern Romania, is celebrated for its brightly painted wooden crosses decorated with colourful patterns, portraits and painted scenes from the lives of the deceased.

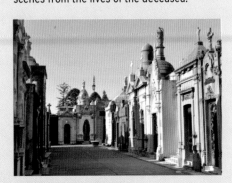

Cementerio de La Recoleta

ZOLLVEREIN COAL MINE

Once at the heart of a heaving industrial plant, the Modernist remnants of Germany's Zollverein coal mine make a fitting venue for today's state-of-the-art cultural centre.

S haft 12 of the Zollverein coal mine is crowned by an unlikely building: the clean lines of horizontal and vertical windows are sandwiched between layers of brick and narrow bands of steel. Behind it looms the giant steel A-frame of the winding tower, legs akimbo, wheels at the ready – an icon of the Ruhr district's great industrial past. The building may look uncompromisingly modern, but it was in fact built in 1932.

Industrial prowess

The first mine on this site was started in 1847 by Franz Haniel, an industrialist who needed coke to make steel, and it was immediately successful. By 1890 the

Family fun Among the attractions at today's coal-mining complex are a park, a swimming pool, a big wheel and – for a short spell in winter – an ice rink.

WHERE ON EARTH?

An anchor point on the European Route of Industrial Heritage, the Zollverein Coal Mine Industrial Complex is located in the suburbs of Essen, in the Ruhr district of North Rhine-Westphalia, western Germany. The nearest airport is Düsseldorf, 15 miles (25km) away. The site can be reached by tram and S-Bahn rail.

Zollverein coal mine had three shafts and was the most productive in Germany, with an output of a million tonnes of coal a year. Eight more shafts had been added by the outbreak of World War One, by which time the area dominated German coal, iron and steel production.

Zollverein remained in the Haniel family until 1920. It was under the ownership of the Gelsenkirchener Bergwerks AG that Shaft 12 was developed, quickly becoming more productive than all the other shafts put together. The building above Shaft 12, the creation of Bauhaus-inspired Fritz Schupp, earned Zollverein a reputation as the most beautiful coal mine in the world. New cokeries above ground added huge and complex structures and machinery to the landscape.

From industry to art

Zollverein survived World War Two virtually unscathed, and continued to develop into the 1970s, but by the early 1980s coal-mining there was no longer profitable. Mining ceased at Zollverein in 1986, coke-making in 1993.

This might have been the end of the story, but with visionary swiftness the state of North Rhine-Westphalia stepped

Industrial overtones The monumental Modernist architecture of the 1930s is a striking reminder of the Ruhr's history as a leading industrial region.

in to preserve the whole complex. Now it serves as a cultural hub, providing space for art and entertainment, performances, workshops, trade shows and family entertainment. Schupp's classic Shaft 12 building has been put to fitting use as the Red Dot Design Museum, showcasing winners of the coveted annual Red Dot Design Award. An industrial heritage trail and guided tours of the complex take visitors around the original machinery of this former powerhouse.

best of the rest...

REGENERATED INDUSTRIAL SITES

■ In the 17th and 18th centuries, Sweden was a noted source of high-quality iron, produced on large, semi-rural industrial estates. One of these was the **Engelsberg Ironworks** in central southern Sweden, founded in 1681. Historic smelting furnaces, kilns and forges have been preserved in some 50 buildings. Painted oxide red, they are set in woodlands.

■ Liverpool, on the northwest coast of England, was one of the world's busiest ports in the 19th and early-20th centuries, before suffering a rapid decline. When the warehouses of **Albert Dock** were built in 1846, they were the first in the country to be constructed of iron, brick and stone, and therefore fireproof. They have now been imaginatively converted into a number of museums and galleries (including Tate Liverpool), hotels, restaurants and entertainment venues. On the Pier Head waterfront just to the north is the ultra-modern Museum of Liverpool, inaugurated in 2011.

■ When completed in 1923, Fiat's **Lingotto Building** in Turin, northern Italy, was the world's largest car factory. The cars were assembled in stages as they moved upwards through the building's five floors, before being tested on a track on the roof and then descending to ground level on a spiral ramp. The factory closed when manufacturing came to an end in 1982, but the building has since been converted into a complex of fashionable shops, performance venues and a hotel, to designs by the leading Italian architect Renzo Piano.

INDEX

A

Abanda Caves, Gabon 80
Abbey Gardens (Isles of Scilly), England 192
Abisko National Park, Sweden 34
Abu Dhabi 41
Abu Simbel, Egypt 8-13
Acre Geoglyphs, Brazil 195
Acropolis, Greece 14-17
Afar Depression, Ethiopia 18-19
Aix-en-Provence, France 301
Akhetaten, Egypt 171
Aladzha Monastery, Bulgaria 157
Albania 45
Albert Dock, England 313
Alcatraz, USA 257
Alcázar (Segovia), Spain 79
Alcázar (Seville), Spain 23
Algeria 142
Al-Hajjarah, Yemen 239
Alhambra, Spain 20-23
Altiplano, Peru 24-25
Amalfi Coast, Italy 54
Anafiotika, Greece 243
Angel Falls, Venezuela 141
Angkor Thom, Cambodia 31
Angkor Wat, Cambodia 28-31
Anse Source D'Argent, Seychelles 280
Antarctic Peninsula 32-35
Antigua, Guatemala 205
Aonni Mineral Water Plant, Argentina 303
Applecross Peninsula, Scotland 121
Aqua Tower, USA 36-37
Arcos de la Frontera, Spain 239
Arena Chapel, Italy 38-39
Argentina
    Altiplano 24-25
    Aonni Mineral Water Plant 303
    Cementerio de La Recoleta 311
    Iguazú Falls 138-41
    Los Glaciares National Park 108-10
    Perito Moreno Glacier 108-9
    Plaza Dorrego 240
    Punta Walichu Caves 109
    San Telmo 240-2
Armenia 157
Astana, Kazakhstan 40-41
Aurora Sky Station, Sweden 34
Auschwitz-Birkenau Memorial and
    Museum, Poland 179
Australia
    Great Barrier Reef 7, 285
    Kakadu rock paintings 142-3
    Kimberley Coast 54
    Lake Eyre 289
    Marree Man 195
    Sydney Harbour 262-5
    Sydney Opera House 27, 263
    Uluru 286-7
Austria
    Eisriesenwelt 219
    Heiligenkreuz Abbey 109
    Melk Abbey 304
    Zentralfriedhof Cemetery 310-11
Auvergne, France 261
Ayers Rock see Uluru
Aysen Fjord, Chile 184

B

Baalbek, Lebanon 160
Babylon, Iraq 171
Badshahi Mosque, Pakistan 61
Banaue rice fields, Philippines 46-47
Banc d'Arguin National Park, Mauritania
    209

Bandelier, USA 183
Banff National Park, Canada 48-49
Barranca del Cobre, Mexico 117
basalt landscapes 253
    Giant's Causeway 252-3
    Iguazú Falls 140
    Staffa 252-3
Basilica of St Mark (Venice), Italy 298
Basilica of San Francisco (Arezzo), Italy
    39
Batak Toba, Indonesia 244
Bath, England 301
beaches 280
    Copacabana Beach 256
    Trunk Bay 280-1
Belgium
    Bruges 301
    Menin Gate 176-8
Belize Barrier Reef 285
Bell Rock Lighthouse, Scotland 50-52
Beppu, Japan 308
Bermuda Islands Barrier Reef 285
Bhutan
    Paro Taktsang 210-11
    Punakha 223
Big Ben, England 95
Big Sur, USA 54-55
Biltmore House, USA 73
Bird's Nest Stadium, China 56
birdwatching
    Cape May 173
    East African Rift Valley 173
    Iguazú Falls 140-141
    Kyushu 173
    Manú National Park 172-3
    Ngorongoro Crater 202-3
    Pantanal 208
Blue Mosque, Turkey 58-61
Blythe Geoglyphs, USA 195
Bolivia
    Altiplano 24-25
    Pantanal 206-9
    Salar de Uyuni 288-91
Bonneville Salt Flats, USA 289
Boqueria Market, Spain 62-63
Bora Bora, French Polynesia 64-65
Borneo
    Kelabit people 129
Borobudur, Indonesia 295
Borough Market, England 63
Bosque del Apache, USA 209
Botswana
    Okavango Delta 209
Brancacci Chapel, Italy 39
Bran Castle, Romania 73
Brazil
    Acre Geoglyphs 195
    Brasília 41
    Christ the Redeemer 257
    Church of St Francis of Assisi (Ouro
        Preto) 304
    Convent of San Francisco 204-5
    Copacabana Beach 256
    Copan Building 37
    Corcovado Mountain 257
    Iguazú Falls 138-41
    Jaú National Park 150
    Manaus Opera House 26-27
    Olinda 204-5
    Pantanal 206-9
    Sugarloaf Mountain 254-7
Bridalveil Fall, USA 141
bridges 112-13
    Golden Gate 112

Ponte Vecchio 113
    Rialto 6, 299
    Sydney Harbour Bridge 264
British Museum, England 167
Bruges, Belgium 301
Bulgaria
    Aladzha Monastery 157
    Burgos Cathedral, Spain 71
Burj Khalifa, Dubai 77

C

Cadiz, Spain 91
Cai Rang floating market, Vietnam 63
Cambodia
    Angkor Thom 31
    Angkor Wat 28-31
    Khmer Empire 29
    Ta Prohm 31
Cambridge, England 71, 137
Canada
    Banff National Park 48-49
    Churchill 34
    Gros Morne 120-1
    Haida Gwaii 128-9
    Jasper National Park 49
    Moraine Lake 48-49
    Niagara Falls 141
    Rocky Mountains 48-49
    Saguenay Fjord 184
    Yoho National Park 49
Canadian National Vimy Memorial,
    France 179
canals, Britain's 147
Canary Islands 133
Canyon de Chelly, USA 183
Cape Elizabeth Lighthouse, USA 53
Cape May, USA 173
Capri, Italy 249
Carcassonne, France 86
Carnac, France 66
Cartagena, Colombia 235
castles
    Alcázar (Segovia) 79
    Bran Castle 73
    Crac des Chevaliers 78-79
    Eilean Donan 79
    Harlech Castle 79
    Heidelberg castle 136
    Qal'at Salah El-Din 79
    San Felipe de Barajas 79
Cave of Crystals, Mexico 80-81
caves
    Abanda Caves 80
    Cave of Crystals 80-81
    Eisriesenwelt 219
    Ellora Caves 31
    Krubera-Voronya 219
    Lascaux Caves 80
    Mammoth Cave 219
    Phong Nha Cave 216-19
    Punta Walichu Caves 109
    Sarawak Chamber 219
    Skocjan Caves 219
Cementerio de La Recoleta, Argentina
    311
cemeteries 311
    Zentralfriedhof Cemetery 310-11
Central African Republic
    Dzanga-Ndoki National Park 150
Centre Georges Pompidou, France 122
Cerdanya, France/Spain 223
Chaco Canyon, USA 183
Chad 142

Chandni Chowk, India 85
Chartres Cathedral, France 68-70
Chatsworth House, England 72-73
Chenonceau, France 73
Chichen Itzá, Mexico 273
Chile
    Aysen Fjord 184
    Easter Island 92-93
    El Tatio 309
    Rapa Nui National Park 92-93
    Torres del Paine National Park 111
China
    Bird's Nest Stadium 56
    Five Flower Lake 44
    Foping National Nature Reserve 145
    Forbidden City 98-101
    Great Wall of China 118-19
    Guangzhou Opera House 27
    Hakka villages 244
    Huanglong Valley 125
    Jade Dragon Snow Mountain 111
    Jin Dian Temple 251
    Shanghai Bund 265
    Sichuan province 44
    Terracotta Army 274-7
    Yuyuan garden 192
Chrysler Building, USA 74-77
churches and cathedrals
    Arena Chapel 38-39
    Basilica of St Mark (Venice) 298
    Basilica of San Francisco (Arezzo) 39
    Brancacci Chapel 39
    Burgos Cathedral 71
    Chartres Cathedral 68-70
    Church of St Francis of Assisi (Ouro
        Preto) 304
    Church of the Annunciation
        (Moldovita) 230-1
    Church of the Holy Cross (Lecce) 304
    Church of the Jacobins (Toulouse) 71
    Church of the Transfiguration (Kizhi)
        229
    Cologne Cathedral 71
    Córdoba Cathedral 23
    Gothic churches in Europe 71
    Kilpeck church 229
    King's College (Cambridge) 71
    Lalibela rock churches 156-7
    Matera 157
    Melk Abbey 304
    Notre Dame (Paris) 71
    Notre Dame du Haut (Ronchamp) 122
    Our Lady of Reims 71
    Romania's painted churches 228-31
    Saint-Denis (Paris) 71
    Sainte-Chapelle (Paris) 71
    St Marco (Florence) 39
    St Paul's Cathedral (London) 304
    San Giorgio Maggiore (Venice) 296
    Santa Maria della Vittoria (Rome) 304
    Santiago de Compostela 295
    Urnes Stave Church 229
    Wieskirche 304-5
Churchill (Manitoba), Canada 34
Church of the Transfiguration (Kizhi),
    Russia 229
cliff dwellings 180-3
coastlines 54
    Big Sur 54-55
    Bora Bora 64-65
    Halong Bay 124-7
Coastwatcher's Memorial Lighthouse,
    Papua New Guinea 53
Colca Canyon, Peru 117

Cologne Cathedral, Germany 71
Colombia
  Cartagena 235
  San Felipe de Barajas 79
Colorado Plateau, USA 25, 114
Colosseum, Italy 57
Commerzbank Tower, Germany 76
Concarneau, France 91
concert halls see opera houses
Congo, Democratic Republic of
  Virunga National Park 202
Copacabana Beach, Brazil 256
Copan Building, Brazil 37
Coral Beach Nature Reserve, Israel 285
coral reefs 7, 282-4, 285
Corcovado Mountain, Brazil 257
Córdoba, Spain
  Cathedral of 23
  Great Mosque of 23
Coruche, Portugal 47
Courtauld Gallery, England 166
Coyoacan, Mexico City 243
Crac des Chevaliers, Syria 78-79
Crater Lake, USA 45
Croagh Patrick, Ireland 103
Croatia
  Dubrovnik 88-91
  Plitvice Lakes 45
Cuba 205
Cuenca, Spain 301
Culloden, Scotland 82-83
Cyclopean Isles, Italy 253
Czech Republic
  Staromestske Namesti 154

D
Damascus, Old, Syria 87
Danakil Desert, Ethiopia 19
Danube Delta, Romania 209
Darjeeling, India 47
Darwin, Charles 104-7
Dead Sea, Israel/Jordan 19
Death Valley, USA 19
Deccan Plateau, India 25
Delhi Old Town, India 84-87
Delphi, Greece 17
Dendera, Egypt 11
deserts 96-97
  Arabian Desert 195
  Danakil Desert 19
  Erg Chebbi 96
  Mohave Desert 19, 195
  White Desert 97
Devil's Tower, USA 253
Dogon people, Mali 129
Doñana National Park, Spain 209
Dubai 265
  Burj Khalifa 77
  Dubai Fountain 279
Dubrovnik, Croatia 88-91
Dzanga-Ndoki National Park, Central
  African Republic 150

E
Easter Island, Chile 92-93
Ecuador 154
  Galápagos Islands 104-7
  Plaza de la Independencia 154
Edinburgh, Scotland 301
Egypt
  Abu Simbel temples 8-13
  Akhetaten 171
  Colossi of Memnon 11
  Dendera temple complex 11
  Great Sphinx 11
  Karnak temple complex 11
  Kom Ombo 11
  Lake Nasser 13

Luxor temple complex 11
  Mount Sinai 103
  Nile Valley 227
  Pyramids of Giza 11
  Queen Hatshepsut Mortuary Temple 11
  Step Pyramid of Djoser 11
  Temple of Horus 11
  Valley of the Kings 276
  White Desert 97
Eiffel Tower, France 94-95
Eilean Donan Castle, Scotland 79
Eisriesenwelt, Austria 219
Ellora Caves, India 31
El Tatio, Chile 308
Empire State Building, USA 76
Engelsberg Ironworks, Sweden 313
England
  Abbey Gardens (Isles of Scilly) 192
  Albert Dock 313
  Bath 301
  Cambridge 137
  canals 147
  Chatsworth House 72-73
  Kilpeck church 229
  King's College (Cambridge) 71
  Lizard Lighthouse 53
  Oxford 137
  Stonehenge 67
  Uffington White Horse 195
  see also London
Ennedi Plateau, Chad 142
Enoshima Lighthouse, Japan 52
Ephesus, Turkey 160
Erg Chebbi, Morocco 96
Essaouira, Morocco 91
Estonia 87
Ethiopia
  Afar Depression 18-19
  Danakil Desert 19
  Lake Tana Monasteries 189
  Lalibela rock churches 156-7
Etosha pan, Namibia 289
Éze, France 239

F
factories
  Aonni Mineral Water Plant 303
  Bodegas Portia 303
  Helicopter Building 303
  see also industrial sites
Fallingwater, USA 37
fantasy homes
  Hearst Castle 196
  Neuschwanstein 196-7
  Tsarkoe Selo 196
finches 106
Fish River Canyon, Namibia 117
Five Flower Lake, China 44
fjords 184
  Fjordland National Park 184
  Gros Morne 120-1
Flatiron Building, USA 74
Foping National Nature Reserve, China
  145
Forbidden City, China 98-101
fountains 278-9
  Dubai Fountain 279
  Trevi Fountain 278
France
  Aix-en-Provence 301
  Auvergne 261
  Canadian National Vimy Memorial 179
  Carcassonne 86
  Carnac 66
  Chartres Cathedral 68-70
  Chenonceau 73
  Church of the Jacobins (Toulouse) 71
  Concarneau 91
  Éze 239

Gordes 239
  Lascaux Caves 80
  Monet's Garden 190-3
  Montségur 83
  Notre Dame du Haut (Ronchamp) 122
  Oradour-sur-Glane 179
  Our Lady of Reims 71
  Palace of Versailles 225
  Pointe Sainte-Mathieu Lighthouse 53
  Pont du Gard 160
  Roncesvalles Pass 83
  Thiepval Memorial 179
  Villa Savoye 37
  see also Paris
French Polynesia
  Bora Bora 64-65
frescoes 38-39, 187, 229, 238

G
Gabon
  Abanda Caves 80
  Loango National Park 150
Galápagos Islands, Ecuador 104-7
galleries see museums and galleries
gardens 192
  Monet's Garden 190-3
Geghard, Armenia 157
geoglyphs 195
  Nazca Lines 194-5
Georgia
  Krubera-Voronya Caves 219
  Svaneti 258-61
geothermal features
  Beppu 309
  Castle Geyser 306-7
  El Tatio 309
  Lady Knox Geyser 308
  Old Faithful 309
  Valley of the Geysers 308
  Yellowstone National Park 306-9
German Chancellery 122
Germany
  Berliner Philharmonie 27
  Cologne Cathedral 71
  Commerzbank Tower 76
  Frankfurt 265
  German Chancellery 122
  Heidelberg 134-7
  Hortus Palatinus 135
  Neuschwanstein 196-7
  Rhine Valley 47, 226-7
  VW Transparent Factory 302-3
  Wieskirche 304-5
  Wurzburg Residence 73
  Zollverein Coal Mine 312-13
geysers see geothermal features
Gherkin, England 76
Gianicolo, Italy 257
Giant's Causeway, Northern Ireland
  252-3
giant pandas 145
giant tortoises 104-7
Giardini di Boboli, Italy 192
Giotto di Bondone 38-39
Giza Pyramids, Egypt 11
Glacier Bay National Park and Preserve,
  USA 111
glaciers 34, 108-11
Glass House, USA 36
Glencoe, Scotland 223
Glenveagh National Park, Scotland 121
Golden Gate Bridge, USA 112
Golden Temple of Amritsar, India 295
Gordes, France 239
Göreme Valley, Turkey 157
gorillas 202
Grand Canyon, USA 25, 114-17
Grand Teton National Park, USA 49
Great Barrier Reef, Australia 7, 285

Great Mosque of Djenné, Mali 61
Great Wall of China 118-19
Greece
  Acropolis 14-17
  Anafiotika 243
  frescoes 187
  icons 187
  Metéora Monasteries 186-9
  Parthenon 14-17
  Santorini 246-9
  Temple of Apollo (Delphi) 17
  Temple of Apollo Epicurius (Bassae) 17
  Temple of Hephaestus 17
Greenland
  Ilulissat Icefjord 34
Greenwich Village, USA 243
Gros Morne National Park, Canada 120-1
Guangzhou Opera House, China 27
Guatemala
  Antigua 205
  Tikal 171, 273
Guggenheim Bilbao, Spain 122-3
Gullfoss, Iceland 141

H
Hagia Sophia, Turkey 59
Haida Gwaii, Canada 128-9
Hakka villages, China 244
Halong Bay, Vietnam 124-7
Harlech Castle, Wales 79
Harmandir Sahib, India 251
Hassan II Mosque, Morocco 61
Hawaii
  Hawaii Volcanoes National Park 130
  Kure Atoll 285
  Mauna Kea 130
  Mauna Kilauea 130-3
  Mauna Loa 130, 132
  volcanoes 130-3
  Waikiki 280
Hearst Castle, USA 196
Heidelberg, Germany 134-7
Heiligenkreuz Abbey, Austria 189
Hemis monastery, Ladakh 210
Hephaestus, Temple of, Greece 17
Hermitage Museum, Russia 167
Hexagon Pools, Israel/Syria 253
Highgate Cemetery, England 311
Hiroshima Peace Memorial, Japan 179
Holland
  Keukenhof garden 192
  Rijksmuseum 167
Hong Kong, China 265
  Victoria Peak 257
Huanglong Valley, China 125

I
Ibiza, Spain 249
Iceland
  Gullfoss 141
  Vatnajökull glacier 34
icy wastes
  Antarctic Peninsula 32-35
  Aurora Sky Station 34
  Churchill 34
  Ilulissat Icefjord 34
  Vatnajökull glacier 34
Iguazú Falls, Brazil/Argentina 138-41
Ilulissat Icefjord, Greenland 34
India
  Chandni Chowk 85
  Darjeeling 47
  Deccan Plateau 25
  Delhi Old Town 84-87
  Ellora Caves 31
  Golden Temple of Amritsar 295
  Harmandir Sahib 251
  Hemis monastery 210

Indus Valley 223
Kanha National Park 144-5
Kerala's backwaters 146
Khajuraho temples 31
Mahabalipuram 31
Namgyal monastery 210
Sripuram Golden Temple 251
Taj Mahal 7, 266-9
Thikse monastery 210
Varanasi 292-5
indigenous people 129
Indonesia
    Batak Toba 244
    Borobudur 295
    Raja Ampat Islands 285
    Sumbanese people 129
industrial sites
    Albert Dock 313
    Engelsberg Ironworks 313
    Lingotto Building 313
    VW Transparent Factory 302-3
    Zollverein Coal Mine 312-13
    see also factories
Indus Valley, India/Pakistan 223, 227
Intramuros, Philipppines, 205
Iran 154
Iraq 171
Ireland
    Croagh Patrick 103
    Glenveagh National Park 121
    Newgrange tomb 276
    Skellig Michael 188
Iron Gates Gorge, Romania/Serbia 117
islands
    Bora Bora 64-65
    Canary Islands 133
    Capri 249
    Cyclopean Isles 253
    Easter Island 92-93
    Galápagos Islands 104-7
    Isola Bella 248
    Isola di San Michele 311
    Isola de Santa Pietro 249
    Mediterranean islands 246-9
    Pitcairn 64
    Ponza 249
    Santorini 246-9
    São Tomé & Principe 64
    Socotra 64
    see also coral reefs
Isola Bella, Italy 248
Isola de Santa Pietro, Italy 249
Isola di San Michele, Italy 311
Israel
    Coral Beach Nature Reserve 285
    Hexagon Pools 253
    Jerusalem, Old 87
Italy
    Amalfi Coast 54
    Arena Chapel 38-39
    Arena di Verona 27
    Basilica of St Mark (Venice) 298
    Basilica of San Francisco (Arezzo) 39
    Brancacci Chapel 39
    Capri 249
    Church of the Holy Cross (Lecce) 304
    Colosseum (Rome) 57
    Cyclopean Isles (Sicily) 253
    Dolomites 261
    Florence 39, 113, 167, 192
    frescoes 38-39, 238
    Gianicolo 257
    Giardini di Boboli 192
    Isola Bella 248
    Isola de Santa Pietro 249
    Isola di San Michele 311
    Lake Maggiore 45
    Leaning Tower of Pisa 95
    Lingotto Building 313
    Matera 157

Matterhorn 174-5
mosaics 298
Mount Etna 133
Mount Vesuvius 133
Paestum temples 17
Perugia 137
Pienza 235
Pompeii 160
Ponte Vecchio 113
Ponza 249
Ragusa 239
Rialto Bridge 6, 299
St Marco (Florence) 39
San Gimignano 236-239
San Giorgio Maggiore (Venice) 296
Santa Maria della Vittoria (Rome) 304
Sistine Chapel 39
Stromboli 133, 249
Trevi Fountain 278
Uffizi Gallery 167
Valley of the Temples 17
Vatican Museums 167
Venice 6, 296-9, 311
Verona 301
Vucciria market 63

J
Jade Dragon Snow Mountain, China 111
Japan
    Beppu 309
    Enoshima Lighthouse 52
    Hiroshima Peace Memorial 179
    Jigokudani Monkey Park 145
    Kinkaku-ji 251
    Kunisaki Peninsula 295
    Kyoto, Ancient 87
    Kyushu 173
    Mount Fuji 102-3
    Ryoan-ji garden 192
Jardin Majorelle, Morocco 192
Jasper National Park, Canada 49
Jaú National Park, Brazil 150
Jemaa el-Fna, Morocco 154
Jerusalem, Old, Israel 87
Jigokudani Monkey Park, Japan 145
Jin Dian Temple, China 251
Jordan
    Jordan Rift Valley 227
    Petra 212-15
    Works of the Old Men 195
Jostedalbreen National Park, Norway 111
Jotunheimen National Park, Norway 111

K
Kakadu rock paintings, Australia 142-3
Kamchatka Peninsula, Russia 133, 308
Kanchanaphisek Lighthouse, Thailand 53
Kanha National Park, India 144-5
Karnak temple complex, Egypt 11
Karymsky, Russia 133
Kazakhstan
    Astana 40-41
    Kelabit people, Borneo 129
Kenya
    Masai Mara National Park 200
Kerala's backwaters, India 146
Keukenhof gardens, Holland 192
Khajuraho temples, India 31
Khao Sok National Park, Thailand 148-51
Khiva, Uzbekistan 215
Khmer Empire 29
Kilpeck church, England 229
Kimberley Coast, Australia 54
King's College, Cambridge, England 71
Kinkaku-ji, Japan 251
Kirstenbosch National Botanic Garden,
    South Africa 192
Klyuchevskaya Sopka, Russia 133

Kom Ombo, Egypt 11
Kotor, Montenegro 91
Kraków, Poland 152-5
Kronotsky, Russia 133
Krubera-Voronya cave, Georgia 219
Kunisaki Peninsula, Japan 295
Kure Atoll, Hawaii 285
Kwandwe Private Game Reserve, South
    Africa 200
Kyoto, Ancient, Japan 87
Kyushu, Japan 173

L
Ladakh 261
Lady Knox Geyser, New Zealand 308
Lahore, Pakistan 61
lakes
    Crater Lake 45
    Five Flower Lake 44
    Lake Baikal 42-44
    Lake Eyre 289
    Lake Maggiore 45
    Lake Nasser 8, 12
    Lake Ohrid 45
    Lake Tekapo 45
    Lake Titicaca 25
    Loch Etive 184
    Moraine Lake 48-49
    Phewa Lake 45
    Plitvice Lakes 45
Lake Tana Monasteries, Ethiopia 189
Lalibela, Ethiopia 156-7
Lascaux Caves, France 80
Latvia 215
La Venta, Mexico 273
Leander's Tower lighthouse, Turkey 53
Lebanon
    Baalbek 160
Leptis Magna, Libya 158-61
Libya
    Leptis Magna 158-61
    mosaics 160
lighthouses 52, 53
    Bell Rock Lighthouse 50-52
Lingotto Building, Italy 313
Little Bighorn, USA 83
Liverpool, England 313
Lizard Lighthouse, England 53
Loango National Park, Gabon 150
Loch Etive, Scotland 184
London
    Big Ben 95
    Borough Market 63
    British Museum 167
    Courtauld Gallery 166
    Gherkin 76
    Highgate Cemetery 311
    London Eye 257
    Royal Artillery War Memorial 178
    St Paul's Cathedral 304
    Tower of London 100
Lord Howe Island, 285
Los Glaciares National Park 108-10
Louvre Museum 6, 7, 162-7
Luxor temple complex, Egypt 11
Lycian Coast, Turkey 54

M
macaws 172-3
Macedonia 45
Machu Picchu, Peru 168-71
Madang Barrier Reef, Papua New Guinea
    285
Madinat al Zahra, Spain 23
Mahabalipuram, India 31
Malaysia 219
Mali
    Dogon people 129

Great Mosque of Djenné 61
Niger Inland Delta 209
Timbuktu 215
Malta 91
Mammoth Cave, USA 219
Manaus Opera House, Brazil 26-27
Manhattan, USA 257, 265
Manú National Park, Peru 172-3
Marché des Enfants Rouges, France 63
markets
    Boqueria Market 62-63
    Borough Market 63
    Cai Rang 63
    Chandni Chowk 85
    Marché des Enfants Rouges 63
    Mercado de la Merced 63
    Plaza Dorrego 240
    Vucciria 63
Marree Man, Australia 195
Masai Mara National Park, Kenya 200
Masdar, Abu Dhabi 41
Matera, Italy 157
Matmata, Tunisia 157
Matterhorn, Switzerland/Italy 174-5
Mauritania 209
Mecca, Saudi Arabia 295
Mediterranean islands 249
megaliths 66-67
    Carnac 66
    Stonehenge 67
Melk Abbey, Austria 304
Memnon Colossi, Egypt 11
Menin Gate, Belgium 176-8
Mercado de la Merced, Mexico 63
Merry Cemetery, Romania 311
Mesa Verde, USA 180-3
Mesoamerican sites 272, 273
    Teotihuacán 270-3
Metéora Monasteries, Greece 186-9
Metropolitan Museum of Art, USA 167
Mexico
    Barranca del Cobre 117
    Cave of Crystals 80-81
    Chichen Itzá 273
    Coyoacan 243
    La Venta 273
    Mercado de la Merced 63
    Mexico City 63, 243
    Mitla 273
    Monte Albán 273
    Palenque 273
    Teotihuacán 270-3
    Tulum 272
Michigan, University of, USA 137
Micronesia 171
Milford Sound, New Zealand 184-5
Mitla, Mexico 273
monasteries
    Aladzha Monastery 157
    Buddhist monasteries 210-11
    Geghard 157
    Heiligenkreuz Abbey 189
    Hemis monastery 210
    Lake Tana Monasteries 189
    Metéora Monasteries 186-9
    Namgyal monastery 210
    New Camaldoli Hermitage 189
    Paro Taktsang 210-11
    Skellig Michael 188
    Thikse monastery 210
    Varlaam monastery 187
Monet's Garden, France 190-3
Monte Albán, Mexico 273
Montenegro 91
Montmartre, France 257
Montségur, France 83
Moraine Lake, Canada 48-49
Morocco
    Atlas Mountains 261
    Erg Chebbi 96

Essaouira 91
Hassan II Mosque 61
Jardin Majorelle 192
Jemaa el-Fna 154
Ourika Valley 223
mosques
Badshahi Mosque 61
Blue Mosque 58–61
Great Mosque of Córdoba 23
Great Mosque of Djenné 61
Hassan II Mosque 61
mountain plateaus
Altiplano 24–25
Colorado Plateau 25, 114
Deccan Plateau 25
Ennedi Plateau 142
Paraná plateau 138
Tibetan Plateau 25
mountain settlements 261
Svaneti 258–61
mountain valleys 223
Pokhara Valley 220–3
Mount Everest, Nepal/China 174
Mughal architecture 86–87, 266–9
museums and galleries
Auschwitz-Birkenau Memorial and
Museum 179
British Museum 167
Courtauld Gallery 166
Guggenheim Bilbao 122–3
Hermitage Museum 167
Louvre Museum 6, 7, 162–7
Metropolitan Museum of Art 167
Prado Museum 167
Rijksmuseum 167
Uffizi Gallery 167
Vatican Museums 167
Myanmar 250–1

N
Namgyal monastery, India 210
Namibia
Etosha pan 289
Fish River Canyon 117
Nan Madol, Micronesia 171
Naqsh-e Jahan Square, Iran 154
nature reserves
Foping National Nature Reserve 145
Jigokudani Monkey Park 145
Sagarmatha National Park 145
Nazca Lines, Peru 194–5
Nemrut Dag, Turkey 276
Nepal
Mount Everest 174
Phewa Lake 45
Pokhara Valley 220–3
Sagarmatha National Park 145
Neuschwanstein, Germany 196–7
New Camaldoli Hermitage, USA 189
Newgrange tomb, Ireland 276
New York City
Chrysler Building 74–77
Empire State Building 76
Greenwich Village 243
Manhattan 257, 265
Metropolitan Museum of Art 167
Statue of Liberty 95
New Zealand
Fjordland National Park 184
Fox Glacier 111
Franz Josef Glacier 111
Lady Knox Geyser 308
Lake Tekapo 45
Milford Sound 184–5
Ngorongoro Crater, Tanzania 198–203
Niagara Falls, USA/Canada 141
Niger Inland Delta, Mali 209
Nile Valley, Egypt 227
Northern Ireland

Giant's Causeway 252–3
northern lights 34
Norway
Jostedalbreen National Park 111
Jotunheimen National Park 111
Oslo Opera House 27
Preikestolen 174
Sognefjord 184
Urnes Stave Church 229
Notre Dame Cathedral (Paris), France 71
Notre Dame du Haut (Ronchamp) France
122

O
Okavango Delta, Botswana 209
Old Faithful geyser, USA 309
Olinda, Brazil 204–5
opera houses 27, 41
Manaus Opera House 26–27
Sydney Opera House 27, 263
Oradour-sur-Glane, France 179
Ourika Valley, Morocco 223
Our Lady of Reims, France 71
Oxford, England 137

P
Paestum temples, Italy 17
painted churches, Romania 228–31
Pakistan
Badshahi Mosque 61
Biafo Glacier 111
Hispar Glacier 111
Indus Valley 227
Palace of Versailles, France 225
palaces 224–5
Alcázar (Seville) 23
Alhambra 20–23
Cliff Palace 180–1, 182
Forbidden City 98–101
Madinat al Zahra 23
Palace of Versailles 225
Potola Palace 224
Topkapi Palace 100
Winter Palace 100, 167,
232–3
Wurzburg Residence 73
Palenque, Mexico 273
Palmyra, Syria 160
Pantanal, Brazil/Bolivia/Paraguay 206–9
Papua New Guinea
Coastwatcher's Memorial Lighthouse
53
Madang Barrier Reef 285
Magic Passage 285
Planet Rock 285
Paraguay 206–209
Paris
Centre Georges Pompidou 122
Eiffel Tower 94–95
Helicopter Building 303
Louvre Museum 6, 7, 162–7
Marché des Enfants Rouges 63
Montmartre 257
Notre Dame Cathedral 71
Saint-Denis 71
Sainte-Chapelle 71
Paro Taktsang, Bhutan 210–11
Parthenon, Greece 14–17
penguins 35
Perito Moreno Glacier, Argentina 108–9
Peru
Altiplano 24–25
Colca Canyon 117
Machu Picchu 168–71
Manú National Park 172–3
Nazca Lines 194–5
Temple of the Sun 170
Perugia, Italy 137

Peter the Great 234
Petra, Jordan 212–15
Phang Nga Bay, Thailand 125
Phewa Lake, Nepal 45
Philippines
Banaue rice fields 46–47
Intramuros 205
Tubbataha Reefs 7, 282–4
White Beach 280
Phong Nha Cave, Vietnam 216–19
Phong Nha-Ke Bang National Park,
Vietnam 219
Phra Sri Rattana Chedi, Thailand 251
Pico del Teide, Spain 133
Pienza, Italy 235
pilgrimage destinations
Borobudur 295
Golden Temple of Amritsar 295
Kunisaki Peninsula 295
Mecca 295
Santiago de Compostela 295
Temple of the Sacred Tooth 295
Varanasi 292–5
Wieskirche 304–5
Pisa, Leaning Tower, Italy 95
Pitcairn, 64
Piton de la Fournaise, France 133
Playa Parguito, Venezuela 280
Plaza Dorrego, Argentina 240
Plitvice Lakes, Croatia 45
Pointe Sainte-Mathieu Lighthouse,
France 53
Pokhara Valley, Nepal 220–3
Poland
Auschwitz-Birkenau Memorial and
Museum 179
Kraków 152–5
Pompeii, Italy 160
Pont du Gard, France 160
Ponte Vecchio, Italy 113
Ponza, Italy 249
Portugal
Coruche 47
Lisbon 235
Potola Palace, Tibet 224
Powell, John Wesley 116
Prado Museum, Spain 167
Prague, Czech Republic 154
Preikestolen 174
Pueblo people 116, 181–3, 244
Punakha, Bhutan 223
Punta Walichu Caves, Argentina 109
pyramids
Step Pyramid of Djoser 11
Giza Pyramids 11
Teotihuacán 270–2

Q
Qal'at Salah El-Din, Syria 79
Queen Hatshepsut Mortuary Temple,
Egypt 11

R
Ragusa, Italy 239
rain forests 26, 150
Raja Ampat Islands, Indonesia 285
Ramesses II 8–9, 10, 13
Rapa Nui National Park, Chile 92–93
Réunion, 133
Rhine Valley, Germany 47, 226–7
rhinos, black 200–1
Rialto Bridge, Italy 6, 299
Rías Baixas, Spain 121
rift valleys
East African Rift Valley 173, 199
Jordan Rift Valley 227
Lake Baikal 43
Riga, Latvia 215

Rijksmuseum, Holland 167
Rio de Janeiro 254–7
rock-hewn architecture
Aladzha Monastery 157
Ellora Caves 31
Geghard 157
Göreme Valley 157
Lalibela 156–7
Matera 157
Matmata 157
Petra 212–15
rock paintings
Ennedi Plateau 142
Kakadu rock paintings 142–3
Lascaux Caves 80
Tassili N'Ajjer National Park 142
Roman Empire 160
Leptis Magna 158–61
Rome 57, 160
Romania
Bran Castle 73
Danube Delta 209
frescoes 229
Iron Gates Gorge 117
Merry Cemetery 311
painted churches 228–31
Rome 57, 160, 167, 278, 304
Roncesvalles Pass, Spain 83
Rorke's Drift, South Africa 83
Royal Artillery War Memorial, England 178
Russia
Church of the Transfiguration (Kizhi)
229
Hermitage Museum 167
St Petersburg 100, 167, 232–5
Tsarkoe Selo 196
Winter Palace 100, 167, 232–3
Rynek Główny, Poland 152–3
Ryoan-ji garden, Japan 192

S
sacred mountains 102–3
Sacred Tooth, Temple of the, Sri Lanka
295
Sagarmatha National Park, Nepal 145
Saguenay Fjord, Canada 184
Saint-Denis (Paris), France 71
Sainte-Chapelle (Paris), France 71
St Marco (Florence), Italy 39
St Paul's Cathedral (London), England
304
St Petersburg, Russia 100, 167, 232–5
Salar de Uyuni, Bolivia 288–91
salt flats 289
Salar de Uyuni 288–91
Samarkand, Uzbekistan 215
Sana'a, Yemen 244–5
San Felipe de Barajas, Colombia 79
San Gimignano, Italy 236–9
San Giorgio Maggiore (Venice), Italy 296
Santa Cruz, Spain 243
Santa Maria della Vittoria (Rome), Italy
304
San Telmo, Argentina 240–2
Santiago de Compostela, Spain 295
São Tomé & Principe 64
Sarawak Chamber, Malaysia 219
Saudi Arabia 295
Savannah, USA 301
Scotland
Applecross Peninsula 121
Bell Rock Lighthouse 50–52
Culloden, Battle of 82–83
Edinburgh 301
Eilean Donan Castle 79
Glencoe 223
Loch Etive 184
Staffa 252–3
Serbia 117

Serengeti National Park, Tanzania 198, 200
Seychelles 280
Shah Jahan 84-87, 266-9
Shanghai, China 192
    Shanghai Bund 265
Shwedagon Pagoda, Myanmar 250-1
Siberia
    Karymsky 133
    Klyuchevskaya Sopka 133
    Kronotsky 133
    Lake Baikal 42-44
    Valley of the Geysers 308
Sigiriya, Sri Lanka 171
Sistine Chapel, Vatican 39
Skellig Michael, Ireland 188
Skocjan Caves, Slovenia 219
skyscrapers 36-37, 74-77
Slovenia 219
Socotra 65
Sognefjord, Norway 184
South Africa
    Kirstenbosch National Botanic Garden 192
    Kwandwe Private Game Reserve 200
    Rorke's Drift 83
Spain 79
    Alcázar (Segovia) 79
    Alcázar (Seville) 23
    Alhambra 20-23
    Arcos de la Frontera 239
    Bodegas Portia factory 303
    Boqueria Market 62-63
    Burgos Cathedral 71
    Cadiz 91
    Cerdanya 223
    Córdoba Cathedral 23
    Cuenca 301
    Doñana National Park 209
    Great Mosque of Córdoba 23
    Guggenheim Bilbao 122-3
    Ibiza 249
    Madinat al Zahra 23
    Moorish Spain 20-23
    Pico del Teide 133
    Prado Museum 167
    Rías Baixas 121
    Salamanca 137
    Santa Cruz 243
    Santiago de Compostela 295
    Timanfaya 133
Sphinx, Great, Egypt 11
Sri Lanka
    Sigiriya 171
    Temple of the Sacred Tooth 295
Sripuram Golden Temple, India 251
stadiums 56-57
    Bird's Nest Stadium 56
    Colosseum 57
Staffa, Scotland 252-3
Stahl House, USA 37
Staromestske Namesti, Czech Republic 154
Statue of Liberty, USA 95
statues
    Christ the Redeemer 257
    Easter Island 92-93
    Statue of Liberty 95
    Terracotta Army 274-7
Step Pyramid of Djoser, Egypt 11
Stonehenge, England 67
Stromboli, Italy 133, 249
Sugarloaf Mountain, Brazil 254-7
Sumbanese people, Indonesia 129
Svaneti, Georgia 258-61
Sweden
    Abisko National Park 34
    Aurora Sky Station 34
    Engelsberg Ironworks 313
    Turning Torso 77

Visby 300-1
Switzerland 174-5
Sydney Harbour, Australia 262-5
Syria
    Crac des Chevaliers 78-79
    Damascus, Old 87
    Hexagon Pools 253
    Palmyra 160
    Qal'at Salah El-Din 79

T
Taiwan
    Taipei 101 77
Taj Mahal, India 7, 266-9
Tallinn Old Town, Estonia 87
Tanzania
    Furtwängler Glacier 111
    Ngorongoro Crater 198-203
    Serengeti National Park 198, 200
Taos Pueblo, USA 244
Ta Prohm, Cambodia 31
Tassili N'Ajjer National Park, Algeria 142
temples
    Abu Simbel 8-13
    Acropolis 14-17
    Angkor Thom 31
    Angkor Wat 28-31
    Apollo (Delphi) 17
    Apollo Epicurius (Bassae) 17
    Athena Nike (Acropolis) 15
    Borobudur 295
    Dendera temple complex 11
    Ellora Caves 31
    Golden Temple of Amritsar 295
    Harmandir Sahib 251
    Hephaestus 17
    Horus 11
    Jin Dian 251
    Karnak temple complex 11
    Khajuraho 31
    Kinkaku-ji 251
    Kom Ombo 11
    Luxor temple complex 11
    Mahabalipuram 31
    Paestum 17
    Paro Taktsang 210-11
    Parthenon 14-17
    Phra Sri Rattana Chedi 251
    Queen Hatshepsut Mortuary Temple 11
    Shwedagon Pagoda 250-1
    Sripuram Golden Temple 251
    Ta Prohm 31
    Temple of the Sacred Tooth 295
    Temple of the Sun (Peru) 170
    Valley of the Temples 17
Teotihuacán, Mexico 270-3
Terracotta Army, China 274-7
Thailand
    Kanchanaphisek Lighthouse 53
    Khao Sok National Park 148-51
    Phang Nga Bay 125
    Phra Sri Rattana Chedi 251
Thiepval Memorial, France 179
Thikse Monastery, Ladakh 210
Tibet
    Potola Palace 224
    Tibetan Plateau 25
    Yarlung Tsangpo Canyon 117
tigers 144-5
Tikal, Guatemala 171, 273
Timanfaya, Spain 133
Timbuktu, Mali 215
tombs 276
    Terracotta Army 274-7
Topkapi Palace, Turkey 100
Torres del Paine National Park, Chile 111
tortoises 106-7
Toulouse, France 71
Tower of London, England 100

Trevi Fountain, Italy 278
Trinidad, Cuba 205
Troy, Turkey 171
Trunk Bay, US Virgin Islands 280-1
Tsarkoe Selo, Russia 196
Tubbataha Reefs, Philippines 7, 282-4
Tulum, Mexico 272
Tunisia 157
Turkey
    Blue Mosque 58-61
    Ephesus 160
    Göreme Valley 157
    Hagia Sophia 59
    Leander's Tower 53
    Lycian Coast 54
    Nemrut Dag 276
    Topkapi Palace 100
Turning Torso, Sweden 77

U
Uffington White Horse, England 195
Uffizi Gallery, Italy 167
Uluru, Australia 286-7
Urnes Stave Church, Norway 229
USA
    Alcatraz 257
    Aqua Tower 36-37
    Bandelier 183
    Big Sur 54-55
    Biltmore House 73
    Blythe Geoglyphs 195
    Bonneville Salt Flats 289
    Bosque del Apache 209
    Bridalveil Fall 141
    Canyon de Chelly 183
    Cape Elizabeth Lighthouse 53
    Cape May 173
    Chaco Canyon 183
    Chicago 36-37
    cliff dwellings 180-3
    Colorado Plateau 25, 114
    Crater Lake 45
    Death Valley 19
    Devil's Tower 253
    Empire State Building 76
    Fallingwater 37
    Flatiron Building 74
    Glacier Bay National Park and Preserve 111
    Glass House 36
    Golden Gate Bridge 112
    Grand Canyon 25, 114-17
    Grand Teton National Park 49
    Hearst Castle 196
    Little Bighorn 83
    Mammoth Cave 219
    Mesa Verde 180-3
    Michigan, University of 137
    Mohave Desert 19, 195
    Mount Shasta 103
    Nankoweap Canyon 116
    New Camaldoli Hermitage 189
    Niagara Falls 141
    Old Faithful 309
    Savannah 301
    Stahl House 37
    Taos Pueblo 244
    Ute Mountain Tribal Park 183
    Walt Disney Concert Hall 27
    Washington DC 235
    Yellowstone National Park 306-9
    Yosemite National Park 141
    see also Hawaii; New York City
US Virgin Islands
    Trunk Bay 280-1
Ute Mountain Tribal Park, USA 183
Uzbekistan
    Khiva 215
    Samarkand 215

V
Valetta, Malta 91
Valley of the Geysers, Russia 308
Valley of the Kings, Egypt 276
Valley of the Temples (Sicily), Italy 17
Varanasi, India 292-5
Vatican 39, 167
Venezuela
    Angel Falls 141
    Playa Parguito 280
Venice, Italy 6, 296-9, 311
Verona, Italy 27, 301
Victoria Falls, Zambia/Zimbabwe 141
Victoria Peak (Hong Kong), China 257
Vietnam
    Cai Rang floating market 63
    Halong Bay 124-7
    Phong Nha Cave 216-9
    Phong Nha-Ke Bang National Park 219
Villa Savoye, France 37
Virunga National Park, DRC 202
Visby, Sweden 300-1
Vucciria market, Italy 63
VW Transparent Factory, Germany 302-3

W
Waikiki, Hawaii 280
Wales 79
war memorials 178, 179
    Menin Gate 176-8
Washington DC 235
waterfalls 141, 185
    Iguazú Falls 138-41
    Niagara Falls 141
    Victoria Falls 141
waterways 146-7
    Britain's canals 147
    Kerala's backwaters 146
wetlands 209
    Pantanal 206-9
White Beach, Philippines 280
White Desert, Egypt 97
Wieskirche, Germany 304-5
wildlife
    Antarctic Peninsula 33-35
    Foping National Nature Reserve 145
    Galápagos Islands 104-7
    Jigokudani Monkey Park 145
    Kanha National Park 144-5
    Kwandwe Private Game Reserve 200
    Lake Baikal 43-44
    Masai Mara National Park 200
    Ngorongoro Crater 198-203
    Pantanal 206, 208, 209
    Sagarmatha National Park 145
    Serengeti National Park 200
    Tubbataha Reefs 282-4
    Yellowstone National Park 308
    see also birdwatching
Winter Palace, Russia 100, 167, 232-3
Works of the Old Men, Jordan 195
Wurzburg Residence, Germany 73

Y
Yarlung Tsangpo Canyon, Tibet 117
Yellowstone National Park, USA 306-9
Yemen
    Al-Hajjarah 239
    Sana'a 244-5
Yoho National Park, Canada 49
Yosemite National Park, USA 141
Yuyuan garden, China 192

Z
Zambia 141
Zentralfriedhof Cemetery, Austria 310-11
Zimbabwe 141

Authors

Derek Barton
Michael Bright
Mary Frances Budzik
Katie Cancila
Marolyn Charpentier
Helen Douglas-Cooper
Marc Funda
Lisa Halvorsen
Solange Hando
Karen Hursh Graber
Michael Kerrigan
Miren Lopategui
Antony Mason
Margaret McPhee
Anna McSweeney
Peter Neville-Hadley
Katie Parla
Robert Sackville West
GeorgeSemler
Ginger Vaughn
Joe Yogerst

Picture Credits

Abbreviations: t = top; **b** = bottom; **l** = left; **r** = right; **m** = middle.
Front cover: Getty Images/Photolibrary/Peter Adams;
End Papers: Superstock/Hemis fr;
1 National Geographic Stock/Speleoresearch & Films/Carsten Peter; **2-3** Shutterstock.com/Kipp Schoen; **4bl** SuperStock/Angelo Cavalli; **4bm** FLPA/Frans Lanting; **4br** 4Corners Images/SIME/ Laurent Grandadam; **5bl, 5bm** 4Corners Images/ HP Huber; **5br** Getty Images/Vetta/Chris Hepburn; **6** Corbis/Hemis/Arnaud Chichurel (© SETE Illuminations Pierre Bideau); **8-9** Alamy/Russell Kord; **10tr** awl-images.com/Julian Love; **10bl** SuperStock/JTB Photo; **11mr** awl-images.com/ Michele Falzone; **11bl** Shutterstock.com/Planner; **12** National Geographic Stock/David Boyer; **13** Panos Pictures/Georg Gerster; **14-15** 4Corners Images/Huber/Reinhard Schmid; **16** 4Corners Images/SIME/Johanna Huber; **17t** Corbis/Ocean; **17bl** Shutterstock.com/Motordigitaal; **18** SuperStock/Marka; **19ml** Still Pictures/ Blickwinkel/R.Gemperle; **19bm** Shutterstock.com/ Galyna Andrushko; **20-21** awl-images.com/Doug Pearson; **22** 4Corners Images/Huber/Günter Gräfenhain; **23t** Corbis/Jean-Pierre Lescourret; **23b** Shutterstock.com/Barone Firenze; **24-25** Shutterstock.com/MP cz; **25tr** National Geographic Stock/Minden Pictures/Pete Oxford; **25bm** Shutterstock Images/Hung Chung Chih; **26** Corbis/Robert Harding World Imagery/Michael DeFreitas; **27t** Getty Images/Altrendo Travel; **27b** Shutterstock.com/Gerry Broughan; **28bl** National Geographic Stock/Kent Kobersteen; **28-29t** 4Corners Images/ Huber/Günter Gräfenhain; **30t** Getty Images/AFP/Tang Chhin Sothy; **30b** Panos Pictures/Dieter Telemans; **31** National Geographic Stock/Steve Raymer; **32-33** Robert Harding/Geoff Renner; **34t** Specialist Stock/Michael S. Nolan; **34b** SuperStock/JTB Photo; **35** FLPA/Minden Pictures/Colin Monteath; **36bm** The Philip Johnson Glass House/Eirik Johnson; **36-37** Arcaid Images/Steve Hall/Hedrich Blessing; **38** The Bridgeman Art Library/Alinari/Scrovegni (Arena) Chapel, Padua, Italy; **39** Photo Scala, Florence; **40, 41** awl-images.com/Jane Sweeney; **42-43** Shutterstock.com/Mikhail Markovskiy; **43t** naturepl.com/Doug Allan; **44t** Shutterstock.com/ Gontar; **44b** SuperStock/JTB Photo; **45tr** National Geographic Stock/Bates Littlehales; **45ml** SuperStock/imagebroker.net; **45br** Hedgehog House/Colin Monteath; **46bl** Corbis/Robert Harding World Imagery/Tony Waltham; **46-47, 48-49** awl-images.com/Michele Falzone; **50-51** Alamy/Ian Cowe; **52t** Getty Images/SSPL; **52b** Ken Kaizuka; **53tm** Shutterstock.com/Mikhail Markovskiy; **53mr** SuperStock/Photononstop; **53bl** SuperStock/Robert Harding Picture Library; **54bm** Shutterstock.com/Freddy Eliasson; **54br** Getty Images/Photolibrary/Ted Mead; **55** Shutterstock.com/Chris Rodenberg Photography; **56** awl-images.com/Cahir Davitt; **57** 4Corners Images/SIME/Massimo Borchi; **58** awl-images. com/Peter Adams; **59** Robert Harding/age fotostock/Jeff Greenberg; **60** Shutterstock.com/ Mikhail Markovskiy; **61t** Lonely Planet Images/Tim Barker; **61bl** awl-images.com/Michele Falzone; **61mr** Getty Images/Donald Nausbaum; **62** 4Corners/SIME/Massimo Borchi; **63t** Alamy/Paul Lindsay; **63bm** SuperStock/Prisma; **64bl** Shutterstock.com/Oleg Znamenskiy; **64-65** awl-images.com/Danita Delimont Stock; **66** Getty Images/Max Homand; **67** SuperStock/F1 Online; **68** SuperStock/Yoshio Tomii; **69tr** 4Corners Images/SIME/Massimo Ripani; **69br** Sonia Halliday Photographs; **70t** Corbis/Sylvain Sonnet; **70b** SuperStock/Hemis.fr; **71t** 4Corners Images/Huber/ Fridmar Damm; **71mr** Corbis/Sylvain Sonnet; **71bl** 4Corners Images/SIME/Massimo Ripani; **72** awl-images.com/Neil Farrin; **73t** SuperStock/ Stock Connection;**73br** 4Corners Images/Huber/ Reinhard Schmid; **74** Shutterstock.com/Songquan Deng; **75** awl-images.com/Jon Arnold; **76t** Alamy/ Nathan Benn; **76bl** Getty Images/Brian Lawrence; **76br** SuperStock/Travel Library Limited; **77bl** Corbis/Art on File; **77br** Getty Images/IMAGEMORE Co, Ltd. **78-79** Rex Features/Roland Kemp; **79tr** SuperStock/age fotostock; **79br** Alamy/Alan Gignoux; **80bl** Robert Harding; **80-81** National Geographic Stock/Speleoresearch & Films/Carsten Peter; **82-83** Alamy/Arterra Picture Library; **84-85** Lonely Planet Images/Richard I'Anson; **86bl** Corbis/SOPA/Massimo Borchi; **86-87** Dreamstime.com/Sbeh; **87mr** Corbis/JAI/Gavin Hellier; **88-89** Shutterstock.com/sergruss; **90** SuperStock/imagebroker.net; **91** Shutterstock. com/Prohasson Frederic; **92-93** SuperStock/ Angelo Cavalli; **94** SuperStock/Robert Harding Picture Library; **95t** SuperStock/Flirt; **95b** SuperStock/Prisma; **96** Corbis/Martin Harvey; **97** naturepl.com/Dan Rees; **98b** Robert Harding/Tao; **98-99** Getty Images/Best View Stock; **100t** Robert Harding/PanoramaStock; **100b** Getty Images/Marco Simoni; **101** Robert Harding/ Christian Kober; **102-103** Robert Harding/age fotostock; **104** Getty Images/Mark Jones Roving Tortoise Photos; **105tl** ardea.com/M.Watson; **105br** Getty Images/Michele Westmorland; **106-107** FLPA/Frans Lanting; **108-109t** 4Corners Images/Huber/Fridmar Damm; **109br** Shutterstock.com/Sebastian Burel; **110** © David Boswell/DBoswell Photography ; **111tr** naturepl. com/Orsolya Haarberg; **111ml** SuperStock/ imagebroker.net; **111br** 4Corners Images/SIME/ Gabriele Croppi; **112** Issac Brooks; **113** 4Corners Images/Stefano Amantini; **114-115** Corbis/ Momatiuk-Eastcott; **116** 4Corners Images/Stefano Amantini; **117t** Corbis/National Geographic Society/John Burcham; **117b** Getty Images/B. Holland; **118-119** 4Corners Images/SIME/Laurent Grandadam; **120-121** Corbis/All Canada Photos/ Bruce Corbett; **122** 4Corners Images/Huber/ Sabine Lubenow; **123** 4Corners Images/SIME/ Massimo Borchi; **124-125** 4Corners/Huber/Günter Gräfenhain; **125tr** Shutterstock.com/modestlife; **126-127** Corbis/Hemis/Romain Cintract; **128** Getty Images/National Geographic/Bill Curtsinger; **129tr** Getty Images/National Geographic/Michael Melford; **129bl** Corbis/Hugh Sitton; **130-131** Getty Images/Toshi Sasaki; **132** naturepl.com/Photo Resource Hawaii; **133tr** FLPA/Frans Lanting; **133bl** naturepl.com/Igor Shpilenok; **134-135** Corbis/ Richard Klune; **135t** 4Corners/Huber/Reinhard Schmid; **136** Alamy/blickwinkel; **137t** Corbis/ National Geographic Society/Greg Dale; **137b** Shutterstock.com/Skowron; 138-139 4 Corners Images/SIME/Antonino Bartuccio; **140t** 4 Corners Images/SIME/Antonino Bartuccio; **140b** Alamy/ David Lyons; **141t** naturepl.com/Gabriel Rojo; 141b Shutterstock.com/Janne Hämäläinen; **142b** Corbis/Ocean; **143** Getty Images/DEA/N.Cirani (Kakadu National Park:www.environment.gov.au/ parks/kakadu/visitor-information/permits; **144b** Alamy/blickwinkel; **144-145t** Alamy/Dinodia Photos; **145b** Robert Harding/Image Broker/ Michael Krabs; **146** SuperStock/Photononstop; **147** SuperStock/Robert Harding Picture Library; **148bl** FLPA/Imagebroker/Bernd Mehmen; **148-149** FLPA/Imagebroker; **150** Getty Images/Tier und Naturfotografie J & C Sohns; **151** SuperStock/age fotostock/Gonzalo Azumendi; **152-153** Shutterstock.com/Pecold; **154t** awl-images.com/ Katie Garrod; **154b** SuperStock/age fotostock; **155** SuperStock/Robert Harding; **156bl** Robert Harding/age footstock; **156-157t** Corbis/George Steinmetz; **157bm** awl-images.com/Travel Pix Collection; **158-159** Shutterstock.com/Christian Wilkinson; **160t** akg-images/Gilles Mermet; **160b** 4Corners Images/SIME/Guido Baviera; **161** Robert Harding/Sergio Pitamitz; **162bl** Robert Harding/ age fotostock/Nacho Calonge; **162-163** Corbis/ Hemis/Arnaud Chicurel (©SETI illuminations Pierre Bideau); **164t** SuperStock/Fine Art Images; **164b** Corbis/Sylvain Sonnet; **165** Corbis/Hemis/ Bertrand Rieger; **166tr** 4Corners Images/SIME/ Susy Mezzanotte; **166bl** SuperStock/imagebroker. net; **167mr** SuperStock/Hemis.fr; **167bl** Corbis/ Bob Krist; **168-169** Getty Images/Kelly Cheng Travel Photography; **170** SuperStock/age fotostock; **171tr** Getty Images/De Agostini/G.Dagli Orti; **171bm** SuperStock/Prisma; **172-173b** SuperStock/Frans Lemmens; **173tr** Shutterstock. com/Steffen Foerster Photography; **174bm** SuperStock/imagebroker.net; **174-175** awl-images. com/Michele Falzone; **176bl** Rex Features/Brian Harris; **176-177** Dreamstime.com/Andyemptag; **178tr** Rex Features/Daily Mail/David Crump; **178bl** Alamy/Robert Preston; **179tr** Corbis/Michael St. Maur Sheil; **179ml** Corbis/Paul Thompson; **179bm** Shutterstock.com/alessandro0770; **180-181** Corbis/Jose Fuste Raga; **182tr** SuperStock/Ernest Manewal; **182b** awl-images.com/Danita Delimont Stock; **183tr** Robert Harding/Gavin Hellier; **183br** Alamy/Carver Mostardi; **184ml** Lonely Planet Images/Holger Leue; **185** Hedgehog House/Colin Monteath; **186-187** Alamy JTB Photo Communications. Inc; **187tr** ALIMDI.NET/WOT; **188tr** awl-images.com/Michele Falzone; **188bl** Getty Images/Robert Harding/Peter Barritt; **189** Corbis/Rob Howard; **190ml** The Bridgeman Art Library/Giraudon/Musee Marmottan Monet, Paris, France; **190-191b** Lonely Planet Images/Diana Mayfield; **191tr** SuperStock/ClassicStock.com; **192tr** Corbis/Harpur Garden Library; **192bm** Shutterstock.com/S.Borisov; **193** Shutterstock. com/Anneka; **194bm** Robert Harding/Odyssey/ Robert Frerck; **194-195** National Geographic Stock/George Steinmetz; **195bm** awl-images.com/ Max Milligan; **196bl** Shutterstock.com/Konstantin Mironov; **196br** Corbis/Visions of America/Joseph Sohm; **197** 4Corners Images/SIME/Olimpio Fantuz; **198-199** awl-images.com/Ivan Vdovin; **200t** FLPA/Frans Lanting; **200bl** naturepl.com/Visuals Unlimited; **200-201b** naturepl.com/Nick Garbutt; **202-203t** Shutterstock.com/Pal Teravagimov; **202bl** SuperStock/NaturePL; **203bm** Alamy/ Ulrich Doering; **204-205** 4Corners Images/SIME/ Antonio Bartuccio; **205mr** SuperStock/age fotostock/Alvaro Leiva; **206bl** SuperStock/ Wolfgang Kaehler; **206-207** Corbis/Yann Arthus-Bertrand; **208** Getty Images/Roy Toft; **209tr** Corbis/Staffan Widstrand; **209bm** SuperStock/Science Faction; **210bl** Shutterstock. com/P.Santibhavank; **210-211** Corbis/JAI/Peter Adams; **212** Shutterstock.com/CJPhoto; **213b** 4Corners Images/SIME/Johanna Huber; **214-215t** Robert Harding/age fotostock/Yadid Levy; **215bm** Shutterstock.com/Edward Kim; **216-217b** Terra Galleria Photography/Quang-Tuan Luong; **217tr** Alamy/Robbie Shone; **218t** Luke Duggleby; **218bl** Getty Images/National Geographic/Carsten Peter; **219** Eisriesenwelt GMBH; **220-221** SuperStock/ Hemis.fr; **222** SuperStock/Robert Harding Picture Library; **223** Lonely Planet Images/Felix Hug; **224** Corbis/Rob Howard; **225** Shutterstock.com/ Crobard; **226-227** 4Corners Images/Huber/Günter Gräfenhain; **227** Shutterstock.com/Frank11; **228** SuperStock/age fotostock; **229t** SuperStock/ Marka; **229b** Shutterstock.com/Mikhail Markovskiy; **230-231** Robert Harding/age fotostock/P.Narayan; **232-233** 4Corners Images/ SIME/FotoSa/Alexander Petrosyan; **234** Shutterstock.com/Sergei Butorin; **235t** SuperStock/Photononstop; **235b** Superstock. com/Prisma; **236-237** SuperStock/Hidekazu Nishibata; **237t** Shutterstock.com/Maugli; **238t** 4Corners Images/SIME/Guido Baviera; **238b** Photo Scala, Florence; **239t** 4Corners Images/SIME/ Guido Baviera; **239b** Robert Harding/age fotostock/Wojtek Buss; **240** Getty Images/ National Geographic/Michael Lewis; **241** awl-images.com/Walter Bibikow; **242** SpecialistStock/Aurora/Peter McBride; **243tr** SuperStock/age fotostock; **243ml** Alamy/Alex Segre; **243br** SuperStock/Travel Library Limited; 244bl Corbis/Ryan Pyle; **244-245t** 4Corners/ Huber/ Günter Gräfenhain; **246-247** Shutterstock. com/Eastimages; **247t** SuperStock/imagebroker. net; **248bl** 4Corners Images/SIME/Antonino Bartuccio; **248-249** SuperStock/age fotostock/ Jan Wlodarczyk; **249b** 4Corners Images/SIME/ Johanna Huber; **250bl** Still Pictures/Sean Sprague; **250-251** 4Corners Images/Huber/ Fridmar Damm; **252-253** SuperStock/age fotostock/David Lyons; **253t** Shutterstock.com/ Pecold; **254-255** 4Corners Images/SIME/Antonino Bartuccio; **256-257** SuperStock/Robert Harding Picture Library; **257t** Getty Images/Michael Regan; **258-259** Lonely Planet Images/Sean Caffrey; **260** SuperStock/imagebroker.net; **261t** Invision/Stephane Remael; **261b** SuperStock/ Photononstop; **262-263** Tourism NSW; **263br** Shutterstock\Debra James; **264-265** PA Photos/ aapnewswire/Mick Tsikas; **265tr** awl-images/ Andrew Watson; **265bm** Shutterstock.com/ leungchopan; **266-267** 4Corners Images/Huber HP/Huber; **268** Shutterstock.com/Carlos Neto; **269tr** Corbis/Alex Masi; **269m** Lonely Planet Images/Sara-Jane Cleland; **270-271** Alamy/Prismo Archivo; **272t** SuperStock/imagebroker.net; **272b** iStockphoto.com/Lubomir Jendrol; **273t** Corbis/ Gianni Dagli Orti; **273b** Shutterstock/Christian Delbert; **274bl** Panos Pictures/Dieter Telemans; **274-275** Corbis/Ocean; 276tm Corbis/ Imaginechina; **276bm** Shutterstock.com/Boris Stroujko; **277t** National Geographic Stock/O.Louis Mazzatenta; **277b** PA Photos/AP/Color China Photo/Lan Shan; **278** awl-images/David Bank; **279** Getty Images/arabianEye/Gerald Donovan; **280-281** awl-images.com/Michele Falzone; **282bl** naturepl.com/David Fleetham; **282-283** SuperStock/NaturePL; **284** Still Pictures/ WaterFrame/Borut Frulan; **285tr** Alamy/Andre Seale; **285ml** Alamy/imagebroker/Norbert Probst; **285br** Eddie Gerald/Alamy; **286-287** 4Corners Images/HP Huber/Huber. (www.environment.gov. au/parks/uluru); **288b** Getty Images/Zack Seckler; **288-289** Science Photo Library/George Steinmetz; **289bm** Robert Harding/age fotostock/ Hoffmann Photography; **290-291** SuperStock/ Travel Library Limited; **292bl** Alamy/David Pearson; **292-293** awl-images.com/Aurora Photos; **294** SuperStock/Prisma/Blum Bruno; **295t** Panos Pictures/G.M.B.Akash; **295b** Shutterstock.com/Luciano Mortula; **296-297** Getty Images/Vetta/Chris Hepburn; **297tl** 4Corners Images/SIME/Olimpio Fantuz; **298** 4Corners Images/SIME/Giovanni Simeone; **299** awl-images.com/Alan Copson; **300-301** awl-images.com/Nordic Photos; **302-303** Photoshot/Picture Alliance/Matthais Hiekel; **303tr** Die Gläserne Manufaktur, Volkswagen Automobilmanufaktur Dresden GmbH; **305** Corbis/Ocean; **306bl** Robert Harding/age footstock/Luis Castaneda; **306-307** SuperStock/ age fotostock/Photri Inc; **307b** SuperStock/ Hemis.fr; **308t** Nature Picture Library/George Sanker; **308b** Shutterstock/Jan Mika; **309** SuperStock/Flirt; **310** Still Pictures/Blickwinkel/ McPHOTO; **311t** SuperStock/imagebroker.net; **311b** SuperStock/imagebroker.net; **312bl** SuperStock/ imagebroker.net; **312-313** Stiftung Zollverein/ Thomas Willemsen

THE BEST OF THE BEST PLACES IN THE WORLD was originated in the UK by the editorial team of The Reader's Digest Association Inc., London. It was created and produced for Reader's Digest by Toucan Books Limited, London.

The Reader's Digest Association Inc., London.
1 Eversholt Street
London NW1 2DN

First published 2012
Copyright © 2012 The Reader's Digest Association Inc.
All rights reserved. Unauthorised reproduction, in any manner, is prohibited without permission, in writing from the publishers.

Reader's Digest is a registered trademark of The Reader's Digest Association Inc., of New York, USA.

This edition published by:
Reader's Digest Book and Home Entertainment (India) Pvt Ltd, Mumbai
Copyright © 2012 Reader's Digest Association India Pvt Limited.

Sold under license in the UK by:
Vivat Direct Limited (t/a Reader's Digest)
157 Edgware Road, London W2 2HR
Copyright © 2012 The Reader's Digest Association Inc.

For Toucan Books Limited
Editorial Director Ellen Dupont
Book Development Andrew Kerr-Jarrett
Senior Editor Helen Douglas-Cooper
Editors Judith Samuelson, Anna Southgate
Designer Mark Scribbins
Picture Manager Christine Vincent
Picture Researcher Sharon Southren
Proofreader Marion Dent
Indexer Michael Dent

For Reader's Digest Books
VP, Chief Content Officer RD International
Neil Wertheimer
International Managing Editor and Book Project Editor
Alastair Holmes

Edited for Reader's Digest by Christine Noble

Prepress origination by FMG, London
Printed in China

Concept code FR2232/G-IE
Book code 400-489 UP0000-1
ISBN 978-1-78020-158-0